REORIENTATION

RECOVERING POLITICAL PHILOSOPHY

SERIES EDITORS: THOMAS L. PANGLE AND TIMOTHY W. BURNS

PUBLISHED BY PALGRAVE MACMILLAN:

Lucretius as Theorist of Political Life
By John Colman

Shakespeare's Political Wisdom
By Timothy W. Burns

Political Philosophy Cross-Examined: Perennial Challenges to the Philosophic Life
Edited by Thomas L. Pangle and J. Harvey Lomax

Eros and Socratic Political Philosophy
By David Levy

Reorientation: Leo Strauss in the 1930s
Edited by Martin D. Yaffe and Richard S. Ruderman

REORIENTATION: LEO STRAUSS IN THE 1930s

Edited by

Martin D. Yaffe

and

Richard S. Ruderman

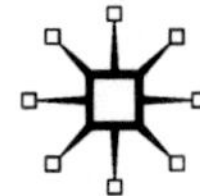

REORIENTATION

First published in 2014 by
PALGRAVE MACMILLAN®
in the United States—a division of St. Martin's Press LLC,
175 Fifth Avenue, New York, NY 10010.

Where this book is distributed in the UK, Europe and the rest of the world, this is by Palgrave Macmillan, a division of Macmillan Publishers Limited, registered in England, company number 785998, of Houndmills, Basingstoke, Hampshire RG21 6XS.

Palgrave Macmillan is the global academic imprint of the above companies and has companies and representatives throughout the world.

ISBN: 978–1–137–32438–2

Library of Congress Cataloging-in-Publication Data

Reorientation : Leo Strauss in the 1930s / edited by Martin D. Yaffe and Richard S. Ruderman.
pages cm.—(Recovering political philosophy)
Includes index.
ISBN 978–1–137–37423–3 (pbk.)—
ISBN 978–1–137–32438–2
1. Strauss, Leo—Criticism and interpretation. 2. Political science—Philosophy. I. Yaffe, Martin D. II. Ruderman, Richard S., 1958–

JC251.S8R46 2014
181′.06—dc23 2013025811

A catalogue record of the book is available from the British Library.

Design by Newgen Knowledge Works (P) Ltd., Chennai, India.

First edition: July 2014

10 9 8 7 6 5 4 3 2 1

For Connie and Anne

CONTENTS

ACKNOWLEDGMENTS

Earlier versions of chapter 1 have appeared previously as "Vorwort des Herausgebers" in Leo Strauss, *Gesammelte Schriften, Band 2: Philosophie und Gesetz—Frühe Schriften*, edited by Heinrich Meier, Stuttgart and Weimar: Metzler Verlag, 1997, ix–xxxiii, and in translation as "How Strauss Became Strauss," in *Enlightening Revolutions: Essays in Honor of Ralph Lerner*, edited by Svetozar Minkov, 363–82, Lanham, MD: Lexington Books, 2006. We are grateful to Heinrich Meier for his kind permission to republish.

Earlier versions of chapters 7 and 9 have appeared previously as "Leo Strauss on the Origins of Hobbes's Natural Science," *Review of Metaphysics* 64, no. 4 (June 2011): 823–55, and "The Problem of the Enlightenment: Strauss, Jacobi, and the Pantheism Controversy," *Review of Metaphysics* 56, no. 3 (March 2003): 605–31, respectively. We are grateful to *Review of Metaphysics* and its editor, Professor Jude P. Dougherty, for their kind permission to republish.

The German originals of appendices A, B, C, D, and E have appeared previously in Strauss, *Gesammelte Schriften, Band 2*, as "Konspektivismus" (pp. 365–75, 620–21), "Religiöse Lage der Gegenwart" (pp. 377–90, 621), "Die geistige Lage der Gegenwart" (pp. 441–62, 623), "Eine vermißte Schrift Farâbî's" (pp. 167–77, 614), and "Zu Abravanels Kritik der Königtums" (pp. 233–34, 615), respectively. We are grateful to J. B. Metzlersche Verlagsbuchhandlung und C. H. Poeschel Verlag, GmbH, for their kind permission to publish translations of these and to Heinrich Meier for his help in arranging for their permission. Thanks especially to the Earhart Foundation of Ann Arbor, Michigan, for its generous financial support for that purpose.

Our series coeditor Timothy W. Burns has been unstinting in his encouragement and judicious in his counsel during the routine and not-so-routine ins and outs, ups and downs of the preparation of this volume. And Daniel Burns, Guy Chet, Kenneth Hart Green, Joshua Parens, and Alan Udoff have provided timely assistance concerning Hebrew and Arabic and related matters.

ABBREVIATIONS

Titles of Leo Strauss's Writings

AAPL	*The Argument and the Action of Plato's "Laws."* Chicago: The University of Chicago Press, 1975.
APT	"On Abravanel's Philosophical Tendency and Political Teaching." In *Isaac Abravanel*, edited by J. B. Trend and H. Loewe, pp. 93–109. Cambridge, UK: Cambridge University Press, 1937.
CaM	"Cohen and Maimonides." Translated by Martin D. Yaffe and Ian Moore. *LSMC* 173–222.
CM	*The City and Man*. Chicago: Rand McNally, 1964.
CuM	"*Cohen und Maimuni*." *GS–2* 393–436.
EMFL	"Einleitung zu *Morgenstunden* und *An die Freunde Lessings*." *GS–2* 528–605.
EP	"Einleitung zu *Phädon*." *GS–2* 485–504.
EPLJ	*Das Erkenntnisproblem in der philosophischen Lehre Fr. H. Jacobis*. *GS–2* 237–92.
EPM	"Einleitung zu *Pope ein Metaphysiker!*" *GS–2* 476–72.
ESG	"Einleitung zu *Sache Gottes, oder die gerettete Vorsehung*." *GS–2* 514–27.
ESL	"Einleitung zu *Sendschreiben an den Herrn Magister Lessing in Leipzig*." *GS–2* 473–75.
FP	"Fârâbî's *Plato*." In *Louis Ginzberg Jubilee Volume*. New York: American Academy for Jewish Research, 1945, 357–93.
FPP	*Faith and Political Philosophy: The Correspondence Between Leo Strauss and Eric Voegelin, 1934–1964*. Edited by Peter Emberley and Barry Cooper. Columbia, MO: University of Missouri Press, 2004.
GA	With Jacob Klein. "A Giving of Accounts." *The College* (Annapolis, MD) 22, no. 1 (April 1970): 1–5.
GA–*JPCM*	"A Giving of Accounts," *JPCM* 457–66.
GS–1	*Gesammelte Schriften*, Band 1: *Die Religionskritik Spinozas und gehörige Schriften*. Herausgegeben von Heinrich Meier. Stuttgart und Weimar: J. B. Metzler Verlag, 1996; 3rd, rev. and expanded ed., 2008.
GS–2	*Gesammelte Schriften*, Band 2: *Philosophie und Gesetz—Frühe Schriften*. Herausgegeben von Heinrich Meier. Stuttgart und Weimar: J. B. Metzler Verlag, 1997; 2nd rev. printing, 1998; 3rd printing, 2004.

GS–3 *Gesammelte Schriften*, Band 3: *Hobbes' politische Wissenschaft, and zugehörige Schriften—Briefe*. Herausgegeben von Heinrich Meier. Stuttgart und Weimar: J. B. Metzler Verlag, 2001; 2nd, rev. ed., 2008.

HBS "How to Begin to Study *The Guide of the Perplexed*." Maimonides, Moses. *The Guide of the Perplexed*. Translated by Shlomo Pines. Introductory Essay by Leo Strauss. Chicago: University of Chicago Press, 1963.

HCR *Hobbes's Critique of Religion and Related Writings*. Translated and Edited by Gabriel Bartlett and Svetozar Minkov. Chicago: University of Chicago Press, 2011.

ISP "The Intellectual Situation of the Present." Appendix C of the present volume.

JPCM *Jewish Philosophy and the Crisis of Modernity*. Edited by Kenneth Hart Green. Albany, NY: State University of New York Press, 1997.

LAM *Liberalism Ancient and Modern*. New York: Basic Books, 1968.

LSEW *The Early Writings (1921–1932)*. Translated and Edited by Michael Zank. Albany, NY: SUNY Press, 2002.

LSMC *Leo Strauss on Maimonides: The Complete Writings*. Edited by Kenneth Hart. Chicago, IL: University of Chicago Press, 2013.

LSMM *Leo Strauss on Moses Mendelssohn*. Translated, Edited, and with an Interpretive Essay by Martin D. Yaffe. Chicago, IL: University of Chicago Press, 2012.

NRH *Natural Right and History*. Chicago, IL: University of Chicago Press, 1953.

ONI "On a New Interpretation of Plato's Political Philosophy." *Social Research* 13 (1946): 326–67.

OPS *On Plato's "Symposium."* Edited by Seth Benardete. Chicago, IL: University of Chicago Press, 2001.

OPSPS "The Origins of Political Science and the Problem of Socrates." *Interpretation* 23, no. 2 (1996):127–208.

OT *On Tyranny*. Revised and Expanded Edition, Including the Strauss-Kojève Correspondence. Edited by Victor Gourevitch and Michael S. Roth. New York: Free Press, 1991.

PAW *Persecution and the Art of Writing*. Glencoe, IL: Free Press, 1952.

PG *Philosophie und Gesetz: Beiträge zum Verständnis Maimunis und seiner Vorläufer*. Berlin: Schocken Verlag, 1935.

PLA *Philosophy and Law: Contributions to the Understanding of Maimonides and His Predecessors*. Translated by Eve Adler. Albany, NY: SUNY Press, 1995.

PLB *Philosophy and Law: Essays Toward the Understanding of Maimonides and His Predecessors*. Translated by Fred Baumann. Philadelphia, PA: Jewish Publication Society, 1987.

PPH *The Political Philosophy of Hobbes: Its Basis and Its Genesis*. Translated by Elsa M. Sinclair. Reprint. Chicago: University of Chicago Press, 1952.[1]

PoP "The Place of the Doctrine of Providence according to Maimonides." Translated by Gabriel Bartlett and Svetozar Minkov. *Review of Metaphysics* 57 (2004): 537–49.

PoR "Progress or Return?" *JPCM* 87–136.

RCPR *The Rebirth of Classical Political Rationalism*. Edited by Thomas L. Pangle. Chicago, IL: University of Chicago Press, 1989.

RSP "Religious Situation of the Present." Appendix B of the present volume.

SA *Socrates and Aristophanes*. New York: Basic Books, 1966.

SCR *Spinoza's Critique of Religion*. Translated by Elsa M. Sinclair. New York: Schocken Books, 1965.

SR "Some Remarks on the Political Science of Farabi and Maimonides." *Interpretation* 18 (1990–91): 1–30.

SSTX "The Spirit of Sparta or the Taste of Xenophon." *Social Research* 6 (1939): 502–36.

TM *Thoughts on Machiavelli*. Glencoe, IL: The Free Press, 1958.

TWM "Three Waves of Modernity." In *An Introduction to Political Philosophy: Ten Essays by Leo Strauss*. Edited by Hilail Gildin. Detroit, MI: Wayne State University Press, 1989.

WIPP *What is Political Philosophy? And Other Studies*. Glencoe, IL: Free Press, 1959.

XS *Xenophon's Socrates*. Ithaca, NY: Cornell University Press, 1972.

XSD *Xenophon's Socratic Discourse: An Interpretation of the "Oeconomicus."* Ithaca, NY: Cornell University Press, 1970.

Other Titles

JMW *The Jew in the Modern World: A Documentary History*. Edited by Paul Mendes-Flohr and Jehuda Reinharz. 2nd ed. New York: Oxford University Press, 1995.

NHE Karl Löwith. *Nature, History, and Existentialism*. Edited by Arnold Levison. Evanston, IL: Northwestern University Press, 1966.

MPP–1 *Medieval Political Philosophy: A Sourcebook*. Edited by Ralph Lerner and Muhsin Mahdi. New York: Free Press of Glencoe, 1963.

MPP–2 *Medieval Political Philosophy: A Sourcebook*. 2nd ed. Edited by Joshua Parens and Joseph C. Macfarland. Ithaca, NY: Cornell University Press, 2011.

Other Abbreviations

Gk. Greek

Ger. German

Heb. Hebrew

{HM} Heinrich Meier (appended to footnote as its author)

Lat. Latin

Lit. literally

{LS} Leo Strauss (appended to footnote as its author)

Note

1. Originally: Oxford: Clarendon Press, 1936. This edition will be referred to as *The Political Philosophy of Hobbes* (1936). It differs from the 1952 reprint in that the latter includes a two-page "Preface to the American Edition" by Strauss, which begins as follows: "For various reasons this study is here reissued in its original form. It is, no doubt, in need of considerable revision. But it still seems to me that the way in which I approached Hobbes is preferable to the available alternatives. Hobbes appeared to me as the originator of modern political philosophy. This was an error: not Hobbes but Machiavelli deserves this honor. But I still prefer that easily corrected error, or rather its characteristic premises, to the more generally accepted views which I was forced to oppose and which are less easily corrected" (p. xv).

EDITORS' INTRODUCTION

Martin D. Yaffe and Richard S. Ruderman

As a young scholar in 1920s Germany, Leo Strauss, under Ernst Cassirer, earned his doctorate with a dissertation on F. H. Jacobi, went on to study with Edmund Husserl and Martin Heidegger, worked on a series of studies on primarily Jewish themes while employed at the Academy for the Scientific Study of Judaism in Berlin, and, as he soon afterward said about his intellectual outlook during his twenties, was "so dominated and bewitched" by the thought of Friedrich Nietzsche "that I literally believed everything that I understood of him."[1] What this perhaps hyperbolic remark seems to have meant is that Strauss was convinced by Nietzsche that "God is dead"—namely that not only the Biblical God but also the high claims of rationalism (Plato's Ideas, Aristotle's *teloi*, the modern scientific reconstruction of human life) had all been shown to have lost their power to convince or compel the modern (or nascent postmodern) soul to assent to their putative truths. Indeed, Truth itself (as a plausible concept) would seem to have breathed its last. And while the charm of Plato continued to hold sway over the young Strauss—he remarked in a reminiscence late in life that he would once have loved nothing less than to have been a rural postmaster who spent his free time raising rabbits and studying the Platonic dialogues[2]—he could only have done so in the somewhat impotent manner of the amused end-of-history thinker looking to fill his days (or, as a hostile critic would later say, "rolling the classics round the tongue like old brandy"[3]), for he remained convinced that a "return to the classics was not possible."

What were the then widely accepted reasons for this supposed impossibility? Advanced thinking of the time (at least in Germany, the most intellectually advanced country in the world) held that modern rationalism had refuted classical thought and had itself then been refuted by the historicist insights of Heidegger, leaving us without God, nature, or reason. By the end of the 1920s, however, Strauss was beginning to suspect that the natural situation of man had not yet been completely obliterated or shown to be a sham, but remained rather as a hidden possibility to be uncovered. That possibility was far from being a simple "given" in the situation of modern men, immediately or directly available to any who sought it. For modern man's situation, as Strauss's studies of Hobbes (whom he took at the time to be the founder of modernity) were beginning to reveal to him, was not a natural but rather a constructed one.[4] Man, according to the early modern philosophers who were dedicated to improving his lot, was no longer to be understood in terms of what he aspired to be. Such longings to transcend his given situation through *eros*, political ambition, an after-world, or such philosophical thought as culminates in some form of metaphysics, were to be understood—and rejected—as so many "imaginary republics and principalities" (Machiavelli, *Prince*, ch. 15). Instead, he should be posited, as it were, as he would have to be in order to achieve scientific and political certainty in his situation. If political science was to achieve the Euclidean certainty that Hobbes sought for it, man would have to be simplified so as to take on the countable and interchangeable nature of numbers. And so, Hobbes rejected all claims of human inequality as the wishful thinking of vainglorious thinkers who mistook their dreams for reality. If men could be understood as equal—or if they could simply view themselves as though they were equal (see *Leviathan*, ch. 15, end of paragraph 21)—they could enter into a social contract that would stabilize their politics and thereby liberate their lives for the safe pursuit of all civilized pastimes. In the absence of any naturally ordered world, Hobbesian man would have to construct one by means of modern science.

Now, the classical philosophers would not have denied that men had always begun from a "made" or "created" world, the world that Plato called the "cave." But that world was created by poets, not scientists or philosophers. And those poets—at least those of the caliber of Homer and Hesiod—offered captivating tableaus of human nature that stood as invitations to their audience to reflect on and deepen their understanding of that nature. Such worlds or caves, then, retained openings to the light, to the natural world outside of any and all societies, such that potential philosophers who detected contradictions in the authoritative poetic accounts could escape from them into the world of nature. But the modern world was to be a construct, not of poets, but of philosophers and scientists themselves. And, since the world of nature could no longer be viewed as one of light but rather of mute darkness (random matter in motion, as Hobbes put it), modern philosophic liberation had an altogether different character than that of classical philosophic liberation. Modernity ultimately came to be the first time in human history when the authority of philosophy itself stood opposed to the search for human nature or any and all timeless truths.

The 1930s marked Strauss's "change of orientation," a change that represented or consisted of his rediscovery of political philosophy and therewith the possibility of an escape from the limitations of modern thought, culminating in a return to classical philosophy. On the suspicion that the natural starting point for philosophical reflection (Plato's "cave") had been lost to us through the construction of an unnatural, man-made world (modern philosophy had, in Strauss's arresting formula, dug for us a "pit beneath the cave"), Strauss set out in the 1930s to test four grand arguments: first, that the modern world was a constructed one that could not, strictly speaking, be considered either natural or rational; second, that the failure of that world to become rational meant that modern philosophy had neither refuted religion nor established its own basis as philosophy; third, that the great medieval political philosophers were not, as was widely thought, convinced that monotheism had fundamentally altered the nature of man but rather that they showed a way back to true rationalism from within changed circumstances; and fourth, that only by reopening the great moral and theological questions as genuine questions (i.e., by admitting man's natural interest in them, irrespective of the external pressures of social, political, and theological actors) could one recover the genuine classical approach to grounding the still possible life of philosophy. This meant that Strauss had to dedicate himself to thoroughgoing reexaminations of the founders of modernity (chiefly Hobbes, whose subordination of the truth to political goals continued to have overwhelming influence, even on his chief critic, Carl Schmitt) and of modern, dismissive Biblical criticism (Spinoza); of the medieval thinkers and their forgotten art of esoteric writing (Farabi, Maimonides); of various misleading efforts of those who would recover earlier thought (F. H. Jacobi, Hermann Cohen, Franz Rosenzweig); and finally, of the ancients properly understood (Strauss began with Xenophon at the end of the 1930s). This collection constitutes the first comprehensive effort to examine Strauss's astonishingly wide-ranging essays and books of the 1930s (some of which having become available only recently to English-speaking readers, including several herein) with a view to their unifying theme of recovering classical political philosophy.

Reorientation: Leo Strauss in the 1930s seeks to explain the "change in orientation" that Strauss underwent during that eventful decade. While Strauss arrived in America in 1937, and only began publishing the books that garnered attention in the 1950s, it was in the 1930s (a decade of much personal as well as political upheaval) that Strauss made the series of fundamental breakthroughs that enabled him to recover, for the first time since the Middle Ages, the genuine meaning of political philosophy and therewith the possibility of recovering classical philosophy. Despite this being a period of extraordinary and wide-ranging productivity, Strauss's research in this period remains overlooked and largely unknown. This has primarily been true in the English-speaking world, since so many of his essays in this period have not been translated into English until quite recently (we add several new translations in this volume). In fact, one major manuscript (*Hobbes's Critique of Religion*) was not published at all until the twenty-first century. The lack of attention paid to this period is unfortunate, for several reasons. During this period, Strauss's manner of writing, though extremely intricate and demanding, was relatively lacking in the allusiveness and extreme restraint that made some of his later works sometimes difficult to access. Second, it is during this period that the reader can follow Strauss, step by step, as he works out his liberation from the "pit beneath the cave" (namely, the artificial situation imposed on man by modern political philosophy and modern science that must be overcome merely to return to the "cave," the natural moral and political consciousness of man from which and only from which it is possible to ascend to genuine classical philosophy). In the 1930s, we see Strauss recovering genuine philosophy.

* * *

The recovery Strauss undertook involved multiple, interlocking investigations. This volume assembles in one place an examination of the various parts of Strauss's project so that the reader can more fully appreciate the manner in which the parts rely on and support one another. In his opening, comprehensive chapter ("How Strauss Became Strauss"), Heinrich Meier focuses on the meaning of "political philosophy" and its centrality to Strauss's project. Unlike those who treated it as a subset of philosophy—a way of thinking about politics that presupposed the existence and validity of philosophy itself as an undertaking—Strauss treated political philosophy as the essential introduction to or vindication of philosophy. This entailed addressing the pre-philosophic political opinions (including the moral and religious opinions) of communities in their fullness, especially in their characteristic view that philosophy was either "vicious or useless" (*Republic* VI). Political philosophy, then, had to perform the function of justifying philosophy before the tribunal of the city. As Meier shows, Strauss came to see that political philosophy's central theme is not "belief and knowledge" but, rather, "law and philosophy." Not different ways of knowing but different ways of life are at issue in the confrontation between reason and revelation. And this means that the relation between reason and belief is one of conflict, not of two alternative ways of knowing the world that can stand side by side or that can be synthesized into some combination.

Steven Frankel looks at the dramatic change in Strauss's understanding of the seminal Jewish apostate Baruch Spinoza. It was, after all, Spinoza, more than any other thinker, who initially convinced Strauss of the impossibility of a return to classical thought. Frankel focuses on the so-called autobiographical Preface to the 1962 English translation of Strauss's *Spinoza's Critique of Religion*. He shows that that Preface, rather than being genuinely autobiographical, is in fact a kind of series of "Socratic dialogues" pitting various philosophical authorities against one another—Martin Buber against Heidegger, Cohen against Spinoza, Rosenzweig against Maimonides, and liberalism against Zionism. Frankel helps us to see that Strauss, rather than trying to show or illuminate the specific historical influences that shaped his youthful (limited) understanding of Spinoza and related questions, had, by 1962, become capable of seeing the ways in which the apparently time-bound disputes of the 1920s and 1930s were in fact iterations (strikingly new ones in many ways) of various permanent questions.

In the only chapter in the volume covering a personal friendship of Strauss, Thomas L. Pangle examines the epistolary exchange with Gerhard Krüger. Krüger was alone among all of Strauss's intellectual friends and acquaintances to join with him in taking a "philosophical interest" in theology. Krüger and Strauss were distinctive in recognizing that the (widely understood) crisis of modern Enlightenment thought lay not so much in its failure to provide a rational ethics with which to replace Biblical ethics, but in its prior failure to adequately meet the challenge to rationalism itself from "supra-rational and contra-rational revelation." Only Krüger was able to share in Strauss's eagerness to elevate consideration of Nietzsche's claim that "God is dead" from the sociological level (a mere description of the religious-mental state of modern European man) to the philosophical level (i.e., to raise the question of whether modern scientific and philosophical thought had indeed refuted revelation in general or even Christian revelation specifically). The correspondence, Pangle shows, proceeds by indicating both the inadequacy of the modern treatment of the religious question and the initial steps Strauss was beginning to take—with the acknowledged assistance of the great medieval political philosophers, chiefly Farabi and Maimonides—toward the adequate and even definitive ancient, Platonic approach to the question. For even if orthodoxy had been marginalized and weakened by the successes of modernity (as Krüger and Strauss each acknowledged), the contemporary call (by men such as Karl Barth and Franz Rosenzweig) for a return to orthodoxy (or at any rate a kind of "'post-modern' neo-orthodoxy") posed (and would continue to pose) a theoretical challenge to philosophy. Strauss traced the inadequacy of the modern approach to its critique of miracles—a critique, he showed, that presupposed "enlightened" man (who could accept nothing on faith) and thereby begged the question. The correspondence, then, shows Strauss completing his escape from the Heideggerian influence (at least with respect to the modern atheistic assumptions toward revelation) with which he was partly entangled when he wrote his first book (*Spinoza's Critique of Religion*). This is marked by his evolving understanding of the "ancient" critique of religion as being, at its deepest, not Epicurean, but Platonic. Now, as Pangle further shows through a brief discussion of Strauss's later consideration (in 1959) of Krüger's final book (*Insight and Passion: The Essence of Platonic Thinking* (1939)), Krüger was not in fact able to follow Strauss's lead or take his hints as to how to recover an adequate understanding of the Platonic approach. For he, no less than Heidegger himself, could not entertain the possibility that Plato supplied the answer to the theological question, in large measure because they still labored under Christian assumptions about the altered and supposedly deepened nature of man brought about by the now-disintegrated Christianity.

Martin D. Yaffe next examines the question of whether in Strauss's understanding Hermann Cohen's efforts at "Platonizing" Maimonides were convincing—and whether Cohen may ultimately have been right that Maimonides is best understood as a Platonist, but for different reasons than those adduced by Cohen. Cohen tried to show that Maimonides presented God as a moral-ideal for humanity, thereby (Cohen thought) siding with Plato over and against Aristotle (who placed intellectual virtue ahead of moral virtue). But, Yaffe explains how Strauss showed that, on this key question of the relative superiority of the intellectual to the moral virtues, Plato was in agreement with Aristotle—and that Maimonides' view of God does indeed comport with Plato's view, properly understood. Moreover, insofar as Maimonides understood the Torah as itself a document of political philosophy that served as a "propaedeutic to philosophy," he was ultimately indeed more a Platonist than an Aristotelian.

In the next chapter, Timothy W. Burns considers two remarkable talks that Strauss gave in 1930 and 1932 on the "Religious" and the "Intellectual" situation of the present. (The two talks, never before translated, are presented in our Appendices B and C.) In these talks, Strauss elaborates, in the wake of his unpublished book review of the sociologist Karl Mannheim (Appendix A), his understanding of the "present" as a curious amalgamation of temporal and permanent concerns. Focusing (in front of his young German-Jewish audience) on "the Jewish problem," Strauss discusses both the "theologico-political *predicament*," and the "theologico-political *problem*." The former is a time-bound, local, if exceptionally pressing, problem for German Jews in the era of nascent Nazism. The latter, however, is a permanent problem, perhaps the central permanent problem: should man be guided by revelation or by his freely-employed reason? In order to see his way to the genuine contours of this problem, Strauss has to begin by showing the inadequacy of the "new thinking" and new theology of Rosenzweig—as well as of the inadequate defense of reason mounted by Mannheim against the greatest philosophical critic of reason, Heidegger. Burns shows the way in which Strauss powerfully demonstrates both the allure and the fundamental dishonesty or incompleteness of "the Present." For the Present, as interpreted by the children of modernity and "ultra-modernity" (what today is called postmodernity), is nothing other than a summing up and dividing of all purported and equally valid "truths" into a sort of "mean" that is meant to satisfy all by satisfying none. "Our" Present—that is, the purported result of our dedication to reason—is characterized by its smug certainty that reason teaches there is no "Truth." Strauss, Burns argues, teaches that the greatest obstacle to reason in "our" time comes not from frankly antirational outlooks such as revealed religion, but from the false reason of modernity and ultramodernity masquerading as philosophy.

Nasser Behnegar, in the subsequent chapter dealing with Strauss's "Comments on Carl Schmitt's *The Concept of the Political*," helps us understand what was, according to Strauss himself, "the pivotal moment" in his life. Schmitt was perhaps the most thoughtful critic of liberalism in Germany at the time. And more than a few features of his critique were apt to interest Strauss. Above all, Schmitt wished to show that liberalism was deeply hostile to the fundamentally political nature of man, a nature that had been illegitimately (if astoundingly successfully) covered over or assumed away by the prestidigitation of Hobbes's "state of nature." Now, insofar as Hobbes had been engaged in a political critique of the political nature of man (i.e., a critique that was meant to advance his brand of politics) it won Schmitt's respect as an unusually successful instance of polemics. But Schmitt, as Behnegar shows through his intricate analysis of Strauss's argument, labors under a massive contradiction: he argues both that man's nature (in the "natural order of things") is political *and* that politics is always fundamentally polemical, that is, time-bound and related to a "concrete political existence." Behnegar's analysis reveals, then, the deepest basis for Strauss's interest in Schmitt: the latter exemplified the tempting but ultimately flawed way of escaping from what Schmitt perceived to be the debilitating tyranny of liberalism by adopting or remaining under the unconscious sway of liberalism's chief assumptions. Those assumptions, at least when inverted, provided the only cogent assumptions—other than "murderous hatred of the Jews"[5]—that lay behind National Socialism. As Strauss memorably puts it in his "Comments": Schmitt's effort at repoliticizing man, tolerant as it was toward any and all convictions that are willing to risk war and death, "proves to be liberalism preceded by a minus sign."[6] Liberalism, that is, considers as true whatever tends toward peace; Schmitt's thought considers as true whatever tends toward war (for only in war can the noble nature of man emerge). Now, as Strauss puts it in a later writing, "we should not behave toward Thrasymachus as Thrasymachus behaves."[7] We see in Behnegar's elaboration of Strauss's "Comments" the first concrete step Strauss was able to take in rejecting liberalism's depoliticization of man without making the apparently concomitant Schmittian error of valorizing war or deadly decision-making. Instead, Strauss points to the Platonic manner of rejecting that depoliticization: we need to raise anew the question of the best regime, a political question (submerged by Hobbes and the liberalism that arose on his basis) that without contradiction reopens the question of the true nature of man and thereby of his satisfaction. Strauss, we see, wishes to salvage Schmitt's natural longing for the full coming-to-be of man's noblest possibilities from the derailment it suffers through remaining enmeshed in the Hobbesian notion that human seriousness is a willed matter (which willing Schmitt promotes and Hobbes sought to end). And, as Behnegar finally shows, it is through Strauss's recovery of the sense of evil as "moral depravity" (as opposed to the "innocent" evil that Hobbes had understood to emanate from unenlightened man) that enabled Strauss, unlike Schmitt, to "restore the connection between politics and morality." Schmitt could not see the moral basis of his condemnation of liberalism because he fundamentally and mistakenly accepted liberalism's view of morality as a private affair. If, instead, we recover the sense of morality as indeed a force in human nature—a force not to be bracketed through a somewhat cowardly retreat to the supposedly neutral, morality-free plane of "theory"—we will finally once again be in a position to engage profitably in the problem represented by the "antagonism between belief and unbelief."

In the following chapter, Timothy W. Burns examines Strauss's arguments in his unfinished manuscript from 1933–34 (translated and published by Gabriel Bartlett and Svetozar Minkov in 2011), *Hobbes's Critique of Religion*, the first extended if ultimately incomplete product that followed on the "change in orientation" that he later identified as having first received public expression in "Comments on Carl Schmitt's *The Concept of the Political*." The echo, in the title, of Strauss's first book (*Spinoza's Critique of Religion*) should not mislead the reader into thinking that Strauss was rehearsing the same arguments with little changed but the names. For not only had Strauss come to see how much more daunting the task modern philosophy had undertaken was in refuting religion in the process of justifying itself as a genuinely rational enterprise; he had also learned how much more penetrating and satisfactory (because more open-minded) Hobbes's critique of miracles was than that of Spinoza (or Descartes). Strauss reveals, in Burns's reading, that Hobbes's critique of religion (which included a critique of classical philosophical politics, insofar as that classical approach had supplied the "dangerous weapon" of incorporeal substances to Christian theologians) was not the result of his materialist philosophy—as the *Leviathan* appears to argue—but became rather the presupposition or foundation of his whole philosophy. Hobbes's procedure involves granting the possibility of a mysterious, all-powerful God (a concession the more polemical Spinoza did not grant)—which possibility renders nature and hence philosophy radically questionable. To contend with—and ultimately to dispose of—this possibility, Hobbes inaugurates a grand "civilizational" project by which man and the world will be transformed in such a way as to render him and it impervious to miracles. As the scientific mind (initially lacking a true foundation) becomes more pervasive, belief in and even interest in miracles can be counted on to fade. This hope in the progress of the human mind proves then to be the foundation of modern rationalism. And, as Burns shows through his discussion of Strauss's later, rather different, analysis of Hobbes's critique in *Natural Right and History*, Hobbes's hope obscured from him the "ultimate futility of all human endeavors" (a futility that Hobbes's materialistic—and even "idealistic"—predecessors recognized all too well).

Joshua Parens's study of Strauss's "Farabian turn" (the phrase is Daniel Tanguay's)[8] provides valuable insight into the thought and extraordinary influence of Farabi on both Maimonides and Strauss. Through a careful examination of a series of very little-known essays on Farabi, Maimonides, and Abravanel, Parens shows that Strauss was far more open in his writings of the 1930s than in his more well-known essays of later years with regard to Farabi's crucial influence on Maimonides. A proper appreciation of that influence enables us not only to interpret Maimonides better, but even to understand the reasons for Strauss's growing tendency to downplay that influence. For Farabi supplies the two keys essential for understanding Maimonides: the centrality of political science and of esoteric writing. Prior to seeing the scope of his debt to Farabi, Strauss was still apt to read Maimonides as turning to "supernatural resources" to supply the defect or limits of natural human knowledge. He still, that is, saw in Maimonides another, if perhaps the greatest, synthesizer of reason and revelation. After seeing that Maimonides shared with Farabi the belief that there could be no synthesis of these two ultimately antagonistic outlooks—and that esoteric writing was the historical and even necessary manner in which that antagonism would have to be carefully expressed—Strauss's understanding of Maimonides (and the struggle between belief and unbelief) deepened considerably. From Farabi, Strauss learned that the political—both political science as means of analysis and the Law as the fundamental social, moral, and psychological aspect of man—was "central" to Maimonides's undertakings in the *Guide*. In turning his focus from "theoretical philosophy" and "metaphysics" to the "Law" and "particular providence," Strauss was able to find a more, not a less, rationalist Maimonides. Moreover, this emphasis on political philosophy—on the effort to resolve on the moral plane the dispute between philosophy and the city and its Law or its gods—revealed to Strauss the Platonic core of Farabi's and Maimonides's approaches. Farabi, Parens shows, was of unusual importance to Strauss, insofar as he was the first thinker to show that it was possible to return to classical thought from within a far-from-classical world, and how to do so.

In his chapter on "The Problem of the Enlightenment: Strauss, Jacobi, and the Pantheism Controversy," David Janssens provides the prehistory of the chief concerns animating Strauss in the 1930s. He does so through a careful and revealing analysis of how Strauss was and was not influenced by the subject of his 1921 dissertation, F. H. Jacobi. Jacobi, a younger friend and admirer of Lessing, became an outspoken and influential critic of the Enlightenment, in both its radical (Spinozist) and its moderate (Mendelssohnian) forms. While despising the latter position as an unconvincing effort to stand between two stools (as well as to replace biblical revelation by the subterfuge of "common sense"), Jacobi had a certain respect for the former as one of the key consistent and rigorous engineers of the Enlightenment outlook. That outlook, which claimed to liberate human understanding and therewith moral and political life from traditional authorities, was recognized by Jacobi as fundamentally destructive of all that could not be made a "clear and distinct" object of rational, scientific thought. By applying radical doubt to the world (in order to ground our knowledge more securely), the early Enlighteners were guilty of reducing "Being or reality to non-Being or Nothingness" (which he termed, in a new coinage, "nihilism"). More importantly (as such and to Strauss's development), Jacobi recognized the nontheoretical and in fact moral impetus behind the modern reconstitution of science and of moral/political life. In order to grant man autonomy, morality had to be reconceived as following the norms that we ourselves generate (following on the model of a science that understands what it creates or posits). But—anticipating Strauss's rediscovery of the crucial importance of the Law—Jacobi saw that only out of obedience to a norm, via heteronomy, "does moral insight emerge." Moreover, Jacobi saw that, to liberate man from heteronomy, the Enlightenment had to "liberate man from the authority of transcendence." While Jacobi understood this "liberation" as amounting to nothing other than a revolt against God—and consequently proposed faith (in both God and in the given world) as the antidote to the Enlightenment's impoverishing of man—Strauss recognized that enlisting transcendence for a moral or political purpose was just as suspect as was condemning it for a contrary purpose. (Strauss reproduced this line of thought throughout the 1920s in his Zionist writings, where he found both the efforts of the political Zionists to liberate the Jews from God, and those of the religious Zionists to enlist God, to be equally guilty of presupposing a "truth" in order to satisfy a human, moral need.) And so, while Strauss was impressed and influenced by many aspects of Jacobi's critique of the Enlightenment, Janssens powerfully demonstrates that he could not and did not share Jacobi's turn to irrationalism, authoritarianism, and faith as an alternative. Indeed, Strauss saw that Jacobi remained enmeshed in modern presuppositions even as he sought to counter them. Janssens completes his analysis of Jacobi and his influence on Strauss with a consideration of Strauss's 1930s writings on Mendelssohn. Eager to defend "natural religion," Mendelssohn rejected all religious doctrines incompatible with the goodness of God. In doing so, Mendelssohn also fell prey to the modern genuflection before autonomy. Thus, Janssens concludes, neither Jacobi nor Mendelssohn made any serious effort to recover the ancient, Socratic outlook. For that, Strauss turned to their common, infinitely more ironic and nondogmatic friend, Lessing (whose *Nathan the Wise* Strauss took to be "the outstanding poetic monument erected in honor of medieval Jewish philosophy").

In the following chapter, Richard S. Ruderman considers Strauss's first publication devoted exclusively to an ancient author, "The Spirit of Sparta or the

Taste of Xenophon." This essay, written shortly after Strauss's arrival in America in 1937, examines Xenophon's *Constitution of the Lacedaemonians.* Both the quiet, bashful nature of Xenophon's writings and the disrepute into which he had fallen by Strauss's time could lead the unwary reader into thinking that Strauss's work was a mere obscurantist scholarly production. Ruderman shows that Strauss's essay was timely without seeking to be so, since the "spirit of Sparta" (the attraction of which having been relaunched in modernity by Rousseau)—namely the longing for total human transformation or perfection through political life—was very much on the march in 1930s Europe. More important, Strauss demonstrated, through a careful reading of the *Constitution*, that Xenophon was satirizing, not praising, the Spartan way of life—and was doing so from the perspective of philosophy. He was thereby able to show that Xenophon was able to demonstrate, in his inimitably unassuming manner, that philosophy—precisely by taking the claims of the city, its founders, and its morality more seriously than did the city itself—would always and inevitably end up critiquing the city and its gods. But, following the Xenophontic Socrates's refusal to separate wisdom from moderation, Strauss presented to his readers two of the crucial features of philosophy that had been obscured or denied throughout the course of modernity: first, it was an essentially theoretical enterprise that neither could nor should seek to transform the world; and second, it could only dismiss politics or ethics (as Heidegger, for instance, did) at the cost of losing the opportunity to engage in the kind of political philosophy that alone could justify its practice as a way of life.

In the final chapter of the volume, Hannes Kerber discusses Strauss's final writing (though unpublished until after his death) of the 1930s, "Exoteric Teaching." While Strauss had made a variety of observations regarding exoteric and esoteric writing throughout the 1930s, and would continue to do so in the 1940s and beyond (most famously in *Persecution and the Art of Writing*), "Exoteric Teaching" is unique in its exclusive focus on European authors (avoiding the medieval Islamic and Jewish authors from whom he had learned of the phenomenon in the first place). In particular, Strauss here considers Lessing (whose writings confirmed and deepened Strauss's suspicions regarding esotericism more than perhaps any others) and Schleiermacher (whose powerful and influential denial that Plato was an esoteric writer Strauss sought to refute). Schleiermacher was not unacquainted with the thesis of esotericism. Moreover, he usefully distinguished esoteric "subject matters" (as in Pythagoreanism) from the esoteric "manner of presentation." He then denied that either view applied to Plato. Kerber shows that Strauss agreed with Schleiermacher in rejecting Platonic esotericism thus understood. For Plato did not follow the Pythagoreans in refusing to discuss "in public" (i.e., in his writings) certain topics and he did not divide his oeuvre into popular or "exoteric" and scientific or "esoteric" writings. There is, in all of Plato's writings, both a comprehensive account of all subjects, so to speak, and a perfect fusion or interweaving of esoteric and exoteric presentations. Schleiermacher, in short, had failed to grasp the specific nature of Plato's intended audience—the potential philosopher—and thus had failed to see that the Platonic mode of education present throughout the dialogues consisted of broaching every subject "exoterically" (i.e., through an appeal to some sort of popular or accepted opinion) and then to move, not "continuously" (as though deepening an essentially correct view with fuller insights), but "discontinuously" via a conversion or "turning-around" of the soul to the "esoteric" level. And, as Kerber points out, Schleiermacher's inability to see Plato's exotericism was connected to his failure to see the *need* for it: Socrates was not engaged in a mere quarrel with polytheism or popular religion (as though striving to purify the object of the Athenians' sound but confused religious longings) but was questioning the "gods of the city of Athens," which gods underwrote the political and moral basis of Athenian life. Schleiermacher's rejection of Platonic esotericism, then, was connected to his failure to see the radical content of Socratic questioning. Finally, Kerber notes perhaps the chief insight or advance made by Strauss in the course of the 1930s due to his deepened understanding of esotericism: while he had still understood Maimonides to be nothing more than a "believing Jew" in his start-of-the-decade *Spinoza's Critique of Religion*, he came to see, by the decade's end, that Maimonides was a philosopher who, through his example and his teaching, made the return to classical philosophy a plausible and indeed compelling possibility.

Our appendices include translations of several fascinating writings of Strauss's from the 1930s that have been unavailable in English till now. In "Conspectivism" (1929), Strauss uncovers the questionable moral motive behind the contemporary effort to replace the notion of timeless truth with something like the "spirit of the age," an outlook not precisely held by anyone at the time, but an assumed conglomeration or averaging of all partial but equally valid outlooks. One cannot help but express Strauss's intention here as being an effort to clarify the nature of "our" cave and to do so in such a way as to incline us to the suspicion that an egalitarian moral motive (and not a genuine theoretical insight) lay behind its novel (and purportedly theoretical) denial that one could escape from the cave. Strauss then critiques at length the efforts of sociologist Karl Mannheim to defend, through conspectivism, rationalism (i.e., the effort to celebrate the fact that multiple philosophies exist that cannot and do not presume to refute one another and thereby to ground themselves).

In "Religious Situation of the Present" (1930) and "The Intellectual Situation of the Present" (1932), both analyzed in detail in this volume by Timothy W. Burns, Strauss undertakes not merely to summarize those respective situations, but to bring a radical critique to bear on the very notion of their importance or existence. Indeed, he shows the very problematical nature of the always-powerful enticement of "the present." Not deeper entanglement with the "present," but a return to the fundamental, original meanings of the Bible and of Plato is what is needed. Through reinforcing or bowing to the moral prejudices of the time, the religious thinkers and intellectuals can be seen as standing athwart Thinking and yelling "stop!"

We should add that the translators of the three foregoing writings have annotated them somewhat sparingly, so as to call attention to Strauss's evidently not considering the German originals ready or worthy to be published as they stand.

"A Lost Writing of Farâbî's" (1936) and "On Abravanel's Critique of Monarchy" (1937) supply intricate supplemental background to Joshua Parens's penetrating discussion of Strauss's studies of medieval political philosophy throughout the 1930s. The former essay proceeds in a somewhat scholarly fashion to disentangle the genuine Farabi from the rather less penetrating version of him transmitted by the Jewish thinker Falaquera—the Farabi who, as Strauss concludes, was "the towering figure who laid the ground for the later development and set down its limits by making his task the revival of Platonic-Aristotelian philosophy as philosophy as such." The latter is a brief but arresting effort to disentangle Abravanel's "theocratic" critique of monarchy from Joseph ibn Caspi's "aristocratic-philosophical" one (both of which are considered more or less identical by the essay under review). In the course of his demonstration, Strauss traces Caspi's argument to a somewhat overlooked passage in Maimonides' *Guide of the Perplexed*, thereby offering a small and early example of how to read Maimonides as an esoteric thinker.

Finally, we present the original, unfinished work "Exoteric Teaching," and "Lecture Notes for 'Persecution and the Art of Writing,'" both analyzed herein by Hannes Kerber. The former supplies Strauss's pre-*Persecution and the Art of Writing* views on exoteric writing in general and the proper way of understanding Plato's exotericism in particular. And the latter supplies a plethora of evidence (much of which was not provided to the readers of the later essay "Persecution and the Art of Writing") from writers both ancient and modern that they employed and had to employ esoteric writing as well as a brief interpretation of *Don Quixote* that establishes it too as a masterpiece of esotericism.

The volume as a whole attempts to introduce the reader to the extraordinary and rapid evolution of Strauss's thought in the 1930s. His efforts at analyzing the current state of thinking (and of the political and religious possibilities thought to constitute our horizon) provide incentive to escape from the cave. And his studies of the medieval philosophers and, through them, the classics, provided him (and us) with proof of the possibility of such an escape. We hope, in presenting these studies, to ensure that Strauss's efforts will no longer be able to be dismissed as essentially Schmittian (or Jacobian) efforts at the authoritarian rejection of democratic modernity, nor as "rationalist" efforts at restoring religion, nor as "pain-loving antiquarianism."[9] For it was in the 1930s that Strauss made the first efforts in 400 years to uncover the true meaning of philosophy and the manner in which to vindicate it as a way of life.

Notes

1. Letter to Karl Löwith, June 23, 1935, *GS–3* 648; trans. George Elliot Tucker, in *Independent Journal of Philosophy* 5/6 (1988): 183; quoted in *JPCM* 63.
2. GA–*JPCM* 460.
3. Brian Barry, *Political Argument* (London: Routledge, 1965), 290.
4. See *HCR*.
5. *SCR* 3.
6. *SCR* 350.
7. *CM* 74.
8. Daniel Tanguay, *Leo Strauss: An Intellectual Biography*, trans. Christopher Nadon (New Haven: Yale University Press, 2007), 7.
9. *CM* 1.

CHAPTER 1

HOW STRAUSS BECAME STRAUSS

Heinrich Meier

Among the great philosophers of the twentieth century, political philosophy had only one advocate. For a long time it seemed to have been dispensed with by history or to have fallen into oblivion, thus to have become a thing of the past in every sense. That political philosophy has been recognized to have a present and ultimately a future is the achievement of Leo Strauss. It is especially this achievement that marks his place in the history of philosophy. And it alone would suffice to draw the keen attention of later philosophers to his oeuvre. For nothing less than their ownmost, their vital and rightly understood self-interest is in question with the disappearance or the recovery of political philosophy. Yet the revolution of thought that Strauss brought about single-handedly has a pre-history. The revolution is preceded by a *periagoge*, or a decisive turn, in Strauss's thought, just as political philosophy itself is based on a periagoge in philosophy. Whoever would like to understand this turn better, whoever is interested in how Strauss became Strauss, can now—with the aid of the first three volumes of his *Gesammelte Schriften*, which appeared between 1996 and 2001 and which come to some 2,000 pages, nearly half of which contain previously unpublished texts and letters—retrace step by step the path of thought that Strauss traversed in the formative period of his philosophy.[1]

The second volume of Strauss's *Gesammelte Schriften* comprises 35 texts that were written between 1921 and 1937. Together with the first and third volumes, which contain the books on Spinoza and Hobbes, as well as the accompanying writings from the same period, it makes accessible—in the original languages (German, French, and English)—Strauss's entire early work up to his emigration to the United States of America in 1938. Well over a quarter of the second volume consists of first publications. Part I makes available once again, after more than six decades, *Philosophie und Gesetz*, a book that marks the beginning of a radically new understanding of Maimonides and his Arabic "predecessors" in the horizon of Platonic political philosophy. The new edition of *Philosophie und Gesetz* is complemented by four important essays from 1936–37 on Farabi,

Maimonides, and Abravanel, which continue the new interpretative approach and are supplemented by previously untranscribed marginalia from Strauss's personal copies. Part I concludes with a brief, previously unknown comment entitled "Zu Abravanels Kritik des Königtums." Part II, entitled *Frühe Schriften*, begins with the first publication of Strauss's doctoral dissertation, *Das Erkenntnisproblem in der philosophischen Lehre Fr. H. Jacobis*, from 1921, and ends with a preface that Strauss wrote in 1937 in Cambridge to an unwritten book entitled *Eine Erinnerung an Lessing*. Between them lie numerous essays, lectures, articles, and reviews, which are presented in chronological order. These include the first publication of "Der Konspektivismus" (1929), "'Religiöse Lage der Gegenwart'" (1930), "Cohen und Maimuni" (1931), and "Die geistige Lage der Gegenwart" (1932).

Leo Strauss's second book-length work, *Philosophie und Gesetz. Beiträge zum Verständnis Maimunis und seiner Vorläufer*, was published by Schocken Verlag in Berlin in time for the festivities surrounding the eight-hundredth anniversary of Maimonides's birth on March 30, 1935. Just a few days later, Ludwig Feuchtwanger announced the new book in a review that began: "The concern that access to Maimonides would be more obstructed than opened up by the vast literature from the anniversary year is eliminated by Leo Strauss's revolutionary writing, *Philosophie und Gesetz*."[2] The volume's appearance on the Maimonides anniversary did not result, however, in either greater circulation or an appreciable public reception. Since it was a publication by a "Jewish author" on a "Jewish subject" with a Jewish publishing house—a circumstance that alone made it possible to publish *Philosophie und Gesetz* in the Germany of 1935[3]—it went virtually unnoticed beyond the few Jewish organs still in existence. Most libraries in Germany were closed to it. It did not even make it into the holdings of some university libraries. The contemporary debate passed over it almost completely in silence.[4] One can therefore say: *Philosophie und Gesetz* had been in print since spring 1935 without ever really having been made public. It remained a book for the few. In addition to the circle of specialists in the thought of the Jewish and Islamic Middle Ages, it reached "initiates" such as Ernest Barker in England, Étienne Gilson in France, and Carl Schmitt in Germany. And it received attention early from friends and acquaintances to whom Strauss himself sent the book: in philosophy, for example, to Hans-Georg Gadamer, Gerhard Krüger, Karl Löwith, Jacob Klein, Alexandre Koyré, and Alexandre Kojève; in Arabic and Judaic studies, to Fritz Baer, Shlomo Pines,[5] Paul Kraus, and Gershom Scholem. Their names may give an indication of the subterranean influence that *Philosophie und Gesetz* exerted from the very beginning.

The Maimonides anniversary was the reason for Schocken Verlag to publish *Philosophie und Gesetz* in 1935. Not so for Strauss. He had not written the book in view of the commemorative year, nor did he even write it as a *book* in the first place. He published it with an eye to his application for a professorship at the Hebrew University in Jerusalem that he decided to pursue in 1933–34 since his grant from the Rockefeller Foundation—which had led him first to Paris from October 1932 to December 1933 and then on to London in order to continue his Hobbes research—ended on September 30, 1934, and he had no hope of securing a position in either France or England. From autumn 1933 on, Strauss tried to get various positions in Jerusalem.[6] After Julius Guttmann, 19 years Strauss's senior and his superior at the Akademie für die Wissenschaft des Judentums (Academy for the Science of Judaism) in Berlin until 1932, had received the professorship for Jewish medieval philosophy in 1934, Gershom Scholem advised Strauss to publish something in Jewish studies as soon as possible in view of another vacant professorship. At the time Strauss had two essays ready for publication that fitted the bill, copies of which had already been circulating for some time and with which Scholem was quite familiar: the study "Maimunis Lehre von der Prophetie und ihre Quellen,"[7] which was completed in July 1931 and was originally to appear in the *Korrespondenzblatt* of the Akademie für die Wissenschaft des Judentums but did not because, for financial reasons, the *Korrespondenzblatt* could not be continued from 1931 on; and an essay of roughly the same length that was finished in September 1933 and that takes Julius Guttmann's *Philosophie des Judentums* published in the same year as the occasion for a fundamental statement and clarification of Strauss's own position.[8] On August 2, 1934, Strauss writes to Scholem: "To follow your advice to publish something soon in Jewish studies, I wrote to Nyberg, the editor of *Monde Oriental*, who had accepted my essay on Maimonides's prophetology and its sources for publication in the 1933 volume of the journal, asking him to print my essay finally." Strauss continues: "So since, as things stand, the publication might be delayed for some time still, I have considered whether it would not be feasible to publish either my Guttmann review or my Maimonides essay or both in Hebrew translation in a Palestinian journal. What do you think about that? And might you know of someone who would undertake the translation?" On December 14, 1934, Strauss is able to tell Scholem about an entirely different publication project: "Thanks to Ernst Simon's and Buber's kind mediation, there is now some hope that my essay on Maimonides's prophetology and its sources, as well as my notes on Guttmann's book, will finally be printed. Schocken Verlag's editor—Dr. Spitzer—writes me that he wants to recommend to Schocken that the essays be published on the occasion of the Maimonides anniversary as soon as a suitable title has been found that would justify the publication of the two at least formally quite different essays together in one volume. I suggest adding a short essay entitled "Die gesetzliche Begründung der Philosophie," in which I discuss the treatment of this theme in Ibn Rushd, Maimonides, and Levi b. Gershom, and then to entitle the volume *Philosophie und Gesetz. Ein Beitrag zur Maimuni-Forschung.* The decision is completely in Mr. Schocken's hands in Jerusalem. I would be enormously grateful to you if you would put in a good word for me with Schocken. An emphatic recommendation by Buber and an evaluation by Schaeder have been sent to Spitzer."[9] *Philosophie und Gesetz* now takes shape so rapidly and so concretely that Strauss is able to inform Guttmann not even six weeks later, on January 22, 1935, about the quite advanced preparations for its publication: "I have already finalized two essays for publication: the review of your book and a short article on the legal justification of philosophy in Ibn Rushd, Maimonides, and Gersonides. The essay on Maimonides's prophetology and its sources I hope to be able to send off in two or three days. And if I still have the time and leisure for it, I want to write an introduction that will motivate the publication of these essays, which are so diverse." We shall soon have occasion to speak of this introduction—the first part of the book, though the last to be written. On March 27, 1935, Strauss is able to report to Guttmann and his other correspondents that the book has been published. In just under three months, the plan had been realized. Strauss announces to Gerhard Krüger in Marburg "that in the next few days you will receive two copies of a booklet, one of which is for you and the other for Gadamer. I would be delighted to hear what each of you thinks of it sometime."

The history of the genesis of *Philosophie und Gesetz* is of interest insofar as it allows an adequate dating of the individual parts of the volume, and the chronology of the four essays making up *Philosophie und Gesetz* deserves, like the chronology of other works that Strauss wrote between 1929 and 1937, some consideration, since during these nine years a far-reaching reorientation of Strauss's thought occurs and his philosophical positions undergo a significant change. Strauss himself drew attention to the fact that after the completion of *Die Religionskritik Spinozas* in 1928 he reached a caesura that was of the greatest importance for his further path of thought. At the end of the long "autobiographical preface" to the English translation of his Spinoza book, he speaks of a "change of orientation," which took the form of a turn away from the premise, sanctioned by a powerful prejudice, "that a return to premodern philosophy is impossible," a premise, as he expressly adds, on which *Die Religionskritik Spinozas* was based. Strauss's change of orientation found its first expression, "not entirely by accident," in the 1932 essay "Anmerkungen zu Carl Schmitt, *Der Begriff des Politischen*."[10] What caused this change of orientation? How is it to be defined more precisely? And what insights does the change disclose? The edition of Strauss's *Gesammelte Schriften*, which in the second and third volumes presents together for the first time all the writings from the decisive years between the conclusion of the Spinoza book and his new beginning in America, places the careful reader in a position to answer these and similar questions himself. A few remarks concerning the development of Strauss's thought, in addition to information about the chronology of his oeuvre,[11] may nevertheless be appropriate.

At the center of Strauss's change of orientation lies the emphatic turn to political philosophy in the sense of a conscious return to a thorough examination of the political opinions and theological convictions that precede philosophy or that are able to place philosophy fundamentally in question. The turn to political philosophy is flanked by both a new hermeneutic openness and the rediscovery of the art of exoteric-esoteric writing. The former is reflected in the maxim that the greatest effort must be made to understand the philosophers of the past exactly as they understood themselves. The latter leads to the insight into the difference that exists, for political as well as philosophical reasons, between the generally accessible teachings and the thought of those philosophers. Each of the three aspects of this turn includes mutatis mutandis the turn away from the "*premise*, sanctioned by a powerful prejudice," that a return to premodern philosophy is impossible. The most important considerations and encounters that contributed to the reorientation sketched only briefly here[12] can be named in abbreviated form: 1) The conclusion reached by *Die Religionskritik Spinozas* that modern rationalism's answer to revealed religion remained insufficient—or that the "offensive critique" failed and the "Napoleonic strategy," with which the modern Enlightenment hoped to defeat orthodoxy, ultimately aroused the suspicion that the Enlightenment was based merely on a "new belief" rather than on a "new knowledge." 2) The question whether the self-destruction of reason is the inevitable consequence of modern, in contrast to premodern, rationalism; and whether radical historicism, in which that self-destruction is most clearly and most resolutely expressed, must not be grasped as the position in which the complex historical development of modern philosophy reaches its end. 3) The judgment that the irruption of a tradition based on revelation into the world of philosophy and the battle fought against this tradition in a manifoldly interlocking way over the centuries maneuvered philosophy into a second, historical cave of increased mediation and artificiality that lies below the "natural" cave in which philosophy, according to the Platonic allegory, begins its ascent; and the resultant view that the historical obstacles that are added to the natural difficulties of philosophizing in the present make necessary a concerted effort, to regain the natural horizon in the form of a historical propaedeutic. 4) The insight into the possibilities that Nietzsche's critique of the principles of the biblical and the philosophical traditions opens up for an original understanding of these principles, as well as the insight into the opportunities that Heidegger's destruction of the tradition offers for an adequate confrontation with the thought of the philosophers of the past, a confrontation oriented completely toward the subject at issue in their thought, when this confrontation is carried out under the guidance of political philosophy. 5) The conclusion that the philosopher in the present has every reason to approach premodern philosophy in the manner not of one who believes oneself able to understand medieval and ancient philosophers better than they understood themselves, but rather of one who wants to give thought to the alternatives and explore paths that lead out of the modern impasse, in short: as one eager to learn from premodern philosophy and open to being overcome by wonder, to being surprised by it.

A momentous surprise awaited Strauss in 1929 or 1930. While reading Avicenna's treatise *On the Divisions of the Rational Sciences* for the first time, he came upon the statement that the treatment of prophecy and divine law is contained in Plato's *Laws*. Avicenna's hint, which Strauss would use more than four decades later as the motto of his last book, his commentary on the *Laws* (the "most pious" and "most ironical of Plato's works"),[13] disclosed to Strauss virtually overnight a new, unhoped-for access not only to the Arabic philosophers Farabi, Avicenna, and Averroes, and to Maimonides, but also to Plato himself. This find at the Berlin National Library meant the birth of Strauss's theme "philosophy and law." A subject to which Strauss had directed his attention primarily for historical reasons turned out to be one of eminently philosophical interest.[14] For Avicenna's sentence said in other words that, long before the irruption of revealed religions into the world of philosophy, Plato had at his disposal the means that the philosophers of the Middle Ages needed and which the Platonic political philosophers used to meet the historical challenge with which they were confronted: that is to say, to understand it philosophically and to make the best of it politically for themselves and for their commonwealths. The Arabic philosophers and Maimonides follow Plato when they grasp the divine law, providence, and the prophet as objects of politics; they rely on the *Laws* when they treat the teaching of revelation, the doctrine of particular providence, and prophetology as parts of political science (and not at all of metaphysics);[15] they move in the horizon of the *Republic* when they regard the founding of the "perfect city" as the raison d'être of revelation.[16] In this sense Strauss can speak of our grasping in Plato the "unbelieving, philosophical grounding of faith in revelation in its origin."[17] The endeavor to ground or to found faith in revelation from the political perspective of the founder distinguishes the rationalism of the Platonic political philosophers from modern rationalism, which is no less interested in a natural explanation of faith in revelation, which ventures no less to gain a philosophical understanding of faith in revelation, but which does not carry out the confrontation from this perspective.[18] And also in contrast to modern rationalism, premodern rationalism begins the confrontation by focusing on the law: It carries out its grounding of faith in revelation as the grounding of the law. Platonic rationalism begins by focusing on the law in the original sense, on the comprehensive order of the commonwealth, an order that unites religion and politics and that, as religious, political, moral law, lays claim to the individual wholly, existentially.[19] Premodern rationalism engages this claim radically in order to understand the law radically. It justifies the law in order to get beyond the law. If the philosophical justification of the law is the mode of understanding the law from the ground up, then it is simultaneously the locus in which the presuppositions of philosophy are engaged, in which the self-knowledge of the philosopher is in question. For with the grounding of the law as the politico-theological order or the way of life of the commonwealth the question of the right of the philosophical life is raised most acutely. This question moves into the center of political philosophy, and since the rationalism of the medieval Platonists is essentially political philosophy, its central theme is not "belief and knowledge" but "law and philosophy": The philosophical justification of the law becomes the grounding of philosophy.[20]

Leo Strauss persistently pursued his new interpretation of the political philosophy of the Islamic and Jewish Middle Ages in the essays and lectures from 1930–37 and rapidly developed it more richly. In the course of this development, the confrontation with the conflict-laden polarity "philosophy and law" becomes not only more profound but also clearer. Several careful statements and several cautious hints in Parts II–IV of *Philosophie und Gesetz* disclose their full significance only in light of the rhetorically bolder essays "Quelques remarques sur la science politique de Maïmonide et de Fârâbî" and "On Abravanel's Philosophical Tendency and Political Teaching." However, given his high regard for the medieval enlightenment—which, as Strauss emphasizes, in contrast to the modern Enlightenment, or the "Enlightenment properly speaking," insisted on the esoteric character of philosophy—Strauss's reticence in all the aforementioned writings (including the "very daring" introduction to *Philosophie und Gesetz*) should not be underestimated.[21] For instance, it is left up to the reader to bring together arguments that interlock but are developed in passages far removed from one another, or important statements able to shed light on one another but that the author "scatters" over various publications, so that the reader thinks them himself and draws the necessary conclusions. Let us give three examples, which lead us beyond Strauss's early writings on medieval political philosophy: First, precisely what Strauss had in view when, at the outset of the Introduction to *Philosophie und Gesetz*, he says that "the critique of the present, the critique of modern rationalism *as the critique of modern sophistry*, is the necessary beginning, the constant companion, and the sure sign of the quest for truth which is possible in our age," becomes clear when one consults the critique of the "Epimethean" physics proper to sophistry with recourse to Plato's *Protagoras* in *Hobbes' politische Wissenschaft*, which he wrote at the same time or had already completed.[22] Second, whoever wants to understand why Strauss (once again in the Introduction) places the word "radicalized" in quotation marks in saying that modern philosophy has "radicalized" the Platonic critique of the natural ideal of courage "in such a way that the character of virtue in courage as such is really denied," or whoever would like to understand Strauss's confrontation with Nietzsche's and Heidegger's "new kind of fortitude" (in which the Introduction culminates) will profit from reading what Strauss has to say in *Hobbes' politische Wissenschaft* about the *radical critique* of the ideal of courage—now without quotation marks.[23] Third and finally, in the context of the same discussion there occurs a statement—expressed most clearly in the revised English version—that clarifies the status of the expositions on the "fundamental difference between Plato and Aristotle" that come at the end of *Philosophie und Gesetz* and that may perhaps puzzle some readers.[24] Of course, there are also modifications of content—and new discoveries. Thus Strauss gains greater clarity roughly in the latter half of 1935 on the political dimension of the philosophical confrontation with revealed religions and on what he terms "philosophical politics." It is expressed, for example, in the account of Farabi's role as founding father of the first great endeavor to recover philosophy and in the observation that the Arabic philosophers attached far greater significance to war and courage than had Plato or Aristotle, as well as in the parallel observation that Hobbes—whom Strauss regarded at that time as the founding father of modern political philosophy—gave primacy to foreign policy in a critical turn against the ancient philosophers.[25] The most important changes in Strauss's position concern, however, his account and—if we look beyond the years 1930–37 for a moment—understanding of Maimonides as a whole. Whereas Strauss still characterized Maimonides in his Spinoza book as an "adherent of revealed religion" and as a "devout Jew," ten years later he is convinced that Maimonides was absolutely not a Jew in his belief; and whereas he had stuck essentially to the traditional reading in his interpretation of the *Moreh nebuchim* in 1928, after careful study of the book he comes to the view, in 1938, that Maimonides with his *Guide of the Perplexed* had succeeded to a far greater degree in doing what Nietzsche had in mind with his *Zarathustra*.[26] Before 1938 the most striking modification that Strauss makes in his new Maimonides interpretation,[27] which he had been developing since 1930, is in "Quelques remarques." There he explicitly distances himself from the view that for Maimonides the dependence of the philosophers on revelation is based on the insufficiency of human reason. It is presumably in view of the claim of insufficiency, which plays a prominent role in the account in *Philosophie und Gesetz*,[28] that Strauss says in retrospect that he moved, "so to speak, contrary to Guttmann's moderate rationalism, on a path via a Jewish Thomism to radical 'rationalism.'"[29] The Abravanel essay, in which the contours of the political philosopher Maimonides emerge particularly clearly through a comparison and contrast with the political theologian Abravanel, doubtless comes very close to the position of "radical rationalism." With its uncommon openness, it forms a transition to the essay "The Literary Character of the *Guide for the Perplexed*," which was written in 1938 with all the more reticence and extreme concentration.[30]

In many respects the introduction to *Philosophie und Gesetz* occupies a special place. It is—notwithstanding the framing remarks, which make express reference to the subsequent texts and without which it could not have been published in 1935—an essay in its own right. Finished in only a few days, it counts among the most brilliant essays that Strauss wrote. Its great themes—the need for a new understanding of the quarrel between enlightenment and orthodoxy, the necessary failure of any attempt to bring about a synthesis of "Jerusalem" and "Athens," the self-destruction of reason as a consequence of modern rationalism, the requirement that the philosophical confrontation with faith in revelation be taken up anew—are programmatic for Strauss's future studies. Almost three decades later, Strauss granted such undiminished validity to the analysis of "atheism from probity," that new "atheism with a good, or also a bad conscience," which "is distinguished from the atheism at which the past shuddered precisely by its conscientiousness, by its morality," that he translated the decisive passages from the introduction word for word into English and included them in his "autobiographical preface."[31] Since the essay gives a vigorous account of the philosophical intention that guides the investigation of the seemingly historical subject of *Philosophie und Gesetz*, it is simultaneously, strictly speaking, an introduction, a text that leads the reader to Parts II–IV, and thus that part that makes the volume a whole. On May 9, 1935, Strauss writes to Kojève from Cambridge: "Just read the introduction and essay no. 1. The introduction is very daring and will interest you already for that reason. And then write me with your reaction. I myself regard it as the best I've written." There is no record of Kojève's judgment. The contemporary reactions we know of from Strauss's circle of friends and acquaintances, however, could hardly be more diverse. They range from Löwith's conjecture that Strauss sided with orthodoxy[32] to Guttmann's assumption that he identifies himself with the position of "modern existentialist philosophy."[33] Klein, whom Strauss had described as *perscrutatorem cordis mei* a few years earlier in a letter to Krüger, confesses a certain helplessness regarding the question to which the last pages of the Introduction give rise: "but *where* is Maimonides's enlightenment supposed to lead us now? I understand full well that an answer is not *immediately* possible: it is the situation in which we find ourselves in the first place: indeed, to anticipate an answer would mean no longer wanting to understand back [*Zurückverstehen-Wollen*]." He has his astonishment lead to the consideration: "Well, one could, *following* your account, arrive at the conclusion: why not orthodoxy, then?! After all, you yourself say something *very, very* important, it seems to me, when you do *not* identify 'probity' with 'love of truth.' And so everything remains open. Which I *myself* have nothing against. But it is clear that people are going to hold that against you."[34] By contrast, for Scholem the most important question by no means remains open. "Shortly," he writes to Walter Benjamin on March 29, 1935, "Schocken will publish for the Maimonides anniversary a book by Leo Strauß (whom I have tried very hard to get appointed to a professorship in Jerusalem) which—a remarkable act of bravery for a book that has to be understood by everyone as one by a candidate for Jerusalem—begins with a thoroughly (albeit completely madly) reasoned, undisguised confession to atheism as the most important Jewish watchword! That even outdoes those first 40 pages of your *Habilitationsschrift*! I admire this morale and regret the apparently consciously and deliberately provoked suicide of such a good mind. The independence of mind to vote for the appointment of an atheist to a teaching post for the philosophy of religion is here understandably to be expected from at most three people." Benjamin responds to the news on May 20: "the book by Leo Strauß is of great interest to me. What you have told me about him fits the pleasant impression I had always had of him."[35]

The early writings presented in Part II of the second volume of the *Gesammelte Schriften* give clear confirmation of a statement Jacob Klein made half a century later, namely that at the time of their first encounter at the University of Marburg in 1920 and in the early years of their friendship thereafter Strauss was primarily interested in two questions: the question of God and the question of politics.[36] The importance of these questions, which form the leitmotif of the articles and reviews from the 1920s—beginning with the first two of Strauss's publications, an intervention in the debate over Zionism and a short essay on Rudolf Otto's book *Das Heilige*—justifies the presentation of all the publications prior to the caesura around 1929 that, along with the dissertation, make up the first group of the *Frühe Schriften*.[37] Strauss himself most likely would not have included these contributions to journals and newspapers in a collection; he did not even gather them together for his personal archive; and he certainly did not consider a later publication of his doctoral dissertation, which he wrote as a 22-year-old under Ernst Cassirer in Hamburg and which in 1970 he called "a disgraceful performance."[38] Yet in view of the fact that the dissertation on Jacobi has since become available in French translation[39] and its translation into other languages is planned, it seemed time to publish a reliable edition of the German original—particularly as the question of God already plays a role in the dissertation. The Zionist articles and statements from 1923–25 allow the starting point of the intellectual development to take on sharper contours, a development on which the "autobiographical preface" sheds light and whose philosophical interest lies in the fact that it testifies to the truth of Plato's *Republic* according to which the ascent of philosophy starts with the political opinions that are obligatory or binding for the individual and is carried out as the gaining of insight into the nature or the limits of those opinions.

The second group of the *Frühe Schriften* comprises texts in which Strauss's "change of orientation" is prepared or is already expressed. Since, with the exception of the Ebbinghaus review, none of them has been published before, they shed still more light on the factors that contributed to that change of orientation, factors that I sketched above in five points. Thus, at the end of the essay on conspectivism, we encounter the question of "how the world in which science arose looked before the irruption of biblical consciousness," which Strauss reinforces with the announcement: "Only in the orientation towards this world is one to gain the horizon in which alone one can now radically question and answer." And we are in a position to pursue how Strauss, beginning with the lecture "'Religiöse Lage der Gegenwart,'" introduces the figure of the "second cave" and develops it step by step, a figure that he first uses in print in the Ebbinghaus review.[40] There is more: The critique of "conspectivism," which Strauss intended to rework into a critique of the "sophistry of our times,"[41] can be read as an early example of Strauss's talent for irony and ridicule or for that "laughter" that "belongs essentially to all enlightenment, be it Platonic or modern."[42] The lecture bearing the title "'Religiöse Lage der Gegenwart'" shows clearly the ease with which Strauss is able to transform a prescribed theme into his own, his ability to raise the theme to the level of the confrontation that seems appropriate to him. In "Cohen und Maimuni" we encounter the first presentation of the new Maimonides interpretation, which in large part found its way into Part IV of *Philosophie und Gesetz*.[43] Finally, "Die geistige Lage der Gegenwart" presents us with Strauss's historical self-reflection as an answer to historical consciousness and sheds light on the role that Nietzsche plays in this self-reflection.

The third section of *Frühe Schriften* contains the introductions that Strauss contributed to the Jubilee Edition of Moses Mendelssohn's *Gesammelte Schriften*. Strauss first wrote them on behalf of the Akademie für die Wissenschaft des Judentums, where he worked from February 1925 to October 1932 and which entrusted him with quite a number of Mendelssohn's philosophical writings.[44] The first two volumes of the jubilee edition that Strauss coedited, the *Schriften zur Philosophie und Ästhetik* II and III 1, appeared in 1931 and 1932. Volume III 2, which Strauss edited alone and on which he had made a great deal of progress by 1932,[45] could no longer be published due to the political circumstances in the 1930s. In addition to his studies of Hobbes and medieval philosophy, Strauss nevertheless continued his work on the edition of *Sache Gottes oder die gerettete Vorsehung*, as well as of *Morgenstunden* and *An die Freunde Lessings*. Strauss published the introduction to *Sache Gottes*, the typescript of which was finished in 1936, as a contribution to the festschrift for Krüger in 1962.[46] By contrast, he would not live to see the publication of the long essay on *Morgenstunden* and *An die Freunde Lessings*, which he likewise completed during his stay in Cambridge:[47] volume III 2, and with it Strauss's account of the quarrel between Mendelssohn and Jacobi about Lessing's Spinozism, which reads like a detective story, appeared only in 1974, several months after Strauss's death, in the continuation of the jubilee edition under Alexander Altmann's direction. After the Second World War, Strauss considered using the unpublished manuscript for an essay on the quarrel over Lessing entitled "A Controversy on Spinoza," which would form the penultimate chapter of a book consisting partly of published essays and partly of some that were still to be written. The volume, which

Strauss estimated would be 350 pages in length and which he planned to publish in 1948, had the working title *Philosophy and The Law: Historical Essays.* The titles of the 12 chapters, which Strauss sketched in a typed outline, read: "I) Modern Jewish philosophy and its limitations. II) Jerusalem and Athens. III) The two faces of Socrates. IV) How to study Jewish medieval philosophy. V) Maimonides's political science. VI) Maimonides's ethics. VII) The literary character of the Guide for the Perplexed. VIII) Fârâbî's treatise on Plato's philosophy. IX) The Law of Reason in the Cuzari. X) Persecution and the art of writing. XI) A controversy on Spinoza. XII) Nathan the Wise."[48] This book project, which was never realized, was replaced by the collection *Persecution and the Art of Writing*, which appeared in 1952.

The chapter on *Nathan der Weise* was never written, like the book Strauss had planned to write about Lessing in Cambridge in 1937. Thus on the author who was particularly important for Strauss's rediscovery of the distinction between exoteric and esoteric speech,[49] we have—besides the few pages that are devoted to Lessing in the essay "Exoteric Teaching" (which was written in December 1939, remained a fragment, and was published only posthumously)[50]—only the preface to *Eine Erinnerung an Lessing*, which concludes the second volume of the *Gesammelte Schriften*. It ends with the words: "Incidentally, the author was not unmindful of the debt of thanks that his nation owes to that great son of the German nation, especially in this moment of farewell." Strauss first wrote "moment of parting" and then replaced "parting" (*Trennung*) with "farewell" (*Abschied*). Toward the end of his life, he recalls in a letter to Alexander Altmann the title of the book on Lessing he had once planned, *Abschied von Deutschland* (Farewell to Germany): "In 1937 I had the intention to give an account of the center of Lessing's thoughts *de Deo et mundo* either in the conclusion of the introduction [to *Morgenstunden* and *An die Freunde Lessings*] or in a separate text (under the title *Abschied von Deutschland*). The decisive points are as clear to me today as they were back then. But 'Making plans is often . . . ' All that I could do was to point my better students emphatically to Lessing and to say on appropriate occasions what I owe to Lessing."[51]

Translated by Marcus Brainard

Notes

1. As in the case of every philosopher, for an adequate study of Strauss's thought it is at least advisable—if not required—that one study his writings in the languages in which they were written. The present essay is a revised and expanded English version of my introduction to *GS–2* ix–xxxiii.
2. Ludwig Feuchtwanger, "Philosophie und Gesetz. Bemerkungen zu zwei neuen Arbeiten zum Verständnis Maimunis," *Jüdische Rundschau* no. 29 (Berlin, April 9, 1935): 7. Feuchtwanger had been the editorial director of the publishing house Duncker & Humblot from 1913 to 1933 in Munich and a close acquaintance of Carl Schmitt since the First World War. At the end of 1932 he published Strauss's essay "Das Testament Spinozas" in the *Bayerische Israelitische Gemeindezeitung* (now in *GS–1* 414–22). On April 15, 1935, Feuchtwanger writes to Strauss: "I recently reviewed your Maimonides book in the *Rundschau*. I enclose a copy of the paper

for you. I feel bad about it because I am well aware of the particularly demanding requirements for being able to judge it: a knowledge of Aristotle and Arabic studies would be the bare minimum. *It would also be necessary to go into the whole of 'existentialist philosophy' and ontology.* [...] In 1932 the author of *The Concept of the Political* spoke to me about you with high esteem; but his praise was quite unnecessary, because I knew your book on Sp. If I had not reviewed your book, no one would have reviewed it in the *Rundschau*. Take that as the extenuating circumstance. [...] *I have high hopes for you as one of a very few who have something to say*" (Leo Strauss Papers, Box 1, Folder 13, Department of Special Collections, University of Chicago Library).

3. Thus in the case of his monograph *Hobbes' politische Wissenschaft*, which obviously dealt with a "non-Jewish subject," all of Strauss's attempts in 1935 to find a German publisher, or at least a German journal that would be willing to publish the study in several parts, came to nothing. The book ultimately appeared in English translation in 1936 under the title *The Political Philosophy of Hobbes: Its Basis and Its Genesis* at the Clarendon Press in Oxford, whereas the German original was not published until 1965.
4. As a peripheral phenomenon, we mention the attack of the National Socialist philosophy professor Hans Alfred Grunsky, who lumped Strauss together with Hermann Cohen, Maimonides, and Philo and then reproached *Philosophie und Gesetz* for a "falsification of Plato" from the point of view of "Jewish prophetism," which struck him as "all the more brazen" since Strauss "knows very well that the concept of the prophet is not Platonic and precisely because it presupposes the notion of revelation, which is completely foreign to Plato" (*Der Einbruch des Judentums in die Philosophie* (Berlin: Junker und Dünnhaupt, 1937), 15–16).
5. Shlomo Pines reviewed *Philosophie und Gesetz* in *Recherches Philosophiques* V (Paris, 1936), 504–7. Almost three decades later he and Strauss edited the epoch-making edition of Maimonides's *The Guide of the Perplexed* (Chicago: The University of Chicago Press, 1963), to which Pines, assisted by Ralph Lerner, contributed a painstaking translation of the *Moreh nebuchim* from the Arabic original, and a historical introduction, and for which Strauss wrote his famous essay "How To Begin To Study *The Guide of the Perplexed*" (xi–lvi; reprinted in *LAM* 140–84).
6. Letters to Fritz Baer from September 24, 1933 and Gershom Scholem from December 7, 1933. (Both letters, as well as all other letters to Scholem cited in the present essay, are located under the signature "Arc. 4°1599/Corresp. Leo Strauss" in the Department of Manuscripts & Archives as part of the collection of the Jewish National and University Library, Jerusalem. Photocopies are located in Leo Strauss Papers, Box 18, Folder 1, Department of Special Collections, University of Chicago Library. Strauss's correspondence with Scholem has been published in *GS–3* 699–772. The letter referred to here may be found on 706–9. *GS–3* also contains the correspondence between Strauss and Gerhard Krüger (377–454), Strauss and Jacob Klein (455–605), and Strauss and Karl Löwith (607–95), all in the original languages in which the letters were written.) On December 7, 1933, Strauss informs Gerhard Krüger: "I have just heard that I have certain prospects of getting the professorship for Jewish medieval philosophy in Jerusalem" (*GS–3* 436). In a letter from December 31, 1933, to Jacob Klein, his closest friend from the 1920s and 1930s, Strauss explains his stance as follows (he apparently knew nothing of Julius Guttmann's candidacy at the time): "My sincere thanks to you, as well as to Krüger and Gadamer, for your Palestine-Buber operation. I have no illusions about the fact that [Simon] Rawidowicz will presumably come out on

top, and I am not even sad about that: Palestine means abandoning Hobbes and thus much else besides. Nevertheless, I cannot afford to leave any stone unturned so that we three aren't left with nothing on October 1st. Besides, I am hoping that, should R. get the position in Jerusalem, the university there will do its best to help me in England or America. *Naturally*, I would like most to stay in England—indeed, *everything* speaks for this country..." (*GS–3* 485).

7. In a letter to Krüger from July 25, 1931, Strauss writes: "I am enclosing my essay for you. I would appreciate it if you would take a look at it soon. Pages 1–5 and 23–37 would be enough for you; the middle section is far too 'medieval'" (*GS–3* 391). On December 7, 1933, Strauss describes the background of the essay to Scholem: "This study is meant as groundwork for a history of prophetology in the Middle Ages for which I have collected a lot of material but which I can begin to elaborate only after the provisional conclusion of my Hobbes study (in two treatises on Hobbes's critique of religion and on Hegel and Hobbes). The idea for this larger investigation of things medieval grew out of several years of work on Gersonides's *Milchamoth ha-shem* and Aristotle- (or Averroes-) commentaries" (*GS–3* 708).
8. On September 15, 1933, Strauss mentions to Klein "that I have written a long review of Guttmann's book, which is destined to become part of my posthumous papers." On September 24, he sends the essay to Scholem. On December 3, 1933, Strauss asks Krüger: "Has he [Klein] given you my Guttmann critique?" On October 10, 1933, Strauss tells Klein: "In the meantime, after a year's hesitation, I sent my Guttmann review to Guttmann. The result was surprising: he was delighted and honored, and he wants to try to get it published" (see *GS–3* 470, 702, 436, and 523).
9. On the same day Strauss writes to Guttmann to the same effect (Leo Strauss Papers, Box 1, Folder 14). The report from November 20, 1933, by the Orientalist Hans Heinrich Schaeder (Berlin) gives the following judgment: "Dr. Strauss combines to an exceptional degree the abilities of a responsible philosophizing that unwaveringly gets to the bottom of the matter and a historical reflection that seeks to be wholly concrete and that does not shy away from any investigation of detail. He has an advantage over others who have oriented their study towards the entire development of the problem of religion and philosophy, with his intimate and sure knowledge of the state of the problem in the Age of the Enlightenment. [...] His studies on the doctrine of prophetology in the Islamic and Jewish Middle Ages, in which he is currently engaged and which he sketches in the two aforementioned unpublished essays, signify, if I understand correctly, the opening up of an essentially new and incalculably fruitful perspective for the judgment of the medieval discussion of the problem of revelation and reason. He finds a way here to elucidate the doctrine of the bringer of revelation no longer with respect to the constricting perspectives of modern Romantic philosophy of religion, but rather based on the tradition of the ancient, in particular the Platonic, doctrine of the state and the laws, and once again to give the ancient division of philosophy its due in the consideration of its continuations in the Middle Ages. For all their subtlety, his studies are just as powerful and courageous in the progression of thought as their language is terse. The historical investigation does not once get lost in antiquarian concerns, but remains ever philosophically relevant. Whoever studies the history of religion and the history of thought in the philosophy of religion today will have much to learn from these studies again and again and will have to take a stand with respect to them. In the areas in which he works,

there are hardly any subjects of inquiry that are more pressing than his and there is hardly anyone better prepared to do the job than he." (A copy of the evaluation is located in Correspondence Leo Strauss, Arc. 4°1599 of the Jewish National and University Library Jerusalem.)

10. *LAM* 257. Consider also Strauss's letter of June 23, 1935, to Karl Löwith (*GS–3* 648). Strauss's "Anmerkungen zu Carl Schmitt, *Der Begriff des Politischen*" has been republished in *GS–3* 217–38. An English translation may be found under the title "Notes on Carl Schmitt, *The Concept of the Political*" in my *Carl Schmitt and Leo Strauss: The Hidden Dialogue*, trans. J. Harvey Lomax (Chicago: The University of Chicago Press, 1995; rev. paperback ed., 2006), 89–120.
11. From the correspondence or based on the dates that Strauss himself entered into his personal copies (P), insofar as they are available, the following chronology can be reconstructed for the writings of relevance to our question: 1929 (P): "Der Konspektivismus"; until December 1930: "'Religiöse Lage der Gegenwart'"; until May 1931: "Cohen und Maimuni"; by July 1931: *Philosophie und Gesetz*, Part IV; circa October 1931: "Besprechung von Julius Ebbinghaus"; end of October/beginning of November 1931: "Disposition" of a book entitled *Die politische Wissenschaft des Hobbes. Eine Einführung in das Naturrecht*; end of 1931: "Vorwort zu einem geplanten Buch über Hobbes"; by February 1932: "Die geistige Lage der Gegenwart"; April–May 1932 (P): "Anmerkungen zu Carl Schmitt, *Der Begriff des Politischen*"; end of 1932/beginning of 1933: "Einige Anmerkungen über die politische Wissenschaft des Hobbes"; 1933–34: *Die Religionskritik des Hobbes*; by September 1933: *Philosophie und Gesetz*, Part II; circa December 1934–January 1935: *Philosophie und Gesetz*, Part III (based on a manuscript from 1932?); January–February 1935 (P): *Philosophie und Gesetz*, Part I; 1934 by May 1935: *Hobbes' politische Wissenschaft*; circa second half of 1935: changes and supplements to the text of *The Political Philosophy of Hobbes* that go beyond the German original; August–October 1935 (P): "Quelques remarques sur la science politique de Maïmonide et de Fârâbî"; November 1935 (P): "Eine vermißte Schrift Farâbîs"; May 1936: "Notes additionelles" to "Quelques remarques sur la science politique de Maïmonide et de Fârâbî"; August 1936 (P): "Der Ort der Vorsehungslehre nach der Ansicht Maimunis"; April–August 1937 (P): "On Abravanel's Philosophical Tendency and Political Teaching."
12. An in-depth confrontation may be found in my *Die Denkbewegung von Leo Strauss. Die Geschichte der Philosophie und die Intention des Philosophen* (Stuttgart/Weimar: J. B. Metzler, 1996), 19–43, and in *Das theologisch-politische Problem. Zum Thema von Leo Strauss* (Stuttgart/Weimar: J. B. Metzler, 2003), 13–48. (An English translation of both texts is contained in my book *Leo Strauss and the Theologico-Political Problem* (Cambridge/New York: Cambridge University Press, 2006), 53–73 and 3–28 respectively.)
13. *AAPL* 1 and 2; "On Abravanel's Philosophical Tendency and Political Teaching," in *GS–2* 198; cf. *Philosophie und Gesetz*, *GS–2* 112, 114, "Quelques remarques sur la science politique de Maïmonide et de Fârâbî," *GS–2* 126, "Cohen und Maimuni," *GS–2* 425, as well as "The Spirit of Sparta or the Taste of Xenophon," *Social Research* 6 (1939): 530–32.
14. After concluding the Spinoza book, Strauss's research concentrated on Hobbes on the one hand and medieval thought on the other. On June 26, 1930, he offers to give a talk in Krüger's Augustine seminar on "Enlightenment in the Middle Ages." He adds the following explanation: "I had begun my work on a Jewish Scholastic—Gersonides—purely in the 'interest of learning' [*als reine 'Lernarbeit'*],

but also because, of course, I have to give the people who pay me some writings or other. I soon saw, however, that the work couldn't be done so mindlessly, simply because the subject is so exciting" (*GS–3* 382).

15. *Philosophie und Gesetz*, *GS–2* 57–58, 59, 90, 111, 116; "Quelques remarques," *GS–2* 125, 126, 132–33, 136–37, 139; "Eine vermißte Schrift Farâbîs," *GS–2* 170; "Der Ort der Vorsehungslehre nach der Ansicht Maimunis," *GS–2* 182–84, 187, 189.
16. *Philosophie und Gesetz*, *GS–2* 60, 114–15, 123; "Quelques remarques," *GS–2* 143.
17. *Philosophie und Gesetz*, *GS–2* 64. Cf. *GS–2* 49, 86, 118; *AAPL* 7–11.
18. Cf. *TM* 288–90, 291–92; furthermore, my *Denkbewegung von Leo Strauss*, 26 (*Leo Strauss and the Theologico-Political Problem*, 60).
19. *Philosophie und Gesetz*, *GS–2* 61; "Quelques remarques," *GS–2* 126. ". . . law is originally nothing other than the way of life of the community. The first things and the right way cannot become questionable or the object of a quest, or philosophy cannot emerge, or nature cannot be discovered, if authority as such is not doubted or as long as at least any general statement of any being whatsoever is accepted on trust" (*NRH* 84).
20. *Philosophie und Gesetz*, *GS–2* 48, 60, 62, 66, 67–68, 78; "Quelques remarques," *GS–2* 125, 128, 152; "On Abravanel's Philosophical Tendency," *GS–2* 198–99.
21. *Philosophie und Gesetz*, *GS–2* 46, 47, 67, 71, 74, 76, 78, 88–89, 115 (cf. the variant to 123, which is found on 612, and "Cohen und Maimuni," *GS–2* 425); "Quelques remarques," *GS–2* 137, 144–45, 148, 152, 156; "Der Ort der Vorsehungslehre," *GS–2* 184, 186–87; "On Abravanel's Philosophical Tendency," *GS–2* 197–98.
22. *Philosophie und Gesetz*, *GS–2* 9–10 (my emphasis, H.M.); *Hobbes' politische Wissenschaft*, in *GS–3* 162–63. On March 27, 1935, Strauss writes to Krüger: "To avoid a possible misunderstanding: 'Sophistry' on the first page of my introduction is meant quite literally (after Protagoras's myth): on the basis of an Epimethean physics (the exposedness of man) to surrender ultimately to what the Athenians say" (*GS–3* 442).
23. *Philosophie und Gesetz*, *GS–2* 14, 25–26; *Hobbes' politische Wissenschaft*, *GS–3* 166–69.
24. "It is not courage which is the highest virtue—self-mastery stands higher, and higher still than self-mastery stand wisdom and justice. *In itself wisdom stands supreme, but justice stands supreme from an exoteric point of view.* This explains why Plato does not assert, as does Aristotle, the superiority of the theoretical life to ethical virtue" (*The Political Philosophy of Hobbes* (1936) 147; my emphasis, H.M.). In *Hobbes' politische Wissenschaft* this passage read originally: "It is not courage that is the highest virtue—moderation stands higher than courage, higher still than moderation stand insight and justice. And in fact it is insight in itself that stands highest, though for man it is justice [that stands highest]. This explains why Plato does not assert, as does Aristotle, the superiority of the theoretical life to ethical virtue" (*GS–3* 167–68). Cf. *Philosophie und Gesetz*, *GS–2* 122–23.
25. "Quelques remarques," *GS–2* 128–30, 136, 142, 150–51, 156–58 (cf. "On Abravanel's Philosophical Tendency," *GS–2* 197, 205–6); *The Political Philosophy of Hobbes* (1936) 161–63. The long paragraph on the primacy of foreign policy is not in *Hobbes' politische Wissenschaft*. It was added to the English text roughly at the same time as Strauss wrote "Quelques remarques." For the importance of this change, consider what Strauss suggests in *Thoughts on Machiavelli*, 298–99 on the ancients and the moderns regarding "the art of war" and what the book

as a whole says about Machiavelli's "spiritual warfare." Cf. my *Denkbewegung von Leo Strauss*, 24–28 (*Leo Strauss and the Theologico-Political Problem*, 59–61). (In 1952, in the foreword to the American edition of the Hobbes book [xix], Strauss formally corrected his mistaken view that Hobbes was the founder of modern political philosophy: "Hobbes appeared to me as the originator of modern political philosophy. This was an error: not Hobbes, but Machiavelli, deserves this honor.")—On October 2, 1935, just prior to completing the manuscript of "Quelques remarques," Strauss writes to Scholem: "What I claimed in this book [*Philosophie und Gesetz*] purely on historical grounds, I have since come to find to be totally insufficient: Cohen was much more right [in claiming that Maimonides was a Platonist] than I ever would have dreamed possible (of course, his reasons are and remain misguided, indeed absurd). What happened there between 900 and 1200 looks completely different than it appears in the light of the reception of Islamic philosophy by Christianity (and this reception—perhaps even more than the specifically modern prejudices—is the reason for the prevailing view). If I have the time and energy, I want to write a book about the *Moreh* over the course of roughly ten years. For the time being I am publishing an introduction to the *Moreh* under the title: Hobbes's political science in its development, which should be published next year by Oxford Press" (*GS–3* 716). On the political dimension of the confrontation with revealed religions into which the Arabic or the modern founding fathers entered in order to recover philosophy, see also my preface to *GS–3* xxiii–xxiv, and the newly discovered letter to Paul Kraus that is cited there.

26. Cf. *Die Religionskritik Spinozas*, *GS–2* 208, 238, 254; *PAW* 81, 124–26; letters to Jacob Klein from February 16 and July 23, 1938, *GS–3* 549–50 and 553–54, respectively. – In the first sentence of "How To Begin To Study *The Guide of the Perplexed*," Strauss states that *Philosophie und Gesetz* was not based on an adequate understanding of the *Moreh*: "I believe that it will not be amiss if I simply present the plan of the *Guide* as it has become clear to me in the course of about twenty-five years of frequently interrupted but never abandoned study" (*LAM* 140). In the manuscript on which Strauss worked from May 19 to August 13, 1960, he first wrote "36 years," which would have put us in 1924, the year in which "Cohens Analyse der Bibel-Wissenschaft Spinozas" was published. Strauss then changed it to "25 years" and underscored it in red, which places the beginning of Strauss's study of the *plan* of the *Moreh* in the period following the publication of *Philosophie und Gesetz*. After having written "The Literary Character of the *Guide for the Perplexed*," Strauss never left any doubt that a philosophical work on the order of the *Moreh* could not be adequately understood so long as the reader did not have its plan clearly in view, that is, as long as it is not also understood as a work of art.

27. In GA the following oral statement by Strauss is recorded: "Maimonides was, to begin with, wholly unintelligible to me. I got the first glimmer of light when I concentrated on his prophetology and, therefore, the prophetology of the Islamic philosophers who preceded him. One day when reading in a Latin translation Avicenna's treatise, *On the Division of the Sciences*, I came across this sentence (I quote from memory): the standard work on prophecy and revelation is Plato's *Laws*. Then I began to begin to understand Maimonides's prophetology and eventually, as I believe, the whole *Guide of the Perplexed*. Maimonides never calls himself a philosopher; he presents himself as an opponent of the philosophers. He used a kind of writing which is, in the precise sense of the term, exoteric. When

Klein had read the manuscript of my essay on the literary character of the *Guide of the Perplexed*, he said, 'We have rediscovered exotericism.'"

28. *Philosophie und Gesetz*, *GS–2* 51–52, 55, 77, 82. As for what status the claim of insufficiency has in *Philosophie und Gesetz*, that can remain open here. Consider on this point 58–59 and 64, as well as the question at the end of the introduction: "Is it [Maimonides's enlightenment] not even in some respects more 'radical,' more dangerous to the spirit of Judaism, than the modern Enlightenment altogether?" In "Quelques remarques" Strauss begins his answer as follows: "Il reste à savoir si Maïmonide, lui aussi, regarde la fondation de la cité parfaite comme la raison d'être de la révélation. *On a pensé* que, selon lui, le but principal de la révélation était la proclamation des vérités les plus importantes, surtout de celles qui ne sont pas accessibles à la raison humaine" (*GS–2* 143, my emphasis, H.M.).
29. As is clear from two letters Strauss wrote to Guttmann, in 1934 Guttmann had sent Strauss a detailed response to his review of *Philosophie des Judentums* (letters from December 14, 1934 and January 22, 1935). Later Guttmann wrote a critique of *Philosophie und Gesetz*, though he did not publish it. On October 10, 1939, Strauss mentions to Klein: "Kraus spoke with Guttmann in Jerusalem. Guttmann told him that he is writing an article against me, to which K. responded that it is too late since in the meantime I have a new interpretation of Maimonides" (*GS–3* 583). On June 22, 1952—Guttmann had died in 1950—Strauss says in a letter to Scholem: "I knew from Guttmann himself about the reply he had begun. He wrote me several years ago (it may be 8–10 years already) that he had ceased to work on the reply because I had given up the standpoint I had held in *Philosophie und Gesetz*. That is correct insofar as I publicly agreed to G.'s thesis about the identity of reason and revelation in the M.A., but my earlier rejection is 'sublated' in my current agreement: I have moved, so to speak, contrary to G.'s moderate rationalism, on the path via a Jewish Thomism to radical 'rationalism,' am now therefore on the right wing (for the right is truth, the left is *sinister*, as no one knows better than you), whereas I stood on the left wing in *Philosophie und Gesetz*: Guttmann ever in the middle. (I am *now* attempting to reach a moderate 'rationalism,' but one that, I am afraid, would be even less acceptable to G. than my two earlier positions). Be that as it may, I am of the opinion that G.'s critique is still highly relevant." When in 1972 Scholem offered Strauss the typescript of Guttmann's critique, which was found in the latter's posthumous papers, Strauss expressed his interest (November 17, 1972; *GS–3* 765). On January 2, 1973, he confirms receipt of it (*GS–3* 765). The essay, which was written between 1940 and 1945, was published by Pines shortly after Strauss's death: Julius Guttmann, *Philosophie der Religion oder Philosophie des Gesetzes?* in *Proceedings of the Israel Academy of Sciences and Humanities* V, 6 (Jerusalem 1974).
30. "On Abravanel's Philosophical Tendency," *GS–2* 197–98, 200–4, 205–6, 207n33, 209, 215, 224–25. "The Literary Character" was published in 1941 and then reprinted in *PAW* 38–94.
31. Compare *Philosophie und Gesetz*, *GS–2* 17, 18, 19, 20, 23, 24–26, with *LAM* 254, 255, 256. The final sentence of the analysis reads: "The last word and the ultimate justification of the Enlightenment is the atheism from probity, which overcomes orthodoxy radically by understanding it radically, that is, free of both the polemical bitterness of the Enlightenment and the equivocal reverence of romanticism" (*Philosophie und Gesetz*, *GS–2* 26). In his "autobiographical preface" Strauss adds what was—though not expressly formulated—no less clearly discernible as the underlying thrust of the critique: "Yet this claim, however eloquently raised,

cannot deceive one about the fact that its basis is an act of will, of belief, and that being based on belief is fatal to any philosophy" ("Preface to Spinoza's Critique of Religion," *LAM* 256).

32. Cf. Löwith's letter from April 15, 1935. Strauss responds to it on June 23, 1935: "Incidentally: I am *not* an orthodox Jew!" (*GS–3* 645–47, 650). On February 14, 1934, Strauss remarks to Scholem in another context: "That I am not orthodox and under no circumstances the right man for an orthodox institute since I cannot make any concessions, I hardly need to tell you" (*GS–3* 711).
33. Guttmann, *Philosophie der Religion oder Philosophie des Gesetzes?* 6; cf. 26–27.
34. Letter from May 6, 1935 (*GS–3* 538–39). The characterization *perscrutator cordis mei* [scrutinizer of my heart] is in Strauss's letter to Krüger from August 19, 1932 (*GS–3* 399).
35. Gershom Scholem, ed., *Walter Benjamin—Gershom Scholem. Briefwechsel 1933–1940* (Frankfurt a. M.: Suhrkamp, 1980), 192–93, 197.
36. "Now, while Mr. Strauss and I were studying we had many, I should say, endless conversations about many things. His primary interests were two questions: one, the question of God; and two, the question of politics. These questions were not mine. I studied [. . .] Hegel, mathematics, and physics" (GA 1).
37. All the publications I knew of in 1997 were taken into account. It may be that still more newspaper articles will turn up in the future. For example, while I was preparing volume 2 for publication the article "*Ecclesia militans*," which was not known in the entire literature on Strauss, was brought to my attention and thus could be included in the first edition of volume 2. In spring 1999, I discovered three articles that Strauss had published in *Der Jüdische Student*, which I edited in the second, revised, and enlarged edition of *GS–1* in 2001: "Bemerkung zu der Weinbergschen Kritik" (1925), "'Die Zukunft einer Illusion'" (1928), and "Zur Ideologie des politischen Zionismus" (1929). And after 2001 I discovered more of Strauss's writings on political Zionism from the 1920s: "Zionismus und Orthodoxie" (1924) and "Quellen des Zionismus" (1924) as well as "Die 'Jüdischen Schriften' Hermann Cohens" which are now contained in an appendix to the third edition of *GS–1* and to the second edition of *GS*–2 (2013) respectively.
38. GA 2.
39. *Revue de métaphysique et de morale* 99, nos. 3–4 (1994): 291–311 and 505–32. The translation is based on a photocopy of the Munich typescript, which I gave to the Department of Special Collections at the University of Chicago in the 1980s.
40. On October 15, 1931, Strauss writes to Krüger: "I have now discovered a fourth man who shares our opinion of the present as a second cave: Ebbinghaus. His lecture *Ueber die Fortschritte der Metaphysik* contains several excellent formulations; I am going to review the booklet in the *D. L. Z.*" (*GS–3* 394–95). On the "second cave," see "'Religiöse Lage der Gegenwart,'" *GS–2* 386–87, "Besprechung von Julius Ebbinghaus," *GS–2* 438–39, "Die geistige Lage der Gegenwart," *GS–2* 451–52, 455–56, 461, *Philosophie und Gesetz*, *GS–2* 14, 45, and *PAW* 155–56. Cf. my *Denkbewegung von Leo Strauss*, 21–28 and 42–43 (*Leo Strauss and the Theologico-political Problem*, 56–61, 72–73).
41. In a letter to Krüger dated February 27, 1931, we read: "Enclosed, then, the piece on conspectivism, which I kindly request you to pass on to Gogarten. I am thinking of developing it in such a way as to fill out the critique to which I allude in the second half, in particular by showing how Mannheim remains completely 'helpless' insofar as he asks about politics as a science and about utopia without having been enlightened by Plato (Pardon the barbaric sentence!).

I give expression to this tendency by entitling the whole thing: Sophistry of Our Times. I shall work in the theses that I expounded in my lecture on the religious situation of the present (the 2d cave, etc.). My hope is that the essay, revised along the lines I am planning now, will seem convincing to you and will amuse you, at least that it will be far better than it is now. Thus: if Gogarten is prepared to recommend the essay, enlarged and improved, to a suitable publisher, whether as a contribution to a journal, or as a separate booklet, then I shall be happy to begin reworking it" (*GS–3* 384). In Leo Strauss Papers, Box 8, Folder 4, there is a two-page, handwritten outline with the title "Sophistik der Zeit" (Sophistry of Our Times).

42. Letter to Krüger from July 17, 1933 (*GS–3* 431).
43. On May 7, 1931, Strauss tells Krüger about the lecture that he had given on May 4 in the auditorium of the Hochschule für die Wissenschaft des Judentums in Berlin: "Last Monday I gave a lecture on Cohen and Maimonides. I attempted to show that Cohen was *nevertheless* right in saying that Maimonides was *basically* a Platonist, and *not* an Aristotelian; of course, one cannot show that as *directly* as did C. In this lecture I made public for the first time my thesis about Islamic-Jewish scholasticism (that it understands revelation within the framework laid out by Plato's *Republic* and *Laws*). Too bad that you were not there; I would have liked to have heard your opinion. You would also have seen just how much I have profited from your lecture course on Plato" (*GS–3* 385).
44. Letter to Cyrus Adler from November 30, 1933 (Leo Strauss Papers, Box 4, Folder 1). When the Akademie ran into financial difficulties at the end of 1931, all its employees had to be given notice.
45. On August 21, 1932, Strauss writes to Krüger that he wants to "conclude" the commentary on Mendelssohn's *Morgenstunden* "if it is at all possible, in the near future." On February 7, 1933, he mentions that he is working on the introduction to *Sache Gottes* (*GS–3* 400, 426).
46. On September 12, 1962, Strauss writes to Krüger: "It was extremely good of you to write to me about my contribution to the festschrift. I thought that it was fitting for the purpose because of your deep interest in Leibniz. I regret that by a grave error of the publisher the error was created that the article had been published before: it was written in 1936 for Volume III b of the Jubilee Edition of Mendelssohn's works, and the volume could no longer appear because of the situation at that time" (*GS–3* 453).
47. On May 31, 1937, Strauss writes to Guttmann, the editor in charge of the Jubilee Edition: "As for the Mendelssohn introduction, I have already decided not to consider at all the effects and consequences of the quarrel [about Lessing's Spinozism]. But the history of the genesis [of *Morgenstunden*] is so opaque and so little explained that a certain thoroughness cannot be avoided, particularly since a material understanding of Chapters XIII–XV of *Morgenstunden* depends entirely on an understanding of its genesis. It is, so it seems to me, of considerable significance that the concept of purified Spinozism never occurs in the whole prehistory [of the quarrel]. Incidentally, I hope to be able to submit the introduction soon for your assessment."
48. Plan of a book tentatively entitled *Philosophy and The Law: Historical Essays*. 5 pages. Leo Strauss Papers, Box 11, Folder 11. At the time of the outline, essays VII, VIII, IX, and X had already been published, a typescript of essay IV existed, which appeared posthumously, and Strauss wrote and published essays II and V later. (Cf. *Die Denkbewegung von Leo Strauss*, Bibliography: A 18, B 29, 31, 36, 38,

61, 129; and *Leo Strauss 1899–1973: A Bibliography* by Heinrich Meier, The Leo Strauss Center, Chicago: A 18, B 35, 37, 42, 44, 67, 137.)

49. In GA 3, Strauss reports in 1970: "In this study [of Spinoza's *Theologico-Political Treatise*] I was greatly assisted by Lessing, especially his theological writings, some of them with forbidding titles. Incidentally, Lessing is also the author of the only improvised live dialogue on a philosophic subject known to me. Lessing was always at my elbow. This meant that I learned more from him than I knew at the time. As I came to see later Lessing had said everything I had found out about the distinction between exoteric and esoteric speech and its grounds." Already in 1948 Strauss had expressed an emphatic word of thanks to Lessing at the end of his lecture, "Reason and Revelation," which he gave at the Hartford Theological Seminary in Hartford, Connecticut: "In conclusion, I would like to name that man to whom I owe, so to say, everything I have been able to discern in the labyrinth of that grave question: Lessing. I do not mean the Lessing of a certain tradition, the Lessing celebrated by a certain type of oratory, but the true and unknown Lessing. Lessing's attitude was characterized by an innate disgust against compromises in serious, i.e. theoretical, matters [. . .] He decided in favor of philosophy." "Reason and Revelation" in *Leo Strauss and the Theologico-Political Problem*, 178.
50. It was first published in *Interpretation* 14 (1986): 51–59. Unfortunately, the editor failed to inform the reader that the text presented is only the first part of a longer work, the manuscript of which breaks off after the heading "II," which marks the unwritten second part. Its fragmentary character may also explain why Strauss chose not to publish the text. However, a note among his posthumous papers reveals the intended structure of the treatise. The plan of Part II contains the following entries: "7. Aristotle's 'exoteric' writings. 8. Cicero. 9. Xenophon. Cyneg. 10. Plato's Letters. 11. Plato's Dialogues. Phaedrus, Rep., Timaeus. 12. Plato on the poets and Hesiod on the Muses. 13. Herakleitus. 14. The big exceptions: Epicurus and Sophists. Cic. Rep. III" (Leo Strauss Papers, Box 12, Folder 2). See now the critical edition by Hannes Kerber in this volume.
51. The letter to Alexander Altmann from May 28, 1971, is printed in Altmann's preface to volume III 2 of the Jubilee Edition (Stuttgart/Bad Cannstatt: Frommann-Holzboog, 1974), viii. (Cf. now *LSMM* 4–5.)

CHAPTER 2

SPINOZA'S CRITIQUE OF RELIGION: READING THE LOW IN LIGHT OF THE HIGH*

Steven Frankel

Strauss's early studies of Spinoza, including his first book, *Spinoza's Critique of Religion* (1930; henceforth *SCR*), have been largely neglected in favor of his later work. Such neglect is understandable: Strauss's work on Spinoza spans his entire career as a scholar and thinker, and includes his discovery of esotericism—which played a critical role in his most authoritative analysis of Spinoza. In addition, Strauss privately conceded problems with the work. In a letter to Gerhard Krüger in 1930, Strauss conceded that he had been compelled to remain silent in public about the presuppositions that were the point of departure for *SCR*.[1] Later he criticized the work publicly for not taking seriously the possibility of return to premodern philosophy (¶¶21, 42). It is somewhat surprising then that more than 30 years later, after its publication in German, Strauss decided to have the book translated into English. Ostensibly to explain his decision, Strauss prefaces the translation with an autobiographical account of the genesis and development of his early views as well as the inclusion of a later essay on Carl Schmitt (1932). One can recognize many of the themes in *SCR*—for example, the tension between Athens and Jerusalem, the inadequacy of the Enlightenment's critique of religion, and the development of Epicureanism, and others—which would preoccupy Strauss over the course of his career. Still, Strauss's decision to resurrect this early work is puzzling.

The studied carelessness with which Strauss handles his autobiographical account is in striking contrast to the attention he pays to the substance of the preface. This becomes clear when we contrast the literary form of the essay with the substantive argument: The literary form is an autobiographical narrative of a young German Jew who seeks to escape the "theological-political predicament" by either returning to the form of Jewish belief or else discovering a political alternative, such as Zionism or liberalism (see ¶¶1–13). After pointing to the difficulties with both of these political alternatives, Strauss seeks a qualified return to Jewish belief mediated by modern thought (see ¶¶14–23). When this proves unworkable, he considers the return to "unqualified Jewish belief" or orthodoxy. This leads him to consider Spinoza's critique of Judaism, and this is presumably the context within which *SCR* was written (see ¶¶24–39). Ultimately, Strauss concludes that Spinoza's critique undermines not only Judaism but also philosophy, and he decides to return to "Jewish medieval rationalism and its classical (Aristotelian and Platonic) foundation" (see ¶¶40–42).

This straightforward account of his intellectual development is undermined by the substance of his argument. Toward the center of his essay, Strauss confounds the account of his development.[2] For example, as a young man, Strauss reports that he was still considering the possibility of return to Jewish thought as mediated by modern rationalism, particularly in the thought of Franz Rosenzweig. According to his autobiographical narrative, he has not yet considered the possibility of return to premodern forms of rationalism, and in fact would not do so until after the completion of *SCR*. This is the conclusion of his autobiographical account: "I began therefore to wonder whether the destruction of reason was not the outcome of modern rationalism, as distinguished from pre-modern rationalism" (¶42).

However, in ¶21 Strauss breaks dramatically from the autobiographical narrative to assert the conclusion of the autobiographical account. After he criticizes Rosenzweig's new thinking, he writes: "One begins to wonder whether our medieval philosophy, and the old thinking of Aristotle, of which it made use, was not more 'empirical'...than an unqualified empiricism" (¶21). In effect, Strauss has moved the conclusion of the autobiography to the middle of the argument. This casts doubt on the central claim of the autobiography, which presents Strauss as gradually discovering the inadequacy of modern reason and the relevance of the ancients. Even if we read this claim as merely an aside or parenthetical remark so that it does not disturb the overall narrative, it is difficult to deny that Strauss is more concerned with emphasizing his conclusions than with giving an account or exploring the historical development of his thought.[3] Throughout the essay, he presents several more examples of interrupting the narrative to emphasize mature judgments that, though they shape his account, emerge only after the biographical period portrayed in the essay. One example, which we shall discuss in greater detail below, is Strauss's hermeneutical maxim of reading the low in light of the high (¶7). This principle supersedes the autobiographical narrative in terms of shaping the content of the essay. Strauss's goal is not to encourage further reflection upon his autobiography or offer an account of his intellectual development, but rather to guide our attention toward his mature thought.

The Theologico-Political Problem

Strauss begins the preface by referring to himself as "a young Jew born and raised in Germany who found himself in the grips of the theologico-political predicament."[4] Unfortunately, Strauss does not explain the nature of the theologico-political predicament, or indicate what specifically about the predicament constrained him. This is less of a mystery than it appears since the preface itself is devoted to explaining how to read Spinoza's *Tractatus Theologico-Politicus* (henceforth *TTP*), which in term is intended as an introduction to Strauss first book on the same topic. In order to see what is at issue, it is useful therefore to remind ourselves of the main themes of the theologico-political predicament as presented by Spinoza.

The *TTP* begins with an account of the role of superstition in political life. The perdurance of superstition creates a theological problem because men imagine a divine source to explain their fortunes, and it also creates a political problem because religious and political leaders are eager to manipulate them in order to solidify their own power.[5] Spinoza focuses on the particular theologico-political problem in Christendom and asks his readers to consider why Christians preach love and practice hatred (P.4.1–2). He goes on to suggest that Christianity has been hijacked and vulgarized by unscrupulous men who pervert its teachings in order to satisfy their ambitions for the wealth and power of ecclesiastical offices. Among their most insidious methods for obscuring and twisting the word of God is the importation of foreign or superstitious ideas into the Bible, particularly "the theories of Aristotelians and Platonists" (P.4.7).[6] Spinoza's account assumes that reason can identify superstition because reason can in principle provide a full account of nature; nonetheless, philosophy is unable to adjudicate disputes among superstitious, passionate individuals. To the contrary, philosophy is quickly transformed into yet another instrument to bolster superstition. The power of superstition also poses a political problem, because as superstitions gain in intensity, the passions that accompany them also increase and threaten the stability of the state.

The theologico-political predicament refers to the superstitious condition of mankind and the subsequent manipulation of those superstitions by religious and political leaders. Spinoza's solution to the problem has both political and theological elements. Theologically, he distinguishes the essential teachings of Christianity so that they can be purged of superstition, and restored in authority. The essential teaching of the Bible, and the minimum requirement for salvation, is the practice of charity and love toward all men. With her foundations restored, Christianity can once again contribute to the peacefulness of society. These few dogmas of Christianity do not exhaust our knowledge of God. Some men may seek and achieve greater knowledge of God; however, such knowledge is not a theological or political requirement for salvation. Politically, the pursuit of this knowledge is irrelevant since it is available to only a few individuals (14.1.49–51). The state needs only to secure safety and security for its citizens. For the most part, it leaves the citizens free to pursue knowledge of God as they see fit—as long as that pursuit is consistent with *caritas*. Spinoza envisions freedom, rather than reason or virtue, as the cornerstone of political life with the hope that reason will flourish under such conditions.[7] Strauss describes this regime as liberal democracy, and identifies Spinoza as its founder.[8]

The general analysis of the theologico-political predicament, directed toward a larger Christian audience, was not the same problem faced by Strauss, "a young

Jew in Germany." The version that Strauss inherited reflected the success of Spinoza's political solution in Germany, as well as its particular reception in the Jewish community. Spinoza's analysis was attractive to German Jews for several reasons: First, Spinoza himself was born a Jew and his argument involves a deep knowledge of Jewish commentaries on the Hebrew Bible. Strauss writes that many of his contemporaries in the Jewish community celebrated Spinoza "on purely Jewish grounds" (¶¶28, 26). Second, Spinoza's solution to the theologico-political predicament provides for a society where both Jews and Christians can live together in freedom despite differences in their private beliefs. Strauss reports that many German Jews believed that, thanks to Spinoza, "the millennial antagonism between Judaism and Christianity was about to disappear" (¶27). The reason for this confidence is that Spinoza had shown Jews that their religious law was purely political, and as a result, had become obsolete with the destruction of the Jewish state. This provided the theological argument for assimilation. Third, Spinoza's analysis of the Jews in Chapter three of the *TTP* not only envisions Jews and Christians living together but also considers the possibility that Jews might rebuild their former state. Certainly, this argument was meant to complement his analysis of the destruction of the Jewish state and not as a political strategy; nonetheless, Spinoza was celebrated by some Jews as the founder of Zionism (cf. ¶11).

Strauss was in the grips of the theologico-political predicament as described by Spinoza. The various solutions that Spinoza suggests, namely secular liberalism, religious liberalism, and Zionism, appear to be the only options available to the young Strauss. The organization of the essay adopts the framework set out by Spinoza, considering each possibility in turn. As we shall see, each solution falls short and the thread connecting these failures is the audacious confidence in the power and capacity of reason to recognize and redress superstition. Spinoza's solutions are political solutions to the problem of superstition since they concede that most people will remain superstitious; nonetheless, they offer strategies for prudently managing superstition. By framing the issue in this way, as a matter of reason ameliorating superstition, Spinoza suggests the political value of religion for a stable community, while undermining the philosophical basis for revelation. The result is that we are left with only unpalatable options. After turning to Spinoza's solutions to the theological political problem, Strauss next considers the modern variants of Spinoza's analysis, Heidegger's atheism, and Rosenzweig's piety. Both fail to resolve the tension between politics, religion, and philosophy: either we reject reason and embrace revelation, or else we reject revelation and, with it, the well-being of our political communities.

Liberalism in Weimar

Strauss reports that the majority of German Jews celebrated Weimar and its historical founder, Spinoza. Although Weimar originated with the defeat of Germany and his humiliation in the Treaty of Versailles, she could trace her roots to a nobler, deeper heritage in the French Revolution, and ultimately Spinoza's account of the theological-political problem. From their point of view, liberal democracy had deep roots in Germany so that their Jewish faith presented no obstacle to assimilation. They interpreted Weimar in the best or highest light, emphasizing its moderate character and its attempt to integrate the "principles of 1789" with the "highest German tradition" (¶2). This tradition includes the recognition of the rights of man and a well-organized government of highly trained civil servants. Under this regime, Jews flourished and participated in the cultural life of the Republic, and Jewish life was strong; it even developed a new "science of Judaism" (¶7). Although the German tradition also included strong anti-Jewish sentiments that dominated medieval society, liberalism corrected this situation by protecting the rights of religious minorities and purging the government of superstitious and irrational goals. No wonder Weimar appeared to German Jews all the more precious and noble.[9]

In direct contrast to this view, the Zionists, with whom Strauss openly sided, viewed Weimar as weak at its very foundations and unable to defend itself when challenged by ruthless enemies who viewed the Jews as outsiders who threatened German *Kultur* with foreign culture and "*Civilisation*."[10] Strauss presents quotations from Goethe, Nietzsche, and Heidegger that demonstrate the resilience of anti-Jewish feelings in Germany (¶8). Ignoring their "precarious situation," the Jews of Weimar clung to the vain hope that liberalism would somehow prevail. Strauss suggests that the election of Hindenburg in 1925 "showed *everyone who had eyes to see* that the Weimar Republic had only a short time to live," because the nonliberal tradition was "stronger in will" (¶3, emphasis added, S.F.). Strauss's phrase suggests that the weakness and vulnerability of Weimar were obvious, yet few, particularly within the Jewish community, recognized it. The problem of superstition comes to light in the first instance as the belief in the durability of liberalism in Weimar.

History appears to have vindicated this Zionist critique of German Jewry. Weimar is likely to be remembered as a cautionary tale of democracy without strength, "of justice without a sword" (¶3). However, the Zionist vision was also limited by the fact it is the product of the liberalism that it criticizes, rather than of the Jewish tradition (cf. ¶11). The difficulty of making a balanced judgment on Weimar is that it requires measuring the low elements against the higher ones. Strauss suggests the following rule of thumb: "It is safer to understand the low in the light of the high than the high in the light of the low. In doing the latter one necessarily distorts the high, whereas in doing the former one does not deprive the low of the freedom to reveal itself fully as what it is" (¶5).[11] To judge Weimar only on its sorry record of weakness and collapse ignores its deeper and nobler roots and "its moderate, non-radical character" (¶2). As a principle of interpretation, taking one's bearings from the highest rather than the lowest possibilities seems to be a prudent rule of thumb.

But this principle is hardly self-evident. Strauss's justification of this principle on the grounds of safety raises the question: safer for whom? In the context of the preface, where Strauss discusses repeatedly the "precarious" situation of the Jews in Weimar and Europe, the primary consideration appears to be the safety of the Jews in the Diaspora (¶¶6–8). His subsequent analysis highlights the dangers involved in ignoring the lowest political elements in favor of dreams about perpetual peace. He takes a particularly severe view of Hermann Cohen's faith in progress and his unwillingness to confront the less palatable side of power and coercion in politics (cf. ¶¶32–33). Cohen was so concerned with interpreting the high in light of the low that he underplayed the reality of the low. He condemned Spinoza "for his Machiavellian-inspired hard-heartedness" only to fall victim to "the opposite extreme" (¶32). But even Cohen appears to be a sober realist compared to the "fantastic flights" that mesmerized those German Jews who feted Spinoza as a savior (¶29). Strauss openly sides with the Zionists' interpretation of the Jewish Question, a position that confirms the wisdom of neglecting the high in politics in order to protect oneself from the low. Nonetheless, as we shall see, his analysis ultimately reveals the serious flaws with its neglect of the high.

Zionism as a Political Solution to the "Jewish Problem"

Spinoza inspired the Zionist movement by suggesting that there is a political solution to the Jewish problem, which involves giving priority to politics over religion.[12] In his critique of purely political Zionism, Strauss draws our attention to the work of Ahad Ha'am (Asher Ginsberg, 1856–1927), "the founder of cultural Zionism." For Ahad Ha'am, the theological questions had been already settled by Darwin and science, both of which had allegedly proven that revelation was false (¶15). This distinction helps to understand Strauss's critique, specifically how Zionism was largely correct in its analysis of liberalism in Germany and yet not able to offer Jews a completely satisfying account of Judaism. In addition, this analysis of a political solution that is theologically inadequate casts the theologico-political problem in sharper relief. The political situation of the Jews involves questions of power and safety as well as theoretical questions about the meaning of Judaism. To read the low in light of the high means to judge political solutions in light of their higher, theoretical considerations. Strauss's analysis shows that, while it is dangerous to ignore practical political concerns, they need to be separated from the higher theological questions. His critique of both the Zionists and the assimilationists confirms this reading.

While Zionism has the virtue of grasping the limitations of liberalism in Europe (cf. ¶6), it does not reject liberalism itself. Instead it attributes the failure of liberalism to the fact that the Jews were at the mercy of other nations. Strauss quotes Herzl on the failure of assimilation: "We are a nation—the enemy makes us a nation whether we like it or not" (¶10). The assimilationists abandon Judaism in the vain hope that they will be welcomed into a universal society. Political Zionism exposes the fact that liberalism, despite its promise of a universal solution to the Jewish Question, cannot create a view of justice strong enough to overcome discrimination. Liberalism cannot eliminate hatred or superstition; at best, it can provide only legal—rather than social—equality. But Strauss does not stop there. He argues that Zionism also betrays Judaism in the belief that it can resolve the Jewish Question by treating it merely as a problem of power, not divine punishment.

The virtue of Zionism was its sober claim that the Jewish Question could be solved by power alone. Even cultural Zionism attempts to combine this view with a project for the revival of Judaism, but its account of the high is vague and unsatisfying. As a result, cultural Zionism tends to slide in opposite directions, "politics (power politics) and divine revelation" (¶12). This result follows from Spinoza's account of the Jewish Question. Cultural Zionism attempts to escape the theological-political grip of Spinoza, but it cannot explain the basis of the high; instead it either ignores the high in the case of political Zionism or reads the high in light of the low in the case of cultural Zionism.

The Highest Goals of Political Life

Strauss exposes the failure of Zionism to resolve the Jewish Question as part of a broader critique of liberalism. Following Spinoza, liberalism advocated the separation of politics from religion on the grounds that such a separation would allow politics to pursue more effectively the goals of safety and security.[13] By focusing on the low, liberalism promised to leave people the freedom to pursue the high in safety. The problem is that this freedom also allows for superstition, and thus liberalism does not solve the problem of discrimination. To do so, liberalism would have to prevent discrimination by severely limiting freedom of speech in both the public and the private sphere. This would, in effect, destroy the private sphere and, with it, the *raison d'être* for the liberalism. The Zionists recognized that the problem of superstition, and more particularly of anti-Jewish beliefs, was not resolved by freedom of thought in the private sphere. To the contrary, prejudice against Jews seemed to spread all the more widely in liberal democracies. Liberalism cannot resolve the Jewish problem, or more generally the problem of the imagination in political life. In Strauss's words, the Jewish Question is an example of an "infinite, absolute problem [which] cannot be solved" (¶12).

The claim that there are permanent problems shifts our attention from the particular perspective of a young Jew in Weimar toward a broader understanding of the limits of liberalism. The Jewish Question is one example of neglecting the high to manage the low. By allowing superstitious men freedom of thought, liberalism contributes willy-nilly to the decline of philosophy and reason in political life. Strauss again breaks from the autobiographical chronology with a judgment that shapes the narrative. As with his claim about judging the lower in light of the higher, he forces us to consider the claim more carefully and reflect on the role of reason in political life. The Jewish problem is "the most manifest symbol" of the political dimension of the "human problem," which cannot be fully resolved (¶12). He contrasts this with the problem of the Jewish individual who has become alienated from his faith. This problem can be resolved by rejoining the Jewish community. However, the larger problem of the Jewish community's relation to other, nonJewish communities cannot be resolved. Liberalism tries to resolve it by finding a common understanding of justice or "a universal human society," which is united by its vision of justice (¶14).

Strauss presents the liberal solution as it appeared to his contemporaries, namely that liberalism was the best solution to the Jewish problem either because

Judaism itself had been refuted (¶14) or because liberalism simply followed from Jewish principles of justice (¶28). Spinoza provides the basis for both claims since his argument is built on the dual premises of criticizing the Biblical teaching while returning to its essential principle, the practice of charity.[14] The principle of charity and toleration has the advantage of a broad consensus among various religious faiths and even nonbelievers. For adherents of the Bible, Spinoza argues that the truest and most accurate reading of the Bible reveals that its deepest teaching, the one most necessary for salvation, is the practice of *caritas*. For all good men—*honestos* as Spinoza calls them—the benefits of this religious view are so apparent that they would embrace it just as enthusiastically whether or not they are believers (*TTP* 14.1.36).[15] In addition, by subordinating all other religious beliefs to charity, liberalism allows a good deal of freedom of thought. Any views, even atheism, are acceptable if they promote charity.[16]

The Question of Return

In his critique of Weimar and Zionism, Strauss had cast a doubt on whether Spinoza's strategy of accommodating all views can work effectively without identifying a firmer theoretical basis for the morality of *caritas*. He concludes that "the Jewish problem is insoluble," by which he means that the "liberal state cannot provide a solution to the Jewish problem" (¶13). Strauss qualifies this claim by admitting that liberalism is better than the alternatives of communism and National Socialism, and that it does provide an "uneasy 'solution to the Jewish problem'" (¶13). Then, in striking contrast to his previous claims, he declares in the next paragraph: "There is a Jewish problem that is humanly soluble" (¶14). This problem, however, is not the wider political problem of the community in a precarious situation, but rather of "the problem of the Western Jewish individual." The individual can return to traditional beliefs and avoid the illusions of liberalism. In this sense, there is hope for solving our "deepest problem" and "most vital need" theoretically, even if this does not end discrimination or superstition (¶14).

In moving from the political situation to the question of individual return, Strauss has not entirely freed himself from the grips of the theologico-political predicament. Although he has explained why a political solution cannot fully solve the Jewish problem, he has not yet exposed the theoretical underpinnings of liberalism. These underpinnings are first revealed when Strauss points out that "some of his contemporaries" believed that return was impossible because the traditional faith "had been overthrown once and for all." But the theoretical legacy of liberalism is more complicated than simply rejecting revelation. This is indicated by the fact that many more of Strauss's contemporaries believed that it was possible to grant science and history complete authority "without abandoning one iota of the substance of the Jewish faith" (¶15). In short, the theologico-political predicament is ambiguous: does it destroy faith or preserve it? In the next section of the essay, Strauss examines the reasons for this ambiguity. As we shall see, both positions are the result of a deliberate ambiguity about the status of Scripture within Spinoza's argument. As Strauss frees himself of Spinoza's theologico-political grip, he parts company with more of his contemporaries.

The path Strauss follows takes him through the intellectual currents of his time. I emphasize that he *follows* this path, which he describes as a "qualified return" or a return mediated by modernity, because it has already been marked out by its founders including Martin Buber and Franz Rosenzweig as "new thinking." As the very title of the movement, "new thinking," indicates, the movement represented a conscious departure from the tradition so that the question of return takes on a radical new meaning. The new thinking has several elements that interested Strauss and explains why he chose to pursue it rather than traditional Judaism. For one thing, the movement assigns authority to "present experience" rather than revealed law or tradition. Further, the new thinking relies heavily on a broader critique of reason and philosophy found in the work of Friedrich Nietzsche, a seminal thinker for Strauss (¶17). Unlike earlier efforts to make Judaism compelling by showing that "the truth of traditional Judaism is the religion of reason," the new thinking rejected reason as a criterion altogether (¶15). The movement followed Nietzsche in arguing that the "return to Judaism requires today the overcoming of what one may call the perennial obstacle to the Jewish faith: traditional philosophy" (¶16).

This critique of philosophy was based not only on its awareness of the limits of reason but also on its thoroughgoing historicism. Following Nietzsche, Rosenzweig argued that "the human soul has no unchangeable essence or limits but is essential historical" (¶20). This claim constitutes the core of historicism's claim to wisdom. The historical dimension of all thought reveals previous claims to wisdom as defective. It allows us to understand previous thinkers better than they understood themselves. Historicism also provides a new approach to tradition: whereas the question of return was also seen as a return to the revealed law, the new thinking claims that we have always selected from the tradition according to the needs of our age; now we can and should do so consciously.

According to the autobiographical account of the narrative, Strauss's turn to the new thinking was motivated by his question of whether a "return to Jewish orthodoxy was not both possible and necessary" (¶24). Yet Strauss does not return to orthodoxy. Instead he launches an investigation of Spinoza's critique of religion to see if there are grounds philosophically that prevent a return. The results of this investigation are less clear in terms of orthodoxy, but point instead to the continuing relevance of ancient philosophy. Like Socrates, who claims in the *Apology* that his lifelong philosophical quest began with his pious attempts to understand and verify the oracle of Delphi, Strauss frames his discovery of philosophy in terms of his pious effort to return to orthodoxy. Whereas Socrates had investigated the belief in the gods of the city, Strauss investigates the superstitions of his age, the belief in historicism under the guise of the "new thinking."

The New Thinking

Strauss begins with Martin Buber's foray into the new thinking in *I and Thou*. Rather than begin with the tradition, he starts with "present experience," which is more immediate and less doubtful. If we are open to an encounter with the divine, that is, if we have not dogmatically accepted the rationalism of Greek philosophy—the path that recognizes only "what man knows by himself"—we may experience an absolute call that comes from outside of man and "goes against man's grain," suddenly becomes more compelling (¶16). This experience finds confirmation in the call of the prophets in the Bible. The prophets too have experienced the speechless "call" of God and, in response, offer a human interpretation. Prophecy, the speechless experience of the absolute, is in principle open to everyone. Our return depends on our experience of the absolute and our recognition of this same experience in the Bible.

Buber's analysis places great weight on our interpretation of the absolute divine experience. But which interpretation of this experience is the truest one? Cannot the experience be tampered with? Is not the experience itself determined by our historical conditions? Buber cannot answer these questions by using reason to judge because he assumes that reason necessarily undermines such an experience. To show us the danger that Buber's position has invited, Strauss invents a dialogue between Buber and Heidegger regarding whether the prophets sought to challenge or affirm the people's security. Although Buber would many years later consider Heidegger's critique, during the 1930s no such dialogue was possible because "[a]t that time, Heidegger expressed his thought about revelation by silence or deed rather than by speech" (¶17). To create a dialogue between Heidegger and Buber, therefore, Strauss has to use later writings from each author that he could not have had access to during this period of his development.[17] The confrontation between Buber and Heidegger once again confounds our efforts to trace Strauss's historical development.

Strauss's dialogue reveals that Heidegger has a "deeper understanding" of the meaning and implications of the new thinking (¶17). Heidegger claims that Buber's interpretation of the absolute is merely wishful thinking. Indeed, against Buber's assertion that the warnings of the prophets do not "go against our grain," Heidegger shows that they merely confirm our wish for security, particularly the security of our moral judgments by providing a "supra-human support for justice" (¶18). Rather than dismiss philosophy, he identifies a goal shared by both ancient philosophy and biblical revelation to find or demonstrate "the security of justice." The desire for justice is in turn related to the desire for the eternal, which does not come into being or pass away. But the new thinking exposes this desire as "stemming from 'spirit of revenge'" rather than from either revelation or reason. Buber had dismissed reason with the confidence that revelation could take its place as the basis for justice. But Heidegger's atheism cuts off this possibility and forces us to confront our terrifying condition of insecurity and uncertainty. For him, terror and cruelty are the true signs of "intellectual probity."[18] There is no ultimate ground for its belief in a *summum bonum*; philosophy can no longer pretend to be anything more than an act of will.

Strauss presents Heidegger's critique of revelation in terms of a critique of the high. In an unmistakable attack on Heidegger, he observes that "[n]ot every man but every noble man is concerned with justice and righteousness and therefore with any possible or extra-human support of justice, or with the security of justice" (¶18). In Strauss's presentation, Heidegger's pursuit of justice takes the form of a demand for "intellectual probity," which in turn attempts to expose every concern for justice with the desire for security.[19] Intellectual probity should not be confused with "the old love of truth."[20] The difference, Strauss, explains, is that probity is more explicit, even dogmatic, about its atheism. As a result, it rejects all attempts to obscure the consequences of atheism, or to pretend that some sort of "semi-theism" is possible.[21] In Heidegger's hands, liberalism's neutrality regarding the high gives way to the explicit rejection of the transcendent and the apparent embrace of the low. Conversely, Strauss shows the common ground shared by reason and revelation, and in fact by all noble men, namely the concern for justice. Strauss's return aims at restoring this common ground rather than showing the victory of one alternative. Of course, this personal attack does not mitigate the force of Heidegger's objections. Instead, it exposes a deeper problem: modern philosophy, which began with a criticism of superstition in favor of reason, now abandons reason as a guide. The result is that philosophy participates in the superstitions that it had previously criticized and the cruelty that it had once abhorred.[22]

Strauss's path of return moves from Heidegger toward the origins of modernity and Spinoza.[23] First, though, he considers a more serious attempt at a qualified return to the Bible offered by Franz Rosenzweig. Paradoxically, Rosenzweig begins his quest to return by denying the possibility of a return to Biblical faith. He draws a distinction between what the authors of the Bible meant and how we understand it today. The former is a historical concern characteristic of what he calls the "old thinking," while the latter is practiced in full awareness of the historical text and our current situation, that is, how the text affects the present situation. It is important to note that Rosenzweig rejects Spinoza's principle of selecting from the text by distinguishing between its essential and unessential parts. Such a distinction can hardly be as objective as it claims, since it presumes the wisdom that it seeks to find in the Bible. Rosenzweig avoids this problem by admitting that a "force" rather than a principle guides our decision. The past, the "whole reality of Jewish life," offers materials for us to select and by virtue of the selection, transform into a living force in our lives. The past becomes a set of resources for building the future, but we are the ones who select from the past.

But as we scrutinize Rosenzweig's selections, we cannot help but notice that vitality is measured by consistency with modern liberal regimes. Thus, for example, Rosenzweig does not find compelling the orthodox view of the Torah's law, which sees it in terms of prohibition and rejection; instead he interprets the law in terms of liberation and transformation. This represents a far more optimistic view of political possibilities and of the fate of liberal societies. Another example of vitality is Rosenzweig's rejection of Biblical miracles. Here vitality is associated with skepticism and science. Rosenzweig claims he did not believe all the miracles reported in the Torah but, rather, claims to be open to belief.[24] The orthodox approach, in contrast, had far less confidence in the judgment of each individual not only because of the limits of reason but also because such individuality could undermine the cohesiveness of the community.

Like Buber, Rosenzweig wishes to make Judaism more consistent with experience, but in practice this means making it more consistent with liberalism. Instead of beginning from the Torah as law, as does Maimonides, for example, Rosenzweig begins from one's awareness of being a member of the chosen people, because such awareness is "the primary condition of the possibility of Jewish consciousness" (¶21). This is at odds with the traditional view that the law as revealed is the basis of the community. Strauss suggests that Rosenzweig consciously begins with chosenness rather than law in order to reshape the tradition so that it is more compatible with Christianity. This is in keeping with Spinoza's liberalism, where Judaism and Christianity are assimilated into a universal religion that stresses *caritas* as the sole requirement for salvation. Rosenzweig did not hope to return to traditional Judaism, but to adapt the tradition so that it would be at home in Weimar. Strauss exposes Rosenzweig's effort to reshape the tradition, yet he does not criticize this reform simply as a betrayal of the tradition. Rather, he wonders how to take one's bearing in such a project: how can one know that one's proposals to change the tradition will result in its preservation or deepening? Has Rosenzweig understood "the old in its depth"? His attempt to transform Judaism in order to make it compatible with liberalism, a regime that is ambiguous with respect to a *summum bonum,* suggest otherwise.[25] By transforming Judaism to meet the needs of liberalism, Rosenzweig has lowered the tradition rather than deepened it.

Strauss also suggests that Rosenzweig's proffered reform has not deepened the tradition, by contrasting him with Maimonides, who similarly attempted to alter the tradition's attitude toward philosophy. Curiously, Strauss approaches the superiority of Maimonides in terms of his method for reshaping the tradition. Maimonides was more loyal to the Jewish People, or at least more careful to preserve the appearance of his loyalty to the tradition, than was Rosenzweig. Nothing exemplifies this better than Maimonides insistence on placing Judaism above philosophy and politics. Strauss says that Maimonides, in sharp contrast to Rosenzweig, wrote Jewish books, not philosophical ones, "as a Jew he gives his assent where as a philosopher he would suspend his assent" (cf. *Guide of the Perplexed* 2.16; HBS xiv). In the preface, Strauss makes the same point in order to contrast Maimonides with Rosenzweig, He points out that [w]hereas the classic work of what is called Jewish medieval philosophy, the *Guide of the Perplexed*, is primarily not a philosophic book but a Jewish book, Rosenzweig's *Star of Redemption* is primarily not a Jewish book but a "system of philosophy" (¶21). The difference between a Jewish book and a philosophic book is that in a Jewish book, the authority of law precedes and is distinguished from the authority of reason.[26] Rosenzweig, however, has already rejected both ancient philosophy and reason as a guide. To make matters worse from Strauss's point of view, Rosenzweig's philosophy is much more consistent with Christianity than is traditional Judaism because its starting point is not the law, but a secondary category like chosenness. In this sense, he treats the tradition as a quarry, or set of resources, for crafting a Judeo-Christian society. This view is important to keep in mind because Strauss will later call attention to Rosenzweig and Cohen's critique of Spinoza, which essentially claims that he was disloyal to his people by exposing its flaws for all to see. In fact, Strauss here shows that Rosenzweig has essentially done the same thing, with even less consciousness of his debt to Spinoza.

The Return to Spinoza

The second half of Strauss's preface (¶¶ 24–42) is devoted to Hermann Cohen's analysis of Spinoza. This is surprising, insofar as Cohen predated Rosenzweig and Buber. Moreover, his analysis stops short of the new thinking in that he holds reason in high esteem, capable of guiding men and teaching them a universal moral law consistent with Jewish law. Possibly Strauss was genuinely more impressed by Cohen than by Rosenzweig. He describes Cohen as "a Jew of rare dedication" who "symbolized more than anyone else the union of Jewish faith and German culture." Nor did Cohen neglect the high. In fact, he "surpassed in spiritual power" his colleagues in philosophy and theology. However, we must be careful not to overstate the influence of Cohen's critique; after all, Strauss largely rejects Cohen's analysis of Spinoza. His tribute to Cohen is actually a refutation of Cohen's approach to philosophy. Indeed, he raises the question of whether Cohen could even be considered a philosopher, suggesting instead that he is a rather limited, if well-meaning, scholar.[27] In short, his presentation of Cohen is from the point of view of the mature Strauss who has thoroughly rejected him.[28]

Yet Rosenzweig's judgment on Cohen plays an important role in Strauss's presentation. Rosenzweig admits that Cohen's treatment of the evidence may not be just; however, Rosenzweig argues that there is a deeper justification for Cohen's position. Spinoza took "for granted the philosophic detachment or freedom from the tradition of his own people" (¶35). Philosophy may appear to confer freedom by detaching one from the community, but this is an illusion on par with the erroneous view that reason provides a liberating vantage point. Rejecting such illusions, Rosenzweig claims that this detachment is nothing more than the rejection of loyalty, love, and sympathy for one's own community. Had Spinoza cared more for his people, he would have helped them reinterpret their tradition "in light of the highest [possibility, or failing that,] if necessary, better than they understood themselves" (¶35). Thus, although the explicit topic of this section of the essay is how to read Spinoza (or how Cohen misread Spinoza), the judgment of Rosenzweig opens the radical question about changing a tradition. Cohen, who was temperamentally conservative, was unable to grasp, "the fact that the continuous and changing tradition . . . [depends on] revolutions and sacrileges" (¶38).

As for Cohen's critical reading of Spinoza, Strauss does show how Cohen helps expose several central and apparently deliberate contradictions in the *TTP.* These contradictions would reappear in Strauss's mature interpretation of Spinoza; however, Cohen was unable to resolve them correctly because of his conviction that he has understood Spinoza better than Spinoza understood himself. This "idealizing interpretation" is a variety of historicism, which explains an author's work as a product of history rather than deliberate choice. Cohen, for example, did not consider that Spinoza's style reflected a deliberate choice in light of persecution and his political project. Strauss playfully and explicitly refutes this, and suggests instead that Cohen "understood Spinoza too literally because he didn't understand him literally enough" (¶37). The difficulty in reading Spinoza correctly is determining whether he means what he says, that is, whether we should read him literally. The question of historical circumstances undoubtedly plays a role in Spinoza's presentation, but in order to measure this influence, we must understand Spinoza's metaphysical project. If Spinoza's assertions contradict his metaphysical teaching, then we are justified in considering his political circumstances to explain his argument.[29] Thus, Strauss's section is meant to guide the reader away from his historicist prejudice to a more thoughtful reading of Spinoza. The claim of the overall narrative is that one can escape Spinoza's theologico-political grip only by reading him correctly.

The Development of Strauss's Interpretation of Spinoza

In addressing Cohen's historicist interpretation of Spinoza, Strauss begins by putting aside the autobiographical narrative to offer an account of Spinoza's metaphysics (¶27). To see more clearly the defects in Cohen's hermeneutics, Strauss begins with a literal reading of Spinoza's political thought. According to this account, Spinoza must be understood as part of modern philosophy's break with ancient philosophy. Spinoza did not initiate this break, but was "the heir of the modern revolt" (¶29). Modern philosophy rejected the theoretical contemplation of nature in favor of a more practical and useful approach. It sought to master rather than contemplate nature. This was part of a political project to improve man's comfort and thereby secure the freedom to philosophize. Spinoza embraces the modern project, but also attempts to restore the "dignity of speculation on the basis of modern philosophy or science" (¶29).

Spinoza's metaphysical starting point is also distinctively modern: all things proceed from the one, but the process is not one of decay or descent, neither is it one of creation. Rather it is an unfolding of individual, particular things that we are to understand *sub specie aeternatatis*.[30] The "last word on the subject" is the *Ethics*, where Spinoza argues that the highest form of knowledge is of particular things.[31] In sharp contrast to the Bible, God is not therefore the highest source of knowledge, but the process or unfolding of nature. Thus, on the question of the high, Spinoza's thought is ambiguous. On the one hand, he maintains the view of ancient philosophy that philosophy is the highest activity for man; on the other hand, his view is not grounded in nature but rather in the endless (and directionless) unfolding of nature.

Spinoza's political project, liberalism, reflects his ambiguity about the status of the high. He begins, or appears to begin, from metaphysical axioms that provide no basis or support for justice.[32] In fact, the goal of politics must be understood in light of the mechanical universe within which it operates. Rather than refer to intellectual or moral virtue, the regime must be directed toward security and comfort. Nor can political leaders rely on some absolute standard of justice (from nature or God) to fix their goal. They must guide man but rather by the tough-minded control of destructive passions and the fostering of more constructive ones through, for example, a commercial society. Spinoza equates the passions with the right of nature, so as to indicate that they are natural, even if they are not directed toward any end other than the striving to persist.

Cohen's Critique of Spinoza

The celebration of Spinoza by German Jews reflects their appreciation of liberalism as a regime that offered them unprecedented opportunities. Spinoza was the saint who inaugurated "a new religion or religiousness which was to become a wholly new kind of society, a new kind of Church" (¶27). That they neglected the Machiavellian elements of his political thought and ignored his rejection of the Biblical God is not surprising given their apparent flourishing in liberal democracy. To his credit, Cohen refused to ignore the less attractive elements of Spinoza's teaching (¶29). He was particularly disturbed by the effort to annul the original excommunication, arguing instead that Spinoza had indeed betrayed the Jewish people. Cohen was not concerned, according to Strauss, with violations of ceremonial law or the denial of Mosaic authorship. Instead, he "condemned Spinoza because of his infidelity in the simple human sense, of his complete lack of loyalty to his own people, of his acting like an enemy of the Jews and thus giving aid and comfort to the many enemies of the Jews, of his behaving like a base traitor" (¶19).

Cohen's particular charges constitute a damning indictment: Spinoza accepts and extends the Christian critique of Judaism. He falsely accuses Judaism of commanding hatred of the enemy. He presents a picture of Judaism as carnal and particularistic in contrast to the universal and spiritual picture of Christianity. His efforts to show Judaism in a poor light lead him to contradict himself by then claiming that prophecy is universal in order to promote the universalism of Christianity. In Spinoza's version of Judaism, the law is particularly devalued as having a purely political, rather than moral or spiritual, role. Having reduced the law to a tribal code, Spinoza suggests that the law's author, the God of Israel, is merely a tribal God. Not only then does Spinoza betray the Jewish people, he also blasphemes God while suggesting that the Torah is "of merely human origin" (¶18).

In Cohen's reading, Spinoza is so filled with malice—"he has no heart for the people, no compassion"—that he grows obsessed with denigrating Judaism by any means necessary (¶30). He does not hesitate, for instance, to praise Christianity or encourage the anti-Jewish views of his Christian readers. He ignores contradictions in his own argument if they undermine Judaism. His betrayal of his people and philosophy is "humanly incomprehensible" and even demonic in that it is rooted in a denial of any standard of morality. Cohen also argues that there was a more comprehensible motive for Spinoza's hostility toward Judaism. Like other Marranos, whose fear of the Inquisition turned into hatred of its causes, namely Judaism, Spinoza aimed his hatred at the victims rather than the perpetrators.

Strauss agrees with Cohen's overall judgment that Spinoza is "amazingly unscrupulous"; indeed, he argues that his own judgment is "in some ways even stronger than Cohen's" (¶31). But Cohen reads the *TTP* too literally and therefore mistakenly thinks that Spinoza genuinely prefers Christianity to Judaism because it appears more spiritual and universal. In his view, Spinoza wishes to ennoble Christianity by convincing Christians to purge themselves of carnal relics of Judaism, that is, by liberating Christianity from Judaism. This is where "Cohen fails" to follow Spinoza's argument.[33] Spinoza's goal according to Strauss was to fashion a liberal society that embraced the freedom to philosophy. The argument that he crafted was not a betrayal of the Jewish people, nor does his primary allegiance to philosophy mean that he is indifferent to the Jewish people.[34] To the contrary, Spinoza provides a society wherein they could be citizens. In addition, the universal dogmas of catholic faith in *TTP* Chapter 14 "are equally acceptable to both Jews and Christians" (¶31). Such a society requires the abrogation of the Mosaic law, but this law had become obsolete with the destruction of the state. Strauss's defense of Spinoza amounts to this: he "liberated Jews in the only way he could think of" given his philosophy (¶31).

Strauss's critique of Spinoza is stronger than Cohen's because Strauss does not ignore the Machiavellian core of Spinoza's project. Cohen was committed to a theologico-political view that combined the Bible with Kant, who viewed God as an "idea" that guarantees the existence of a universal moral law discoverable by reason. The "idea" of God is the basis of morality, as well as of the optimistic belief in the ultimate triumph of Good over Evil.[35] Kant's moral law is realizable first only in particular states, but it points toward a universal moral order, grounded in international law and enforced by a league of nations. In Cohen's version of creation and providence, the politics generates the theology. In other words, we need the "idea" of God to justify a certain political order. Reason comes to theology's aid to help determine the requirements of a universal and just political order, and instructs theology on its presuppositions.

But all of these beliefs are exposed as superstitions, albeit salutary superstitions, within the confines of Spinoza's metaphysics. Cohen's thought and his interpretation of Spinoza have a clear sense of the high, and he seeks wherever possible to read the low in light of the high. According to Strauss, this leads to various problems within Cohen's own thought. For example, he tends to cover over the criminal violence and destruction that attend revolutions. Similarly, he sees the purpose of punishment solely in terms of promoting the well-being of the criminal. In his single-minded attention to the high, Cohen appears to ignore the low altogether. He "ignored the harsh political verities which Spinoza had stated so forcefully" (¶36). In this, one wonders whether he did not help to prepare the generation of Jews who did not have "eyes to see" the disaster that was approaching. In any case, this tendency to neglect the low renders Cohen a woefully inadequate interpreter of Spinoza because "the kind of interpretation which Spinoza calls for is not idealizing, since his own doctrine is not idealistic" (¶36).

Strauss focuses our attention on two related problems in Cohen's interpretation that expose the problem that emerges with his idealizing philosophy.

First, Cohen is unable to conceive of the relation between reason and revelation as anything other than harmonious. In addition, Cohen cannot grasp the meaning of Spinoza's denial of any natural support for the high. Both examples point us directly to Maimonides and imply that not only did Cohen misinterpret Spinoza and Maimonides incorrectly but also that Maimonides's point of view was superior.

Cohen claims that Spinoza's interpretation of Judaism does not recognize the universalism of the prophets. For instance, Spinoza draws our attention to Maimonides's claim that a person cannot be saved unless he believes in Mosaic revelation. This view suggests that obedience rather than reason is primary to piety. Similarly, Maimonides claims that a non-Jew can be considered pious if he performs the Noahide commandments as commandments of God, adding that if a non-Jew performs them because they are rational, he is neither pious nor wise. Its wisdom teaches that reason cannot supplant piety as a source of political authority. Finally, Maimonides suggests that the Torah's commandments themselves are not rational, but are meant to address and cure idolatry, "an irrational practice." Maimonides begins from the opinions of the community before determining the best way to enlighten the tradition. Irrational opinions may justify the commandments while reason itself may not.[36] Leaving aside Spinoza, Strauss reports that the Jewish tradition, as per Joseph Caro, confirms this view. Cohen ignores those elements of the Jewish tradition, which suggests a tension between wisdom and piety because he overestimates the power of reason and its compatibility with the law.

The other example that Strauss chooses focuses on the question of the highest good. Cohen points out the following contradiction in the *TTP*: Spinoza claims that Moses's law is a divine law, that is, it points man toward the highest good or intellectual love of God; yet, he denies that the Mosaic law aims at the highest good. Strauss denies that this is a contradiction, because Spinoza does not mean the law is divine in the sense of aiming toward salvation or even intellectual knowledge of God. Rather, Spinoza means that the law is divine because it is *believed to be divine* by Christian readers whom Spinoza addresses. There is no divine law in the sense of a law with natural or rational ends. Cohen has not come to grips with the fact that neither God nor reason supports the moral law. Spinoza's morality is always tied to a relentless egoism. Following his teacher Machiavelli, Spinoza conceives of nature in terms of individuals struggling to persist in their own being. Nothing stands apart from or above this struggle that would allow us to judge it in moral terms.

Cohen wants to understand the tradition as something that we can shape by understanding the low or superstitious in light of reason, or the high. Despite Strauss's insistence on understanding the low in light of the high, he rejects Cohen's reading of the Jewish tradition. The reason for this is that Cohen has not escaped the horizons set out by Spinoza. He "does not come to grips with the fact that Spinoza's critique is directed against the whole body" of Jewish teachings and tradition (¶39). He believed that Spinoza had refuted orthodoxy, especially miracles and law. Furthermore, Cohen agrees with Spinoza's opposition to rabbinical Judaism, which put great emphasis on ceremonial law. Modern

Judaism has liberated itself from the rabbinical view of law. Cohen's understanding of Judaism, by virtue of which he attacks Spinoza, is grounded in the "historical understanding of the Bible," which in fact was originated by Spinoza. Cohen recognizes that his understanding of Judaism, for example, his distinction between mythical and historical elements of the Bible, is not consistent with "our traditional exegesis." In short, Cohen offers a more positive view of Judaism as rational, but ultimately his understanding of Torah is consistent with, and rests on Spinoza. Cohen's attempt to understand Spinoza better than he understood himself failed; in fact, Spinoza understood Cohen better than Cohen understood himself.

Strauss's Judgment on Spinoza

Strauss concludes the Preface by summarizing his argument in *SCR* on the consequences of Spinoza's critique of religion. Spinoza claims to refute orthodoxy, and its particular claims about the divine inspiration of every word of the Bible, that Moses was the author of the Torah, the account of miracles as violations of natural law, etc. The *TTP* did succeed in refuting orthodoxy, but only if orthodoxy makes claims that it cannot defend. But if Orthodoxy responds by making less ambitious claims, for example, by admitting that such claims "cannot claim to possess the binding power peculiar to the known," than Spinoza has not refuted orthodoxy (¶40). Biblical religion ultimately rests on the claim that God's will is unfathomable. This is the premise by which all orthodox claims are possible.

Spinoza has succeeded only in showing that there are contradictions in the Biblical narrative but this only undermines an overly ambitious variety of orthodoxy, which claims paradoxically to know the ways of God. Traditional Judaism, however, makes no such claims and thus "cannot be refuted by experience or by recourse to the principle of contradiction" (¶40). Spinoza was forced to overreach by claiming to know more than he could about the whole of things, and he had resort to mockery and ridicule in the place of argument to unseat religion. This reveals his critique as fundamentally resting on an act of will or a decision rather than reason. By exposing the defects of Spinoza's critique, Strauss does not mean to suggest that orthodoxy has triumphed over philosophy. Rather, he wishes to show the defects inherent in the Enlightenment's political project, which leaves men freedom without guidance. The "self-destruction of reason" in modernity invites another kind of return, a return to a preliberal thought. Such a return requires an investigation into method by which "heterodox thinkers of earlier ages wrote their books" (¶42).

Conclusion: Progress or Return?

As we have seen, Strauss presents an autobiographical account meant to explain the development of his understanding of Spinoza in the Preface to the translation of his first book on Spinoza. But a careful examination of the Preface reveals the fact that Strauss is neither explaining the development of his thought, nor simply giving an account of his life as a young man. This becomes clear when we pay attention, for example, to the fact that Strauss's mature judgments guide his presentation of the autobiographical materials. His assertion that it is safer to understand the low in light of the high is particularly important in this regard. But what does Strauss mean by the "high"? Strauss forces the reader to puzzle out this critical question, which is the key to understanding the essay.

Instead of identifying the meaning of the "high," he provides an account of his efforts to escape "the grips of the theologico-political predicament" bequeathed to modernity by Spinoza. This escape or liberation initially takes the form of return, particularly a return to revelation. But this attempt to return proves exceptionally difficult because Spinoza's critique of revelation profoundly shapes the way subsequent thinkers understand the tradition. Significantly, Spinoza is ambiguous about the source and meaning of "the high"; specifically, he is unclear whether the divine law is in some sense true or whether it is merely the product of superstition. This ambiguity allows for a variety of readings of Spinoza, which were pursued by Strauss's community in Germany. The more optimistic interpretation affirmed the divine foundation of morality, while others took Spinoza's atheism as corroborating the new virtue of "intellectual probity." Neither view, however, managed fully to escape Spinoza's grip and appreciate the possibility of return. Strauss suggests that the liberation from Spinoza is possible if we read Spinoza carefully, that is, if we understand his political project, including his ambiguous treatment of the high, in light of his metaphysics that denies the possibility of the high. In other words, the political project must be understood as an attempt to obscure Spinoza's view of nature, which is entirely indifferent to human flourishing.

To liberate oneself from the grip of Spinoza means to understand his project and also to recognize an alternative to his metaphysical and political views. Strauss suggests that this is possible because Spinoza has not succeeded in refuting revelation. "The genuine refutation of orthodoxy would require the proof that the world and human life are perfectly intelligible without the assumption of a mysterious God.... [M]an has to show himself theoretically and practically as the master of the world and the master of life" (¶40). Spinoza has not done this; instead, in his attempt to do so he has overstated the capacity of reason to provide a full account of the whole and thereby rendered it questionable as a rational activity. To the clear-sighted descendants of Spinoza, philosophy appears to be the result not of rational inquiry, but an act of will. This permits the provisional triumph of orthodoxy, but without reason. Invariably, orthodoxy descends into fanaticism. Strauss envisions a "return" to a piety that is checked by reason, and a philosophy that is mindful of its limitations. Thus the restoration of the "high" requires the simultaneous recovery of reason and revelation as potential candidates for the best life. Nor is the possibility of such a recovery a matter for despair. Since we have the important works of medieval and ancient philosophy, we need only to excavate how such issues appeared to thinkers before Spinoza. In teaching us to read Spinoza carefully, Strauss also teaches us to read his predecessors carefully.

Since Strauss himself was not an observant Jew, it is easy to conclude that philosophy has, in his eyes, already ultimately overcome revelation in its claims to the high.[37] In fact, Strauss appears to say as much: "Philosophy or science, the highest activity of man, is the attempt to replace opinion about 'all things' by knowledge of 'all things'; but opinion is the element of society; philosophy or science is the attempt to dissolve the element in which society breathes, and thus it endangers society." The result is that philosophy "must respect the opinions on which society rests" without "accepting them as true."[38] Thus, even if we attribute to Strauss the view that philosophy is the highest or best activity for man, we cannot avoid the political problem of accommodating this view to our community, which rests on a settled standard of justice. This tension between conventional opinion and philosophy resembles the Platonic cave. Yet this tension has been entirely obscured by modern philosophy, as exemplified in Spinoza's metaphysics, which claims that nature offers no support to either reason or revelation. In this sense, believers and philosophers are in the same predicament: in order to restore a sense of the high, they must first liberate themselves from the cave beneath the cave.[39]

Notes

*Strauss published two editions of the autobiographical preface: the first as a preface to the translation of *SCR* and the second as part of a collection of essays in *LAM*. The two versions are nearly identical except that in the latter version Strauss divides several of the longer paragraphs into shorter ones so that where there are 42 paragraphs in the original essay, while there are 54 paragraphs in the later edition. Another important difference is that in the later edition, Strauss refers to himself as being in the "grips" of a theologico-political problem. This change, from "grip" is discussed below (see note 22). This essay uses the paragraph numbering from the original essay in *SCR*. My thanks to Professors Terence Marshall, Thomas Meyer, Richard Polt, Timothy Sean Quinn, John Ray, and Martin D. Yaffe for their thoughtful comments (and objections) to this essay.

1. Strauss's letter to Krüger is dated January 7, 1930 (*GS–3* 380–81). He blames his "boss," Julius Guttmann, for preventing him from writing more explicitly. For an overview of the correspondence between Krüger and Strauss, see Thomas L. Pangle, "Light Shed on the Crucial Development of Strauss's Thought by his Correspondence with Gerhard Krüger," chapter 3 of the present volume.
2. One of Strauss's central hermeneutical principles is that careful authors have developed their own manner of writing by studying other careful writers. In general, therefore, "we learn to write by reading. A man learns to write well by reading well good books, by reading well most carefully books which are carefully written" (*PAW* 144). Strauss's commentaries on philosophical texts offer guidelines for reading carefully. One method that he frequently employs, for example, is counting the number of paragraphs to determine the central paragraph (cf. *PAW* 24–25).
3. A good example of this is David Janssens's fine study, *Between Athens and Jerusalem: Philosophy, Prophecy, and Politics in Leo Strauss's Early Thought* (Albany: SUNY Press 2008), 8–26. Janssens begins by attempting to follow Strauss's preface as an account of his early thought, but is quickly forced to cite other materials and

sources to fill in the picture even to explain the meaning of Strauss's description of the "theological-political predicament."

4. The original essay indicated that Strauss was in the "grip" of the theologico-political predicament. Strauss decided to make "grip" plural in the subsequent edition. His choice may reflect the fact that he believed the theologico-political predicament had multiple sources and expressions. I wish to thank Thomas Meyer for directing me to this difference and its possible meaning.
5. For a more extended analysis of the theologico-political predicament, see my "Politics and Rhetoric: The Intended Audience of Spinoza's *Tractatus Theologico-Politicus*," *Review of Metaphysics* 52 (1998–99): 897–924.
6. See my "Review Essay of Martin D. Yaffe's translation and commentary of Spinoza's *Tractatus*," *Interpretation* 32, no. 2 (Spring 2005): 171–78.
7. Spinoza also hoped to mitigate the damage done by theology, by creating a universal faith whose only requirement was the practice of charity. In addition, he prescribed political institutions based on power rather than theology, which were more consistent with the natural asocial nature of man. Finally, by liberating philosophy from politics and theology, he enlisted the help of science in promoting the well-being of the citizens.
8. Spinoza "was the philosopher who founded liberal democracy, a specifically modern regime" (¶27).
9. Allan Arkush, "Leo Strauss and Jewish Modernity," in *Leo Strauss and Judaism: Jerusalem and Athens Revisited*, ed. David Novak (Lanham, MD: Rowman & Littlefield, 1996), 115.
10. See Steven Smith, "How to Commemorate the 350th Anniversary of Spinoza's Expulsion," *Hebraic Political Studies* 3, no. 2 (Spring 2008): 173.
11. Emil Fackenheim also identifies this passage as critical to understanding Strauss, but Fackenheim thinks that Strauss has not fully confronted the low as revealed in the Holocaust. See his "Leo Strauss and Modern Judaism," in Emil Fackenheim, *Jewish Philosophers and Jewish Philosophy*, ed. Michael Morgan (Bloomington: University of Indiana Press, 1996), 103, 104.
12. Contrast this position with Hannah Arendt's critique of Zionism. After the war, Strauss continued to defend Israel on the grounds that it restored national pride (see his letter to *National Review* in *JPCM* 413–14.). The preface was written in August 1962, less than 3 months after Eichmann was hung in Jerusalem. Strauss's endorsement of Zionism on the grounds of restoring Jewish pride stands in sharp contrast to Arendt's *Eichmann in Jerusalem*, written during the same period.
13. See *TTP*, chapter IV.
14. Strauss explains in his 1959 Spinoza seminar: Spinoza insists that "[w]e must go back to the Scriptures. And this Scripture is the document of revealed truth, and forget everything which the theologians claim to know. And in that moment—up to this point he says, by implication, there is only one authority: the word of God as delivered in the Bible. Then he turns it around. We must even examine the authority of the Bible.... That the Bible itself is true and divine cannot be assumed. It must be found out. Perhaps it is not true and divine, or is only partly true and divine. Therefore, to repeat, the argument of this work is ambiguous throughout. There is a Biblicist argument, based on the accepted authority of the Bible, but only of the Bible, as the word of God, and there is another argument which questions this very premise. The real teaching of Spinoza is not the Biblicist argument, but the other one" (29).

15. After quoting this passage, Strauss observes that the dogmas of universal piety "must be of such a kind that all moral men, all decent men, regardless of whether they are Confucians or Christians, or Greek pagans for example, would never disagree. But this must somehow be in accordance with the Bible. That is the difficulty. The dogmas must be acceptable to all decent men. Now I hope the philosophers are decent men. Must they not also be dogmas which are acceptable to the philosophers? And philosophers according to Spinoza cannot believe in a legislating God, in a God who exercises providence. That's the problem. . . . after having said that the Bible demands nothing but charity, meaning love of neighbor—therefore, opinions are free. But Spinoza knows that this principle . . . necessarily has theoretical premises. . . . If that is so, the denial of these theoretical principles must be prevented. And if the philosophers by definition deny these principles, the philosophers must be persecuted" (Lecture 9, p. 172). The solution, Strauss suggests, is that philosophers must pay lip-service to the essential dogmas, even if they do not believe in them (cf. 176–77).
16. See *PAW* 193–96.
17. Richard Velkley shows how Strauss's thought acquired a "renewed and deeper engagement with Heidegger in the 1950s as Strauss acquired the publications of [Heidegger's] later thought." See *Heidegger, Strauss, and the Premises of Philosophy* (Chicago: University of Chicago Press, 2011), 69.
18. See Nietzsche, *Human, All Too Human*, sec. 120 and 227 (trans. Marion Faber and Stephen Lehmann [Lincoln: University of Nebraska Press, 1984], 87, 140–41).
19. "Heidegger's political engagements show that the furthering of [the renewal of the question of being] takes precedence over any considerations of the good, the moral, and the just, as these have been understood in the philosophic tradition as having some universal articulation, reflecting ends (happiness, perfection, virtue) inherent in human nature or reason" in Velkley, *Heidegger*, 93.
20. See *PLA* 137–38 (endnote 13).
21. Ibid.
22. Strauss makes this point quite sharply in *WIPP* 26–27: "The crucial issue concerns the status of those permanent characteristics of humanity, such as the distinction between the noble and the base." He goes on to associate the neglect of these characteristics with Heidegger: "It was the contempt for these permanencies which permitted the most radical historicist in 1933 to submit to, or rather to welcome, as a dispensation of fate, the verdict of the least wise and least moderate part of his nation which it was in its least wise and least moderate mood, and at the same time to speak of wisdom and moderation. The biggest even of 1933 would rather seem to have proved, if such a proof was necessary, that man cannot abandon the question of the good society, and that he cannot free himself from the responsibility of answering it by deferring to history or to any other power different from his own reason."
23. Strauss will argue that "the ultimate justification of Spinoza's critique is the atheism from intellectual probity, which overcomes orthodoxy radically by understanding it radically, i.e., without the polemical bitterness of the Enlightenment and the equivocal reverence of romanticism" (¶39).
24. Buber and Rosenzweig did not succeed in preserving the substance of the Jewish tradition. Their strategy, which Strauss describes in *Philosophy and Law* as "internalization," manages to reinterpret the claims of the Jewish tradition (e.g., creation, miracles, revelation, and prophecy) so that they would no longer conflict with "intellectual probity." For a lucid outline of *Philosophy and Law*, see Eve Adler, "Translator's Introduction," *PLA* 1–20.

25. Hobbes is less ambiguous and therefore more revealing than Spinoza on the question of the greatest good. See *Leviathan*, chapter 11.
26. As Hillel Fradkin points out: "there are according to Maimonides different sciences of the law, or more precisely two: the legalistic science of the law or jurisprudence and the true science of the law. The *Guide* is devoted to the latter." See Fradkin, "A Word Fitly Spoken: The Interpretation of Maimonides in the legacy of Leo Strauss," in *Leo Strauss and Judaism: Jerusalem and Athens Revisited*, ed. David Novak (Lanham, MD: Rowman & Littlefield, 1996), 59.
27. "Cohen commits the typical mistake of the conservative, which consists in concealing the fact that the continuous and changing tradition... [depends on] revolutions and sacrileges" (¶38). By "conservative," Strauss does not mean politically conservative. (Cohen's left-wing political views, including his endorsement of socialism and his hostility to capital punishment, are well known.) Rather, Strauss means by "conservative" a strong orientation toward preserving the tradition that precludes questioning and challenging it.
28. As Strauss admits in 1972, it had been many decades since he had read Cohen seriously: "I grew up in an environment in which Cohen was the center of attraction for philosophically minded Jews who were devoted to Judaism; he was the master whom they revered. But it is more than forty years since I last studied or even read the *Religion of Reason*, and within the last twenty years I have only from time to time read or looked into some of his other writings." See "Introductory Essay to Hermann Cohen," *JPCM* 267.
29. This also explains a host of apparent contradictions in Strauss's explanation of Spinoza. For example, Strauss says that the *Ethics* is the first and last word of Spinoza, but he praises Cohen for beginning with the *TTP*, which he says is more revealing.
30. See Richard Kennington, "Analytic and Synthetic Methods in Spinoza's *Ethics*," in *On Modern Origins: Essays in Early Modern Philosophy*, ed. Pamela Kraus and Frank Hunt (Lanham, MD: Lexington Books, 2004), 205–28. For an extended discussion of Kennington's argument, see Joshua Parens, *Maimonides and Spinoza: Their Conflicting Views of Human Nature* (Chicago: University of Chicago Press, 2012), 193–212.
31. But Strauss praises Cohen for focusing his study on Spinoza's *TTP* rather than the *Ethics*, a method that Strauss himself follows in his own writing and teaching (¶39). In his seminar on Spinoza in 1959 at the University of Chicago, for example, Strauss promises to turn to the *Ethics* after reading the *TTP* and the *Political Treatise*, but does not do so.
32. The ambivalence runs throughout Spinoza's critique of the Bible. Spinoza wishes to use the Bible to establish a liberal society, which in turn, calls into question the very foundations of that society. As Strauss wrote in his 1936 study of Hobbes: "Exactly as a Spinoza did later, Hobbes becomes an interpreter of the Bible... to make use of the authority of Scriptures for his own theory, and then... to shake the authority of Scriptures themselves." Cited in Leora Batnitzky, "Leo Strauss and the 'Theologico-Political Predicament,'" in *The Cambridge Companion to Leo Strauss*, ed. Steven B. Smith (New York: Cambridge University Press, 2009), 47.
33. In *PAW* 187, after claiming that Spinoza deliberately contradicts himself and that we should always resolve these contradictions by accepting the "the statement most opposed to what Spinoza considered the vulgar view," Strauss says that "[o]nly by following this rule can we understand Spinoza's thought exactly as he himself understood it and avoid the danger of becoming or remaining the

dupes of his accommodations." Here Harry Wolfson takes the place of Cohen as an author who explains Spinoza's contradictions with historical reasons, that is, reasons "primarily based, not on Spinoza's explicit statements, but on the history of the author's life." Wolfson "admits that he is trying to understand Spinoza better than he understood himself" (*PAW* 188).

34. "[T]he *Treatise* is linked to its time, not because Spinoza's serious or private thought was determined by his 'historical situation' without his being aware of it, but because he consciously and deliberately adapted, not his thought, but the public expression of his thought, to what his time demanded or permitted. His plea for 'the freedom of philosophizing,' and therefore for 'the separation of philosophy from theology,' is linked to its time in the first place because the time lacked that freedom and simultaneously offered reasonable prospects for its establishment" (*PAW* 192).
35. See also "Introductory Essay to Hermann Cohen," *JPCM* 280: Cohen's "'optimism' was too strong."
36. On the importance of the distinction between wisdom and piety in Maimonides, see Raymond Weiss, *Maimonides' Ethics: The Encounter of Philosophic and Religious Morality* (Chicago: University of Chicago Press, 1991).
37. This is Werner Dannhauser's argument in "Athens and Jerusalem or Jerusalem and Athens" in *Leo Strauss and Judaism: Jerusalem and Athens Revisited*, ed. David Novak (Lanham, MD: Rowman & Littlefield, 1996), 155–71. See Hilail Gildin's useful rejoinder, "Déjà Jew All Over Again: Dannhauser on Leo Strauss and Atheism," *Interpretation* 25, no. 1 (Fall 1997): 125–33.
38. See "On a Forgotten Kind of Writing," in *WIPP* 221–22.
39. Philosophy may not disagree with Spinoza's conclusions as much as his presentation of those conclusions. In his essay on Kurt Riezler, Strauss presents a disagreement between Socrates and Thucydides on whether the high is supported by nature, or whether it is vulnerable precisely because it lacks support. Thucydides appears to deny the existence of such support, but nonetheless is not indifferent to its existence. See "Kurt Riezler," *WIPP* 260.

CHAPTER 3

THE LIGHT SHED ON THE CRUCIAL DEVELOPMENT OF STRAUSS'S THOUGHT BY HIS CORRESPONDENCE WITH GERHARD KRÜGER

Thomas L. Pangle

The rather complex private correspondence between Leo Strauss (1899–1973) and Gerhard Krüger (1902–72) runs from late 1929 through 1935.[1] Readers will presumably be acquainted with Strauss, but a few words are in order to introduce Krüger—whose fulfillment of his great promise was severely hindered by the oppression of National Socialism and then, in his early fifties, was cut short by strokes that left Krüger mentally incapacitated.[2]

Like Strauss, Krüger studied at the University of Marburg, a center of Kantian thought that, starting in 1923, experienced the electrifying teaching of Heidegger (whom Strauss encountered when, after completing his dissertation at Hamburg under Cassirer, he went to Freiburg in 1921 to study with Husserl). Krüger completed his "Habilitation" in 1929 with a dissertation that was published in 1931 as *Philosophy and Morality in the Kantian Critique*.[3] This book's unusual stress on Kant's "anthropology," or analysis of lived human experience, indicates the impact of Heidegger. At the same time, the book's unusual insistence on the affinities between Kant's doctrine, as one of obedience to higher law, and the thought of St. Augustine indicates Krüger's sharing with Strauss, though from a Christian perspective, deep interest in the resurgence of morally and intellectually demanding theology—a reawakening led by Karl Barth, Franz Rosenzweig, Friedrich Gogarten, and Rudolph Bultmann (with the last of whom Krüger was especially close). Above all, the book testifies to Krüger's growing conviction, shared with Strauss and also Jacob Klein, that classical Greek philosophy (to which Heidegger had given fresh access but which he regarded as historically surpassed) contained decisive wisdom about the human condition that modern philosophy had covered over and lost.

This trajectory is articulated at the conclusion of Krüger's Kant book, the last sentence of which reads: "That the decisive question remains true, even if it does not find an answer, the example of Socrates can teach to whoever asks as did he." Strauss, in the retrospective 1964 Preface to the German edition of his Hobbes book, says: "the final sentence of Krüger's Kant book, which corresponded completely to my view at that time and with which I would still today, with certain reservations, agree, explains why I turned entirely to 'the true politics' and why I did not write about Hobbes as a Hobbesian." In a letter to Krüger of June 1, 1931 (*GS–3* 387), in which Strauss reacts to his receipt and first perusal of Krüger's Kant book, Strauss writes: "I have already flown through the introduction and the conclusion, which give a clear picture of your *direction*: instead of understanding Plato in the light of Kant—as do the neo-Kantians—on the contrary, to put into question Kant and us through Plato."

Krüger's second book, published in 1939, is entitled *Insight and Passion: The Essence of Platonic Thinking.*[4] In 1959, Strauss paid this book the high compliment of referring to it repeatedly in his seminar on Plato's *Symposium* (the transcript of which has been published by the University of Chicago Press in 2001 as *On Plato's Symposium* (*OPS*)). Strauss introduced Krüger as "a very philosophic interpreter" (*OPS* 39)—a high compliment, coming from Strauss. But I believe that the subsequent references Strauss makes to Krüger's book in the course of the seminar indicate that Strauss found himself more and more dissatisfied with Krüger's interpretation, and indeed with Krüger's whole approach to interpreting Plato. The core inadequacies of Krüger's approach, in Strauss's eyes, are already visible in the correspondence of the 1930s, in the comments Krüger makes about Plato when Krüger takes issue with Strauss, and in Krüger's failure to respond to Strauss's countercriticism. In general, Strauss found that Krüger interpreted Plato not sufficiently on Plato's own terms, but still too much in the light of the conventional approach, rooted in the tradition of Christian Platonism (see the last sentence of the unsent draft of a letter from Strauss of December 25, 1935, *GS–3* 450); this is perhaps the most important respect in which Krüger remained under the spell of what Strauss called that "powerful prejudice" according to which it is impossible to return to an understanding of Plato exactly as Plato intended himself to be understood.

Let me now focus in on the immediate philosophic context of the correspondence. What at that time bound the two together in their distinctive critical posture toward modern rationalism was not merely the shared conviction that the thought underlying the Enlightenment had become evidently a failure, and that hence the entire modern civilization rooted in the Enlightenment had entered a state of protracted crisis—that conviction was shared by many who had experienced the philosophic impact of Heidegger, and his predecessor Nietzsche. What distinguished Strauss together with Krüger, even from Strauss's closest intellectual friend and interlocutor Jacob Klein, was the pair's growing confirmation of the suspicion that at the heart of modernity's failure and crisis was the unanswered *theological* question—the un-disposed-of challenge to rationalism from suprarational and contrarational revelation. Again in the Preface to the German edition of his Hobbes book, explaining the development of his thought around 1930, Strauss writes:

> The re-awakening of theology, which for me is marked by the names of Karl Barth and Franz Rosenzweig, appeared to make it necessary to investigate how far the critique of orthodox theology—Jewish and Christian—deserved to be victorious. Since then the theologico-political problem has remained *the* theme of my investigations....The philosophic interest in theology linked me with Gerhard Krüger; his review[5] of my Spinoza book[6] expressed my intention and my result more clearly than I myself had done.[7]

We learn now, when we read Strauss's long letter to Krüger of January 7, 1930 (*GS–3* 378–81), that the latter's review was so helpful in part because Strauss had—in this letter—explained to Krüger the intention and result of the book, while prefacing this explanation with the disclosure that part of the reason for the book's deplorable obscurity was the fact that Strauss's "boss," and more generally the institute where he worked (The Academy for the Scientific Study of Judaism), compelled him to remain silent in public about the true presuppositions that were the point of departure for the book.

This revealing letter to Krüger of January 7, 1930 clarifies and extends what can be gathered from published writings concerning the meaning, for Strauss, of the "philosophic interest in theology" that Strauss reports he shared with Krüger. I would put the key points as follows. Krüger assisted and reinforced Strauss's discovery that modern philosophic rationalism had failed in the grand theological-political project that was its most profound aim. Prior to the Enlightenment, all of post-classical Western Civilization was dominated by biblical revelation as supremely normative—by biblical law, in either its Mosaic, or Islamic, or Christian versions. The deepest motivation and meaning of the Enlightenment was the liberation of civilization from that domination, and, more positively, the replacement of suprarational revealed law, as the supreme civilizational norm, with rational or scientific supreme norms. Strauss and Krüger agreed that this vast cultural revolution had been partly successful—but only partly: modern, Enlightenment rationalism managed to eject revelation from its cultural or civilizational throne, while endowing mankind with unprecedented material, technological power. Modern rationalism failed, however, to discover any adequate moral authority or norms, rooted in reason and science, that could take the place of the previous civilizational guidance by revelation. The consequence has been an ever more obvious spiritual vacuum, apt to be filled by cultural irrationalism of all sorts, and accompanied, in the realm of so-called philosophic rationalism, by desperate or even fanatical recoil from all serious rational thought about foundations. As Strauss put it in his 1951 Preface to the American edition of his Hobbes book, describing the perspective from which that book was written, in the early 1930s: "I had seen that the modern mind had lost its self-confidence or its certainty of having made decisive progress beyond premodern thought; and I saw that it was turning into nihilism, or what is in practice the same thing, fanatical obscurantism."

This crisis of modern rationalism compels a reopening of the possibility that it is necessary to return to revelation—either simply, to traditional orthodoxy; or to what we might today call "postmodern" neo-orthodoxy. And each of these possibilities was powerfully expressed in the 1920s: the first above all by Karl Barth, and the second above all by the "New Thinking" proclaimed by Franz Rosenzweig (to whose memory Strauss dedicated his Spinoza book). What prevented Strauss and Krüger (or at any rate the side of Krüger to which Strauss was drawn) from embracing either orthodoxy or neo-orthodoxy is implied in Strauss's characterization of theirs as a shared "philosophic interest" in theology: Strauss and Krüger approached theology not as theologians, but as philosophic men. They saw the revival of orthodox and neo-orthodox theology as a *challenge*, which had to be met, and disposed of, if genuine (rationalist) philosophizing, if philosophic science—if philosophy as a way of life—were to be tenable for a serious human being.

In his letter to Krüger of January 7, 1930 Strauss writes that the question animating his Spinoza book was: "how was it possible, that the Enlightenment has been *victorious*?" Strauss then proceeds to provide an illuminating, and, so far as I know, otherwise unavailable, summary of the position from which he wrote the book—a summary that affords, in his words, a "share in the insufficiently-clear apparent core of my reflections."

Strauss begins by explaining his dissatisfaction with the answer to his question commonly given by the contemporary new theologians, and expressed by Rosenzweig. They try to respond to the question by asserting that the Enlightenment was victorious *only* "over Scholasticism, but *not* over Revelation," *not* over "the world of the Bible." The "sign of the inadequacy of this answer"—the inadequacy of this attempt to confine the victory of the Enlightenment—Strauss finds in the present status of the Enlightenment's critique of *miracles*:

> the concept of the miraculous is biblical, and, as a consequence of the Enlightenment, this concept has lost its power and its truth. (It is today an embarrassment: just read, please, carefully Rosenzweig's *Star of Redemption* pp. 119ff.;[8] Rosenzweig has recognized, that the problem of miracles is central; and how does he have to "*interpret*" the enlightenment critique of miracles, in order to be able to maintain the miraculous—and what does he have to regard as miraculous!).

Having indicated the gross inadequacy of the answer typified by Rosenzweig, Strauss next asks: "But now what has the Enlightenment achieved in regard to miracles?" Strauss answers: "It has achieved only this. That it itself, that is, that the *already* enlightened human being, is immune to miracles; it has created a position that is unreachable by miracles." But—Strauss counters: "the miraculous is, however, according to its own meaning, only capable of being experienced as a miracle on the foundation of faith—and thereby, the Enlightenment offensive is thus rendered impotent."

"At this point, at the latest," Strauss continues, "it becomes clear that the Enlightenment does not owe its victory to assertions of the scientific refutation of revealed religion." Instead, "its victory is thanks to a certain *will*, that one may, with a grain of salt, characterize as Epicurean." And "*this* will," Strauss declares, "appears to me to be no foundational justification for the Enlightenment, against revealed religion." "The clear indication of this," Strauss submits, "is the fact, that it is evident to anyone who has even only an intellectual grasp of what prayer is, that the understanding, grounded in the Epicurean disposition, of religion, is inadequate" (see also *SCR* 207–8). Now, given this, Strauss continues, it follows that "in order for the social victory of the Enlightenment—a nonbinding state of affairs—to become total, there must emerge *another* will against revealed religion." Strauss says that he sees "such a will disclosed in Machiavelli, Bruno, and Spinoza," and "reaching its most extreme representation in Nietzsche, and its completion in—*Being and Time*." "I mean," Strauss continues, "in the interpretation of the *call* of conscience, and in the answer given there to the question; *who* then is calling?" It is "from Heidegger's *Dasein*-interpretation that for the first time an adequate *atheistic* interpretation of the Bible may be possible." Strauss seems to be concluding when he writes: "religion is then for the first time overcome, when it can be given an adequate atheistic interpretation." But his statement of the thought that constitutes the foundation of his first book in fact concludes with an abrupt new tack: "So: the victory of the Enlightenment, that is, the victory of the 'scientific view of the world'—which I *only* understand to include the loss of the possibility of believing in miracles—is justifiable solely on the ground of a resolute *conviction* [*bestimmten* Gesinnung], not on the ground of this 'worldview' itself."

This complex and ambiguous statement by Strauss of the thought underlying and animating his Spinoza book makes clear the impact of Heidegger's *Being and Time* on Strauss; and at first, or reading only this far in the letter, one gets the impression that Strauss is indicating that he wrote his Spinoza book from a position that was fundamentally Heideggerian, as regards the decisive issue.[9] But: what Strauss says later in this same letter, more specifically about the contents of the Spinoza book, indicates a deep uneasiness with the previously elaborated quasi-Heideggerian position. Strauss writes that in his Spinoza book, "I sought to make clear for myself the various grounds for atheism; *that is the reason for* the apparently typological presentation of the first sections of my work." In thus clarifying the various grounds of Heidegger's atheistic predecessors, above all Spinoza, Strauss was in effect bringing to clear view the various grounds underlying Heidegger, on which Heidegger stands. Strauss was clarifying the historical-philosophic grounds that Heidegger is apparently making firm through his atheistic phenomenological analysis of the call of the conscience. But these historical-philosophic grounds Heidegger himself has failed to bring to light. Strauss is in effect going historically deeper than, and thus criticizing, Heidegger. Strauss is clarifying the various versions of, first, the "Epicurean" will to atheism; and then, secondly, the additional and distinct modern Enlightenment will to atheism—the two of which together comprise the "resolute conviction" (*bestimmten Gesinnung*) that precedes, culminates in, and is presupposed by, is meant to be vindicated by, Heidegger's phenomenology of the conscience.

This letter to Krüger thus helps us to see that Strauss's Spinoza book is in fact also tacitly intended to be a critical interrogation of Heidegger's unarticulated and insufficiently investigated historical-philosophic grounds for atheism. The Spinoza book brings to sight both the strengths and the troubling shakiness of those grounds.[10] And this letter to Krüger—written a year after the book was completed, as Strauss notes—shows that Strauss is now aware that he did not himself sufficiently appreciate, when he wrote the book, how *very* problematic were the implications he was showing, or discovering. For Strauss goes on to say, coming to the close of this letter: "That this orientation, starting from my presuppositions, can no longer justify itself, I of course concede to you." Strauss had opened the letter by expressing his "heartfelt thanks" to Krüger for the latter's previous letter (this important letter has unfortunately not survived), and its critique of Strauss's whole position in the Spinoza book: "most heartfelt thanks for your letter," that "will substantially contribute to transforming my general uneasiness about my work into concrete doubts, and transformations of my previous questions."

As we learn from the next surviving letter to Krüger, written half a year later (on June 26, 1930; *GS–3* 382–83), Strauss soon stumbled across the source from which he was to discover the path out of the aporia in which he found himself. Strauss writes to Krüger with a request to be invited to give a seminar in Krüger's class on Augustine the coming winter, and explaining his request in the following words:

> I had begun my work on a Jewish Scholastic—Gersonides—as a work of "pure scholarship," and also because I must deliver some concoction to the people who pay me. But soon I observed that the work was not so boring to carry on, simply because the subject is exciting. It concerns the problem of that moderate (i.e. non-atheistic) enlightenment, about which I have learned so much from your Kant work.

Strauss proceeds to summarize what he has discovered thus far about the distinctive character of the "moderate" or nonatheistic Judeo-Arabic medieval enlightenment—in contrast to the modern "moderate" enlightenment, typified by Krüger's reflections on Kant, but also probably by Strauss's own work on Mendelssohn (and also in contrast to the medieval Christian-Scholastic enlightenment).

To begin with, Strauss formulates what he has found the Judeo-Arabic version *shares* with the eighteenth-century moderate enlightenment: "prevalence of belief in providence, as belief in the good God over and above the God who calls one to account; and *therefore* belief in the sufficiency of reason." Then Strauss outlines what he has found *distinguishes* the Judeo-Arabic moderate enlightenment from the eighteenth-century moderate enlightenment: *first*, the "primacy of theory," as opposed to the "primacy of morality (veneration of Socrates)" in the eighteenth-century enlightenment; *second*, and linked to the preceding, in the Judeo-Arabic moderate enlightenment, "natural right" or natural law plays no role, or at least not anything like the role that it plays in

Christian medieval thinking—whereas, in the eighteenth-century moderate enlightenment, the moral law is developed as a "natural right" that demands a new and specific kind of constitutional law. This leads immediately to the *third* and most important contrast: in the Judeo-Arabic moderate enlightenment, the place of natural right or natural law is taken by the divinely revealed positive law of Moses, or of Mohammed—which divinely revealed law is, however, reconceived and reinterpreted as fully intelligible in the light of the principles of Plato's *Republic*. Moses and Mohammed are reconceived and reinterpreted as "philosopher-lawgivers"; and the scriptural law itself is reconceived and reinterpreted as the "*sole* sufficient and binding norm, leading life to the happiness that consists in theorizing." Strauss concludes that the Judeo-Arabic middle ages "has, through the link to the ancient idea of the concrete *nomos* [law] and *nomothetes* [lawgiver], a much greater possibility than does the natural right-preoccupied 18th century of accepting the concrete order of revelation."

Now in the Spinoza book, Strauss had already given some attention to the Judeo-Arabic critique of religion, and its relation to the modern Enlightenment's critique. He had done so in the first place through his discussion in the opening chapter (*SCR* 46–49 = 13–17) of "Averroism"—"a tradition which has remained active for about five hundred years." But as the preceding words suggest, Strauss had seen and stressed continuity rather than contrast:

> Three tendencies and traditions of very different origin underlie seventeenth-century criticism of religion. They are traditionally designated by the names Epicurean, Averroist and Machiavellian. From an early time they were in such close association that it becomes difficult to characterize the general movement of criticism of religion in the seventeenth century by one name rather than by another.

Strauss had been interested not so much in the authentic philosophizing of Averroes himself or his predecessors as in the Western European tradition believed to have grown out of Averroes: "in Christian Europe knowledge of the true Averroes is more and more replaced by the legend of Averroes." Strauss had taken notice of "Averroism" not as a profound critique of, or even engagement with, revelation but as an attempt to conceive of religion as "needed for the guidance of the ignorant many, for the sake of law and order." And the sixth chapter's lengthy discussion of Maimonides had treated the latter as a target of Spinoza's critique of religion. From this perspective, Maimonides came to sight in rather conventional garb, as a kind of Jewish scholastic who made use of philosophy conceived as Aristotelian natural science to defend revealed creationism against rationalist natural science. "According to the inner structure of Maimonides's science," Strauss writes, "the insight into the insufficiency of the human understanding—an insight gained on the basis of Aristotelian science, in principle prior to the introduction of the central theological presupposition—motivates the recourse to revelation; this insight inclines man to the acceptance of revelation" (*SCR* 158 = 141).

In contrast, the letter of June 26, 1930 shows that what has revolutionized Strauss's approach to the medieval Judeo-Arabic "moderate" Enlightenment is the stress Strauss now places on the link to "antiquity" as meaning especially the link to *Plato*, and his *Republic*. In the Spinoza book, Strauss sees only the Aristotelianism of Maimonides; Strauss is unaware of Maimonides's profound debt to *Plato* and above all Plato's *political* philosophy—as *the* decisive way of addressing the theological question. In the Spinoza book, Strauss still thinks that: Maimonides's context of thought may be summed up as a nexus of scientific reasoning" (*SCR* 161 = 144). To be sure, Strauss does make "ancient" Greek philosophic-critical theology a major theme in the Spinoza book. But the ancient philosophic-critical theology he has in mind is *Epicurean*, which he takes as the most serious (even the sole serious) ancient critical-theological thought. Similarly, in the earlier letters to Krüger, Strauss equated "ancient" theological criticism with "Epicurean" philosophic theology (see esp. 380: "ancient [Epicurean] critique"). From this new letter of June 26, 1930, however, we see that in the preceding six months it has begun to dawn on Strauss that what is most profound and valuable in the medieval Judeo-Arabic thinkers is the guidance they give back to *Plato*—as above all a *political* philosopher: that is, to a Plato, and to Platonic dialogues, that are *radically different* from what is conventionally understood by *modern* scholarship, shaped by the tradition of Christian or Augustinian Platonism. What Strauss has begun to discover through Maimonides and his Muslim teachers, above all Farabi, is a Plato whose dialogues and political philosophy have to be completely reinterpreted, as *the* philosophic key to meeting the challenge posed by revelation, seen as "the theologico-*political* problem" (see also the draft of Strauss's unsent letter of December 25, 1935, 449–50).

This becomes still more explicit in the next two surviving letters from Strauss to Krüger. The first, dated February 27, 1931 (*GS–3* 383–84), refers to Strauss's delivery on December 21, 1930, of his lecture entitled "Religious Situation of the Present"—in which for the first time Strauss spoke in public of the modern historical-spiritual condition as that of humans dwelling in "a cave, beneath that cave," which is described in the Platonic Socrates's famous image at the beginning of Book Seven of the *Republic*. The second letter, dated May 7, 1931 (*GS–3* 384–85), refers to a public lecture Strauss has just given on Hermann Cohen and Maimonides, which, Strauss reports, is his first public presentation of his thesis that "the Islamic-Jewish Scholastics understood revelation within the framework laid out in Plato's *Republic* and *Laws*." In this letter Strauss speaks of "how much I have profited from your Plato lecture." In other words, Strauss continues to speak as if his own incipient recovery of the genuine Platonic philosophic understanding of and response to revelation is in accord with, and even helped by, the development of Krüger's thinking.

This goes with the strong suggestion of the earlier, first letter mentioning Plato (June 26, 1930, *GS–3* 382–83), where Strauss writes as if he is moving in Krüger's direction—that is, toward a quest for the grounds of what Strauss there calls a "moderate" or "nonatheistic" Enlightenment. BUT: do

Strauss and Krüger agree in their understanding of what this "nonatheistic Enlightenment" means? Above all, do they agree on the meaning of the "possibility" Strauss refers to as: "the philosopher's 'acceptance' of the concrete order of revelation?"[11] To what extent is this *expressed* closeness to Krüger giving voice to Strauss's self-understanding at this time frankly and straightforwardly, OR, to what extent is Strauss writing in a manner designed to try to begin to *entice* his friend to join in pursuing a path of self-discovery, along which Strauss has already proceeded much further—far enough to see that the truths Strauss is beginning to unearth from his study of Plato, guided by the medieval Judeo-Arabic thinkers, will require a radical and wrenching, even agonizing, self-transformation on the part of Krüger: the profundity, and the crux, of which self-transformation, Strauss knows from his own transformation in the intervening months? This much is clear: in the correspondence of the two subsequent years, it becomes more and more evident that, and why, Krüger cannot follow Strauss. Krüger cannot bring himself seriously to entertain the possibility that Plato supplies *the answer* to the theological question; and this is chiefly because Krüger remains tied to the thought that Strauss identifies as the core of historicism.

In a December 27, 1932 letter (*GS–3* 419–22) replying to Krüger's expressed reservations about Strauss's contention that all specifically "modern" thought dwells in a "cave beneath Plato's cave," Strauss writes: "the 'substantial and historical core' of historicism is, *as you correctly say*, 'the factual domination of Christ over the post-classical world.' What follows from that, for him, who does *not* believe, who thus denies the right, that is the divine right, of this domination?" Strauss answers: "the immediate consequence—in Heidegger among others—is: Christianity has brought to light facts of human life, that were unknown or inadequately known to ancient philosophy"; this means, "fundamentally: after the disintegration of Christianity, there remains, and first becomes possible, philosophy that preserves the 'truth' of Christianity; it is as such deeper and more radical than ancient philosophy." Strauss continues: "maybe this consequence is correct—but it must be as such proven. And this is possible only on the basis of a *direct* confrontation of modern with ancient philosophy. So much on the legitimation of my project as regards Hobbes—I mean, the direct confrontation with Plato."

These letters to Krüger allow us to observe the point of departure from which Strauss set out on the journey, taking up the rest of his life, confronting Socratic with non-Socratic thought, ancient and modern, and thereby vindicating ever more powerfully Socratic political philosophy—as the decisive response to the most fundamental and all-encompassing question.

In subsequent letters to Krüger, Strauss tries repeatedly to give his friend leading or thought-provoking clues to *precisely* what *sort* of questioning it is that one can find to be the decisive questioning, in the Platonic–Socratic dialogues, if the dialogues are studied correctly—and that means in liberation from all modern scholarship, with its post-Christian and historicist prejudices. Sadly, Krüger seems never to have caught on.

Two of the passages giving such clues seem to me to be especially helpful. In the letter of December 27, 1932 that I quoted just previously Strauss writes:

> Granting the greater *depth* of post-Christian philosophy: but, is depth what counts? Is the perspective of depth not itself a Christian perspective, that for its part requires proof? Is depth identical with radicalism? Is it not perhaps the case, that "depth" is not *really* radical? Depth is at home in self-examination. Self-examination presupposes a standard. The question as to the standard is the radical question. I find, that the moderns on the whole have neglected this question, while they apparently or really have demanded self-examination.

A year and a half later, on August 18, 1934 (*GS–3* 439–42), responding to his reading of a later Kant essay by Krüger, Strauss returns to this point and elaborates, as regards Kant, in the following most revealing words: "I do not know whether one should proceed on the basis of the distinction between theoretical and practical knowledge as much as do you, following Kant. As important as this difference is, it seems to me to be secondary. Practical knowledge is knowledge *of* an obligation, *on the basis* of an obligation." "But," Strauss continues, "more fundamental than obligation is, *what* is obligatory and what, 'merely for us humans,' *takes on* the character of the obliging. Platonic philosophy is concerned with the character of this what—which does not in itself have the character of a law in the precise sense." For Kant, "the question about the law first emerges in connection with the *application* of the standard to human beings." More generally, "modern morality is from the beginning conceived as an *applicable* morality, and, I believe, despite the incomparable radicalization it undergoes in the Kantian morality, this (latter) still is in this sense specifically modern." In profound contrast, Plato's critical philosophy, while understanding itself to be "summoned by the law, asks, not so much about the law, but rather about the right ordering of human life—and therefore about the principle of the ordering." Strauss interjects this poignant remark: "But I am writing as if we just yesterday had a conversation, and am not taking account of the fact that these indications are perhaps comprehensible only for me." By this time, Strauss had left Germany for good.[12]

In 1958 there was published by Karl Alber Press a collection of essays Krüger had written before his brain strokes, entitled *Freedom and World Administration* (*Freiheit und Weltverwaltung*). Krüger sent a copy to Strauss, eliciting a letter of June 21, 1958 (*GS–3* 450–51) in which Strauss expresses his "heart's joy" in hearing again from Krüger through the book, which Strauss says he has read twice. "How near we come in the questions and even in the general direction in which we seek the answers! Your discussions of the division between the Ancients and the Moderns has especially taught and delighted me." But then Strauss proceeds to expatiate on how and where he departs from Krüger:

> you concede, it seems to me, the necessity of distinguishing between the human as physical-earthly being with its inadequate perspectives, and the human as absolute wayfarer, who is on his way to *the* Truth. A corresponding distinction would also be necessary as regards the essential tension between the *ariste politeia* [best regime]

and the actual "natural community"—not to mention the fundamental difference between the highest *praxis*, which is only *theoria*, and all other *praxeis*. . . .

Decisive, I believe, is the difference in regard to the "natural community." Its "naturalness" is doubtful, because in the strict sense only the *ariste politeia* is natural (cf. the problem of the *agathos aner* [good man] in contrast to the *agathos polites* [good citizen] in [Aristotle's] *Politics* III). To take the extreme Platonic expression of this state of things, the *polis* is the cave—there exists a necessary tension between the *polis* and philosophy (for that very reason the *ariste politeia* needs the *kalon pseudos* [noble lie]). The problem becomes hidden, but not solved, when one replaces the *polis* by the *ethnos* [nation].

Notes

1. In *GS–3* 377–454, Heinrich Meier has made these letters available through painstaking editorial work, and in his introduction has brought intelligent learning to bear in framing their context (esp. *GS–3* XXVIII–XXX). Unless otherwise noted, all page references will be to this edition; italics in quotations from Strauss and Krüger are in the original.
2. For a fuller account of Krüger's career, see esp. the obituary by Krüger's lifelong friend Hans-Georg Gadamer in *Archives de Philosophie* 47 (1984): 353–63.
3. *Philosophie und Morale in der Kantischen Kritik* (Tübingen: Mohr, 1931; 2nd ed. 1967).
4. *Einsicht und Leidenschaft: Das Wesen des platonischen Denkens* (Frankfurt: Klostermann, 1939; 2nd ed. 1948; 3rd ed. 1961).
5. In *Deutsche Literaturzeitung* 51 (December 20, 1931): 2,407–12. An English translation, by Donald J. Maletz, was published in the *Independent Journal of Philosophy*, vol. 5/6 (1988): 173–75. Quotation is from the latter.
6. *Die Religionskritik Spinozas als Grundlage seiner Bibelwissenschaft: Untersuchingen zu Spinozas Theologisch-politischem Traktat* (Berlin: Akademie-Verlag, 1930; repr., Hildesheim: Georg Olms, 1981); republished in *GS–1* 1–362; English translation by Elsa Sinclair published as *Spinoza's Critique of Religion* (New York: Schocken, 1965). All references here will be to pages of the latter, abbreviated as *SCR*, sometimes with equation marks in parentheses indicating page numbers of the German original (printed in the margins of *GS–1*).
7. When Strauss agreed to have an English translation of his Spinoza book executed and published, his revision profited from Krüger's critical suggestion, at the close of his review (175), that "the specific divisions provided by the table of contents would very much facilitate the reading if they were still more detailed and indicated in the text by more than dashes."
8. Franz Rosenzweig, *Der Stern der Erlösung* (Frankfurt am Main: J. Kauffmann Verlag, 1921), 119–42, subtitled "Über die Möglichkeit, das Wunder zu erleben" [On the Possibility of Experiencing Miracle]; trans. William W. Hallo (New York: Holt, Rinehart and Winston, 1971), 93–111, or Barbara Galli (Madison, WI: University of Wisconsin Press, 2005), 101–21.
9. This is not ruled out by what Strauss says when he goes on to express in very personal terms the *distinctive* way in which he shares in the "will" and the "conviction" [*Gesinnung*] that he sees animating modern atheism: "I must justify myself [*mich rechtfertigen*] before the forum of the Jewish tradition": and "truly, without any philosophy-of-history reflection," but "simply because I hold it to be not

defensible [*nicht vertretbar*] that I abandon out of thoughtless lightness and indolent comfort a cause, for the sake of which my ancestors took upon themselves everything conceivable." It is this Jewish moral passion, for self-justification before the tribunal of his ancestors, that Strauss indicates he understands to be driving his relentless quest for the truth about the most momentous question.

10. See esp. *SCR* chap. 5, sec. C, 144–46 (= 126–28), "The Premises and the Limitation of the Critique of Orthodoxy"; also 123, 179; and Ch. 7, sec. A, 193–200 (= 182–90), "Calvin's Position as Immune to [*unerreichbar für*] Spinoza's Critique" as well as sec. B., 200–4 (= 190–94), "The Illusion of the Critique." See also Krüger's review, 175: "The general discussion about the difference between modern and ancient thought receives here for once an 'existential' sharpness: Strauss shows *in concreto* how much the modern 'disposition of method, of culture' (44; 71) is a *historical antithesis*, that is, an unprovable negative life-decision opposed to that past which believed in revelation."
11. See Strauss's highly paradoxical formulation in *Philosophy and Law*'s first chapter, which Heinrich Meier informs us (*GS–2* xvi n11; trans. as n11 of ch. 1 in the present volume, above) was originally completed in September 1933: "It is in the *Laws* that Plato undoubtedly stands closest to the world of revealed law, since it is there that, in accordance with a kind of interpretation anticipating the philosophic interpretation of the revealed law among the medieval thinkers, Plato transforms the 'divine laws' of Greek antiquity into truly divine laws, or recognizes them as truly divine laws. In this approximation to the revelation without the guidance of the revelation we grasp at its origin the unbelieving, philosophic foundation of the belief in revelation."—*PLA* 76.
12. Krüger's leading student, Klaus Oehler, reports that in 1951 "Krüger asked me, 'Do you know who Leo Strauss is?'—to which I had to reply at that time that I did not. Then he said to me: 'If Leo Strauss had not been compelled by the German political situation to depart, philosophy in Germany would have taken a different direction.'" Klaus Oehler, *Blicke aus dem Philosophenturm: Eine Rückschau* (Hildesheim: Georg Olms, 2007), 185; see also 179.

CHAPTER 4

STRAUSS ON HERMANN COHEN'S "IDEALIZING" APPROPRIATION OF MAIMONIDES AS A PLATONIST

Martin D. Yaffe

Hermann Cohen's "Characteristics of Maimonides's Ethics" appeared in 1908, in a collection of essays on Moses Maimonides by various German Jewish scholars.[1] Cohen's essay was the subject of a 1931 lecture by the young Leo Strauss to the Academy for the Scientific Study of Judaism in Berlin, entitled "Cohen and Maimonides."[2] At that time, as Strauss later recalled, Cohen was "the center of attraction for philosophically minded Jews who were devoted to Judaism...the master whom they revered."[3] Strauss's lecture vindicates his older contemporaries' reverence for Cohen to the extent that it shows Cohen to be an extraordinarily helpful (if ultimately inadequate) guide for understanding Maimonides when one starts, as they do, from modern premises, that is to say, from premises supplied by the (modern) Enlightenment. Cohen himself, Strauss shows, reveres Maimonides as an enlightened Jew, indeed as a role model for modern enlightened Jews like himself, and in this regard interprets Maimonides as a Platonist rather than, more conventionally,[4] as an Aristotelian. Strauss endorses Cohen's Maimonides interpretation—up to a point. He demurs at Cohen's retrofitting onto Maimonides his own, "idealizing" way of interpreting Jewish sources.[5] Accordingly, Strauss's lecture probes the merits and shortcomings of Cohen's "idealizing" appropriation of Maimonides and offers a corrective.

Strauss's corrective emerges from three interconnected criticisms: 1) Cohen's reverence for Maimonides as an enlightened Jew is paradoxical. 2) Cohen's interpretation of Maimonides as a Platonist rests on the unsustainable claim that Plato unlike Aristotle privileges ethics over philosophy; rather, both Plato and Aristotle privilege philosophy over ethics. 3) Cohen's interpretation likewise rests on the further unsustainable claim that Maimonides privileges ethics over philosophy; rather, like both Plato and Aristotle, Maimonides too privileges philosophy over ethics. In what follows, I consider each criticism in turn, along with Strauss's corrective.

Cohen's Reverence for Maimonides as an Enlightened Jew

What Strauss finds paradoxical about Cohen's reverence for Maimonides has to do with Cohen's notion of an enlightened Jew. Strauss argues as follows. The term "enlightened Jew" is, on the surface, self-contradictory. Judaism (the Torah) emerges historically within a mythical horizon. By its own lights, then, the Torah would seem oblivious to science. But "enlightenment" means scientific enlightenment. Hence Judaism and enlightenment would seem at bottom incompatible. Admittedly, one might wish to construe the Torah's distinctive doctrines—creation, providence, etc.—as compatible in retrospect with comparable scientific doctrines. Yet this would not prove that the original authors of the Torah understood its doctrines in that way. Nor, being anachronistic, would it be consistent with the principles of modern critical (scientifically-enlightened) historical investigation. One would need to show in addition, or instead, that the Torah as understood by its original authors somehow enjoins scientific enlightenment. As Cohen points out, this in fact is what Maimonides claims. Since the Torah's enjoining scientific enlightenment is not evident from a merely literal reading, however, Maimonides interprets the Torah allegorically.[6] Thus, for example, he identifies *ma'aseh bereshith* and *ma'aseh merkabah*[7] allegorically with Aristotelian cosmology.[8] Cohen takes Maimonides's allegorizing as a precedent for his own idealizing interpretation. Strauss finds this paradoxical.

The paradox shows up in that Maimonides's allegorizing and Cohen's idealizing interpretation differ in their respective aims. Both differ as well, of course, from literal interpretation. Maimonides's allegorizing agrees with literal interpretation in aiming to understand the Torah's original meaning. The difference between them turns on whether the original meaning is to be understood by limiting oneself to a plain-sense reading of the text, as, say, modern biblical criticism does,[9] or whether instead it is to be understood by inferring an inner meaning of which the plain text is merely the outward expression, as Maimonides's allegorizing does. In contrast to both modern biblical criticism and Maimonides, Cohen claims to understand the Torah *better* than its original authors.[10] Rather than simply interpreting the Torah, he consciously reinterprets it. Yet doing so, he claims, is in line with the Torah's real intention. Here Cohen appeals partly to modern biblical criticism and partly to Maimonides. Like modern biblical criticism, Cohen rejects allegorizing as historically dubious. Like Maimonides, however, he is guided by the biblical prophets' intrabiblical critique of the Torah's laws about animal sacrifices to the effect that those laws had an ulterior purpose. According to Maimonides, the laws in question were meant in the long run to wean worshipers from animal sacrifices altogether and to habituate them to focus instead on what really matters to the Torah.[11] Cohen takes Maimonides's allegorizing reading, as it were, literally. According to Cohen, what really matters to the prophets—and hence retroactively to the Torah—is not animal sacrifices as such but the pure worship of God which enjoins human beings to ethical action. That is to say, with their putative assertion that the laws about sacrifices point to enjoining human beings to ethical action, the prophets look beyond the Torah's mythical horizon toward a more enlightened horizon. They thereby set in motion an ongoing, biblically sanctioned struggle for the progressive development of reason for the sake of ethical action. Cohen appeals to that intrabiblical precedent, so construed, while going beyond it.[12] Appropriating Maimonides as his enlightened role model, he radicalizes the prophets' reinterpretation of the laws about sacrifices by regrouping *all* the Torah's laws around the intention the prophets are seen to attach to those particular laws—progressive enlightenment for the sake of ethical action. Such, in brief, is the drift of Cohen's idealizing interpretation. Even so, says Strauss, it differs from Maimonides's allegorizing in a paradoxical way.

The paradox is this. For Maimonides, enlightenment would seem to mean replacing the Torah's original mythical horizon with a horizon constituted by Aristotelian cosmology. Paradoxically, however, Cohen polemicizes against Aristotelian philosophy as fundamentally misguided—indeed as a betrayal of philosophy as understood by Aristotle's teacher Plato, namely, as has been said, philosophy for the sake of ethical action.[13] To avoid the paradox, Cohen interprets Maimonides at bottom as a Platonist rather than the Aristotelian he seems to be on the surface. Before examining Cohen's Maimonides interpretation, then, Strauss considers Cohen's claim about Aristotle and Plato.

Cohen's Claim that Plato unlike Aristotle Privileges Ethics over Philosophy

Notwithstanding the polemical character of Cohen's complaint against Aristotle, Strauss corroborates much of what Cohen claims differentiates Aristotle from Plato. As regards Plato, Cohen's claim reduces to three points. First, Plato, or Plato's Socrates, is concerned only with the question of the just life.[14] Second, the question of the Good (as the highest and most urgent question, which emerges from and guides the question of the just life) is an ongoing question that is never fully disposed of but keeps showing up in day-to-day moral questions.[15] Third, moral questions are inseparable from political life as such.[16] Now, lest the question of the Good as the highest and most urgent question be thought to be merely self-evident and not distinctive to Plato as Cohen claims, Strauss subjects this part of Cohen's claim to a brief thought-experiment. Under what conditions, Strauss asks, would the question of the Good *not* be the highest and most urgent question? Two conditions suggest themselves: first, if the just life were *not* questionable, that is to say, if we knew what the Good is; and second, if human life were *not* the most important thing. As it happens, these same two conditions characterize Aristotle's philosophy, as Strauss points out and Cohen also recognizes. First, as Cohen says of Aristotle: "The moral is not a problem for him."[17] (In corroboration, Strauss quotes Aristotle himself on the aim of ethical inquiry: "we are inquiring not in order to know what virtue is but in order to become good.")[18] Second, as Cohen also says of Aristotle: "His metaphysics is directed toward the universe."[19] (Again, Strauss quotes Aristotle in corroboration: "it is absurd to believe that politics or prudence is the most serious [knowledge] if man is not the best thing in the cosmos.")[20]

Strauss's thought-experiment lets him differentiate Aristotle from Plato in agreement with Cohen without being distracted by the polemical character of Cohen's complaint against Aristotle—so as to be able to examine the validity of Cohen's complaint free of polemics. Since Strauss's focus here is on Aristotle and Plato in the context of Maimonides, he postpones that examination till discussing Maimonides directly. Meanwhile he reformulates Aristotle's differences from Plato nonpolemically:[21] First, whereas Platonic-Socratic philosophy is concerned with the question of the just life, Aristotle restores the possibility of the life spent in pure contemplation, or theorizing (*theôrein*), originally exemplified in the Pre-Socratic philosophers but "called into question by Plato's Socrates." Second, whereas Platonic-Socratic philosophy is questioning about the good of human life, hence about "the true state," Aristotelian philosophy is "pure contemplation of existing [things] and understanding of Being." Finally, whereas the aim of Platonic-Socratic philosophy is inherently political, for Aristotle "politics moves into second place."

Before proceeding to Maimonides, Strauss is prompted to ask: Does it not follow from Aristotle's privileging of pure theorizing over political inquiry that Aristotle is enlightened in the full sense of the word? Why does Cohen nevertheless consider Plato more enlightened? The answer, Strauss goes on to say, has to do with Cohen's extending the struggle against myth as taken up by the biblical prophets to a struggle against pure theorizing as such. Mythical man is said to concern himself exclusively with the cause of the world in the sense of its *origin*—its *whence* or *wherefrom*. Only (biblical) religion, says Cohen, raises the question of the cause of the world in the sense of its *purpose*—its *whither* or *whereto*. Aristotle, being concerned with the world's origin only, therefore remains within the horizon of the mythical. That is to say, even though the highest knowledge according to Aristotle is knowledge of God, Aristotle's God is not the biblical God, who manifestly enjoins ethical action.[22] Cohen infers that if the biblical God is to become the object of knowledge, as for Maimonides, this change must affect theorizing too. Thus Maimonides in *Yesodei ha-Torah*, when discussing the commandment to love and fear God, asks what is the *way* to love and fear of God, and answers that it is knowledge of the *world*, that is to say, (Aristotelian) physics.[23] Here Maimonides, by interpreting physics in connection with the putative moral purposiveness of the biblical God, is seen to go beyond Aristotle's own understanding of physics (and therefore of metaphysics or theology). In Cohen's expression: when knowledge of God becomes knowledge of the biblical God, theorizing itself is "*uprooted*."[24]

Cohen's Claim that Maimonides like Plato Privileges Ethics over Philosophy

Nevertheless Strauss faults Cohen for ascribing to Maimonides a Platonism conceived, or rather misconceived, as philosophy for the sake of ethical action. The fault shows up in Cohen's misconstruing Maimonides's negative theology. Maimonides argues that assigning positive attributes to God is incompatible with God's unity and uniqueness.[25] Even so, positive knowledge of God, as human beings' highest possibility, remains possible. What Maimonides denies of God are attributes that amount to defects, or privations. Positive attributes, properly understood, are "negations of privations." To call positive attributes negations of privations is not to say something trivial. For example, to call God "powerful" is not to say merely that He is "not weak," but that His existence suffices in bringing forth things other than Himself.[26] Here Cohen consciously interprets Maimonides in line with his own theology—although he alerts his reader to this fact and invites him to double-check. (Strauss will respond to Cohen's invitation in a moment.) In Cohen's interpretation, rather than simply denying positive attributes, Maimonides is replacing immanent or absolute attributes, that is, attributes characterizing God as such, by transitive ones—attributes describing God in His correlation with the world. By limiting our knowledge of God to knowledge of that "correlation," Cohen is saying that God is knowable not as the object of metaphysics but only as a moral being, or rather as the *paradigm* or (in Cohen's word) *Idea* of morality. In short, Cohen says Maimonides equates "negations of privations" with what Maimonides calls "attributes of action" (which Cohen interprets to mean moral action).

Strauss finds three difficulties here. First, the passage that Cohen claims equates "negations of privations" with "attributes of action" instead differentiates these as *two* ways of stating something of God.[27] Second, according to Maimonides some negations of privations do *not* involve correlations—for example, "God lives" means no more than "God is not without life," "not ignorant," "not dead," etc.[28] Third, whereas Cohen is content to say that in the Torah God is revealed exclusively as a moral being,[29] Maimonides sees a need to explain why the Torah limits itself to revealing God in that way, given that God also has attributes that concern His actions vis-à-vis the extra-human world.[30] In Maimonides's explanation, revealing God's moral attributes is needed specifically for the existence and guidance of human beings in political communities. To obscure the difference between God's moral actions and His actions vis-à-vis the extra-human world, as Cohen does here, is to assume that morality (human morality) is the purpose of the world. This is in fact the view Cohen ascribes to Plato in contrast to Aristotle.[31] But does Maimonides teach otherwise than Aristotle here, Strauss wonders? Maimonides recognizes the opinion that according to "our" view—the view of those who believe in the creation of the world (in contrast to those who adhere to Aristotle's doctrine that the world is eternal)—the ultimate purpose of the world can be asked about and that its purpose is for the human race to worship God.[32] Yet Maimonides rejects this opinion by saying that the world has no purpose besides God's free will or wisdom and by referring to how small human beings are as compared to the cosmos (understood in Aristotle's terms as the spheres and separate intelligences). Moreover, Maimonides appropriates Aristotle's distinction between dianoetic and ethical virtues by teaching that moral perfection is lower in rank than intellectual perfection, since moral perfection concerns the mutual relations of human beings and is at bottom useful only for an individual human being in relation to others, whereas intellectual perfection benefits the individual alone and simply.[33] In short, Strauss finds Cohen's basic assertion—that knowledge of God as knowledge of the God of Israel "uproots" theorizing—in need of correction.

In correcting it, Strauss notes how Maimonides rethinks Aristotle's distinction between moral and intellectual perfection. On remarking that whereas the moral man depends on others the wise man is self-sufficient to the degree that he is wise, Aristotle adds that the wise man may also experience incidental benefit to himself from those who collaborate in his theorizing.[34] Maimonides inverts Aristotle's addendum in saying instead that those who understand for themselves may also benefit others by helping them understand.[35] Maimonides's inversion invites an explanation. Strauss looks for it in Maimonides's account of prophecy, since while Maimonides like Aristotle teaches that the philosopher is superior to the moral man, unlike Aristotle he teaches also that the prophet is superior to the philosopher. "Hence," Strauss infers, "if there is a limitation, a calling into question, an uprooting of the Aristotelian ideal in [Maimonides], then it must show up in his *prophetology*."[36] Strauss therefore turns to Maimonides's account of prophecy.

In Maimonides's account, the prophet is a philosopher and more. He can surmise future events by bodily visualizing them in front of him. Exercising his vivid power of imagining as well as that of knowing, he can present philosophical insights figuratively so as to communicate them to the unphilosophical multitude.[37] His imaginative power matches that of statesmen, lawgivers, diviners, and magicians (miracle-workers)—yet he exceeds any or all of these by being philosopher, statesman, lawgiver, diviner, and magician combined. The Torah accords the highest rank of prophecy to Moses, a lawgiving prophet,[38] but does not spell out exactly what distinguishes him from the others: knowledge? statesmanship? divination? magic? The basic question here, says Strauss, is: What is ultimately important about prophecy—what purpose or need does it ultimately address?

Maimonides, Strauss admits, offers only an implicit answer. Strauss sketches it as follows,[39] before pointing to its likely source in Maimonides's Muslim predecessors. Human beings, diverse and contrary as they are individually, need socializing by a leader who can bring about agreement among them through law. Leaders divide into lawgivers and governors; governors, unlike lawgivers, presuppose laws already in place. Lawgiving itself can aim either at the perfection of the body only or at the perfection of the body in service to the soul. The latter sorts of laws are called divine laws, and their promulgators prophets. Since the perfection of the soul is the perfection proper to a human being as such, the purpose of prophecy is the founding of a political community whose aim is the proper perfection of human beings. That is to say, the prophet must be a philosopher, statesman, diviner, and magician combined in order to be the founder of the perfect or ideal political community.

Is this implicit answer Maimonides's own answer? Strauss corroborates it by citing Shem Tov ibn Falaquera,[40] who in turn cites Avicenna to that effect.[41] Of the three moments of prophecy besides philosophy (*sc.*, statesmanship, divination, magic), Avicenna ranks statesmanship highest. Accordingly, he treats prophecy as part of politics. Strauss quotes Avicenna as saying in that context: "The first purpose of the lawgiver in lawgiving is the division of the city into three parts: leaders, artisans, and guardians."[42] Avicenna's prophetic lawgiver thus aligns the class divisions of his city with those of Plato's *Republic*. Like Maimonides's other Muslim predecessors, he understands himself in general as a student of Plato and Aristotle, as Strauss also shows.[43] Yet at bottom Avicenna et al. take their bearings by Plato rather than Aristotle. Strauss returns to the difference between Plato and Aristotle to discover why.

As has been said, Plato and Aristotle differ over whether philosophy consists in asking about the Good (Plato) or in pure contemplation and understanding (Aristotle). In Plato's view, Strauss goes on to say, asking rightly about the Good needs a preparation—a detour consisting of such questions as: What is the soul? What are its parts? What is science (or knowledge)? What is being? What is the One? etc. These are the same questions Aristotle asks apart from questions about the Good. But this means that contemplation and understanding as set forth in Aristotle's treatises are already worked out in Plato's dialogues. If so, Plato does not disagree with Aristotle that human happiness means pure contemplation and understanding, or that these are a human being's highest possibility.[44] They disagree in how they approach this possibility. Whereas Aristotle sets or leaves philosophers free of political obligations, Plato forces them to live up to those obligations.[45] For Plato, philosophy is not absolutely sovereign. In Strauss's words: "The [Platonic-Socratic] philosopher who has elevated himself in the beholding of the truth about the beautiful, just, and good in *purity*, lives and *wants* to live in it, is *bound back* to the state by the harsh command of the lawgiver, which considers the order of the whole and not the happiness of the parts."[46]

Now Strauss points out that what Plato requires—philosophy's standing under the law—is given in the age of the revealed religions. Accordingly, philosophers who live in that age must defer to the law—by seeking legal authorization to philosophize through deriving philosophy as a legal obligation and by keeping under wraps (or secret) the freedom they take in interpreting the law in that way (that is to say, exoterically). Yet because the law the philosophers defer to is already given through a prophet, they no longer need to make it the main theme of their philosophizing, as does Plato. Like Aristotle, they can ask metaphysical questions apart from, and at more length than, the question of the just order of human life. They still need to justify and understand the law, however; and when they do, it is within the horizon established by Plato. Here Strauss recalls Avicenna's identifying the prophetic lawgiver with the founder of the Platonic state. "But this," Strauss infers, "means that *revelation, the Law, is understood in the light of Plato*."[47]

Conclusion

"All honor to the God of Aristotle; but truly he is not the God of Israel," says Cohen pivotally in interpreting Maimonides.[48] Strauss agrees with Cohen's pivotal statement, though not entirely in Cohen's sense. Interpreting Maimonides as a Platonist, Cohen nevertheless criticizes him for appropriating Aristotle's theology while underestimating how Aristotle's downgrading of ethics endangers philosophy in what Cohen takes to be Plato's meaning, namely, philosophy for the sake of ethical action.[49] At the same time, Cohen adds that Maimonides could overlook this danger more easily since he saw the privileging of ethics safeguarded by the Torah. Strauss notes that in calling Maimonides a Platonist, Cohen is on to something. Even so, Strauss finds Cohen's "idealizing" interpretation misleading in its gratuitously substituting ethics for law as understood by Maimonides and his predecessors.[50]

Notes

1. Hermann Cohen, "*Charakteristik der Ethik Maimunis*," in *Moses ben Maimon: Sein Leben, seine Werke und sein Einfluß*, ed. W. Bacher, M. Brann, and D. Simonsen (2 vols. in 1; Leipzig: Gustav Fock, 1908; reprint, Hildesheim and New York: Olms, 1971), I, 63–134. Unless otherwise indicated, page numbers to Cohen's essay refer to this volume. Cf. Cohen, *Ethics of Maimonides*, trans. Almut Bruckstein (Madison, WI: University of Wisconsin Press, 2002). No attempt has been made to harmonize my renderings of Cohenian passages with Bruckstein's considerably freer renderings. "*Charakteristik der Ethik Maimunis*" is reprinted in Cohen, *Jüdische Schriften*, ed. Bruno Strauss, intro. Franz Rosenzweig (3 vols.; Berlin: C.A. Schwetschke & Sohn, 1924), III, 221–89; also in Cohen, *Kleinere Schriften IV, 1907–1912*, ed. Hartwig Wiedebach (Hildesheim and New York: Olms, 2009), 161–269.
2. CuM 393–436; CaM 173–222.
3. Strauss, "Introductory Essay for Hermann Cohen, *Religion of Reason out of the Sources of Judaism*," *LAM* 233; originally in Cohen, *Religion of Reason out of the Sources of Judaism*, trans. Simon Kaplan, intro. Leo Strauss (New York: Ungar, 1972), xxiii.
4. See, for example, Julius Guttmann, *Die Philosophie des Judentums* (München: Verlag Ernst Reinhardt, 1933), 174–205; *Philosophies of Judaism*, trans. David W. Silverman (New York: Holt, Rinehart and Winston, 1964), 172–207; Guttmann concludes his account of Maimonides by speaking matter-of-factly about Maimonides's "*theistische Aristotelianismus* [theistic Aristotelianism]," 205; trans. 206–7. See also Isaac Husik, *A History of Medieval Jewish Philosophy* (New York: Macmillan, 1916), 216–311; Husik speaks of Maimonides's "evident purpose... to harmonize Judaism and philosophy, to reconcile the Bible and Talmud with Aristotle," 236.
5. See Hermann Cohen, *Religion der Vernunft aus den Quellen des Judentums* (2nd ed.; Frankfurt am Main: J. Kauffmann, 1929), 78, 89–90, 94, 172, 303–4, 307; cf. Cohen, *Religion of Reason*, 68, 77, 81, 148, 260, 263. Cf. also Cohen, "*Die Bedeutung des Judentums für den religiösen Fortschritt der Menschheit* [The Significance of Judaism for the Religious Progress of Humanity]," *Jüdische Schriften*, I, 18–19; reprinted as "*Die Bedeutung des Judentums für den religiösen Fortschritt*," *Kleinere Schriften IV*, 429; "The Significance of Judaism for the Progress of Religion," ibid., 456.
6. Cf. Strauss, *Die Religikonskritik Spinozas*, in *GS–1* 197; *SCR* 148.
7. The two Hebrew expressions mean, respectively, "The Account of the Beginning" (Genesis 1) and "The Account of the Chariot" (Ezekiel 1 and 10).
8. See Moses Maimonides, *Guide of the Perplexed* Part I, Introduction (trans. Shlomo Pines, intro. Leo Strauss [Chicago: University of Chicago Press, 1963]), 6; henceforth *Guide* I, Introduction (Pines 6).
9. Cf. Strauss, *Die Religikonskritik Spinozas*, in *GS–1* 321–25; *SCR* 258–62.
10. Here Cohen emulates his own philosophical authority Immanuel Kant, who claims to be able to understand Plato better than he understood himself. See *Critique of Pure Reason* A314 = B370.
11. See *Guide* III 32 (Pines 529–31).
12. CuM 401–2; CaM 184–86. Here Strauss quotes *Religion der Vernunft*, 44; cf. *Religion of Reason*, 38 (translation modified, M.Y.): "Against every routine approach, the insight must prevail that progress in religious knowledge has been accomplished

through the revision and reinterpretation of the sources, while these themselves remain preserved in their individual layers and have been at most rearranged or given different emphasis." This sentence of Cohen's serves to answer the (rhetorical) question of his which Strauss quotes immediately beforehand (CuM 401; CaM 185–86): "And it is a question whether such reshaping is not the best form of annihilation [of the mythical]." *Religion der Vernunft*, 204; cf. *Religion of Reason*, 175. The translation of the latter sentence is Strauss's own; see *SCR* 24–25 or *LAM* 250.

13. "*Charakteristik der Ethik Maimunis*," 70–72, 82–84 (cf. Bruckstein, 14–19, 51–55). CuM 403–405; CaM 188–90.
14. In Cohen's words, which Strauss quotes: "Ethics as the doctrine of man becomes the center of philosophy." (CuM 413; CaM 201) See "*Charakteristik der Ethik Maimunis*," 63–64 (cf. Bruckstein, 2).
15. In Cohen's words, which Strauss also quotes, these show up as "ever new questions, [with] every new solution only raising new questions" (CuM 413–14; CaM 201). See "*Charakteristik der Ethik Maimunis*," 70 (cf. Bruckstein, 15).
16. In Cohen's words (commenting on Plato's *Crito*), which Strauss quotes as well: "There is no self-consciousness that is to be acquired without regard for the state and without being guided by *the idea* of the state" (CuM 414; CaM 201). Strauss quotes Cohen, *Ethik des reinen Willens* (Berlin: Bruno Cassirer, 1904), 250; references to the *Ethik* in the text of Strauss's lecture are to this edition, whose pagination differs slightly from the 2nd, revised edition and its subsequent reprints (2nd ed., Berlin: Bruno Cassirer, 1907; cf. 7th ed., Hildesheim and New York: Olms, 2008)—although the changes in the reprints have to do with the addition of an editorial apparatus, etc., only; the corresponding page number in the revised editions is 265.
17. CuM 414; CaM 202. Strauss quotes "*Charakteristik der Ethik Maimunis*," 70 (cf. Bruckstein, 15).
18. *Nicomachean Ethics* 1103b7f.
19. CuM 414; CaM 202. Strauss quotes "*Charakteristik der Ethik Maimunis*," 72 (cf. Bruckstein, 17).
20. *Nicomachean Ethics* 1141a20ff.
21. CuM 414; CaM 202.
22. CuM 416; CaM 204–5.
23. Moses Maimonides, *Sefer HaMada'/The Book of Knowledge*, ed. and trans. Moses Hayamson (Jerusalem: Boys Town, 1963), 35b.
24. CuM 416, with 408, 421, 422; CaM 205, with 195, 211, 212. The emphasis is Strauss's.
25. See *Guide* I 52, 56 (Pines 117–18, 131).
26. See *Guide* I 53, 58 (Pines 122, 136).
27. CuM 418f.; CaM 208. See *Guide* I 59 (Pines 142) with I 58 (Pines 136).
28. CuM 419; CaM 208. See *Guide* I 58 (Pines 135f.).
29. See Cohen on Exodus 34:6–7: *Religion der Vernunft*, 109; *Religion of Reason*, 94. Cf. Cohen on Micah 6:8: *Religion der Vernunft*, 39; *Religion of Reason*, 33.
30. CuM 419; CaM 209. Quoting Exodus 33:19, Strauss cites *Guide* I 54 (Pines 123ff.) but also calls attention to *Guide* 3.54 (Pines 635ff.).
31. "*Charakteristik der Ethik Maimunis*," 71 (cf. Bruckstein, 17).
32. CuM 420; CaM 210. Strauss cites *Guide* III 13 (Pines 452ff.).
33. CuM 420; CaM 210f. Strauss cites *Guide* I 54 (Pines 123ff.), with Aristotle, *Nicomachean Ethics* X 7, 1177a34–b1.

34. *Nicomachean Ethics* 1177a32ff.
35. CuM 421; CaM 212. Strauss cites *Guide* II 37 (Pines 373–74), with II 11 (Pines 275). The emphasis is Strauss's.
36. CuM 422; CaM 212. Throughout his lecture, Strauss calls Maimonides by his traditional Hebrew acronym, RMbM (for "Rabbi Moshe ben Maimon"; vocalized as "Rambam").
37. CuM 422; CaM 212–13. Strauss cites *Guide* II 38 (Pines 377–78).
38. In contrast, Abraham is prophetically inspired in the highest degree but only instructs or teaches; and the post-Mosaic prophets only exhort their addresses to obedience to the Law given by Moses. CuM, 423; CaM 213–14. Strauss cites *Guide* II 39 (Pines 378f.);
39. CuM 423–24; CaM 214–15. Strauss cites *Guide* 2.40, III 27 (Pines 382, 511–12.).
40. CuM 424; CaM 216. Strauss cites Shem Tov ben Joseph ibn Falaquera on *Guide* II 40, in *Moreh ha-Moreh*, ed. Yair Shiffman (Jerusalem: World Union for Jewish Studies, 2001), 289–90.
41. Avicenna, *Healing: Metaphysics X*, trans. Michael Marmura, in *MPP–1* 99–111 or *MPP–2* 78–88; or Avicenna, *The Metaphysics of 'The Healing', A Parallel English-Arabic Text = al-Ilahīyāt min al-Shifā'*, trans. Michael Marmura (Provo, UT: Brigham Young University Press, 2005), 364–68. For a fuller discussion, see *PG* 97–108 or *GS–2* 98–109; *PLA* 111–20.
42. CuM 425; CaM 217. See *MPP–1* 104 or *MPP–2* 84; *The Metaphysics of 'The Healing'*, 370.
43. CuM 424–26; CaM 216–18.
44. That is to say, in Strauss's paraphrase of Plato, Platonic philosophers live in the belief that they have already been relocated during life to the Islands of the Blessed (*Republic* 519c). CuM 426; CaM 218.
45. Plato "*compels*" them "to care for others and to guard them" (*Republic* 519d–520a). CuM 426; CaM 219. The emphasis is Strauss's.
46. CuM 426; CaM 219. The emphases are Strauss's.
47. CuM 427; CaM 220. The emphasis is Strauss's. Strauss traces the provenance of the merging of philosophy, statesmanship, divination, and magic in the prophetology of Maimonides and his Muslim philosophers through, for example, Cicero's *De divinatione* I.40.89, though he adds (while acknowledging that more needs to be said) that its ultimate provenance is Platonic. See CuM 428; CaM 220. For his somewhat fuller discussion, see *PG* 117–22 or *GS–2* 118–23; *PLA* 127–33.
48. CuM 416, 421, 428; CaM 204, 211, 221. See "*Charakteristik der Ethik Maimunis*," 81 (cf. Bruckstein, 50).
49. CuM 427; CaM 219. Strauss quotes "*Charakteristik der Ethik Maimunis*," 87 (cf. Bruckstein, 64): "[Maimonides] underestimated the danger residing in the depreciation of ethics in Aristotle. And from his standpoint he could overlook this danger more easily, *since he saw the value of ethics kept safe in his religion*." The emphasis is Strauss's. I have used the translation of these sentences found in *PLA* 133.
50. CuM 428–29; CaM 221–22.

CHAPTER 5

STRAUSS ON THE RELIGIOUS AND INTELLECTUAL SITUATION OF THE PRESENT

Timothy W. Burns

This chapter focuses on two talks of startling freshness given by Leo Strauss in 1930 and 1932, translated into English for the first time by Anna Schmitt and Martin D. Yaffe.[1] Addressed to a Jewish audience, the talks were given in the most politically unsettled years for Germany, and the richest, intellectually, for German Jews. Among the topics they address is "[t]he Jewish problem, whose urgency in the age of National Socialism perhaps does not need to be proved [any]more to anyone." Since the talks address other problems of both "modernity and ultramodernity," or what today goes by the name postmodernism, their questions are still with us, in sometimes sharpened, sometimes degraded, forms. The talks offer guidance for those who wish to liberate themselves from the crippling presuppositions through which Strauss himself had—as we see here for the first time—fought his way to clarity.

To better grasp the talks' significance, it may be helpful before examining them to note an often-overlooked distinction between what Strauss, in the opening paragraph of the autobiographical preface to *Spinoza's Critique of Religion*, calls the "theologico-political *predicament*," on one hand, and the study of the "theologico-political *problem*" that he later identifies as the theme of his life's work,[2] on the other. The former was a narrower problem for German Jews, one that is bound up with historicism. As Strauss explains, the German thought to which German Jews opened themselves in the nineteenth century "was understood to be German essentially." It was in this respect unlike the Greek thought to which Maimonides and others had opened themselves in the period of Spanish Jewry, which "was understood to be Greek only accidentally." As a result, German Jews had not only a political dependence on Germans (the Weimar Republic) but a "spiritual dependence." For even the most cosmopolitan of German thinkers attempted to understand their nation's thought through its "culture," which was Christian and hence excluded Jews.[3] This was the "predicament" faced by

German Jews who had hoped, on the basis of liberalism, that the difference between Jews and non-Jews would become a matter of indifference, or who thought the state, at least, should remain neutral on that difference. That hope proved to be misguided. Strauss's attempt, as a morally serious young man, to solve his predicament had led him to political Zionism, on one hand, and to the theology of Karl Barth and Franz Rosenzweig, on the other.[4] Zionism had arisen as an attempt to solve the Jewish predicament politically by establishing a liberal, secular state for Jews. But this, even when combined with cultural Zionism—as eventually became the case—meant in truth a rejection of the Jewish tradition, that is, of belief in creation, miracles, and the divine law; it meant in truth a rejection of Judaism. However necessary as a political response to the abiding rejection of the Jew as Jew within the modern liberal state, it could provide no answer to the spiritual or moral longings of serious Jews.

As for Rosenzweig's theology, while Strauss respected the attempt of this friend and colleague[5] to renew Jewish theology for the modern Jew, the two talks before us indicate the ground of his deep dissatisfaction with it. That ground is linked to his recovery of the thought to which Maimonides and Spanish Jewry had opened themselves—that is, the recovery of genuine Socratic-Platonic philosophy—and the uncovering of the roots of its modern alternative, initiated by Spinoza, Hobbes, and Descartes. It is linked to the recovery of the permanent and universal theological-political *problem*. Awareness of that permanent problem, and of the two major philosophic attempts at solving it, points the way to a means for the individual Jew to solve his contemporary "predicament." In these talks, we see for the first time Strauss's recovery of the thought of Maimonides and Plato and hence of the theological-political problem.

That recovery entails likewise the rejection of or liberation from the thought of another representative of the "new thinking." As Strauss indicates, these talks take place against the rise, both meteoric and serious, of Heidegger.[6] They are, to be sure, explicitly directed against the historicism of the sociologist Karl Mannheim, who failed indeed to face the great problem that Heidegger and his better students did face. But in their relentless attack on the historicist doctrine that all thinking is determined by the present—by a thinker's time—the talks move inevitably if quietly against the radical historicism of Heidegger. They show us the vital concerns that had been uncovered by Heidegger and his guide, Nietzsche, and the recovery, which they inadvertently made possible, of genuine philosophizing—of philosophizing that begins by naively asking fundamental questions in search of eternally true answers. To this end, they provide an initial sketch of a nonhistoricist account of the historicism that emerged out of early modern philosophy, one that brings historicism into focus as a "cave beneath the cave." They provide an account of modern philosophy that begins (in Strauss's case) with historicist presuppositions and that ends up turning them, like a balloon, inside-out.

In his initial effort to strip down to its serious intention the assigned topic of his first talk, "Religious Situation of the Present" (1930), Strauss recasts the topic as "The Intellectual Situation of the Present" and then "The Question of the Present," and, finally, "What is the right life? How should I live?" The second talk, "The Intellectual Situation of the Present" (1932), is then, even in its title, a reworked version of the 1930 talk. Moreover, the second talk has, as it seems to me, the rhetorical intention of stressing, on one hand, the original and ever reerupting intention of the moderns, that is, the return to Greek philosophy over and against stale scholasticism, or Greek philosophy minus the biblical tradition, and on the other, the dead end that historicist thinking holds for the question of the right way of life, and, on the basis of that finding, the possibility of beginning again that was opened up by Nietzsche. The recovery of Platonic philosophizing that makes both of these arguments possible is found in the first talk. I will therefore focus my attention on the first talk, as the *arche* of Strauss's new orientation, using the second talk to clarify some of its points, and will bring to bear upon it earlier, contemporaneous, and later writings of Strauss, especially his correspondence with Karl Löwith.

* * *

In his opening remarks, Strauss distinguishes between the many contemporary writers on religion and the few who have "thought thoroughly," and among the latter he further distinguishes between commentators and the very few genuinely authoritative thinkers. Only these very few, he asserts, are worth addressing. And of more interest to "us Jews" among them is "Franz Rosenzweig," of whose teaching Strauss promises to give an exposition, after a preliminary "clarification of the topic." In the talk that has come down to us Strauss never arrives at "Rosenzweig's doctrine and its difficulty." The talk is therefore wholly given over to the preliminary clarification.

The clarification proceeds in six steps: 1) a reduction of the assigned question (the religious situation of the present) to its serious purport, viz., "what is the right way of life?"[7] 2) the summoning of a goddess, "the Present," to warn against any naive pursuit of an answer to this serious question that is simply true or transcends the present; 3) an account of the difficulties with the attempt to find nontranscendent but synthetic answers in the present, that is, the difficulties with "conspectivism"; 4) Over and against the historicist understanding of the multiplicity of answers to fundamental questions, the original, *Socratic* explanation; 5) an account of the additional difficulty to philosophizing that arose through the authority of biblical revelation, as the first "cave beneath the cave"; and 6) a sketch of the unsuccessful modern attempt to eliminate this additional difficulty, resulting in a new authority, a new "cave beneath the cave," that is, historicism. The clear theme of the talk is one of wresting oneself free of the present as from a sub-cave that is mistaken as the true or authentic human situation.

This theme helps to explain what might otherwise appear as a somewhat petulant initial tearing away of the onion layers of the assigned topic in order to reach the serious question that lies beneath it. Strauss conveys in this initial section the impression of one who, having liberated himself from the present sub-cave, is being asked to give a description of its walls and has thus been assigned what is, he bluntly asserts, "*not a serious* topic." The remainder of the talk is intended to justify this assertion, which in other circumstances could appear graceless but which is here intended to free morally serious Jewish youth from the "tyrannical conviction" under which they have posed their topic.

Strauss makes clear that he knows his listeners will be taken aback by this opening, and at the same time he plants the beginning of doubt about their position, by conjuring up a beautifully attired, knowing, powerful goddess, "the Present," who warns them against the naive effort to pose the question of the right life. This is perhaps the most poetic rhetorical device that Strauss ever allowed himself, and echoes Socrates (e.g., the Laws in the *Crito*) and Nietzsche (e.g., the Free Spirit in the *Genealogy of Morals*). The goddess proclaims that each age has its truth and, proudly possessed of this knowledge, she laughs at the naiveté of those who in the past sought a permanent answer to the question of the right way of life. She is told by her understanding (in a brief dialogue with it) that her virtue or duty to be honest with herself does not permit her to fight a direct assault on the quest for truth. Her laughter at naiveté is, she declares, "no naïve laughter" but "reflective" and benevolent: she exculpates earlier generations, who sought the truth and who, finding in fact only the truth of their present, of their age, did against their will what she now *prescribes* to her children, the children of the present. Enthroned high above the past, she does not sternly forbid the search for eternal truth, but instead charmingly appeals against it to her listeners' sense of what is fitting or becoming of them as rational beings: It is now rational to want only the truth of the present.

The summoned goddess's claim to knowledge rests, then, on her reflective, backward glance at the past, and her moral admonition rests on the claim that man is rational; her appeal is found, Strauss declares, in the mouths of "the most agile, most progressive, most expert, most lively children of our time." Through their mouths she appeals daily and everywhere to what is trendy over and against what stodgy old goats might say. Strauss is aware that what he will be saying may be mistaken as the position of a stodgy old goat. He therefore takes up her admonition. But where, he asks, does one encounter "the present" to which she directs one for guidance?

It is allegedly to be found in the competing groups, parties, etc., that are engaged in a struggle to lead the present: to be led by the present means to *withhold* devotion to any one group and instead to synthesize the various competing groups into a coherent totality. Strauss is here speaking of Karl Mannheim's "conspectivism" (or "relationalism"), of which he had written a critique the previous year.[8] He repeats now the most salient features of that critique: 1) Conspectivism's mere reporting of philosophic positions stands in striking contrast to the full, difficult, long, "immense" effort of a Kant, a Marx, or a Nietzsche that is required to arrive at their respective positions; it offers *Reader's Digest* versions of them, the very opposite of the genuine search for understanding.[9] 2) Conspectivism's origin is in a superficial, lazy reading of texts, an openness to what appears to be novel in those texts, and a desire to write about it, to reduce conflicting theories to "keywords" and their connections; the result is inevitably a jargon-laden, sloppily conceived, amusingly superficial synthesis. 3) Conspectivism displays a "sham understanding," a "stale and cowardly mishmash," a failure to take "*seriously* the great men who dominate the present."

In making this third and final criticism of Mannheim's conspectivism, Strauss refers at length to the work of "a philosopher in the full sense of the word. Completely unknown just five years ago, today his name and work are talked of everywhere." He refers, of course, to Heidegger:

> This philosopher in his main work has, among other things, written a few pages about idle talk, what it means and what it inflicts. That was meant as a, so to speak, purely factual statement, not as the author's appeal to spare him from idle talk. What happened? A woman—the noble word "lady" obviously forbids itself—reads this philosopher, and before she can even have the slightest idea of what the man really means, she goes around in London and yaks and yaks. She found the paragraph on idle talk certainly "very fine"; she has understood him in *this* sense; but she did not understand him in such a way that she would finally, finally shut her unbearable trap. (RSP)

Strauss himself had, eight years earlier, seen and been deeply impressed by Heidegger's "precision, and probing, and competence . . . seriousness, profundity, and concentration in the interpretation of philosophic texts."[10] That he refers here to Heidegger without naming him stands in contrast to those many who were now doing so.[11] That he refers to him *only* here should not blind us to the deep impact that Heidegger's thinking had on him. As the passage we have quoted makes clear, Heidegger's philosophic thought represents in a sense *the* alternative to "conspectivism," and of any attempt by social scientists like Mannheim to claim an authoritative position on the right way of life. At the same time, as we will see below, Heidegger represents a deepening of the problematic historicism that lies behind Mannheim's conspectivism. Heidegger, not Mannheim, is the serious target of this talk. Before spelling out how this is so, we must first examine its second half, in which Strauss indicates that he has found his way out of historicism. Indebted to Heidegger, Strauss will now move in a direction that Heidegger might have taken but did not take, that is, to an investigation that leads out of historicism. How, exactly, has Strauss freed himself from it? How does he defend the activity of asking naive questions, questions about the right way of life, from the claims of historicism and its specific "radical reflectiveness"?

* * *

Here as elsewhere, Strauss attempts to understand fully and sympathetically the historicists and the young men who are vaguely dissatisfied with the present.[12] The very attempt of Mannheim's conspectivism, and the difficulties with that attempt, begin to show the way. In seeking a synthesis of present positions that would yield an intelligible whole or totality of them, conspectivism asserts the equivalence of all positions in the present, in order to avoid the necessary blindness or partiality of any one position. In its search for guidance, it wishes to do justice to all the positions, while the partisans of those positions cannot do justice to one another's positions. In seeking to avoid the blindness of partisanship, it aims to know or see the truth. Yet this motive that has come into sight as prompting the search—the desire to know the *truth* about the present—is ill served by treating all positions as equivalent, since some of the positions may be simply untrue and hence not worthy of being made part of the intended synthesis. More importantly, assuming that a synthesis of them all is possible, one may still be left without the truth, since it is possible that "*all* present standpoints rest on a mistaking of the fundamental facts," or *all* present standpoints are perhaps "ideologies." To know whether or not this is so, to know the present as it truly is, one must "first of all be free of the present. This freedom does not fall into our laps; we must win it for ourselves." The motive to know the truth about the present impels the thoughtful person to seek an ascent out of the present.

This first step away from the present still assumes that knowledge of the present is the goal, the vitally desired knowledge. But this first step allows one to call into question this goal. For having taken a step out of the present, one sees that while there has always been a "present," an era, in which human beings lived, it was not something that serious people felt a compelling need to be concerned with as the source of guidance. As Strauss puts it in the second talk, "[t]houghtful people concerned themselves with the eternal." So too with us: the present is our fate, but "our *fate* is *not* our *task*." Strauss extends this point beyond Mannheim's conspectivism, to encompass "today's man" generally: "This is the principal mistake to which today's man keeps succumbing: the attempt to determine the task from the fate. This attempt is absurd if there is *no* God: then fate is chance, and if God *is*, then fate is providence, and we are not allowed to want to play God."[13] If our particular present is the product of mere chance, then it has no serious claim to direct our lives; if it is on the other hand the result of God's providence, then we must bow to that God and seek his guidance rather than being guided by a willing of the present. Making one's fate one's task falls, we may say, somewhere in-between these two, in a confused, half-conscious attempt to find a sacredness in the blind historical development that has produced the contemporary absence of the sacred.

Having expressed this problem with historicism more broadly—and, incidentally, brought out its theological intention—Strauss applies it to Mannheim in particular: "This error manifests itself also in the will to synthesis: even if each standpoint may *be* a synthesis *in fact*—it is nonetheless *never willed as* a synthesis; what has been willed is always the *truth*. We have to look straight *ahead*; we *never* come to know what we have to do by being reflective." The "reflectiveness" of historicism, its bearing in mind the historical experience of the failures of past attempts to arrive at the truth, the historical experience of finding in those attempts only the truth synthesized from particular epochs—all of this has now mistakenly turned this *result*, the failures, into its *goal*.

But a return to a naive questioning, on whose necessity Strauss insists, over and against the sophistication of historical "reflectiveness," is no simple thing. If historicism is right in its interpretation of the multiplicity or anarchy of teachings of the past, then escape from one's time or "the present" is indeed impossible, and it would make little sense to attempt vainly to transcend it. In bidding his listeners, as he again now does, to examine the question "concerning the right life" as a question susceptible of an answer that is *not* bound by one's present, Strauss must establish the possibility that historicism's prescribed "reflectiveness," on the failure of past attempts to answer this question rests in truth on a dubious, dogmatic interpretation of the failure in question. The historicists have, as he says, been turning this failure of past attempts to understand the truth "into a theory," and asserting thereby "the *inevitability* of failure." One must instead, he argues, take seriously that failure as a warning about the possible grounds of failure, in the effort to get at the truth. Examining those possible grounds is "truncate[d]," however, by "the dogmatic assertion that there are no eternal truths." A dogmatic assertion of our present threatens to short-circuit the ascending outside of it that has now begun.

But an investigation of such grounds of failure outside the historicist explanation of those grounds presupposes that the "experience" of such failure is—contrary to the historicists—*not* peculiar to the present: past thinkers also underwent this "experience" of multiplicity of failure but explained it in a different, nonhistoricist manner. Is this really the case? Strauss now argues that it indeed is. After posing the question "what about the historical *experience* of this failure?" he presents *Socrates* as the first to have posed this question. And he presents a sketch of the allegory of the cave as Plato's answer to this question, stressing as he does so the painful character of the ascent out of the cave, and that the one who ascends would be, upon redescending, "completely incomprehensible and laughable" to his companions down below. "Thus Plato presents the difficulties of philosophizing, the *natural* difficulties. If they are so extraordinary, is it any wonder that there are so many conflicting opinions?" This alternative Socratic or Platonic explanation of the multiplicity or "anarchy" of opinions is the means to transcend the reigning historicist interpretation of that multiplicity, the means to overcoming the dogmatic fatalism of the historicists that would short-circuit the escape out of the present.[14]

Yet serious historicists deny that there is a "nature" to man such that one can speak of "natural difficulties." The "natural world" or "nature," so far from being understood by a Socrates or Plato, was (according to historicists) merely the Greeks' *project*, a "construction of the human understanding," as Strauss will put it two pages hence. In their articulation of Western man's historical existence, historicists point in particular to the transformation of Western man that occurred by dint of the biblical doctrine of the revealed, creator God.[15] Has the doctrine of creation not, they ask, deepened man by disclosing among other things the contingency of all that exists, or made doubtful the alleged natural or necessary limits to all possible change?

Strauss confronts this claim in a remarkable fashion. The "natural" difficulties of philosophizing set forth by Plato—difficulties of "man as man, as a sensual-intellectual being"—are indeed no longer the only difficulties. The natural difficulties were reiterated by Alexander of Aphrodisias and quoted by Maimonides in *Guide of the Perplexed*[16]—a clear case of transcendence of time and place in awareness of difficulties—but more importantly, to Alexander's list of three natural difficulties Maimonides explicitly added a fourth: the unconditionally authoritative, revealed writings of Scripture, which had diminished the freedom to philosophize. Far from being changed or determined in his understanding by the biblical doctrine of creation, Maimonides now comes to sight as in agreement with Plato and Alexander. He found or presented the revealed writings of the Bible *not* as offering a radically new way of thinking or existing, in a hitherto unknown awareness of the contingency of all existence, but instead as an historically added *impediment to philosophizing*. Philosophizing was no different and no less possible in principle than it had ever been; it was merely impeded by an additional difficulty.

In this presentation of Maimonides's assertion of a difficulty to philosophizing added since the time of Plato, we see clearly for the first time the effect of Strauss's rediscovery of both Plato's importance for medieval Arabic and Jewish thinkers, and of esoteric writing. As late as 1928, Strauss had not understood Maimonides's professed belief in creation and in the Mosaic Law as exoteric.[17] We see here the first evidence that he now does so. And as Strauss makes explicit in his use of the same Maimonidean passage two years later, he takes Maimonides's surface statement as requiring the reader's own reflection or puzzlement in order to grasp its radical import. Maimonides himself speaks, after all, of the fourth, added difficulty to philosophizing as consisting merely in a habituation and schooling in writings that indicate God's corporeality. Strauss remarks:

> Now surely there were many Greek writings in which the gods were presented corporeally. Why did these writings not compromise Greek philosophy? It is therefore not being accustomed to writings in general, not having grown up in a tradition in general, but rather being accustomed to *very specific* writings, having grown up in a tradition of a *very specific* character: namely, in a tradition possessing an *authority*, as *unconditional* as that of the *tradition of revealed religions*. The fact that a tradition based on revelation entered the world of philosophy increased the *natural* difficulties of philosophizing by adding the *historical* difficulty.
>
> In other words: The natural difficulties of philosophizing have their classical depiction in Plato's allegory of the cave. The historical difficulty may be illustrated by saying: there *now* exists another cave *beneath* the Platonic cave. (ISP)

Strauss's rediscovery of the distinction between the esoteric and the exoteric, and of the significance not only of Aristotle but also of Plato for Maimonides, now comes to the fore in a striking presentation (in both talks) of revealed religion as creating, in Maimonides's view, a "cave beneath the cave," something out of which to ascend to the right life, the philosophic life.

As we know from a much later talk, this rediscovery occurred in conjunction with Jacob Klein's study of Plato, at the time that Strauss was studying Maimonides and Hobbes, just as he was finishing his Spinoza book. Assisted by Klein's rediscovery of the importance of the dramatic character of the Platonic dialogues—even of sections that appear to be philosophic treatises[18]—Strauss was able now to grasp with two hands the significance of Avicenna's statement, in *On the Division of the Rational Sciences*, that "the treatment of prophecy and the Divine law is contained in the *Laws* [of Plato]." (Strauss's first public reference to this passage appears in "Cohen und Maimuni," May 4, 1931).[19] He could now see that the medievals considered Plato to have understood and settled the challenge to philosophy posed by biblical prophecy or revelation. The momentousness of this rediscovery of esotericism in the works of Maimonides and of philosophers in Islamic countries, and thereby of the significance of Plato,[20] cannot be overestimated. The multiplicity or anarchy of philosophic teachings, which had appeared to Strauss and his contemporaries to be evidence of the insurmountable, unpredictable blindness of one's time and place to certain truths and of unpredictable openness to other truths, began now to appear to him instead, in the works of the greatest thinkers, as rhetorical accommodations to human weakness and to historical manifestations of that weakness. The situation created by historicism would eventually compel him to put more public stress on this rediscovery of esotericism than would have been the case otherwise,[21] but the rediscovery is already assisting Strauss in the recovery of the naive, natural question of the right way of life.

Now the fundamental teaching of historicism, as Strauss stresses in his talk two years later, entails a claim to final knowledge of a truth whose content may be lost to future generations only at the price of a rebarbarization. That teaching is that awareness of the radical contingency of all beings, owing to the fundamental thrown-ness of human existence, permits us, in our present, to *know* that all thought is historical. Historicism claims for itself this knowledge, available to no previous age, as a central truth allegedly revealed through the historical process. Proponents of historical consciousness argue that

> historical consciousness will go away if humanity unlearns what it has learned arduously enough over the past centuries; the renunciation of historical consciousness is identical with the relapse into a stage of lesser reflection.
>
> Let us pause here for a moment. Historical consciousness is—one cannot emphasize this strongly enough—according to its own view a stage of higher awareness: we know *more* than the earlier generations; we know more deeply, more profoundly, than the earlier ones that everything human is historically conditioned. (RSP 245–46)

The recovery of Platonic-Socratic philosophizing must, then, somehow answer this claim; it must show that, to the contrary, full awareness of the possibility of the radical contingency of human existence was faced by Plato's Socrates and seriously answered—not just turned away from or neglected—by him.

The recovery of Platonic-Socratic philosophizing was a recovery of the significance of dialectic, or of the Socratic "turn to speeches," illustrated in the allegory of the cave. We can better understand this recovery, as an answer to the problem of contingency, by considering the opposing, historicist, or existentialist position of Strauss's friend and Heidegger's student, Karl Löwith. As Löwith saw things, Plato's student Aristotle *presupposed* that the universe is eternal; he was therefore not at all open to the question of "existence," of radical contingency; he never raised the question of why something is at all, but instead took existence *for granted*, neglected it. "To Aristotle, existence meant an unquestionable element within the essential structure, order, and beauty of a dependable and clearly defined cosmos, which includes the existence of rational animals called men."[22] Again, to Aristotle, "existence as such—that there is something—was an unquestionable element within the essential structure, order, and beauty of an always existing cosmos without beginning and end, including the existence of rational animals called men."[23] Löwith went so far as to claim that "the Greeks" regarded "the physical cosmos...as something divine."[24] He accordingly found that the medieval doctrine of the creator God not only made the problem of causality—of the possibility of the contingency of all beings—clearer than it might otherwise later have been to the moderns, but that the medievals were the first even to *see* this problem, to open it up as a problem. "On the level of Aristotle, one can inquire only into the existence of something already existing," whereas for Thomas Aquinas, "existence is an exceptional category, undefinable by a 'what' or essence."[25] To Löwith, finally, the problem of contingency is fully understood and faced only at the end of modernity, with Heidegger: "With the loss of faith in this cosmos and with the loss of faith in Christianity's creator God, contingency in a thrown, meaningless world comes to the fore"; "If the universe is neither eternal and divine (Aristotle), nor contingent but created (Augustine), if man has no definite *place* in the hierarchy of an eternal or created cosmos, then, and only then, does man *begin* to '*exist*,' ecstatically and historically."[26] Someone living in our age might well desire, Löwith notes, to readopt the ancient view of an "immutable natural order" or "divine creation," but he can now do so only as a choice "between the one or the other 'project' or *Weltentwurf*," and such a choice now "would still be an existential attitude and decision."[27] And so, seeing Strauss arguing now for a serious return to the ancients, to "natural man," Löwith was dumbfounded. As he told Strauss,

> [W]hatever one might say against progressive models of history, I do agree however with them inasmuch as I also find that Christianity fundamentally modified ancient "naturalness." With a cat or a dog "nature" does indeed always come out again, but history is too deeply anchored in man for Rousseau or Nietzsche or your future hero of natural being and understanding to succeed in restoring something which already died out in late antiquity.... Only when you are able to convince me that stars, heaven, sea and earth, generation, birth and death give you... natural answers to your unnatural questions, will I be able to agree to your thesis.[28]

Strauss replied: "You confuse the Greek man-in-the-street, and as far as I am concerned also the Greek poet, with the Greek philosopher.... Plato and Aristotle never believed that 'stars, heaven, sea, earth, generation, birth and death give' them 'natural answers to their unnatural questions'.... Plato 'flees,' as is well known, from these 'things' (*pragmata*) into the *logoi*, because the *pragmata* give no answer directly, but are mute riddles."[29] Dialectics is needed, we may say, because the sensible properties that a being manifests depend for their existence on a mind being there to perceive them, which means that something other than the sensible properties must be there, or there is *nothing* there without man. What that something that is there *is*, however, is elusive, and there is nothing that guarantees its permanence; perhaps, as Hesiod indeed had claimed, it and everything else that is came into being from nothing. And so the possibility does open up, for the ancients no less than for medieval thinkers and for moderns influenced by them, that being is by a creator god or gods, a possibility that is to be excluded, insofar as it can be excluded, by the turn to the speeches, by dialectics. At stake in dialectics, conducted through examination of moral opinions of a believer or a potential believer, is the alleged evidence for the existence of gods who are said to come out of, or to make beings come out of, nothing[30]—the moral experiences connected to the experience of divinity. Telling in this regard is that Löwith, on the basis of Emil Fackenheim's research on Farabi, Algazel, Avicenna, and Maimonides—research assisted by Strauss—finds that to the "Arab and Jewish Aristoteleans of the tenth and twelfth centuries" existence "is a pure accident."[31] It does not for a moment occur to Löwith that Aristotle himself may have taken this position quite seriously.

That Strauss was prepared to see in dialectics the Platonic approach to this problem was due in part to his prior investigation of modern philosophy, which had been underway since his doctoral thesis on Jacobi and had been enlivened by a study of Hobbes with Julius Ebbinghaus;[32] it had to this point born its fullest fruit in what became *Spinoza's Critique of Religion* (1928; published in 1930). In preparing to write that first book, Strauss had accepted "the conditions of the historical consciousness," but in such a way as already to be leading in a direction that would take him out of it. One who thinks within the conditions of that consciousness, he had argued, has an advantage over both Spinoza and his chief antagonist, Calvin, neither of whom recognized the "conditionality" of his cause, and both of whom therefore denied "every right to the opposite position." This shortcoming was more consequential in the case of Spinoza, who was deprived thereby of a "true critique" of revelation; for Spinoza, "every critical argument, any presupposition, . . . is preceded by the conviction that one can judge the truths of religion from a theoretical stance outside the domain of obedience and belief."[33] A true critique, Strauss had argued, would be one that does not (as Spinoza's had) deduce fear of God from profane fear but would instead be one that knows (from experience) "what the fear of God, and the stirrings of conscience entailed by it, actually is." Openness to this nonprofane fear in the religious believer as a genuine experience is something Strauss clearly thinks the "historical consciousness" had made possible for him and even, one could say, obligatory to those within it who wished, as he did, to assess whether the moderns' victory over religious orthodoxy was in every respect deserved. He elaborates helpfully on the lack of this openness in Spinoza's thought by contrasting Spinoza's "critique of legalism" with that of St. Paul:

> In this context nothing is less justified than Spinoza's appeal to Paul's criticism of legalism. In Paul, the deepest awareness of sin rebels against legalism, while Spinoza's rejection of the Law rests on the rejection of obedience as such, and rests ultimately on the absence of any awareness of sin. Spinoza is a *homo liber* and a *homo fortis*, to whom radical stirrings of conscience and moments of ultimate despair are unknown. He either did not know or deadened in himself the characteristic

> experiences that are connected with the interest in revelation. In any case, he did not subject them to critique.

Spinoza, in short, lacked "reflection on the conditions of the possibility of a critique of religion," reflection that arises, to repeat, "under the conditions of the historical consciousness."[34] Such "reflection" is what we see Strauss renouncing in the talks before us, in favor of naiveté or a return to our natural situation. But it had had the great benefit of leading him to see the need for an internal critique of religion, a critique that took seriously the need to consider the believer's experience of sin, of a guilty conscience, if the rational life were to truly ground itself. It had thereby prepared him to see that in dialectic, Socrates indeed takes that experience seriously, and to criticize as late as 1928 Freud's repetition of Spinoza's failure to do so.[35]

To put this somewhat differently, Strauss realized already—as we can see in the phrase "the characteristic experiences [of conscience] that are connected with the interest in revelation"—that (as he formulates it later), "the moral man as such is the potential believer."[36] He was therefore prepared, as he might not otherwise have been, for seeing—with the help of Avicenna—in the Platonic dialogues precisely such an "internal critique" of faith in a creator god and of the possibility of the contingency of all existence, of its coming to be out of nothing, that such a god would inevitably entail, an internal critique that begins by seeing sin not as "animal evil" but as "moral depravity."[37] He could see now, in other words, the Platonic dialogues' attempt to settle this matter through the "common ground" of believer and philosopher. As he later says, the Socratic-Platonic philosopher assumes a "provisional acceptance of the accepted opinions" of the city, or of "'natural' valuations";[38] he sees obedience to divine law or the problem of divine law as "the common ground" between the Bible and Greek philosophy."[39] And so the characteristic of Maimonides's rationalism—that it begins by placing oneself under the law, in obedience to the law—now appeared in this new, startling light.[40] Strauss now began to see that characteristic in the way that he subsequently described it:

> We are again confronted with the question, Why philosophy? or, Why science? This question was in the center of discussion in the beginnings of philosophy. One may say that the Platonic dialogues serve no more obvious purpose than precisely this one: to answer the question, Why philosophy? or, Why science? by justifying philosophy or science before the tribunal of the city, the political community... [or] before the tribunal of the law.[41]

Strauss came to realize (as he had not, when writing the Spinoza book) that Maimonides and Plato, no less than and perhaps more than Heidegger, had indeed engaged in the kind of critique absent from Spinoza and the moderns generally, and had done so through dialectic.[42] With this, he directly experienced ancient thinking that was both alive and nonhistoricist.[43] Strauss therefore asserts firmly now that the natural view is fully recoverable, here and now, as much as it was for Maimonides despite (in his day) the authoritative writings of the Bible. He presents "the hope . . . that some day humans will be able to be natural again," by dint of our "need to know," breaking out in our "question concerning what is right." While he holds out no possibility of an ascent from the cave as possible for the whole of humanity, he does hold out the possibility of a recovery of a natural ignorance, that is, a recovery of the cave, from the "cave of modernity" beneath it.[44]

⋆ ⋆ ⋆

But what, then, did Strauss find to be the substantive result of the Socratic "turn to the speeches" that begins with the common ground of the moral experiences of the believer or potential believer—a result altogether different from the characteristically modern, historicist position? What is learned through dialectic can be gleaned, Strauss suggests in this talk, through an awareness of the pains that the dialectical ascent out of the cave entails, pains upon which he lays stress. Just what those pains are, however, he does not tell his listeners—at least not directly. From a later talk we know that, in contrast to Klein, Strauss found that the result of dialectic was the realization of the insufficiency or problematic character of the moral life, which becomes visible in a sufficient number of cases to the potential believer himself. As a result, "The tension between philosopher and the polis is . . . the highest theme of political philosophy."

> I attached much greater importance than Klein did and does to the tension between philosophy and the city, even the best city. . . . Philosophy is as such transpolitical, transreligious, and transmoral, but the city is and ought to be moral and religious. . . . To illustrate this point, moral man, merely moral man, the *kaloskagathos* in the common meaning of the term, is not simply closer to the philosopher than a man of the dubious morality of Alcibiades. . . .
>
> This view of philosophy was derived from my study of premodern philosophy. It implies that modern philosophy has a radically different character. . . . In modern times the gulf between philosophy and the city was bridged, or believed to have been bridged. . . . If we call moralism the view that morality or moral virtue is the highest, I am doubtful if it occurs in antiquity at all.[45]

A crucial part of what he learned at this time from his reading of Plato was "confirmed," Strauss goes on to say, by his examination of the roots of historicism in modern philosophy.

> I was confirmed in my concentration on the tension between philosophy and the *polis*, i.e., on the highest theme of political philosophy, by this consideration. What distinguishes present-day philosophy in its highest form, in its Heideggerian form, from classical philosophy is its historical character; it presupposes the so-called historical consciousness. It is therefore necessary to understand the partly hidden roots of that consciousness. . . . Politics and political philosophy is the matrix of the historical consciousness.[46]

The results of an investigation of modern philosophy, then, by exposing the roots of historicism in modern political philosophy, provide an important confirmation of what Strauss had learned from Plato at this time.

This helps us understand why, having presented the Bible as something Maimonides saw as producing a "cave beneath the cave," Strauss turns, in the conclusion of his talk, to presenting modern philosophy's struggle against the Bible and its doctrine of creation and providence—that is, modernity's effort to remove this fourth impediment to philosophy—as having brought into being a *new* cave beneath the cave, one that we now inhabit. A sketch or map of "the struggle of the entire last 3 centuries," he asserts, which sought to "destroy" the biblical impediment to philosophy and thereby restore "philosophy in its natural difficulty," is contained in Maimonides's brief account of the biblical impediment to philosophizing.

This modern, Enlightenment struggle characterized itself as a struggle against "prejudices," as opposed to the classic philosophic struggle against appearance and opinion, but (as the later talk especially makes clear) the "prejudice" it chiefly had in mind was biblical faith in the creator God and His miracles.[47] What this modern struggle has achieved, however, Strauss argues, is "not the freedom of questioning, only the freedom of saying No instead of the traditional Yes. (Mortality versus immortality, chance versus providence, atheism versus theism, passion versus reason)." And this achievement was bought at the price of an "entanglement" in the biblical tradition of providence in such a way as to hide that entanglement, by causing awareness of the tradition itself to dissolve. But finally, *both* of "[t]he pillars on which our tradition rested, Prophets and Socrates-Plato, are torn down since Nietzsche," with the result that the question of the right way of life "has . . . regained its full sharpness."

> We can no longer read Plato's dialogues superficially, in order to notice admiringly that old Plato already knew this and that; we can no longer polemicize against him superficially. And the same with the Bible: we no longer think without evidence that the prophets were in the right; we ask ourselves seriously whether it was not the kings who were in the right. We really must begin *entirely* from the beginning.
>
> . . .
>
> But we cannot answer immediately as we are; for we know that we are deeply entangled in a tradition; we are yet much further down than Plato's cave dwellers. We must raise ourselves to the *origin* of the tradition, to the level of *natural ignorance*. If we wanted to concern ourselves with the present situation, we would be doing nothing other than the cave dwellers who describe the interior of their cave. (RSP)

The outcome of the modern struggle was, then, two-fold. On one hand, it resulted finally in the tearing down of the tradition, achieved by Nietzsche, so that a truly fresh start is now possible, with nothing taken for granted. On the other, it resulted in the creation of a new cave beneath the cave, a new claim to authoritative knowledge against the philosophic life, a new "entanglement" in the biblical tradition of providence.[48] We may square the two results by saying, provisionally, that Nietzsche's tearing down of the tradition achieved its result only through continued entanglement in the tradition of providence, so that to make a genuinely fresh start, to make the return to the ancients sought by Nietzsche, we need to climb out of the new cave beneath the cave created by the tradition.[49] Understanding that "entanglement" will therefore help us to understand both the genesis of historicism out of modern philosophy and how it confirmed what Strauss had learned from Plato.

★ ★ ★

Strauss first sketches three examples of this entanglement, and then offers a six-point "Example" of it in the moderns' addressing of "The Problem of Creation." The first three examples illustrate how the Enlightenment arrived at its "No" (to immortality, providence, theism, and understanding) through its appropriation of aspects of the biblical tradition of providence, with opponents of enlightenment appropriating in turn aspects of enlightenment thought. So religious intolerance was fought by the Enlightenment in the name of the biblical principle of love of neighbor, and later, the Enlightenment understood God as a construct by "internalizing the purposes of God into mankind: self-redemption of mankind, self-assurance of immortality (museum, etc.), assuming the role of providence." Late opponents of the Enlightenment, that is, religious believers, for their part reinterpreted traditional notions in light of the Enlightenment's successes: "E.g., revelation is understood as being a human product, as morals and as form, not as law; creation is understood not as being the creation of the world, but as what is binding in advance on human beings." (Here Rosenzweig's thought seem to be intended.)[50] Strauss's objection to this mutual "entanglement," this series of reactions and counterreactions, is that it was carried out with no questioning of the foundation. "Ex[ample]: [in the] concept of the 'irrational'—rationalism [is] understood in the narrowest sense," that is, only as *modern* rationalism, as he calls it in the opening of *Philosophy and Law* (1935). His suggestion is that modern rationalism, in its activist battle with biblical faith, took over certain activities and presuppositions of that faith, in such a way as to make this rationalism questionable as genuine rationalism, and, whatever its initial success in advancing the acceptance of atheism, to make it easy for believers or potential believers to appropriate or dismiss as unimportant the findings of modern enlightenment rationalism.

What Strauss has in mind becomes clearer in the second part of the account of the "entanglement" of modernity in the tradition of biblical providence, the six-point example of "The Problem of Creation." This "example" is a telescoped picture of the whole development of modernity, in its protracted response to (as he says in Point #1) the biblical, radically free, creative God who works miracles. It provides the first outline of what Strauss would later call a nonhistoricist account of historicism—of the development of the doctrine taken for granted or neglected by Heidegger. He begins (as it seems to me) with Spinoza, who presented a new, materialist metaphysics that would correspond with the recent discoveries in physics (Point #2: "miracles are unworthy of God as the perfect being"). But as Strauss had already argued in *Spinoza's Critique of Religion*, the *effective* part of Spinoza's critique was not his materialist metaphysics; it was instead the "positive" critique, that is, the claim that the mind disposed to a scientific explanation of things, the mind that had progressed from ancient superstition and ignorance, was far better able to understand the truth about miracles than were their alleged witnesses in the remote past. This positive critique arose from Spinoza's teaching: he had not only attempted to explain miracles scientifically but had done so with a consciousness of the superiority of the scientific mind over what is ancient and therefore backward or barbaric. "Reason must become *Geist* in order to be able actively to experience its more than royal freedom, its sovereignty which is incapable of being shaken by anything."[51] And as *Geist*, reason does not take seriously the Calvinist position that a creator-God is behind all that is and can work miracles in accord with his will—the position that is compatible with or the theological equivalent of "skepticism."

What Strauss was discovering at the time of these talks, through his work on Hobbes (articulated in the manuscript he left unfinished and unpublished, *Hobbes's Critique of Religion*) is that this most effective part of the modern critique of revelation, this secular advance and triumph of the "positive mind," was in fact *intended* to be such—to be the very means of defeating the challenge posed by revelation, in its most radical, Calvinist form. For unlike Spinoza, Strauss was discovering, Hobbes—along with Descartes—had *granted* to revelation the possibility that the world is indeed radically contingent, that is, that it is possibly the work of a hidden, deceptive God. To secure the possibility of a mechanistic-materialistic physics against this serious possibility, they had conceived a novel science based on "a retreat into consciousness," from which the positive mind would prescribe its own laws to nature, so that man would become the owner or possessor of nature. (Point #3: "Modern physics understands nature completely on its own terms: No scientific proof of God possible." And Point #4: "Nature a construct of the human intellect.") But to secure a ground for this new science, a science that had granted so much to revelation—to "avoid the cavils of the skeptics," as Strauss would later put it[52]—a transformation of the given world and of human beings was needed. A new moral-political teaching, aiming at a change in orientation of everyone—a grand civilizational project—would be the means to the *grounding* of the new science, over and against the claims of religious believers. The new science as a retreat into consciousness requires and anticipates this result. The civilizational project is an attempt to replace providence, to dispel the mundane fear that was thought to lie behind the need for gods by world transformation; it is a "rebellion" against a harsh, meaningless nature by a science that could offer humanity the true goods of this world withheld by religious doctrines and the manipulation of clerics. This modern attempt represents a modification of the Epicurean orientation, such that its concern is no longer with liberating the philosophic individual from fear (of the *numen*) but instead with securing the *happiness* of all, by defeating those earthly political powers that have used the delusion of religion and its imaginary "other-worldliness" to cheat their peoples of the genuine goods and which have disrupted the civil peace.[53]

For in their "No" to immortality, the early moderns had denied the naturalness of a concern for immortality; they held that it was an artificial, biblically-induced concern, one supported by biblical "tales." Relatedly, they denied the naturalness of human sociability. Both of these denials stand in marked opposition to the Platonic Socrates, who saw the desire for immortality both as natural and as a desire that proved to express itself in the human concern for justice or morality. With its "no" to immortality, modern thought turned away from the Socratic *questioning* of moral opinion through dialectic, and hence from the questioning of the (sometimes buried) hope for immortality.[54] The early moderns' attempt thus evinced an "entanglement in the tradition" of providence insofar as it represented a "rebellion" against a niggardly nature and against an allegedly artificially induced desire for immortality and an attempt to overcome it with a new, this-worldly morality that was compatible with the new materialist-mechanistic physics. The attempt was aware of itself as "progressive," over the "prejudices" of the peoples of biblical faith. This is the "historical consciousness of the Enlightenment."

Historicism arises as a "correction" of that consciousness.[55] The first major indications of a need for its correction began to occur precisely as the modern civilizational project seemed to have reached success. "Now, around 1750 the structure of mechanistic physics and the politics resting on it is completed: the consciousness of its problematic comes into the foreground."[56] The early moderns' attempted "enlightenment" of human beings, with its expectation that the kind of happiness indicated would emerge from this enlightenment, produced two reactions, one philosophic, found in "Hume and above all Rousseau," the other more political, found initially in Burke but more broadly in the "historical school" that dominated German jurisprudential and political thought throughout the nineteenth century.

The first—the philosophic—reaction to the modern teaching had two related parts: a return of the very skepticism about causality that the early moderns' civilizational project had attempted to expel, and an attempt to find a workable political substitute for the now fully discredited doctrine of Christian natural law and for the conscience, the means of that law's promulgation, which had been undermined by the new science and the political doctrine of the state of nature. The reaction comes in Rousseau:

> One sees that the promise of enlightened politics (Hobbes, Encyclopedia) to create the just order through the propagation of mechanistic physics and anthropology cannot be kept; one sees it (one, that is, Rousseau) because one learns to see again from Plato the problem "science-politics . . . society needs 'religion.'"[57]

Rousseau's teaching was grounded in an awareness of the looming political-moral threat to the new science and to the civilizational project on which it rested. He attempted to preserve that project, by articulating on one hand an idea of happiness that would be compatible with the new understanding, and on the other, a notion of the general will—something tribal, preceding any social contract, and sustained by a civil religion—that could replace the discredited Christian natural law doctrine. Perhaps on account of his partial recovery of the Socratic-Platonic awareness of the incapacity of most human beings to live in the light of science, Rousseau's presentation, in the *Second Discourse*, of the accidental development of man's very humanity in history—his replacement for the biblical account of creation and its support of the Christian doctrine of the conscience—was written in such a way that Kant could take it to be a vindication of divine providence.[58] But it was of a providence now understood to be fully scrutable as a development, through the pursuit of low ends, toward humanity's present, developed peak. That peak, as Kant establishes in his critique of practical reason, is the full development of prudence and the "good will," a version of Rousseau's "general will."[59] There is thus a further "entanglement," within the philosophic tradition, with the biblical notion of providence, within the Enlightenment itself.

Rousseau and Kant were nonetheless both attempting to secure the victory of science or reason, and therefore attempting to correct the political or civilizational project through which reason or science was to be vindicated. The other reaction to the limited success of the early modern civilizational project was directed by more strictly political concerns that nonetheless were informed by both a philosophic skepticism and a faith in divine providence. This reaction is most visible in the "historical school," which Strauss had been examining as early as 1925[60] and whose primary concern was not philosophic but political-theological. Of this second—political—reaction Strauss says, in a letter to Löwith, "historical consciousness is a result of the discontent of modernity with itself."[61] The way toward the development of this school of thought was paved, Strauss later argued, by Burke, whose opposition to theory or metaphysics was founded in a kinship with "the skeptical tendencies of his contemporaries Hume and Rousseau" and who adhered to a faith in divine providence (as transformed by modernity).[62] Burke's skepticism gave him the same disposition toward philosophic theory or metaphysics as that of Calvin, and therefore an understanding of the beautiful as a thing divorced from reason, and of the best political constitution as one that is by chance, or "grown." He argued for "prescription," that is, he championed the doctrine that the liberties of a people belong by right to them because they have belonged to them time out of mind, without any reference to a higher law; they were written before (*prescriptum*) and therefore trump any other appeals, including the appeal to natural law. To Burke, the justice of what history had "accidentally" produced was vouchsafed by his belief in (scrutable) providence.

These twin developments paved the way, however, for a further development of the modern civilizational project in Hegel, who now took man's actions in history as the proper subject of *theoretical* life, of a new metaphysics that was not about the whole or eternity but the development of spirit (*Geist*) through History. (Point #5: "The whole of 'culture,' and religion with it, is understood by analogy with this construction [of nature], as a construction of the human spirit.") Hegel argued (famously) that the development of rational human consciousness was at an end: History was over, its development fully surveyable and comprehensible as the accidental development of *Geist*. While his philosophy of history significantly enhanced the status of man within the whole, it had the effect of leaving almost no one satisfied.

Over and against Hegel's doctrine the historical school attempted to maintain an undetermined future for significant human action, one that would provide an alternative to the revolutionary or bourgeois-supportive appeals to modern "natural law." It looked for objective but nonuniversal or particular standards within the history of a given people or tribe. History was to supply peoples with the moral standards formerly sought in revelation or in nature. But when the historical school's attempt at discovering objective but nonuniversal standards in a particular history failed, its premise, the historicity of man, was not abandoned, but instead maintained as a hitherto unknown dimension of human existence. At the same time Kierkegaard, also in rebellion against Hegelian rationalism, articulated the possibility of "a human life which has a significant and undetermined future," living authentically, in the face of death,[63] that is, what became "existentialism." The ground of modern science—the alleged advanced consciousness—now became questionable, as representing one particular consciousness among many and one that, moreover, lacked depth. In Strauss's brief description of this anti-Hegelian thinking, we meet up again, it seems, with the thought of Rosenzweig. (Point #6: "Novel understanding of the original religious attitude [in contrast to mysticism]: the demanding God who summons before him. The abandonment of creation remains.")

This six-part "example" of the entanglement of modernity in the biblical tradition of providence thus begins to expose the hidden "roots" of the alleged experience of "history" as a dimension of human existence. And—to move now to the outcome of the development that Strauss here sketches—Nietzsche, having accepted the fundamental premise of the historical school, deconstructed *both* pillars of the tradition, biblical and philosophic, calling into question both the Christian God and the philosophic enterprise of "plebian" Socratic philosophy against the man of *megalopsychia*.[64] Nietzsche, Strauss would later suggest, came close to recovering classical rationalism. Judging "theory" to be deadly to "life," he faced this alternative: he could "insist on the strictly esoteric character of the theoretical analysis of life—that is, restore the Platonic notion of the noble delusion—or else he could deny the possibility of theory proper and so conceive of thought as essentially subservient to, or dependent on, life or fate."[65] He did the latter. And so in his effort to build a bridge back to the natural man of antiquity, instead of restoring Platonic esotericism—as Strauss himself has now begun doing—Nietzsche promulgated his doctrine of the eternal return, to combat modernity's faith in the progress of humanity toward the degraded notion of "happiness" offered through the abolition of suffering. He offered a cosmological doctrine that called for "endurance," over and against the

> millennia-old pampering due to belief in creation and providence. The rebellion against the indifference of the universe, against its aimlessness, which lies at the root of *modern* civilization, is an essential part of this pampering.[66]

In sum, the early moderns attempted to eliminate the obstacle posed to philosophizing by the Bible and thereby restore the natural situation; they attempted to secure a new kind of natural science, a constructivist science, by transforming human consciousness, through a humanly providential transformation of the world. The attempt held human fear of a nature indifferent to human suffering to be conquerable by dint of awareness of scientific progress in conquering nature. Historicism arose as a makeshift political-philosophic-theological effort to correct this attempt, to provide a morally satisfying human life by grounding moral meaning in a "sacred" process of human history. When this attempt, too, proved to be a failure, the alleged historical dimension of life was not abandoned, but was now considered a "discovery." Heidegger's "radical historicism" seeks to provide the philosophic, ontological ground of this historical consciousness, to demonstrate that the experience of contingency is a true or genuine experience.

We draw the following conclusion. The recovery of Socratic dialectics, which in the best cases produces a liberation from the moral and political opinions of one's cave and to the philosophic life, was "confirmed" for Strauss by bringing to light the hidden roots of historicism, which arose owing to what was a serious mistake about human beings on the part of modern political philosophers. Over and against the historical consciousness, Strauss has recovered in Plato the preliminary, dialectical ascent to the philosophic life. This recovery was the *prerequisite* of his understanding of the deficiencies of early modern thought that had called into being historicism as a reaction to that thought.[67] What Strauss realized, on the basis of his recovery of Plato, and of the pains entailed in the dialectical ascent from the cave, was what one might call the inevitability of the failure of the modern attempt at enlightenment, and so of the rise of the historical consciousness against it. He provides here an initial sketch of the nonhistoricist account of historicism that would permit the true fresh, tradition-less start that Nietzsche's tearing down of the tradition had otherwise made possible.

* * *

As should be clear by now, this talk, which begins with a critique of Mannheim, expands into an implicit critique of the more powerful, more serious, more radical historicism of Heidegger, the proponent of what Strauss calls, in the second talk, "radical *reflection*." To grasp better this implicit critique of Heidegger and its ramifications, political and philosophic, a preliminary statement on the relation of Mannheim and Heidegger is in order.

Mannheim was a follower of, among others, Max Weber (and for a time a friend and colleague of Weber's brother Alfred, in Sociology, at Heidelberg), and a founder of "the sociology of knowledge." But on the crucial issue of whether reason could provide ethical or moral guidance, Mannheim broke with Weber.[68] For Weber had, for his part, been led by his reading of Nietzsche to see the depth, seriousness, and vitality of the life of religious faith. Repulsed by the emerging shallow world ruled by science—a world of "specialists without spirit or mind, and voluptuaries without heart"—he had declared the impossibility of answering the question of the right way of life (leading to the famous fact/value distinction). While Weber had, out of intellectual probity, held on to the life of scientific reasoning "as a vocation," and attempted to explain the specific path that had led to it, he was closer to Heidegger than to Mannheim on the central issue of the impossibility of a rational ethics. As Strauss later put it,[69] Mannheim had attempted, over and against Weber, to show that reason and argument could reach agreement on the fundamentals—that the urgent question of the right way of life could and must be settled not, as theologically inclined thinkers like Rosenzweig were claiming, by a return to revelation, nor, as thinkers like Schmitt and Jünger were claiming, through *political* authority, but by examining the *present* as the fruitful locus of all divergent opinions.[70]

Given his confidence in the possibility of rational guidance of nations, it is not surprising that Mannheim's *Ideology and Utopia* included an attack on Heidegger: "He who would wish to have the irrational where, *de jure*, the clarity and astringency of reason should still hold sway, is afraid of looking in the eyes of the mystery in its proper place." Heidegger responded to this attack in his 1931–32 winter semester lectures on Plato, in which he examined at length the *Republic's* image of the cave. We recall that in that image, he who ascends out of the cave, sees the truth and returns, is laughed at, and told that it is not worth going up. Heidegger turns these laughing critics of the philosopher into Karl Mannheim and his students: The philosopher, Heidegger says,

> would be told he was one-sided, he was, coming from somewhere, holding (in their view) a one-sided attitude; and presumably, nay, certainly, they have down there a so-called "sociology of knowledge," with whose help he would be informed that he was operating with so-called ideological prerequisites, which of course gravely disturbed the community of collective opinion in the cave and therefore had to be rejected.

Mannheim's thought belongs, in short, to "cave prattle."[71] It thus came about that both Strauss and Heidegger critiqued Mannheim by means of Plato's allegory of the cave—Strauss first, and Heidegger a year later.

Yet Heidegger manifestly differs from Strauss both in thinking that the ascent from the cave can never be transhistorical or without "reflective reflectiveness," and in thinking, at the same time, that the inhabitants of one's cave can and ought to be transformed, one and all, by the one who has ascended out of it in a resolutely historicist manner. To Strauss, this is evidence that Heidegger no less than Mannheim failed to recover genuine Socratic philosophizing, inhabiting instead the historicist cave beneath the cave, and would as a consequence remain fundamentally in the thrall of "the present." Strauss makes this substantial agreement between Heidegger and Mannheim, and its political consequence, explicit in a talk he gave in 1940. Mannheim's attempted dialectical synthesis of the opinion of the present is, Strauss states, absurd, *unless* one assumes a progress in consciousness that god is dead, that is, unless one is expecting a new, atheistic morality. This new atheism would be opposed to the biblical morality, to progress, to the brotherhood of man, equality of dignity of all men, etc., and would favor courage and steadfastness.[72] The synthesis for which Mannheim held out a hope could become actual through *Heidegger's* thought, but in a way that Mannheim, who was fundamentally a liberal, would have found abhorrent.

The welcoming posture toward the present and its answers to the question of the right way of life is, to be sure, far more obvious in Mannheim than in Heidegger. In the year before this talk was written, Heidegger and Ernst Cassirer had engaged in their famous debate at Davos, and the significance of Heidegger's defeat of Cassirer lay, for Strauss, in the fact that Cassirer had silently dropped the claim that ethics is possible, while Heidegger faced squarely the problem of the impossibility of ethics.[73] Facing this impossibility goes hand-in-hand with Heidegger's stance against liberal pluralism—of which Mannheim's "conspectivism" was the latest version—as degraded, not permitting an experience of the Call of Being but instead ensnaring the spirit in everydayness and utility.

Heidegger himself claimed indeed that there are no ethics in his thought. For despite the fact that we find ourselves existing among other human beings, existence of an other is, he argues, always as an "other," an "also being there," and not as anything demanding reciprocity of behavior. (In the language of Rosenzweig or Buber, the "other" is for Heidegger not a "thou.") To Heidegger, being with others is a being "together," but not a being *with* each other. To be sure, the "confrontation with the other" that our contemporary postmodernist democratic theorists tend to rely upon as the basis of an "ethics" is an outgrowth of Heidegger's thought, but whether it permits the determination of one's authentic being, through resoluteness to be itself in the face of its certain death—upon which Heidegger insisted—is doubtful. It would seem instead to foreclose such determination, which Heidegger thinks is required for the "proper" (*eigentlich*) existence, through the solicitude and concern that it would provide. There is no ethics for Heidegger, secondly, because the resoluteness against one's anticipated death lacks a definite aim.[74] Heidegger stands for the individual's engagement or decision, with the claim that the authentic, knowing subject is ever the subject engaged with finitude, death.

Yet as Strauss had noticed, there is, despite his denials an "ethics" or moral teaching in Heidegger.[75] Heidegger's "resolute" human proves to be actively engaged with the present (over and against the merely imagined) into which he is "thrown." Heidegger stresses indeed that death permits us to become aware of our individual temporality, of our being in time, but death is also for him, as Löwith points out, the hidden motive of all historicalness (*Geschichtlichkeit*) which is the substance of existence, that is, of being engaged resolutely in something and exposed to one's fate. A resolute existence is one that "renews the possibilities of the past by way of its anticipating resolve," that is, by way of facing death. Resolute existence subjects our "today" to criticism when and as it is merely living on the past. But as it "hands itself over to itself," taking upon itself responsibility for its individual being, through resolute anticipation of death, it also hands over to itself past possibilities. It is only these combined deeds, in fact, that lead to a "there and now" (a *Da*) for oneself, a historical "situation"[76] in which the resolute human is not a spectator or critic, but actively engaged.[77] "Being present now on behalf of 'one's time,'" or the "resolution into the world-historical situation" is required,[78] and with it, eternity is given up. By "one's time" Heidegger may not mean the vulgar version of Mannheim, but there is no other "world-time" than the vulgar version.[79] And in 1933, the "being present now on behalf of one's time" meant becoming a Nazi leader of Freiburg University. At that point Strauss, who had already seen the path to which "resoluteness" was leading Heidegger, ceased reading him for 20 years.[80] Those who would attribute to Strauss, with the greatest perversity imaginable, sympathy with Heidegger's National Socialism mistake Strauss's recovery of eternity for a recovery of the radically historical here and now.

For just as he took for granted the tradition of atheism that had yielded the current situation, Heidegger took for granted the superiority of the moral, engaged, political life. His radical historicism is driven, one might say, by the desire for an elevated, morally committed life of decision, in the face of our apparent thrownness. It *must* reject philosophy as having been practiced in ignorance of this thrownness, as having been practiced in fact as an escape from this thrownness, which allegedly reveals itself to one who faces death authentically. Heidegger must claim of philosophy that its search for universal causes is no more than the attempt to avoid our thrownness, to avoid the thought that out of nothing everything comes to be. He needs this doctrine in order to recapture the resoluteness of the Christian moral life, but atheistically. He must in fact avoid anything approaching certainty of death, since that would result in *resignation* and not in the agitation he seeks. Moral men may be drawn to living authentically and enthused in the being-toward death prophesied by Heidegger. But such *Existenz* is possible only if one in fact resists apodictic certainty of death and resignation to it, in order to elicit experiential awareness of death so as to call forth a noble life of some sort—in order to experience, through confrontation with the experience of death, a "call" of Being. Heidegger needs, no less than biblical faith, a Being that calls and that is responsible for bringing all beings into being from nothing.

The idealizing philosophy of Hegel against which Heidegger, with so many others, rebelled, allegedly dilutes the reality of death, which alone can make one's being "still there" manifest. This is what one may call the absolute empiricism of Heidegger; the thinking being is the being aware that he will die. Now Strauss for his part does not dispute this, or run for cover in the "old thinking." On the contrary, on the basis of his recovery from the tradition, his bringing to light the roots hidden by the tradition, he finds that the new thinking of Heidegger merely continues, despite its claims to a stern facing up, the *hiding* of eternity (and hence of one's mortality) begun by Hobbes and continued in Hegel.[81] While Strauss does not in this talk venture such a critique of Heidegger, he does stress its fundamental ground, in his account of Plato's cave allegory: he stresses the terrible pains that, according to Plato's Socrates, are experienced by one ascending from the cave. Among those pains is, of course, the genuine awareness of mortality and, as that awareness is made through dialectic about the just and the noble into knowledge, the accompanying awareness of the lack of cosmic support for one's deepest wishes—which find their responses in the shadows on the cave wall—or, in Heidegger's terminology, the awareness that the Call is an echo off the cave walls, unheard after the (dialectical) ascent, that is, precisely as the genuine knowledge of death is made clear.

These fundamental differences between Strauss and Heidegger are reflected in their respective approaches to ancient texts. In "The Word of Nietzsche: God is Dead," Heidegger makes clear that a hermeneutic is always required and at work in reading them; he claims that one cannot understand thinkers *better* than they understood themselves, yet one cannot but understand them *differently* than they understood themselves. He defends this distinction by criticizing the "layman" who arrogates a right to himself.

> Not only must any commentary gather the substance from the text, it must imperceptibly and without being too insistent, add something of its own to it, from its substance. This supplement is what the layman, regarding what he takes to be the content of the text, always feels as an interpolation; it is what he, with the right he arrogates to himself, criticizes as arbitrary. A proper commentary, however, never understands the text better than its author understood it, though it certainly understands it differently. Only this difference in understanding must be such that it encounters the same thing which the explicated text is meditating.[82]

Strauss, with a deep irony, presents himself as the layman who would understand thinkers as they understood themselves.

Yet while radicalizing historicism, and hence further encrypting one in the cave beneath the cave, Heidegger had opened the way, without intending it, to an ascent out of that secondary cave. Strauss found, with the help of Klein, more compelling than Heidegger's teaching the examination of the roots of the "tradition" that Heidegger's *Destruktion* of the tradition had exposed:

> While everyone else in the young generation who had ears to hear was either completely overwhelmed by Heidegger, or else, having been almost completely overwhelmed by him, engaged in well-intentioned but ineffective rearguard actions against him, Klein alone saw why Heidegger is truly important: by uprooting and not simply rejecting the tradition of philosophy, he made it possible for the first time after many centuries—one hesitates to say how many—to see the roots of the tradition as they are and thus perhaps to know, what so many merely believe, that those roots are the only natural and healthy roots.... Klein was the first to understand the possibility which Heidegger had opened *without intending it*: the possibility of a genuine return to classical philosophy, to the philosophy of Aristotle and of Plato, a return with open eyes and in full clarity about the infinite difficulties which it entails.[83]

As Strauss put it in 1940, "Heidegger had made it clear that Plato and Aristotle have not been refuted, because they had not been understood by modern philosophers," yet "Heidegger's interpretation of Aristotle... is no more than a beginning."[84]

* * *

We have examined what was to be the clarifying preface to a talk on "Franz Rosenzweig's doctrine and his problematic." While the promised talk on

Rosenzweig has not come down to us as such, it is not difficult to see, from the few allusions to his teaching that we have noted, that Strauss now found Rosenzweig, no less than Heidegger, to be entangled in a modern tradition that he neglects, to be reliant upon an Enlightenment critique of the creator God that he has not examined.[85] And despite the differences between Rosenzweig and Heidegger, what Strauss argues here against historicism applies to the one as to the other. To Strauss, the historical consciousness that leads to an enthrallment to the present is a tyranny, a sub-cave, presided over by a bewitching goddess—something from which one ascends to lead a genuine human life. What is entailed in that life can be understood only through a naive, careful reading of the Platonic dialogues. But it is clear that from that present Strauss does not take flight into the mystical eternity of "blood" or nationhood of an allegedly eternal people, as does Rosenzweig. Strauss instead finds in Plato the ground for a resignation to one's own mortality. Like Strauss, Rosenzweig claimed, to be sure, that the starting point of all thinking about the whole is "man in the plainest sense as he still exists,"[86] yet he too engages in an analysis of *Existenz* that is "reflective," aware of its "historical existence."

In the talk he gave two years later, moreover, Strauss notes the deleterious effect, for an honest investigation of the right way of life, of Rosenzweig's historicism. After chronicling the rise of political and cultural Zionism out of the failed hopes of liberal assimilation, Strauss explains in that talk how this movement actually meant that what had been understood by the tradition as the revealed word of God and His Law were instead being understood, in the Enlightenment manner, as a product of the human mind. It thus *clouded* the central issue of the right way of life—the issue of faith or reason. Rosenzweig is presented as an example of how this clouding affects even outstanding men in the ranks of the Jewish "consolidation" movement:

> Those Jews of our time who took an active part in the consolidation process, who in this way came to accept the Law and who have not been driven mad by the difficulty of believing in God, conceive of the Law differently than the Jewish tradition. I recall the outstanding man of this group, Franz Rosenzweig, who reproaches Jewish orthodoxy for de facto having granted priority to prohibitions over commands (e.g., with respect to שבת [*shabbos*; i.e., Sabbath]); in contrast, he wants to regard prohibitions only as the other side of commands. In his struggle against the rigidity of the Law, he goes so far as to want to dissolve entirely the distinction between *minhag* [custom] and *din* [law]. (RSP)

What Strauss notes here concerning Rosenzweig's alteration of the tradition, his accommodating "development" of it, is further elaborated upon and critiqued in the autobiographical preface to *Spinoza's Critique of Religion*, where Strauss speaks of Rosenzweig engaging in a "conscious and radical historicization of the Torah."[87] And over and against Rosenzweig's praise of the justice of Cohen's condemnation of Spinoza, on the ground that Spinoza should have remained faithful to a "living and hence changing tradition," "deepening" the old by reshaping it and thereby annihilating it, Strauss remarks:

> This is indeed the question: whether the loyal and loving reshaping or reinterpretation of the inherited, or the pitiless burning of the hitherto worshiped is the best form of annihilation of the antiquated, i.e. of the untrue or bad.... Is the conservatism which is generally speaking the wise maxim of practice also the sacred law of theory?[88]

Strauss, far from being "conservative" in his thinking, equates the hermeneutic "new thinking" of Rosenzweig (as well as the neo-Kantianism of Cohen) with the wise principle of conservative political practice, and *rejects* it as utterly inappropriate to theory, that is, to thinking, to an individual's serious pursuit of the truth.[89]

It is, in short, only once one has wrested oneself free of the historicizing attempts of the "new thinking," and begins to takes seriously what a return to genuine religious orthodoxy would mean, that the theologico-political problem comes to sight in its natural form. The true initial situation of the Jew is not merely as a member of a specific people, but as someone who confronts the revealed *Law*. This is how Maimonides begins his guidance of a perplexed youth—as if he were a believing Jew and even an enemy of philosophy. For as Strauss puts it in "A Giving of Accounts," "[P]hilosophy is subversive...the virtue of the philosopher's thought is a certain kind of *mania*, while the virtue of the philosopher's speech is *sophrosyne*."[90] True radicalness of *thought* will always be accompanied by an apparent conservatism. We who have grown up within modernity, in which the difference between genuinely independent thinking and thinking aimed at and hence limited by political ends has become obscured, are invited by the apparently conservative Strauss to recover this radical insight.

Notes

1. See Appendixes B and C of the present volume. I wish to thank Devin Stauffer and Stuart Witt for their helpful comments on an earlier draft of this essay.
2. The autobiographical "Preface to the English Translation" (hereafter referred to as "Preface to *SCR*") written in 1962, appears in the English translation, by Elsa M. Sinclair, of *Die Religionskritik Spinozas als Grundlage seiner Bibelwissenschaft Untersuchungen zu Spinozas Theologish-Politischen Traktat* (Berlin: Akademie-Verlag, 1930), reprinted in *GS–1* 1–361; *SCR* 1–31 (also in *LAM* 224–59 or *JPCM* 137–77). The statement on the theological-political problem appears in the German "Preface" to *Hobbes Politische Wissenschaft* (Neuwied am Rhein und Berlin: Hermann Luchterhand Verlag, 1965), the first publication of the original German manuscript of PPH. An English translation of the German Preface, by Donald J. Maletz, appeared in *Interpretation, A Journal of Political Philosophy* 8 (1979–80), 1–3 and is reprinted in *JPCM* 453–56.
3. Preface to *SCR* 1, 3.
4. These two alternatives, though distinct, were not mutually exclusive for German Jewish youth. On Rosenzweig's association with and influence upon German Zionist youth movements, see Paul Mendes-Flohr, "Rosenzweig and the Kameraden: A Non-Zionist Alliance," *Journal of Contemporary History* 26, no. 3/4 (September 1991): 385–402.

5. Strauss's first book, *Spinoza's Critique of Religion,* is dedicated to the memory of Rosenzweig. Between 1922 and 1925 Strauss worked at the *Freies Jüdisches Lehrhaus* in Frankfurt-am-Main, founded by Rosenzweig, and published articles in *Der Jude* and the *Jüdische Rundschau.* Thanks to Michael Zank, English translations of these are available in *LSEW* 63–137.
6. On the relation between Rosenzweig and Heidegger, Strauss recommends (in note 14 to the Preface to *SCR*) Karl Löwith's *Gesammelte Abhandlungen: Zur Kritik der geschichtlichen Existenz* 68–92. The German title of the essay is "M. Heidegger und F. Rosenzweig, ein Nachtrag zu Sein und Zeit.'" An English translation of the essay appeared as "M. Heidegger and F. Rosenzweig, or Temporality and Eternity" in *Philosophy and Phenomenological Research* 3, no. 1 (September 1942), 53–77. It appears as "M. Heidegger and F. Rosenzweig: A Postscript to *Being and Time*," in *NHE* 51–78.
7. Rosenzweig and Heidegger, too, attempt to set aside the superfluous and arrive at "the one" thing that is driving toward decisions "because the traditional contents of modern civilization no longer prove indisputable." *NHE* 55–56.
8. "Conspectivism" (1929), an unpublished review of Mannheim's *Ideology and Utopia.* Translated in Appendix A of this volume.
9. Strauss's impatience with what I have called "*Reader's Digest*" versions of serious thought is already present in his criticisms of Walter Kinkel's *Herman Cohen: Eine einfuuhrung in sein Werk* (Stuttgart: Strecker und Schröder, 1924), made in 1925. Strauss decries the dissolution of the "precision and consistency of Cohen's thought" for the sake of "popularity." See "The 'Jewish Writings of Hermann Cohen' by Dr. Leo Strauss" (*Jüdishe Wochenzeitung fur Cassel, Hessen und Waldeck,* Year 2, Nr. 18, May 8, 1925), 1–3. Translated into English by Michael Zank in "More Early Writings by Leo Strauss from the Jewish Weekly for Cassel, Hessen and Waldeck (1925–28)," *Interpretation* 39, no. 2 (Spring/Summer 2012), 109–37.
10. See "Existentialism," a talk given in February 1956 to the Hillel Foundation of the University of Chicago, in *Interpretation* 22, no. 3 (Spring 1995): 303–20. "Existentialism owes its overriding significance to a single man: Heidegger. Heidegger alone brought about such a radical change in philosophic thought as is revolutionizing all thought in Germany, in continental Europe, and is beginning to affect even Anglo-Saxony. I am not surprised by this effect. I remember the impression he made on me when I heard him first as a young Ph.D. in 1922. Up to that time I had been particularly impressed, as many of my contemporaries in Germany were, by Max Weber, by Weber's intransigent devotion to intellectual honesty, by his passionate devotion to the idea of science, a devotion that was combined with a profound uneasiness regarding the meaning of science. On my way north from Freiburg where Heidegger then taught, I saw in Frankfurt am main Franz Rosenzweig whose name will always be remembered when informed people speak about Existentialism, and I told him of Heidegger. I said to him: in comparison with Heidegger, Weber appeared to me as an orphan child in regard to precision, and probing, and competence. I had never seen before such seriousness, profundity, and concentration in the interpretation of philosophic texts. I had heard Heidegger's interpretation of certain sections in Aristotle. Sometime later I heard Werner Jaeger in Berlin interpret the same texts. Charity compels me to limit the comparison to the remark that there was no comparison. Gradually the breadth of the revolution of thought which Heidegger was preparing dawned upon me and my generation. We saw with our own eyes that there had been no such phenomenon in the world since Hegel" (304). See also "An Unspoken

Prologue to a Public Lecture at St. John's College in Honor of Jacob Klein, in *JPCM* 450: "Nothing affected us as profoundly in the years in which our minds took their lasting directions as the thought of Heidegger.... Certain it is that no one has questioned the premise of philosophy as radically as Heidegger."

11. This disposition—a public modesty for the sake of serious thinking, especially with respect to the work of Heidegger—is not peculiar to this talk. Much later, in the course of describing the impact of Heidegger on himself and Jacob Klein, Strauss speaks of the "all too justified abhorrence" of "publicity" or "the limelight." "An Unspoken Prologue to a Public Lecture at St. John's College in Honor of Jacob Klein," in *JPCM* 449. Similarly, in a talk written in 1940, Strauss speaks of the quiet serious work being done in German Postwar thought and, without mentioning himself, presents his own position, over and against that of Heidegger. "The Living Issues of German Postwar Philosophy" (1940), were published as an appendix (115–40) to *Leo Strauss and the Theologico-Political Problem*, by Heinrich Meier (Cambridge: Cambridge University Press, 2006). That talk also provides a helpful roadmap of the period's leading thinkers as their thought appeared to Strauss.
12. On this point, see "The Living Issues of German Postwar Philosophy," 133. And on the failure of the German intellectual authorities, liberal as well as Marxist, to understand the youthful critics of the present, see "German Nihilism" [April 1941], *Interpretation* 26, no. 3 (Spring 1999): 362: "Those opponents [of thinkers like Spengler, Schmitt, Jünger, Heidegger] committed frequently a grave mistake. They believed to have refuted the No by refuting the Yes, i.e., the inconsistent if not silly positive assertions of the young men. But one cannot refute what one has not *thoroughly* understood. And many opponents did not even *try* to understand the ardent passion underlying the negation of the present world and its potentialities. As a result, the refutations confirmed the nihilists in their belief."
13. What Strauss may have in mind here by "fate" is (among other things) the experience of "existence," allegedly made possible by both medieval theology and its belief in the creator God and by the alternative to that belief, articulated by Farabi and Avicenna, that what is, is the product of *chance*. See Emil L. Fackenheim, "The Possibility of the Universe in Al-Farabi, ibn Sina, and Maimonides," in *Proceedings of the American Academy for Jewish Research* 16 (1946–47), 39–70, which is explicitly indebted to Strauss. Already at the time of this talk Strauss had been directed by Avicenna to Plato's *Laws* for the understanding of "prophecy," and would have encountered there the Athenian Stranger's remarkable and troubling claim that we are the playthings of the gods, that is, of chance (*Laws* 804b–c).
14. Strauss elsewhere presents historicists as echoing Calvin in seeing the multiplicity of philosophic opinions as "disgraceful." *NRH* 18, and "On The Bible Science of Spinoza and His Predecessors," in *LSEW* 185.
15. Heidegger, "Was ist Metaphysik?" in *Wegmarken*, ed. F.-W. von Herrmann (Frankfurt: Klostermann, 1976), 119–20; "What is Metaphysics?" *Pathmarks*, ed. W. MacNeill (Cambridge: Cambridge University Press, 1998), 95–96. See also Karl Löwith, "Heidegger: Problem and Background of Existentialism," *NHE* 29, 38–44, and in the same volume, "M. Heidegger and F. Rosenzweig," *NHE* 67–68. Cf. Löwith's letters to Strauss, July 13, 1935 and August 18, 1946. Finally, see Strauss's letter to Gerhard Krüger, December 27, 1932: "The 'substantial and historical core' of historicism is, as you correctly say, 'the factual domination of Christ over the post-classical world.'... The immediate consequence—above all in Heidegger—is: Christianity has brought to light dimensions of human life,

that were unknown or inadequately known to ancient philosophy;... [this means] most fundamentally: after the disintegration of Christianity, there remains, and first becomes possible, a philosophy that preserves the 'truth' of Christianity; it is as such deeper and more radical than ancient philosophy. Maybe this consequence is correct—but it must be as such proven. And this is possible only on the basis of a direct confrontation of modern with ancient philosophy. That is the legitimation of my project as regards Hobbes—I mean, the direct confrontation with Plato." Translated by Thomas L. Pangle in "The Light Shed on the Crucial Development of Strauss's Thought by his Correspondence with Gerhard Krüger," chapter 3 in the present volume, pp. 129–130 above.

16. The Maimonidean text to which Strauss refers and which he partially quotes is *Guide* I 31 (ed. Munk, 34b–35a).
17. See "On the Bible Science of Spinoza and His Precursors" (1926), *LSEW* 173–200, esp. 178–81. This work is a roadmap, required by Julius Guttmann, for what would become *SCR*, completed in 1929 and finally published in 1930; the same understanding of Maimonides is present in *SCR*. It must be stressed that Strauss's rediscovery of exotericism in Maimonides goes much beyond the recognition of esotericism, driven by a fear of persecution, to be found in Spinoza's writing: Strauss had already recognized such esotericism as early as 1924. See, for example, "Cohen's Analysis of Spinoza's Bible Science," *LSEW* 140–72, especially 148, 151, 153, 158.
18. See "Preface to *Hobbes Politische Wissenschaft*," *JPCM* 454; "An Unspoken Prologue to a Public Lecture at St. John's College in Honor of Jacob Klein," *JPCM* 450; and GA-*JPCM* 462–63: "We have rediscovered exotericism."
19. CuM 424–26; CaM 216–19. I use here the translation from Avicenna that Strauss used for the epigraph of his *AAPL*. A translation of the whole passage, by Michael Marmura, reads as follows: "the treatment of kingship is contained in the book by Plato and the book by Aristotle on the regime, and the treatment of prophecy and the Law is contained in their two books on the laws." *MPP–1* 97 or *MPP–2* 75.
20. On the meaning and significance of this recovery of and return to Plato, over and against radical historicism, that is, Heidegger, see Thomas L. Pangle, "The Light Shed on the Crucial Development of Strauss's Thought by his Correspondence with Gerhard Krüger," and Christopher Bruell, "The Question of Nature and the Thought of Leo Strauss," in *Klesis, Revue Philosophique* 19, Special Issue, *Autour de Leo Strauss*, ed. Timothy Burns and Lucien Oulahbib (June 2011): 92–101.
21. That situation may perhaps best be appreciated by the counterclaims against a return to classical thought made by his friends Löwith and Krüger. On Löwith, see below, notes 22–31. On Krüger, see note 15, and see the letters to Krüger, January 7, 1930, June 26, 1930, February 7, 1931, May 7, 1931, and Pangle, "The Light Shed on the Crucial Development of Strauss's Thought by his Correspondence with Gerhard Krüger."
22. Löwith, "Nature, History, and Existentialism," *NHE* 29.
23. Löwith, "Heidegger: Problem and Background of Existentialism," *NHE* 42.
24. Löwith, "The Fate of Progress," *NHE*, 160.
25. Löwith, "Heidegger: Problem and Background of Existentialism," *NHE* 43.
26. Löwith, "Nature, History, and Existentialism," *NHE* 29.
27. Löwith, "Heidegger: Problem and Background of Existentialism," *NHE*, 49.
28. Löwith to Strauss, August 18, 1946.
29. Letter to Löwith, August 20, 1946. See also *PPH* 142–43: "Confronted with this absurd conclusion [that Anaxagorean, 'Epimethean' physics... necessarily

leads...to subjection to 'what the Athenians *believe*'] Plato does not without further ado oppose to materialist-mechanistic physics a spiritualist-telelological...but keeps...to what the 'Athenians' *say*." And see *NRH* 117ff.

30. See "The Problem of Socrates" (1956), *Interpretation* 22, no. 3 (Spring 1995): 329.
31. Löwith, "Heidegger: Problem and Background of Existentialism," *NHE* 44. See Emil L. Fackenheim, "The Possibility of the Universe in Al-Farabi, ibn Sina, and Maimonides" (cited by Löwith, *NHE* 44n8) and consider especially 54n16 and 68n30–69n31. Fackenheim repeatedly thanks Strauss for his assistance in this research.
32. See "Preface to *Hobbes Politische Wissenschaft*" in *JPCM* 453, and GA–*JPCM* 461.
33. "On the Bible Science of Spinoza and His Precursors" (1926), *LSEW* 186.
34. Ibid., 185.
35. "Sigmund Freud, The Future of an Illusion" (1928), *LSEW* 211.
36. APT 99–109, esp. 108; see also 103ff., esp. 103, 106, 109. FP 388; "The Law of Reason in the *Kuzari*," *PAW* 140–41; Preface to *SCR* 29, and see also SSTX: [P] olitical life and philosophic life...are incompatible in the last analysis: political life, if taken seriously, meant belief in the gods of the city, and philosophy is the denial of the gods of the city" (532). "[T]he large majority of men, the philosophers of the past thought, would be deprived of the very basis of their morality if they were to lose their beliefs" (535).
37. "Comments on *Der Begriff Des Politischen* by Carl Schmitt," *SCR* 344–45. The German original was published as *Die Religionskritik Spinozas als Grundlage seiner Bibelwissenschaft Untersuchungen zu Spinozas Theologisch-Politischem Traktat* (Akademie-Verlag, Berlin, 1930). See also Preface to *SCR* 19.
38. FP 383. *PAW* 17. See also Strauss's account of Platonic dialectic in *PPH* 136–69. See also *RCPR* 181: "[T]he reasoning is in Plato's dialogues integrated into the human drama. The reasoning is frequently, not to say always, faulty––deliberately faulty, as it should be within an imitation of human life."
39. "Progress or Return?" *RCPR* 248; cf. 246. See also Strauss's letter to Voegelin, February 25, 1951: "I believe still today that the *theioi nomoi* is the common ground of the Bible and philosophy––humanly speaking." *FPP* 78. See also Leo Strauss "On the Interpretation of Genesis" [1957], *L'Homme* 21, no. 1 (janvier–mars 1981): 6, where Strauss refers to "the agreement as well as the disagreement between the biblical and the Greek heritage."
40. See the very last topic listed in the outline of the 1932 talk: " v.) *Plato and the Nomos* and *Revelation*."
41. How to Begin to Study Medieval Philosophy," 216–17. See also "On Classical Political Philosophy," *WIPP* 92. That Strauss had already arrived at this understanding at the time of these talks is evident from the concluding part of CuM 419–29; CaM 209–22.
42. What we see here corresponds, in other words, to what Strauss later calls "the self-destruction of historicism": "The study of earlier thought, if conducted with intelligence and assiduity, leads to a revitalization of earlier ways of thinking. The historian who started out with the conviction that true understanding of human thought is understanding of every teaching in terms of its particular time or as an expression of its particular time, necessarily familiarizes himself with the view, constantly urged upon him by his subject matter, that his initial conviction is unsound. More than that: he is brought to realize that one cannot understand the thought of the past as long as one is guided by that initial conviction," *PAW* 158.

One might add that with the Platonic attention to the problem of contingency, the case for Heidegger's "metaphysics of presence" to explain the alleged blindness of the ancients to contingency loses its force.

43. As he later expressed this in a general principle, "By bringing the process to light, we free ourselves from the power of the result." "The Living Issues of German Postwar Philosophy," 134.
44. Strauss elaborates on the "pit beneath the cave" in "How To Study Spinoza's *Theologico-Political Treatise*," *PAW* 155–56.
45. GA–*JPCM* 463–64.
46. GA–*JPCM* 464.
47. Spinoza had attributed belief in miracles to "prejudice" (*SCR* 134ff.), and already in *SCR*, Strauss had distinguished this struggle against prejudice from the natural struggle of classical philosophy against "appearance and opinion" (*SCR* 178–81).
48. In "The Living Issues of German Postwar Philosophy" Strauss credits Nietzsche with introducing him to the notion of an artificial cave protecting one from the elementary problems, a cave visible as "the pre-modern tradition (of providence) and also of "the modern tradition" (138–39).
49. For a helpful elaboration on Strauss's understanding of Nietzsche's (flawed) attempt to return to the ancients, see his correspondence with Löwith, June 23, 1935, Löwith's response on June 28, 1935 and July 13, 1935, and Strauss's rejoinder on July 17, 1935. These were published, with English translations, in *The Independent Journal of Philosophy* 2 (1978): 5–12, and ibid. 4 (1983): 105–19. See especially Strauss to Löwith, June 23, 1935: "I think that you do not take seriously enough those intentions of Nietzsche which point beyond Nietzsche's teaching. You do not enter into these enough. For it is not sufficient simply to stop where Nietzsche is no longer right; rather one must ask whether or not Nietzsche himself became untrue to his intention to repeat antiquity, and did so as a result of his confinement within modern presuppositions or in polemics against these."
50. See *PLB* 9.
51. *SCR* 135, 146.
52. *NRH* 169–70, 172; cf. 311–12 and 319 with 20 and 29–30.
53. *Die Religionskritik Spinozas*, 50–51, 61, 209–10, 224; see also *PLB* 17, and Preface to *SCR* 29.
54. See Christopher Bruell, "The Question of Nature and the Thought of Leo Strauss," *Klesis: Revue Philosophique* 19 Special Issue, *Autour de Leo Strauss*, ed. Timothy Burns and Lucien Oulahbib, (June 2011): 92–101.
55. "Living Issues of German Postwar Philosophy," 135.
56. Strauss to Löwith, August 20, 1946.
57. Ibid. See also the first part of Chapter 6 of *NRH*.
58. See *NRH* 316 and the accompanying note 102.
59. GA–*JPCM* 463–64: "The high point was reached in Kant's teaching on the primacy of practical, i.e., moral reason, a teaching prepared to some extent by Rousseau: the one thing needful is a good will, and of a good will all men are equally capable."
60. See the review of Paul de Lagarde's work in *LSEW* 90. And for an extended examination of the Historical School, see *NRH*, Ch. 1.
61. Strauss's letter to Löwith, August 20, 1946. To the quoted statement, Strauss adds "Cf. Savigny, *Beruf*." Friedrich Carl von Savigny was one of the founders of the German Historical School of jurisprudence; it stood in opposition to appeals to modern rationalist natural law doctrine (*Vernunftsrecht*) which, with the export of

the principles of the French Revolution by Napoleon, were being made all over Europe. *Beruf* refers to his 1814 pamphlet *Vom Beruf unserer Zeit für Gesetzgebung und Rechtswissenschaft* (new edition, 1892). For a discussion of the Historical School and its preparation by Burke's doctrine of "prescription," see Strauss's Autumn, 1963 University of Chicago course on Vico, 10–12 of the original transcript. See also the second part of Chapter 6 of *NRH*.

62. *NRH* 311–12. On Burke's embrace of Democritean-Epicurean physics as the ground of his skepticism, see *NRH* 311–12 with 169–70 and 172. On his faith in divine providence as behind and observable in the humanly unintended or accidental results of history, see *NRH* 316ff.
63. *NRH* 320–21.
64. See the last sentence of this section, where Strauss refers to *megalopsychia*. Cf. CuM 407; CaM 194.
65. *NRH* 26.
66. Strauss to Löwith, June 23, 1935, emphasis added. On the moderns's "rebellion" to which Strauss here alludes, and the role of biblical faith in that rebellion, see *CM* 41–43. Strauss there suggests that while the modern resolve to liberate man from nature appears, to the moderns themselves, to be less naive than Aristotle's understanding of nature, it is better understood as a failure of resignation, a disappointed hope in the existence of a caring God and a consequent, confused sense of a "right to rebel," in order to do for humanity what such a God would have done. See Timothy Burns, "Leo Strauss on the Origins of Hobbes's Natural Science," chapter 7 of the present volume, note 20, pp. 142–44.
67. See "The Living Issues of German Postwar Philosophy," 134: "[W]hen studying the genesis of historical consciousness, we look at it with the eyes of pre-modern philosophy—we stand on the other side of the fence."
68. Contrast Colin Loader, *The Intellectual Development of Karl Mannheim* (Cambridge: Cambridge University Press, 1985), 25–27, 96–101.
69. "The Living Issues of German Postwar Philosophy." Mannheim is discussed on 129–130.
70. As Strauss makes clear in his 1932 review of Schmitt's *The Concept of the Political*, he considered Schmitt to have succumbed, through historicism, to a version of "presentism." "Comments on *Der Begriff des Politischen*" (1932), published in translation in *SCR* 331–51. As Strauss argues, to Schmitt, "'all mind is only present mind'; 'all mental concepts [of the spiritual-intellectual sphere]...can be understood only from the concrete political existence' and...'all political concepts, ideas and words have a polemical meaning'" (*SCR* 331). Schmitt had, to be sure, hoped to launch a *critique* of the present, of liberalism. And he had accordingly been critical of Mannheimian liberal syntheses: "Agreement at any price is possible only as agreement at the price of the meaning of human life, for such agreement is possible only when man abandons the task of raising the question regarding what is right, and when he abandons this question, he abandons humanity" (*SCR* 348). To this extent, there is agreement between Strauss and Schmitt. But to Schmitt, the state of nature is to be returned to over and against "civilization," in the manner that Heidegger recommends being toward death, over and against "everydayness": "Affirmation of the state of nature does not mean affirmation of war, but 'relinquishment of the security of the *status quo*.' Security is relinquished, not because war is something 'ideal,' but because one must return from 'dazzling representation,' from the 'comforts and convenience of the existing *status quo*,' to the 'cultural or social void,' to the 'mysterious, unimpressive origin,' to 'undefiled,

uncorrupted nature,' so that 'by virtue of pure, unpolluted knowledge...the order of human things' may arise afresh'" (*SCR* 348). So too, Schmitt thinks that evaluating the political "would be a 'free, untestable decision'" (*SCR* 349). His true aim, according to Strauss, is against atheistic, this-worldly, anarchistic socialism and technology; liberalism merely gets in the way of this real aim, as would-be mediator, whom he would gesture aside with contempt, in the name of "the opposite spirit and faith, which it seems, does not yet have a name" (*SCR* 350–51). Strauss may imply that that name is National Socialism *or* some kind of otherworldly activism. Schmitt has in any event not yet escaped liberalism, according to Strauss; he remains entangled in a polemic against it. "This involvement is no accidental failure but is the necessary consequence of the principle that 'all concepts of the spiritual-intellectual sphere...can be understood only from the concrete political existence,' and that 'all political concepts, ideas and words have a polemical meaning'" (*SCR* 351). Strauss finds that this principle is "itself altogether based on liberal presuppositions" (*SCR* 351). That is, it begins with the prepolitical right of the individual. Schmitt's "presentism," as it were, causes him to be unable to get outside of liberalism.

71. *Gesamtausgabe* 34, 86. This, and the Mannheim statement about Heidegger are quoted by Rüdiger Safranski in *Martin Heidegger: Between Good and Evil* [translation of *Ein Meister aus Deutschland*], trans. Ewald Osers (Cambridge, MA: Harvard University Press, 1998), 214.
72. "The Living Issues of German Postwar Philosophy," 129–30. Consider also Strauss's brief remark, in the 1929 review of *Ideology and Utopia*, on Mannheim's treatment of fascism, and the following remark in the autobiographical preface to *SCR*: "It was obvious that Heidegger's new thinking led far away from any charity as well as from any humanity" (*SCR* 9). Strauss argues in the Preface to *SCR* that biblical thinking would be an explicit, key component of the new synthesis: "Heidegger wishes to expel from philosophy the last relics of Christian theology like the notions of 'eternal truths' and 'the idealized absolute subject.' But the understanding of man which he opposes to the Greek understanding of man as the rational animal is, as he emphasizes, primarily the Biblical understanding of man as created in the image of God. Accordingly, he interprets human life in the light of 'being towards death,' 'anguish,' 'conscience,' and 'guilt'" (*SCR* 12). Contrast Karl Löwith, who finds Heidegger's fundamental concepts—death, conscience, guilt, anxiety, fear, and corruption—to have a "hidden history" in "the Christian tradition," such that Heidegger was "unconsciously" prevented from presenting certain acts (like suicide) as consistent with an independent, resolute existence. "M. Heidegger and F. Rosenzweig," in *NHE* 67–68. See also Ch. 3 of the same volume, "Heidegger: Problem and Background of Existentialism": "I think it would be very difficult to refute the so-called 'nihilism' of existential ontology, on theoretical as well as *moral* grounds, unless one believes in man and world as a creation of God or in the cosmos as a divine and eternal order—in other words, unless one is not 'modern'" (*NHE* 38). "The fundamental limitation of Greek ontology is, in regard to the problem of Being, that it understands man's being and Being in general in orientation to the *world* as *cosmos* and *physis*, and in regard to the problem of Time, that it takes its orientation from what is *present* and *always present* or eternal" (*NHE* 39–40).
73. "There was a famous discussion between Heidegger and Ernst Cassirer in Davos which revealed the lostness and emptiness of this remarkable representative of established academic philosophy to everyone who had eyes. Cassirer had been

a pupil of Hermann Cohen, the founder of the Marburg neo-Kantian School. Cohen had elaborated a system of philosophy whose center was ethics. Cassirer had transformed Cohen's system into a new system of philosophy in which ethics had completely disappeared: it had been silently dropped. He had not *faced* the problem. Heidegger did face the problem. He declared that ethics is impossible and his whole being was permeated by the awareness that this fact opens up an abyss." "Existentialism," 304. For a helpful analysis of the discussion at Davos, see Peter Eli Gordon, *Continental Divide: Heidegger, Cassirer, Davos* (Cambridge: Harvard University Press, 2010), Ch. 4.

74. As Löwith explains, "only when a decision is in the making, is the necessary vagueness of its 'for what' replaced by a definite aim. To make up one's mind depends on the actual possibilities of the historical situations. Hence, Heidegger refuses to be positive or even authoritative as to existential liabilities....The resolve, thus does not come to any conclusion; it is a constant attitude, formal like the categorical imperative and through its formality open to any material determination, provided it is radical." "M. Heidegger and F. Rosenzweig," *NHE* 66.
75. GA–*JPCM* 457–66. "What I could not stomach was his moral teaching, for despite his disclaimer he had such a teaching. The key term is 'resoluteness,' without any indication as to what are the proper objects of resoluteness" (GA–*JPCM* 461).
76. *Sein und Zeit*, 299.
77. As Strauss puts it in "The Intellectual Situation of the Present," "[t]he 'free decision of the person' that does not want to depend on any justification 'does not take place in a vacuum.' It is conditioned by the *history* in which the person concerned stands."
78. *Sein und Zeit*, 385; cf. 383–84, 299–300, 391
79. *Sein und Zeit*, Sections 78–81. See Karl Löwith, "M. Heidegger and F. Rosenzweig," *NHE* 73–74.
80. "There is a straight line which leads from Heidegger's resoluteness to his siding with the so-called Nazis in 1933. After that I ceased to take any interest in him for about two decades." GA–*JPCM* 461.
81. See *NRH* 175–76, and Timothy Burns, "Leo Strauss on the Origins of Hobbes's Natural Science," chapter 7 of the present volume.
82. Nietzsche's Word: "God Is Dead," in *Holzwege* (1950), trans. Julian Young and Kenneth Haynes as *Off The Beaten Track* (Cambridge: Cambridge University Press, 2002), 160.
83. "An Unspoken Prologue to a Public Lecture at St. John's College in Honor of Jacob Klein," *JPCM* 450, emphasis added. See also GA–*JPCM* 457–66. "In 1925 Heidegger came to Marburg. Klein attended his classes regularly, and he was, naturally, deeply impressed by him. But he did not become a Heideggerian. Heidegger's work required and included what he called *Destruktion* of the tradition....He intended to uproot Greek philosophy, especially Aristotle, but this presupposed the laying bare of its roots, the laying bare of it as it was in itself and not as it had come to appear in the light of the tradition and of modern philosophy. Klein was more attracted by the Aristotle brought to light and life by Heidegger than by Heidegger's own philosophy. Later Klein turned to the study of Plato, in which he got hardly any help from Heidegger. Klein convinced me of two things. First, the one thing needed philosophically is in the first place a return to, a recovery of, classical philosophy; second, the way in which Plato is read, especially by professors of philosophy and by men who do philosophy, is

wholly inadequate because it does not take into account the dramatic character of the dialogues, also and especially of those of their parts which look almost like philosophic treatises" (GA–*JPCM* 462).

84. "The Living Issues of German Postwar Philosophy," 135 and 137.
85. See also on this point *PLB* 8–9.
86. *Kleinere Schriften* (Berlin: Schocken, 1937), 363. Quoted by Löwith in "M. Heidegger and F. Rosenzweig," *NHE* 55.
87. Preface to *SCR* 8–15, 22–28, esp. 14.
88. Preface to *SCR* 25; cf. 27 on Cohen. Strauss is aware that in the passage of Cohen's *Religion of Reason Out of the Sources of Judaism* (*Religion der Vernunft*, ch. X, §19) that he here quotes, Cohen himself rhetorically puts the question of annihilating the tradition. See CuM 401; CaM 185–86.
89. See also "The Living Issues of German Postwar Philosophy," 115: "We may go so far as to say that, generally speaking, German philosophy implies a more or less radical criticism of the very idea of civilization and especially of modern civilization—a criticism disastrous in the political field but necessary in the philosophical, in the theoretical field."
90. GA–*JPCM* 463. Cf. *SA* 137 and 281–82, with *CM* 229–30.

CHAPTER 6

CARL SCHMITT AND STRAUSS'S RETURN TO PREMODERN PHILOSOPHY

Nasser Behnegar

By his own account Strauss's "Anmerkungen Zu Carl Schmitt, *Der Begriff des Politischen*" (hereafter referred to as "Comments")[1]—the only German essay he published in English—marks the pivotal moment of his life, the moment when he first expressed the possibility and even the necessity of a return to premodern philosophy:

> The present study [his book on Spinoza, which was completed in 1928] was based on the premise, sanctioned by powerful prejudice, that a return to pre-modern philosophy is impossible. The change of orientation which found its first expression, not entirely by accident, in the article published at the end of this volume ["Comments," originally published in 1932] compelled me to engage in a number of studies in the course of which I became ever more attentive to the manner in which heterodox thinkers of earlier ages wrote their books.[2]

What is at stake in this reorientation Strauss indicates by recollecting a train of reasoning from Spinoza to Nietzsche that terminates in the dethroning of reason and the "victory of orthodoxy" over philosophy.[3] While he could not reject the logic of this development, Strauss had philosophical, political, and even religious reasons for being dissatisfied with its outcome, which dissatisfaction led him to wonder whether "the self-destruction of reason" is "the inevitable outcome of modern rationalism as distinguished from pre-modern rationalism."[4] Thus, for Strauss the fate of rationalism or philosophy came to depend on the soundness of premodern philosophy. Although Strauss does not explain here the substance or the power of the objection against premodern philosophy, he implies that the "Comments" disarms that objection, at least insofar as he understood it then. Being the first "expression" or articulation[5] of his change of orientation, the "Comments" is his first meaningful step toward the vindication of philosophy or the life of reason.

But is not Strauss being somewhat forgetful here? After all, in 1931 Strauss published a review of *On the Progress of Metaphysics* in which he praised Ebbinghaus for rejecting the modern "prejudice that *the* truth has not already been found in the past." There he speaks for the first time of his notion of modernity as a cave beneath the natural cave, and of the necessity of the historical recovery of the original cave "from which Socrates can lead us to light."[6] Given that Ebbinghaus was in Strauss's mind in 1964–65 (he refers to him in his introduction to *Hobbes' politische Wissenschaft*),[7] it is more likely that his disregard of that review is due to his sense of its inadequacy. There Strauss argues that modern progress has led to "the anarchy of systems" and that the proper response to our ignorance is to read old books with the aim of learning from them or to move from our historical ignorance to the natural ignorance that was the starting point of Socratic thinking. Yet it is possible to break with the Socratic tradition while knowing the natural cave and the natural ignorance: "In [a horizon beyond liberalism] Hobbes completed the foundation of liberalism" ("Comments," ¶35).[8] A return to premodern philosophy requires a criticism of the roots of the modern philosophy as well as of its results. The Ebbinghaus review does not even examine these roots, which come to view only in an attempt to carry out a radical criticism of modernity.

According to Strauss, it was "not entirely by accident" that his questioning of the modern rejection of premodern philosophy found its first expression in the "Comments." That there is at least some essential connection between Schmitt's thought and Strauss's turn to premodern philosophy is evident from the startling final sentences of the "Comments": "A radical critique of liberalism is thus possible only on the basis of an adequate understanding of Hobbes. To show what can be learned from Schmitt in order to achieve that urgent task was therefore the main concern of our comments" (¶35). Since Strauss in the "Comments" characterizes Hobbes as the founder of liberalism, this adequate understanding of Hobbes is necessarily a critical one.[9]

What precisely did Strauss learn about Hobbes through his criticism of Schmitt's position? This question, which Strauss identifies as the main concern of the "Comments," receives scant attention in the most impressive and influential account of this exchange. For Heinrich Meier, Schmitt is a political theologian, a man whose political position rests on his Catholic faith; Strauss a political philosopher, a man whose views (political or otherwise) rest on evidence available to man as man; and the gulf dividing them is an "insuperable" one.[10] When one frames the encounter between Schmitt and Strauss as that between a political theologian and a political philosopher, the theme of the critique of modernity is apt to disappear, and so it does in Meier's reading. Whether Meier's understanding of Schmitt is correct is beyond the scope of this chapter;[11] it is, however, necessary to point out (as Meier himself initially acknowledges) that it does not accord with Strauss's exposition of Schmitt's position.[12] For Strauss, Schmitt is a critic of modernity who is also a modern man, an opponent of liberalism whose position in part rests on liberal presuppositions, presuppositions incompatible with those of Biblical faith and of premodern philosophy.

The "Comments" is an extraordinary record of one serious man understanding another. "You've got to read this [the 'Comments']," Schmitt said to his assistant. "He saw through me and X-rayed me as nobody else has."[13] The "Comments" not only marks the moment of Strauss's return to premodern philosophy; it also marks the moment in which Strauss's prodigious interpretive powers came into their own. Strauss follows Schmitt's arguments in their own terms—step by step—until he arrives at the true foundation of his position. We witness Strauss's attention to contradictions, both between different statements of Schmitt's and between a statement and what is implied in an argument; his grasp of the difficulties that caused these contradictions; and his uncanny gift of discerning which side of a contradiction expresses Schmitt's deeper opinion. In the end Strauss understands Schmitt better than Schmitt understood himself because he tries to understand Schmitt exactly as he understood himself. In exposing Schmitt's numerous contradictions, he at the same time reveals Schmitt's thoughtfulness; he reveals him as a modern man trying to break through the modern prison. The "Comments" is indeed "very critical,"[14] but it is also very helpful in a way that few criticisms are. Schmitt's grateful reception[15] testifies to this as it does to his own intellectual seriousness, for such criticisms, as it hardly needs saying, are not always taken as the gifts that they are.

In the interpretation that follows, I attempt to identify the roots of the controversy between premodern and modern philosophy as they manifest themselves in the "Comments." I do this by focusing on the twists and turns of Strauss's argument. But to makes these intelligible I reproduce Strauss's argument in a manner that necessarily suffers in comparison to the original.

Schmitt's Intention and Strauss's Hermeneutic Principle

The "Comments" begins with a contradiction that is not fully resolved until the very end of the work. Schmitt's exposition of the concept of the political is an attempt to understand the state radically, for the state presupposes the political. This attempt has become necessary on account of the contemporary dissolution of the consensus regarding the purpose of the state (as evident in the tension between the limited liberal state and the total state of democratic or mass movements). Thus, the contemporary crisis has caused Schmitt to raise and address a general question, the question of "the order of human things," which Schmitt identifies with the question of the state (¶1). Yet, Strauss observes that this account, derived from Schmitt's own statements, is inconsistent with Schmitt's "general principles of understanding," which deny the existence of "eternal truths," understand all concepts of the spiritual sphere "in terms of their concrete political existence," and maintain the polemical character of "all political concepts, presentations, and words" (¶2). Strauss thus tries to understand Schmitt in light of his own principles of understanding. Schmitt's attempt to answer the question of the state rests on the premise that "the political precedes the state," which premise is asserted in opposition to liberalism, the movement in which the modern goal of neutralization and depoliticization has reached "its greatest efficacy" (¶3). Since liberalism attempted to construct the rational society by denying the political (through its individualism, and its insistence of autonomy of the spheres of economics, ethics, art, and religion), the failure of liberalism has persuaded Schmitt that an adequate account of the state must first posit the political: "Schmitt's basic thesis is completely dependent on the polemic against liberalism; it can only be understood as a polemical thesis, 'only from concrete political existence'" (¶3). While the guiding question of Schmitt's treatise is unpolemical, universal, and transhistorical, his attempt to prepare an answer to it is completely polemical, concrete, time-bound.

Yet Strauss implies that there is something philosophical about Schmitt's polemic against liberalism. Schmitt sees the failure of liberalism in its self-contradictory character: its attempt to banish the political from the world leads only to carrying out politics "by means of anti-political speech" (¶4). He objects to liberalism because it obscures reality: "Liberalism has not killed the political, but merely killed understanding of the political" (¶4). Accordingly, his intention is not to bring down liberalism by provoking the indignation of the masses; rather, he attempts to find a genuine alternative to liberalism (¶5). Of the difficulties of this task he has a rare grasp. Liberalism may contradict reality but liberal thought is "astonishingly consistent" and saturates the intellectual and moral horizon of European man. Accordingly, he maintains that liberalism has not been replaced by any other system even in thought, which assertion provokes Strauss's extraordinary assessment: "by this awareness he [Schmitt] stands alone among the opponents of liberalism, who usually carry in their pocket a fully-worked out illiberal theory" (¶6). Strauss suggests, and the essay ultimately proves, that Schmitt himself is forced to use liberal elements not just for rhetorical reasons but because his own thought is entangled with them. To his credit, Schmitt was to some extent aware of this state of affairs and therefore presented his work in a provisional manner. From this Strauss draws a principle of interpretation: "the critic is in duty bound to consider more wherein Schmitt differs from the prevailing view than wherein he follows it" (¶6). This means that when one sees a contradiction in Schmitt's thought it is likely (all things being equal) that the nonliberal element is expressive of his deeper opinion.

Hobbes's State of Nature and the Idea of Culture

Strauss here argues that Schmitt's concept of the political (his contention that the distinction between friends and enemies is the ultimate political distinction) is meant to provide a radical criticism of the idea of culture as the intellectual framework within which the state is to be understood. This criticism in turn leads him to restore and reexamine Hobbes's notion of the state of nature as the true ground of the state.

But what is culture? And why does Schmitt's polemic against liberalism lead him to criticize it? According to Strauss, the philosophy of culture is "the ultimate self-consciousness of liberalism" (¶14). Liberalism subordinates the state to society; the former does not rule but protects the latter. The philosophy of culture maintains that all human affairs (both the state and society) are the product of the sovereign creation of the human mind. It thus incorporates idealism's critique of earlier thought (its contention that the human mind orders our reality) into the liberal understanding of both the state and society. It further divides society into different independent domains (economics, aesthetics, morality, etc.) with their own independent criteria. This means, for instance, that morality, the ultimate distinction of which is between good and evil, cannot have authority over economic and aesthetic affairs, which have their own ultimate distinctions (profitable and unprofitable; beautiful and ugly). It thus protects different domains of society, especially the world of art and business, from intervention from other domains in the affairs of the state, expanding the liberal spirit of the society. Now, Strauss observes that some of Schmitt's comments give the impression that he merely wants to recognize the political as an independent domain along with the other domains. In other words, it appears that Schmitt wants to elevate the place of the state (giving it the same autonomy enjoyed by the different spheres of society) while preserving the liberal aspirations for autonomy (¶8). But other comments show that this cannot be his intention: "the distinction between friend and enemy is '*not equivalent and analogous*... to those other distinctions'; the political does *not* describe 'a new *domain* of its own'" (¶7). Indeed, Schmitt's concept of the political does more than preserve the autonomy of politics. The distinction between friend and enemy (enemy meaning public enemy) presupposes the possibility of war, and the possibility of men physically killing each other is the extreme possibility not only in politics but also in all human life. In such a situation, this distinction simply becomes the authoritative distinction. The claims of artists, businessmen, and moralists give way to that of the statesmen when the existence of a country is threatened. While such threats do not always exist, their ever-present possibility casts its light on the normal situation. Schmitt's concept of the political is meant to establish the authority of the political (¶9).[16]

But the authoritativeness of politics is incompatible with the understanding of politics as a kind of cultural phenomenon: no creation of the human mind can exercise an authority over that mind. Strauss discerns in Schmitt a desire to criticize the whole notion of culture. He notes that Schmitt expressly maintains that in order to define the political one must begin not with the genus to which the political belongs but with what is specific to the political. Since no adequate definition of a thing can do without its genus, Schmitt's choice of a partial definition of the political implies that he intends to pioneer "a path to an original answer to the genus question by using the phenomenon of the political to push the most obvious answer [culture] ad absurdum" (¶7). Strauss shows what is entailed in Schmitt's will to deny that politics is fundamentally a cultural phenomenon by deconstructing the idea of culture. Culture is the cultivation of nature, and therefore presupposes the notion of nature. The liberal notion of culture as the sovereign creation of the mind is possible "only if the nature being cultivated has been presupposed to be the *opposite* of mind, and been *forgotten*" (¶10). A critical inquiry into this notion of culture demands that one should articulate the natural state of men. While Hobbes's civil state is consistent with the liberal notion of culture, his account of the state of nature in some ways mirrors Schmitt's concept of the political. Hobbes's state of nature is a state of war, not in the sense of actual fighting but of known disposition to fighting. Hobbes's state of nature is "the genuinely *political* status" (¶11). Accordingly, Strauss notes that Schmitt restores "the Hobbesian concept of the state of nature to a place of honor" (¶11).[17] Politics is not fundamentally a cultural phenomenon because politics is the natural state (order) of man. For Schmitt politics is natural because "there is a *primary* tendency in human nature to form *exclusive groups*."[18]

While Schmitt restores the seventeenth-century concept of the state of nature, he also changes much of its content, turning it into a political state. Strauss exposes the difference between the Hobbesian concept of the state of nature and Schmitt's own concept:

> For Hobbes, it is the state of war of individuals; for Schmitt, it is the state of war of groups (especially) nations. For Hobbes, in the state of nature everyone is the enemy of everyone else; for Schmitt, all political behavior is oriented toward *friend* and enemy. (¶12)

Strauss suggests that Schmitt's notion is the truer one, for Hobbes's account is corrupted by his polemical intention. Hobbes conceived the state of nature as the war of all against all because he wanted to show the necessity of abandoning the state of nature (¶12). The two accounts are more than just different; they are opposed to each other; insofar as Hobbes's state of nature was designed with the view of being negated, it is the presupposition of the liberalism against which Schmitt is fighting. This is already evident in the political teaching that Hobbes himself draws from the state of nature. Hobbes rejects Schmitt's contention that a political community has the right to "demand... from the members of its own nation *the readiness to die*" (¶13). Hobbes conceives of the public good in a way that leads "to the ideal of civilization, that is, to the demand for rational social relations of humanity as *a single* 'partnership in consumption and production'" (¶13). By being the founder of the ideal of civilization, Hobbes is also the founder of liberalism: his articulation of that right to secure mere life "has fully the character of an inalienable human right, that is, of an individual's *claim* that takes precedence over the state" (¶13).

The philosophy of culture presupposes Hobbes's state of nature. Schmitt's critique of the philosophy of culture leads him both to restore the cognitive claim of this forgotten basis and to criticize its content: "Schmitt returns, contrary to liberalism, to its author, Hobbes, in order to strike at the root of liberalism in Hobbes' express negation of the state of nature" (¶14). While Hobbes negates the state of nature, Schmitt affirms it. By observing this Strauss goes beyond Schmitt's own self-understanding. Though by the time of the second edition of "*The Concept of the Political*" Schmitt may have become aware of a tension between his position and that of Hobbes (¶14n), it is doubtful that he conceived of Hobbes as his fundamental adversary. Perhaps he failed to see this because he was impressed by Hobbes's argument for obedience to the state (individuals ought to obey the state because it protects them) and by Hobbes's recognition of what Strauss calls here "the natural evil of man" (¶13). Nonetheless, Strauss's contention remains valid. Whether he knew it or not, Schmitt's thought involves a confrontation with Hobbes's concept of the state of nature. This is the theme of Strauss's final section, which theme explains the otherwise surprising final sentences of the work.

From Necessity to Morality: Schmitt's Confrontation with Hobbes

In the final section of the "Comments," Strauss shows step by step that Schmitt's moral aloofness hides an intense moral seriousness. He takes us from Schmitt's claim that one only needs to recognize the reality of the political, to the claim that one only needs to recognize its necessity, to the claim that one must recognize its desirability, and finally to the claim that the political is a demand of moral seriousness. On the one hand, he traces this movement to reflections that require the abandonment of the fundamental premise underlying the Hobbesian concept of the state of nature. On the other hand, he traces Schmitt's resistance to that movement (or his will to conceive of the political in amoral terms) to his acceptance of that premise.

Strauss begins with Schmitt's claim that it is immaterial whether one recognizes "the political as desirable or detestable" so long as one recognizes its undeniable reality (¶15). He observes that Schmitt's intent here is the opposite of that which animates value-free social science. He does not want to leave open but to close "all possibilities for taking an evaluative stance toward the political" (¶15). Any attempt to evaluate the political presupposes a standpoint higher than the political. Any such attempt leads to degradation of the political: "the political is constituted by reference 'to the real possibility of physical killing' of men by men; and 'there is no rational purpose, no norm however correct...that can justify men's killing one another for its own sake'" (¶15). But if the political cannot be evaluated, how can it be a guiding principle for the state? The political could be a guiding principle if it were inescapable, if it were a basic and necessary character of human life (¶18). Schmitt sometimes is satisfied with less. Since according to him all concepts are related to their time, he occasionally writes as if it is enough to know that the political constitutes our present reality, that today men still form exclusive groups with the view of the possibility of war (¶16). This response, however, is inadequate, for existing groups act with a view to the future and "there is *today* a powerful movement striving toward the total elimination of the real possibility of war and hence the abolition of the political" (¶17; emphasis added, N.B.). Since Schmitt's position is especially directed against such movement, Strauss argues that he, more than others, cannot ignore its hope for the future. Schmitt is not always oblivious to this difficulty. Accordingly, he argues that every attempt to abolish the political or the possibility of war has to take a political form if it is to succeed: it has to become a "war against war." But such wars are likely to be especially inhumane, for the enemy is understood to be the enemy of humanity and hence a monster. The attempt to preserve humanity by eliminating war only leads to an increase in inhumanity. Even if the pacifists win they will lose, because the inhumanity that such a war engenders forces men to form exclusive groups to defend themselves from each other (¶18). Politics cannot end because the dangerous character of man cannot be eliminated: "the thesis of man's dangerousness is the ultimate presupposition of the position of the political" (¶19).[19]

Having articulated what at first glance appears as a perfect summary of Schmitt's position, Strauss argues that this train of thought is "not Schmitt's last word, and it is certainly not the most profound thing that he has to say" (¶20). Schmitt cannot maintain the inescapable necessity of the political, because he cannot claim to know that man will always be evil or dangerous. Schmitt himself "qualifies the thesis of man's dangerousness as a '*supposition*,' as an 'anthropological confession of *faith*'" (¶21). As we shall see, Strauss shows that given his understanding of human evil Schmitt could not rule out the possibility of man becoming tame in the future (¶26). This means that the attempt to end all war does not need to take place through a "war against war." Schmitt's argument for the inescapability of the political presupposed the existence of at least one political opposition (between pacifists and nonpacifists), but this opposition could disappear because nonpacifists can gradually disappear (¶22). Man may escape his political situation. Hence, the political is important to Schmitt neither because he recognizes its reality nor because he recognizes its necessity, but because he recognizes its desirability. He does not merely posit the political but says yes to it (¶23).

Why does Schmitt affirm the political? In other words, why does he affirm the dangerousness of man? Schmitt argues that political actions are motivated by existential as opposed to normative considerations. But, Strauss argues, one cannot politically affirm the political: the dangerousness of man cannot be affirmed existentially, because one cannot wish one's enemies to be dangerous (¶ 24). It can be affirmed only morally. Strauss discerns two different moral sentiments that inform Schmitt's affirmation of the political, and which generally characterize the position of the Right: warlike morality and authoritarianism. One can affirm the dangerousness of man because one honors men who can defend their country; one can also affirm it because it renders authority necessary.[20] Strauss argues that Schmitt's preference for authoritarianism over anarchism, and not his preference for bellicose nationalism over international pacifism, is the true motive for his affirmation of the political, partly because Schmitt raises the question of the dangerousness of man in the context of a world state that does not face threats from the outside (¶25). But why does Schmitt prefer authoritarian political theories to anarchistic theories?

Strauss does not explicitly raise this question, but he does implicitly answer it in the course of a criticism of Schmitt's effort to ground authoritarian political theory in a thesis about human evil. For Schmitt "the quarrel between the authoritarian and the anarchistic theories concerns whether man is by nature evil or good. But 'evil' and 'good,' here are '*not* to be taken in a specifically *moral* or ethical sense' but are to be understood as 'dangerous' and 'undangerous'" (¶26).[21] Strauss clarifies with the help of Schmitt the meaning of the two ways of understanding human evil. An evil man can be either a defective human being or a blameless man whose natural powers are harmful to others. The latter was the sense in which seventeenth-century thinkers such as Hobbes and Spinoza understood human evil. Schmitt regards evil in the latter sense as a possible and even the preferable basis of his political theory, while Strauss denies this possibility. Strauss shows this by first stating the reasons that led Hobbes to develop this notion of evil: "Hobbes had to understand evil as *innocent* 'evil' because he denied sin; and he had to deny sin because he did not recognize any primary obligation of man that takes precedence over every claim *qua* justified claim, because he understood man as by nature free, that is, without obligation" (¶26). This understanding of human evil is compatible not only with liberalism but also with anarchism: "Once one understands man's evil as the innocent 'evil' of the beast, but of a beast that can become astute through injury and thus can be educated, the limits one set for education finally become a matter of mere *supposition*" (¶26). Schmitt then had attempted to ground his authoritarian political theory on a view of man that actually supports the position of his opponents.[22] According to Strauss, Schmitt's attempt at a radical criticism of liberalism requires him "to return to the view of human evil as moral baseness or depravity; only in this way can Schmitt remain in harmony with himself if indeed 'the core of the political idea' is 'the *morally* demanding decision'" (¶26). Strauss's use of this passage from *Political Theology* makes it clear that the notion of human evil as moral depravity is necessary not because it preserves the thesis of man's dangerousness but because it restores the connection between politics and morality that Schmitt had discerned in that earlier work, a connection that apparently had become obscured by the time he wrote *The Concept of the Political.* Insofar as authoritarian governments are necessary to correct the moral depravity of man, Schmitt's affirmation of the political, his choice of authoritarian political theory over and against liberal and anarchistic ones, is rooted in his concern with morality.

Indeed, Strauss makes this point explicit by noticing the moralizing character of Schmitt's "polemic against the ideal that corresponds to the negation of the political," an aspect of his polemic that Schmitt tries to conceal (¶27). I invite the reader to see how Strauss in two passages from Schmitt discerns his moral condemnation of that ideal and the method by which he conceals it (¶27). Here I will address only the substance of his condemnation. While the ideals of liberals and anarchists may be high, their goal threatens the seriousness of human life by creating societies in which entertainment becomes the object of human attention: "it is impossible to mention politics and the state in the same breath as 'entertainment'; politics and the state are the only *guarantee* against the world's becoming a world of entertainment; therefore, what the opponents of the political want is ultimately tantamount to the establishment of a world of entertainment, a world of amusement, a world without *seriousness*" (¶27). But why would serious men in effect will a world without seriousness? Strauss finds an answer to this question in "Schmitt's description of the modern age as the age of depoliticization" (¶28). Politics and the possibility of war have survived in the modern age, but Schmitt notices that the matters over which men quarrel have changed: theological matters in the sixteenth century, metaphysical matters in the seventeenth, moral matters in the eighteenth, economic matters in the nineteenth, and technological matters in the twentieth. He notices a law governing these changes: "the 'tendency' toward neutralization,' that is, the striving to gain a ground that 'makes possible security, clarity, agreement, and peace'" (¶28). This law receives its original motive in the desire "to avoid the quarrel over the right faith." But Strauss brings out the cost of this desire: "it is always possible to reach agreement regarding the means to an end that is already fixed, whereas there is always quarrelling over the ends themselves: we are always quarreling with each other and with ourselves only over the just and the good (Plato, *Euthyphro* 7B-D and *Phaedrus* 263A)" (¶28).[23] The goal of modernity is a peaceful order, an order that is desired for the sake of humanity, but this goal requires human beings to "relinquish asking the question of what is right; and if a human being relinquishes that question, he relinquishes being a human being" (¶28).

If the price of peace is the abandonment of the question of what is right, the price of seriously raising this question is the ignition of quarrels that follow from the problems inherent in this question. Schmitt is an authoritarian but his fundamental concern is neither warlike morality nor physical or spiritual security: "The affirmation of the state of nature does not mean the affirmation of war but 'relinquishment of the security of the status quo'" (¶29). He turns away from the security, comfort, and ease of civilization to nature in its purity so that out of pure knowledge of that nature "'the order of the human things' can arise again" (¶29).

We have followed Strauss as he moves from the surface claim that the political is an inescapable necessity to the deeper but hidden claim that the political is a demand of morality. We noted that he catches Schmitt moralizing while concealing that moralizing. The question naturally emerges as to the source of Schmitt's confusion. If the affirmation of the political is ultimately a moral affirmation, how are we to understand Schmitt's polemic against the primacy of morals over politics? The most obvious explanation is that by morality Schmitt only means humanitarian morality, the very morality that negates the political (¶30). Schmitt is in a way trapped by his opponents' conception of morality. He is not trapped in the sense that he cannot pass a moral judgment on humanitarian morality. He does condemn it, though he conceals this condemnation. He is trapped because he accepts its premise, namely, that all morals are essentially private matters (see his contention that no norm can justify men killing each other). He tries not to defend the political in moral terms because morality as he understands it is incompatible with the political, which has "the character of transprivate *obligation*" (¶31). Morality as he understands it may recognize obligatory duties, but it cannot recognize obligatory duties to one's community. Accordingly, Schmitt has to give political obligation a different basis and a different meaning: "obligation cannot be conceived as such, as duty, but can be conceived only as inescapable necessity" (¶31). He is thus forced to repeat the crucial aspect of Hobbes's teaching regarding natural right, which he himself regarded as "the characteristic presupposition of the 'individualistic-liberal society'" (¶31). Strauss thus lays bare the difficulty that led Schmitt to assert the inescapability of the political and to conceal his moral judgment as soon as his subject forces him to stop maintaining this assertion (¶31). Schmitt cannot recognize the moral authority of the community over the individual, presumably because he agrees with Hobbes that "man is by nature free, that is, without obligation" (¶26). If Schmitt's true motive for the affirmation of the political is concern with the preservation of the serious life (a life that recognizes obligations to one's community), his affirmation of the political is a substitute for a morality that is unavailable to him because he accepts the basic premise of Hobbes's political philosophy—politics as a prosthetic for a mutilated morality.

Having explained Schmitt's tendency to deny and to conceal the moral concern informing his affirmation of the political, Strauss shows the price he pays for "the affirmation of the political in abstraction from the moral" (¶32). To affirm the political in this way is to affirm a state of affairs in which men orient themselves, toward the "dire emergency," toward war. He who affirms the political is silent about the cause for which men fight and thus "comports himself *neutrally* toward all groupings into friends and enemies" (¶32). Schmitt is against liberalism's will to neutralization, its tendency to put off decisions facing man for the sake of peace, but "his eagerness for *any* decision *regardless of content*" presupposes a kind of neutrality. His decisionism avoids deciding between different answers to the question of what is right:

> He who affirms the political as such respects all who want to fight; he is just as *tolerant* as the liberals—but with opposite intention: whereas the liberal respects and tolerates all "*honest*" convictions as long as they merely acknowledge the legal order, *peace*, as sacrosanct, he who affirms the political as such respects and tolerates all "*serious*" convictions, that is, all decisions oriented to the real possibility of *war*. (¶32)

Schmitt's polemic against liberalism, perhaps like every polemic, becomes entangled with its opponent: "the affirmation of the political as such proves to be liberalism with a minus sign" (¶32).[24]

Strauss, nonetheless, discerns a rational provisional purpose for Schmitt's polemic against liberalism in his work: "The affirmation of the political as such can... only *prepare for* the radical critique of liberalism" (¶33). He refers to Schmitt's observation in *Political Theology* on Donoso Cortés: "He 'despises the liberals, whereas he respects atheistic and anarchistic socialism as his mortal enemy'" (¶33). Men like Cortés and Bakunin turn their gaze away from liberalism so that they can look at the other as the enemy. By tolerating intolerant positions while negating liberalism, the affirmation of the political paves the way for this attitude. In Schmitt's deeper view liberalism needs to be negated not because it is the enemy, but because its compromises and its penchant for putting off decisions through endless debates obscure the real field of the battle: "The polemic against liberalism can therefore only signify a concomitant or preparatory action: it is meant to clear the field for the battle of decision between the 'spirit of technicity,' the 'mass faith that inspires an anti-religious, this worldly activism', and the opposite spirit and faith, which, as it seems, still has no name" (¶33). Schmitt's real enemy is the most extreme development of the spirit of modernity, and he treats this enemy with extraordinary respect. For instance, in "The Age of Neutralization and Depoliticization" (the second essay in Schmitt's text) he argues against liberals who deny to technicity its spiritual character. In this respect, he seems more interested in seeing the real issue facing man than in defeating an opponent. Accordingly, Strauss argues that neither the polemic against liberalism nor the affirmation of the political is Schmitt's ultimate concern: "His last word is 'the order of the human things'" (¶33).[25]

But this is not always his last word. The polemic against liberalism, which could only legitimately serve as a preparatory measure, sometimes becomes for him the goal of his reflections. Similarly, his decisionism (liberalism with a minus sign) is not simply a provisional position. According to Strauss, Schmitt is confused, and he traces this confusion to his principle of understanding. His entanglement with the polemic against liberalism "is no accidental failure but the necessary result of the principle that 'all concepts of the spiritual sphere . . . are to be understood only in terms of concrete political existence,' and that 'all political concepts, presentations, and words' have 'a *polemical* meaning'" (¶34). Whereas earlier he identified these as two principles (¶2), he now treats them as one: if all concepts must be understood in terms of their concrete political existence, and if all political concepts are polemical, all concepts are in fact polemical. The result is a complete politicization and historicization of all concepts. Strauss observes that Schmitt rejected this principle of understanding "*in concreto* . . . by opposing his unpolemical concept of nature to Hobbes's polemical concept of the state of nature; and he fundamentally rejects this principle by expecting to gain the order of human things from a 'whole knowledge,'" a knowledge that can be gained only through a return to "pure and uncorrupted nature" (¶34). Despite this movement, he could not completely free himself from this principle, which Strauss notes is "bound to liberal presuppositions." The natural freedom of man and the consequent understanding of the state of nature that can guide man only through being opposed comes to mind here. If Strauss's suggestion is correct, Schmitt was entangled in a polemic against liberalism because he failed to succeed in his attempt at a radical criticism of liberalism.

Strauss unambiguously endorses Schmitt's launching the radical criticism of liberalism, but he shows that Schmitt has failed to complete this task: "his critique of liberalism occurs in the horizon of liberalism; his illiberal tendency is restrained by the still unvanquished 'systematics of liberal thought'" (¶24). To complete what Schmitt started one needs to gain a horizon beyond liberalism and one needs to show that Hobbes's establishment of liberalism in such a horizon was somehow flawed. While Strauss sides with Schmitt against Hobbes, he clearly regards Hobbes as the greater thinker. Whereas Schmitt failed to complete his critique of liberalism in the horizon of liberalism, Hobbes "*completed* the foundation of liberalism" in a horizon beyond liberalism (¶35; emphasis added). Hence, it is doubtful that one can undermine Hobbes's position by exposing its inconsistencies. The radical criticism of Hobbes has to address the truth of the foundational premises of his thought. By bringing out the human cost of liberalism, Schmitt's work makes it possible for us to look into these premises with eyes not blinded by modern promises. His entanglement with liberal premises has the virtue of identifying these premises and their power. Of these, nothing is more fundamental and powerful than the thesis that man is by nature free, that is, without obligation. Accordingly, the radical criticism of liberalism or a return to premodern philosophy requires above all the restoration of the notion of human evil as moral depravity (¶26). Only through such a restoration can a consistent alternative to liberalism or modern philosophy emerge. This restoration also bears on the cause of philosophy or rationalism. Others have noted that this conception of morality, unlike that of Hobbes and Spinoza, can serve as a bridge between philosophy and revealed theology, potentially allowing one to walk (as opposed to leap) from one position to the other.[26] The restoration of the older conception of morality can serve as such a bridge because theoretical disputes turn into serious quarrels only insofar as they are connected with moral disagreements (¶28): the antagonism "between unbelief and belief, is ultimately not theoretical but moral."[27] If "revelation or the polemic against revelation is what makes the acceptance of classical politics impossible for Hobbes,"[28] if premodern philosophy's apparent inability to deal with the problem of revelation is the living justification of the modern break with the past, Strauss's discovery of a bridge between premodern philosophy and revealed theology may well be the decisive insight that makes possible a return to premodern philosophy. But there is also a more elementary and related consideration. If morality is indeed a force in human nature, this restoration bears on the right of reason to rule man, for the freedom that is gained through abstraction from man's nature is no freedom but self-imposed slavery.

Notes

1. The original essay was published in 1932 in *Archiv für Sozialwissenshaften und Sozialpolitik* 67, no. 6. It is also available in *GS–3* 217–38. In 1965 Strauss attached a translation by E. M. Sinclair with the title of "Comments on *Der Begriff des Politischen* by Carl Schmitt" to *Spinoza's Critique of Religion*. He permitted this translation to appear in Carl Schmitt, *The Concept of the Political*, trans. George Schwab (New Brunswick, NJ: Rutgers University Press, 1976). In 1965 he also attached the original German article to *Hobbes' politische Wissenschaft*. It is a testimony to the importance of this article that it is the only one (in any language) that Strauss published four times.
2. *SCR* 31.
3. *SCR* 28–30.
4. *SCR* 30–31.
5. David Janssens has correctly noticed in Strauss's unpublished writings from 1931–1932 evidence of a development toward this reorientation, but he does not give due weight to the decisive questioning that manifests itself first in the "Comments." Accordingly, he interprets "expression" to mean only "publication" ("A Change of Orientation: Leo Strauss's 'Comments' on Carl Schmitt Revisited," *Interpretation* 33, no. 1 (Winter 2005): 100).
6. *LSEW* 214–15.
7. *JPCM* 453.
8. There are two translations of Strauss's review of Schmitt: Sinclair's (referred to in note 2) and J. Harvey Lomax's, which is attached to Heinrich Meier, *Carl Schmitt and Leo Strauss: The Hidden Dialogue*, trans. J. Harvey Lomax (Chicago: University of Chicago Press, 1995), 91–119. I have used both translations, occasionally modifying them when appropriate. For ease of reference, I have used paragraph numbers.

9. This critique presupposes Schmitt's very high opinion of Hobbes. In the "Introduction" to the German edition of his Hobbes book, Strauss writes:Carl Schmitt, in quiet unconscious opposition to Ebbinghaus, asserted in his essay, "The Concept of the Political" (..., 1927) that Hobbes is "by far the greatest and perhaps the only truly systematic political thinker." Schmitt's judgment about the greatness and significance of Hobbes, a judgment which corresponded to my feelings or taste at that time, strengthened, understandably, my interest in Hobbes" (*JPCM* 453).

   In the "Comments" Strauss observes that by 1932 Schmitt had changed his assessment of Hobbes, though not sufficiently.
10. Meier, 43.
11. The opposition between political theology and political theory is not so clear in Schmitt's writings because his conception of political theology is informed by the modern notion of secularization: "all significant concepts of the modern theory of the state are secularized theological concepts" (*Political Theology*, trans. George Schwab (Chicago: University of Chicago Press, 2005), 36). For a defense of Meier's reading, see Anna Schmidt, "The Problem of Carl Schmitt's Political Theology" *Interpretation* 36, no. 3 (Summer 2009): 219–52.
12. Meier in several places acknowledges the profound tension between his reading of Schmitt and Strauss's text. Although "original sin" is "an expression never once uttered by Strauss," in Meier's reading of Schmitt this notion is "the deepest foundation" of the political (53). Meier notes that "Schmitt's affirmation of the political, in Strauss's interpretation, is the affirmation of the 'state of nature,'" but in his own view "Schmitt denies that men ever existed or could exist in a state of nature" (39, 49). Whereas Strauss traces Schmitt's historicism to his acceptance of liberal presuppositions, Meier traces it to his Christianity (83). Meier even goes so far as to assert: "Leo Strauss's critique 'overlooks' what is decisive for Schmitt" (69). The quotation marks around the verb imply that Strauss deliberately distorted Schmitt's teaching by turning it into a philosophical doctrine.
13. Ibid., xvii.
14. Ibid., 8n. The quoted words are Schmitt's.
15. Schmitt supported the publication of the "Comments," helped secure a fellowship for Strauss, and years later attached the "Comments" to the American edition of *The Concept of the Political* (ibid., 8, 8n, 9n).
16. He thus can equate the question of the state with that of the order of human things.
17. Schmitt, *The Concept of the Political*, 65.
18. Strauss, "Letter to Schmitt, September 4, 1932," in Meier, 124.
19. In the course of this reasoning, Strauss in effect separates the true element of Schmitt's notion of the state of nature from its questionable element (the dangerous or evil character of man). The true element is the unpolemical account of that state which he opposes to Hobbes's polemical account. For Schmitt, the state of nature is a political state and is composed not of "individuals but of totalities" and "not every totality is an enemy of every other totality" (¶16). This part of the account only shows that the political is possible but not necessary.
20. In a letter to Schmitt, Strauss sees a connection between bellicose nationalism and authoritarianism: men are so resistant to obedience that "they can be unified, only in a unity *against*—against other men" ("Letter to Schmitt, September 4, 1932," in Meier, 125).

21. According to Schmitt, authoritarian theories can assume that man is evil "in a specifically *moral* or ethical sense" or in an amoral sense so long as they assume that man is dangerous. Schmitt even seems to prefer an amoral understanding of evil to a moral one. For instance, he discerns a connection between the theological notion of original sin and the political notion of evil, but he does not like theological interference: it "generally confuses political concepts because it usually shifts the distinction into *moral* theology" (Schmitt, *The Concept of the Political*, 65). He seems to prefer Machiavelli, Hobbes, and Fichte to Catholic reactionaries because the former only assumed "the reality and the possibility of the distinction of friend and enemy" (ibid.).
22. Schmitt's "correction" of Hobbes's view of evil may avoid the anarchistic potential of Hobbes's notion but at the price of complete confusion. Whereas Hobbes wants to combat human evil, Schmitt speaks of it "with an unmistakable *sympathy*" (¶26). By encouraging men to be evil one may buttress the need for government, but, Strauss argues, such admiration is a kind of aestheticism, which Schmitt criticizes as a path to the universal economization of life (¶8, ¶26), and it is absurd in itself because it is an admiration for a defect, for man's need to be ruled (¶26).
23. Strauss omits the noble, which is mentioned along with the just and the good in the passage from *Euthyphro*, which omission is justified by the passage from *Phaedrus* as well as by Schmitt's criticism of aestheticism. The noble is less controversial than the just and the good. Note also that for Schmitt theological and metaphysical issues are more controversial than moral ones, while Strauss seems to suggest the opposite.
24. While his polemic against liberalism is in truth motivated by a concern for morality, his affirmation of the political as such leads to an even greater alienation from man's moral concerns, for peace is more akin to justice than war (see note 22 above).
25. This abbreviated phrase of Virgil is literally how Schmitt's book ends, but Strauss obviously means that the concern for the right order of human life is Schmitt's ultimate concern.
26. *SCR* 204.
27. *SCR* 29.
28. *HCR* 26.

CHAPTER 7

LEO STRAUSS ON THE ORIGINS OF HOBBES'S NATURAL SCIENCE AND ITS RELATION TO THE CHALLENGE OF DIVINE REVELATION

Timothy W. Burns

Leo Strauss's unfinished manuscript, *Hobbes's Critique of Religion* (1933–34),[1] which Gabriel Bartlett and Svetozar Minkov have now translated into English,[2] belongs to the period that Strauss identifies as the crucial one in his intellectual development, when he underwent what he calls, in the 1965 preface to *Spinoza's Critique of Religion*, his "change of orientation." He moved at this time from the premise that a return to premodern philosophy was impossible to the recognition that such a return is possible. That change had as its foundation the recognition, noted in his review of Carl Schmitt's *Concept of the Political*, that the modern attempt to see human evil as bestial and hence innocent evil, was inferior to the starting point of Socratic dialectic, wherein evil is seen as moral depravity.[3] The unpublished and unfinished Hobbes manuscript from this period provides us with some important, if provisional, results of the ten-year study of Hobbes that Strauss undertook in his effort to understand the roots of the peculiar situation at which the project of modern rationalism had arrived. In it, Strauss argues that Hobbes's positivist-phenomenalist science ("methological materialism" or "hypothetical materialism") is a result of the somewhat unexpected realization that, as a working hypothesis, the omnipotent God has to be assumed to be behind nature, rendering nature unintelligible. That is, Strauss argues that according to Hobbes, the doctrine of an omnipotent God creating the world ex nihilo at each moment—a doctrine that Calvin, as well as the Islamic Kalâm, had come to adopt—had to be initially granted as a possibility, if revelation were to be refuted. Twenty years later, in *Natural Right and History* (1953), Chapter 5, Strauss offers what appears to be a different account of the origin of Hobbes's natural science; there he argues that it resulted from Hobbes's recognition of the impossibility, for knowledge of anything, of conceiving of mind as derivative from matter and hence subject to the flux of mechanical causation, as both Hobbes and some pre-Socratics had wished to conceive of mind. This article examines the similarities and differences between the two arguments, and attempts to explain why and to what extent Strauss abandoned his earlier argument in favor of the one he later articulated in *Natural Right and History.*

I

To better grasp the intention of the earlier work, it may be helpful to first consider Strauss's remarks about its immediate predecessor, *Spinoza's Critique of Religion.* Both books manifest what Strauss later (in his 1965 German Preface to *The Political Philosophy of Hobbes*)[4] describes as his "philosophic interest in theology," an interest prompted by the failure of modern philosophic rationalism's attempt to liberate the West from biblical revelation and direct it by rational norms. As Thomas Pangle has shown in his very helpful explication of that preface and of the Strauss letter to Gerhard Krüger of January 7, 1930,[5] Strauss understood his *Spinoza's Critique of Religion* to be a book on Heidegger, in two senses. First, it was originally conceived from a position that was fundamentally Heideggerian as regards the theological question: Strauss himself continued, as he tells Krüger, to have the "will" (*Wille*) and "stance" (*Gesinnung*) of the Enlightenment, and Strauss understood that will or stance to have reached "its completion in *Being and Time*—I mean in the interpretation of the call of conscience, and in the answer given there to the question" of who is calling, that is, the atheistic answer. Second, Strauss undertook an explication of the historical forms of pre-Heideggerian philosophic atheism precisely in order to clarify the various grounds of Heidegger's atheistic predecessors; the resulting work clarified the various modern versions of the "Epicurean" will, the "stance" (*Gesinnung*) that he found merely *presupposed* in, though meant to be *vindicated* by, Heidegger's *Dasein*-interpretation, a stance Heidegger himself had failed to bring to light.[6]

As Strauss explains in the letter to Krüger, the Enlightenment's attempt to defeat revelation depended on its refutation of the possibility of miracles. Summarizing the findings of his Spinoza book on the achievement of the Enlightenment with respect to miracles, Strauss claims that achievement to be limited to this:

> that the already enlightened human being, is immune to miracles; [the Enlightement] has created a position that is unreachable by miracles. But a miracle is, according to its own meaning, only capable of being experienced as a miracle on the foundation of faith—and thereby, the Enlightenment offensive is thus rendered impotent. At this point,... it becomes clear that the Enlightenment does not owe its victory to assertions of the scientific *refutation* of revealed religion. It owes its victory to a certain will, which one may, with a grain of salt, characterize as Epicurean. This will seems to me to be no foundational justification for the Enlightenment, against revealed religion.... [I]n order for the social victory of the Enlightenment... to become total, there must emerge another will against revealed religion. Such a will I see disclosed in Machiavelli, Bruno, and Spinoza... reaching its most extreme representation in Nietzsche, and its completion in *Being and Time*—I mean in the interpretation of the call of conscience, and in the answer given there to the question: who is calling? It is in Heidegger's *Dasein*-interpretation that for the first

> time an adequate atheistic interpretation of the Bible becomes possible. Religion is then for the first time overcome, when it can be given an adequate atheistic interpretation. Therefore: the victory of the Enlightenment, that is, the victory of the "scientific view of the world"—which I *only* understand to include the loss of the possibility of believing in miracles—is justifiable only on the ground of a certain intellectual stance (*Gesinnung*), not on the ground of this "worldview" itself.

The victory of the Enlightenment that had come about through the activity and spread of modern natural science was not, Strauss had concluded, a victory that was justified; not the findings of science, but the will and stance behind those findings, were responsible for the limited victory, and the stance was unable to sustain a justification of itself against the alternative stance—unable, that is, to defeat the most radical position of revelation, that of Calvin, as Strauss had brought out in *Spinoza's Critique of Religion* (and as he reminds us, in footnote references to *Spinoza's Critique of Religion*, in *Hobbes's Critique of Religion*).

Second, and relatedly, Strauss had come to recognize that the modern enlightenment project was failing. Here is how he puts his recognition of that failure in the 1951 Preface to the American edition of *The Political Philosophy of Hobbes*,[7] describing the perspective from which that book was written:

> I had seen that the modern mind had lost its self-confidence or its certainty of having made decisive progress beyond pre-modern thought; and I saw that it was turning into nihilism, or what is in practice the same thing, fanatical obscurantism.

As noted above, and as both *The Political Philosophy of Hobbes* and *Philosophy and Law* reveal, Strauss had in this situation already worked his way out of the "powerful prejudice" against a return to premodern philosophy. But he still sought to unearth the fullest or strongest version of the modern attempt to dispose of the theological-political problem, and in the process to understand the peculiar impetus behind modern (as opposed to ancient) natural science. And he did so while simultaneously (in other researches and writings) clarifying ancient/medieval rationalism. It is possible that in his long study of Hobbes Strauss might have discovered a more satisfactory critique of miracles, and hence of revelation, than he had found in Spinoza, or a better understanding of the relative success and failure of the Enlightenment.

II

The opening of *Hobbes's Critique of Religion* suggests that he may have. Strauss claims that while Spinoza's *Theologico-Political Treatise* is bolder than *Leviathan*, the boldness is "bought at the price of renouncing the proper foundation of the critique [of religion], which is found much more in the *Leviathan* than in the *Theologico-Political Treatise*" (*HCR* 23 / *GS–3* 267). For while Spinoza had remained a metaphysical or systematic materialist, Strauss was persuaded by Tönnies's argument that Hobbes's natural philosophy is *not* "a materialistic metaphysics" but instead the "foundation of modern natural science" (*HCR* 24 /

GS–3 267–68), and hence that the critique of religion is not a "byproduct" of Hobbes's natural philosophy, as indeed Strauss himself seems to have thought it to be when he wrote the Spinoza book.[8] Hobbes's critique is instead, initially, an "integral feature" of his political science, and even a "presupposition of modern politics" (*HCR* 25, 26 / *GS–3* 269, 270). His critique of the philosophic politics of classical antiquity, the denial of their acceptability, itself rests on the "polemic against revelation" (*HCR* 26 / *GS–3* 270). For since an effective political order required the elimination of "fear of powers invisible," Hobbes had to overcome the Christian teaching on hell, and ancient philosophic politics, far from being helpful on this score, had provided theologians with the "dangerous weapon" of the doctrine of incorporeal substances that supported the teaching on hell.

But in undertaking his critique of revelation for the sake of an effective political order, Strauss claims, Hobbes's critique *became* the "presupposition of Hobbes's philosophy in general" or "the genuine founding (*Grundlegung*) of... his whole philosophy" (*HCR* 28, 30 / *GS–3* 272, 274). What Strauss means by this remarkable claim emerges late in the text. Before explaining it, he attempts to account for the fact that *Leviathan* seems to show that the very opposite is the case—that the critique of revelation "rests on [Hobbes's] elaborated philosophic teaching," that is, on a materialist physics. Against this, Strauss argues that the "structure of *Leviathan*" *conceals* the "real foundation of the critique of revelation"; the critique that we see in *Leviathan* is *not* one that "sets forth his actual opinion unequivocally." Instead, Hobbes proceeds "by beginning with fully or mostly orthodox-sounding statements, in order to lead these statements afterwards, in a more or less veiled manner, *ad absurdum*" (*HCR* 28, 30, 32 / *GS–3* 272, 274, 277). And to understand the true foundation of the critique of revelation in *Leviathan*, Strauss argues, one must "extract the truly foundational elements of the critique of revelation" (*HCR* 30 / *GS–3* 275). Roughly the first half of Strauss's manuscript consists of this extraction. That is, there Strauss attempts to lead the reader in the direction that Hobbes wished to lead the attentive reader. And that direction is toward the manifestation of a *deficiency* in the surface argument of *Leviathan*, a deficiency of which Hobbes was aware.

For example, the first part of Strauss's argument (to *HCR* 45 / *GS–3* 293) details Hobbes's critique of immaterial substances on the basis of Scripture, and hence Hobbes's critique of the possibility of suffering eternally in hell. But:

> It... is... not to be doubted that it was *fully clear to Hobbes* that the denial of spirits, taken by itself, would not suffice to secure the absolute unity of the civil power—that is, the absolute exclusion of a spiritual power. For since Hobbes has to carry out his critique of spiritualism on the basis of Scripture, he has to acknowledge the dualism of God and creation as Scripture understands it, and therefore the possibility of *miracles*." (HCR 45 / *GS–3* 292–93, emphasis added in the first phrase)

And while writing *Leviathan* Hobbes "could not exclude this possibility insofar as he did not *openly* want to renounce his belief in Scripture." The result is that while Hobbes provides a critique of spiritualism in order to secure an absolute unity for the civil power, "[b]ecause this critique does not exclude the possibility of miracles, it has holes in it that can be filled in only with a special investigation" (*HCR* 45, 46 / *GS–3* 293, 294). The whole critique of Scripture on the basis of Scripture is, Strauss eventually says, "exercised only *fictitiously* and only *subsequently* on the basis of Scripture, [but] in truth and *originally* on the basis of philosophic presuppositions thoroughly independent of Scripture." So while Strauss goes through that critique, it "is not," he states, "that critique of religion which we identified at the outset as the presupposition of both Hobbes's political science and his philosophy in general" (*HCR* 64 / *GS–3* 314).

What, then, is the latter critique? Strauss first identifies its "foundation" as "*Epicureanism*"—by which he means not the doctrine of Epicurus "but rather an interest natural to man, a uniform and elementary outlook (*Gesinnung*), which merely found its classic *expression* in the philosophy of Epicurus" (*HCR* 64, 65 / *GS–3* 315–16). So at least to this point in his work, Strauss has arrived at something like the position that he had concluded with respect to Spinoza in his first book: whatever Hobbes's genuine critique of revelation may be, the Epicurean *Gesinnung* is its foundation. According to Strauss, both the "will for the critique of religion" and the "structure of the critique" is "predetermined by this stance," one that is revived generally in the seventeenth century and one that entails a mechanistic determinism.[9] "Hobbes's critique of the religious tradition presents itself as a post-Christian modification of Epicureanism" (*HCR* 67 / *GS–3* 317), that is, Socianism, a latitudinarian Christianity that was the unitarian universalism of his day.[10] Epicurean unbelief is likewise *presupposed* in the "historical critique" of Scripture that Hobbes uses to attack the knowability of revelation, rather than being a *consequence* of that critique (*HCR* 75–81 / *GS–3* 327–34). To attack those who believe in the revealed character of Scripture, Hobbes was aware, and wished his attentive readers to be aware, he had to move from such an attack on the knowability of revelation to an attack on its possibility. And at this point in his argument Strauss refers the reader, in a footnote,[11] to those pages in *Spinoza's Critique of Religion* where he had spelled out the inadequacy of Spinoza's attempted critiques of orthodoxy and of the unfathomable God. That is, Strauss signals that Hobbes, who had become aware of these deficiencies, goes beyond Spinoza in the reach of his critique, and Strauss aims in the rest of the book to spell out in what way it does so.

Strauss accordingly moves from Hobbes's critique of the tradition to his critique of the possibility of revelation (HCR 81ff. / *GS–3* 334ff.). Here again, Hobbes does not "express" his denial of this possibility but "leads the reader to it" (*HCR* 82 / *GS–3* 334). Hobbes begins, as he had in the critique of the tradition, by "granting" the revealed character of Scripture. He presupposes the impossibility of prophecy on the "conviction" that "it is impossible that God speaks," on the rejection of "inspiration," etc. (HCR 82, 84 / *GS–3* 337, 338). But this is not decisive concerning the possibility of revelation. And now (*HCR* 85 / *GS–3* 338), Strauss states the point most clearly, and with the ground now cleared, it seems, he lays out the issue to which Hobbes has led us:

> If God is omnipotent and incomprehensible, one can indeed prove that human *statements* about God's activity to be *absurd*, but one can never refute the claim that

> God's *activity* is carried in a manner fully *incomprehensible* to man, that therefore God in particular brings forth, in a fully incomprehensible, supernatural manner, dreams and visions, that, in contrast to the natural products of the imagination, have as their purpose and content the divine guidance of man. In other words, as long as the presupposition of the incomprehensible omnipotence of God, as long as the possibility of miracles is not shaken, the impossibility of prophecy and revelation has not been proven. The critique of revelation leads further, therefore, to a critique of miracles: *the critique of miracles is the center of the critique of religion.*

The footnote accompanying this statement again points us to passages in *Spinoza's Critique of Religion*, this time to passages arguing that the positive or scientific mind rests on a "will," not on an establishable progress of consciousness, at least in the case of the Spinozistic Enlightenment.[12] This is the point, in other words, at which Spinoza's positive critique of revelation undermined itself. Is the same true of Hobbes's critique? To answer this, Strauss now turns, in Part C of the chapter (*HCR* 85ff. / *GS–3* 339ff.), to Hobbes's critique of miracles.

The central argument of the believer concerning miracles is that everything that is is miraculous. Given God's omnipotence, no distinction between supernatural works of God and natural occurrences is even possible; since God can and does do all that he wants, all "natural" occurrences are as incomprehensible as supernatural ones. In other words, there is no nature, and there is no such thing as "cause," properly speaking (i.e., necessity). In Hobbes's effort to show that miracles are not knowable for believers, he *grants* this presupposition as a possibility, according to Strauss, making it the foundation of his science. To make his case, Hobbes "must, taking over the presupposition of his opponents, argue on the basis of belief in the omnipotence of God," and is thereby "compelled to negate the possibility of natural knowledge." Now Strauss argues that this clearly does not "correspond to Hobbes's real view," which is that natural knowledge *is possible.* This opinion Strauss calls "the genuine presupposition of his critique of miracles." Hobbes, he stresses, "had no reason for regarding natural science as impossible." But having made the "concession to his opponents" of an omnipotent God, having had therefore skepticism "at first only imposed from without," Hobbes was led to a position in which the skepticism became "an integral element" of his thought (*HCR* 89–90 / *GS–3* 343–44).

For, to say that miracles are unknowable owing to the unknowability of an omnipotent God is a critique that "leads only to *Calvin's* teaching on miracles" (*HCR* 90 / *GS–3* 344), that is, to a teaching that Strauss had explained in his *Spinoza's Critique of Religion* as left unrefuted by Spinoza.[13] Hobbes, having arrived at this position, will move beyond it and thus beyond the failure of Spinoza. But, Strauss argues, "this fundamental failure of his critique of religion [to answer Calvin's teaching on miracles] does not come to Hobbes's awareness." In what appears to be a speculation on Strauss's part as to the path that Hobbes's thinking took, he tells us that Hobbes's initial apparent success brings him "into an apparently hopeless situation, a situation of such a kind that he can believe that in being freed from it, that he has once and for all put revealed religion behind him" (*HCR* 91 / *GS–3* 345).

In support of this claim, Strauss reviews the steps that he sees Hobbes as having taken. Hobbes wished to "attack revealed religion in general," and so placed himself "on the ground of belief in the omnipotence of God" (ibid.), adopting his "opponents' presupposition" that "everything which is has its ground in the incomprehensible works of God," and therefore, "there is *nothing* to comprehend." "In other words, in order to refute his opponents, he moves . . . to the complete abandonment of the idea of *nature* as a *comprehensible order*." But in doing so, "Hobbes makes questionable, *at the same time*, revealed religion and natural reason." This is the "hopeless situation" in which Hobbes found himself—presumably long before he wrote *Leviathan*. "How," Strauss asks, "can he liberate himself from this predicament, from this situation that seems completely hopeless?" (ibid.)

Strauss then describes retreat into consciousness as the liberation, or at least the beginning of the liberation, from the situation (*HCR* 91–92 / *GS–3* 345–46):

> He liberates himself from this situation, and at the same time from the power that brought him into this situation, by withdrawing to a dimension that is removed from the grip of God (and of a God who is thus not in fact *omni*potent, or rather, who does not make full use of his omnipotence). This dimension is the world of *consciousness*, that is, a world that is as much of the material that is given to him as of principles freely created by him. God may dispose of nature as he wants; in the extreme case, he could even annihilate it, but insofar as *I* only remain, my representations of nature remain, and with them the material and basis of science. This material takes the form of science in being developed according to principles that we ourselves create at will, which principles are thus to a higher degree in our power than are the representations (which remain even through the fictitious destruction of the world): even if nature is annihilated, the possibility of science would survive so long as *I* survive, and insofar as the material of science (the ideas given to us), as well as its form (the principles of knowledge created by us) are in our power. But the possibility of a genuine natural science has not yet thereby been vouched for. For the causes of the natural things that are sought for by this science are not perceptible, and therefore do not belong to the world of our ideas, nor are they created by us in the way in which the principles of knowledge are; they are, therefore, in no sense in our power, but are simply in God's power. Since nature, as created by an omnipotent God, is beyond our grasp, natural science is possible only in this way, that, starting from the ideas given to us in accord with the principles of knowledge that we ourselves create, we arrive at the *possible* causes of natural things in terms of these principles, without our ever being able to know, or needing to know, whether the causes that we assume are possible are the real ones.

Modern, phenomenalist-positivist science, which understands the principles of science as a construction of the mind, and understands the causes that it posits for phenomena as hypothetical, emerges owing to a concession to the unknowability of the world, a concession made in order to overcome the challenge to knowledge posed by the possible existence of the unfathomable will of an omnipotent God.

Strauss claims that "[t]his concept of natural science is the presupposition of Hobbes's thesis that miracles are, in principle, not knowable to natural reason"

(*HCR* 93 / *GS–3* 347). As the footnotes indicate, Strauss bases this claim on arguments made by Hobbes before and after *Leviathan*.[14] In a footnote (*HCR* 93n239 / *GS–3* 347n239), he explains why the presupposition is not found in *Leviathan*:

> Hobbes's explicit justification of this thesis does not allow for an immediate recognition of his real view (see above, n. 222). Cf., in this connection, the following paragraph.

The "*explicit* justification of this thesis," which Strauss had already spelled out (on *HCR* 85–87 / *GS–3* 339–40), is that Scripture tells us that miracles are knowable not to everyone but only to the elect. After stating that the hypothetical or (merely) possible causes of "natural events" can or do serve as the "explanation" of them and hence, too, of miracles, Strauss explains (in the subsequent paragraph) Hobbes's "civilizational" project. And it is this, he now indicates, that allows Hobbes the final road out of his difficulty, and is something that Hobbes does indeed indicate in *Leviathan* (*HCR* 93–94 / *GS–3* 347–48):

> The science that enables man to explain nature enables him at the same time to explain "miracles." Experience shows that the less natural-scientific knowledge men have at their disposal, the more they are inclined to regard processes as miraculous. In this sense it is true that miracles are only directed to the "elect": the "elect" are precisely those same poor in spirit who are without any scientific culture. Hence, one can expect that, with the progressive cultivation of natural science, belief in miracles will lose more and more of its significance, ultimately disappearing entirely. For natural science is still in its beginnings, and gradually even the unwise multitude will be educated and thereby become mistrustful of reports of miracles that come from a dim past, that is, from an age in which there was no science. Modern science, which excludes the possibility of miracles so little that it rather has as its actual foundation a concession to that possibility, secures itself subsequently against that possibility by claiming, on the basis of the consciousness of progress that belongs to it, and thus on the basis of a historical reflection, that belief in miracles is relative to the prescientific stage of humanity.

When Hobbes speaks in *Leviathan* (Chapter 37) about miracles being knowable only to the elect, he is indicating there, according to Strauss, that the "elect" are those without any scientific culture, and that the more men are enlightened by the new science about possible causes of unusual phenomena, the less the multitude will believe claims of miracles, and the more the belief in them will seem to be something that "belongs to the prescientific stage of humanity" (*HCR* 94 / *GS–3* 349). The "securing" of science is thus achieved through an initial granting of the possibility that all things are miraculous, and the *subsequent* claim, "on the basis of the consciousness of progress that belongs to it," that belief in miracles belongs to a prescientific age.

Now—with the exception of the argument concerning the granting of the unintelligibility of the world—Strauss had already, in *Spinoza's Critique of Religion*, made the argument concerning the awareness of the positive mind's progress as the most effective critique of religion—*much* more effective, indeed, than Spinoza's systematic critique—but had there shown it to be inadequate. (See above, notes 11 and 12). What he has now discovered, it seems, is that this awareness, and the civilizational project upon which it depends for its authentication, is, for Hobbes, the sole basis of the new science, and is the sole basis precisely because Hobbes, unlike Spinoza, has granted to the believer the possibility that the world is the unfathomable work of what he calls, in *Leviathan*, the "incomprehensible" God. And having granted this possibility, Hobbes grasps what Spinoza denies or obscures—the degree to which modern rationalism rests on the hope in progress of the human mind.

III

The final part of *Hobbes's Critique of Religion* is a comparison and contrast of Hobbes and Descartes, whose response, in the *Meditations*, to the *Deus deceptor* argument appears so strikingly similar to the argument, which we summarized above, that Strauss has put together from works of Hobbes other than *Leviathan*. Strauss promises that the comparison of Hobbes with Descartes will allow us "to see the genuine basis of Hobbes's critique of religion," which is "by no means the new science as such" (*HCR* 94 / *GS–3* 348). What he seems to mean is the following. No modern scientific finding of material causes, nor any reflections on the right method of understanding causes, moved Hobbes to doubt the possibility of miracles. Rather, Hobbes "arrives at the new science by first carrying out a response to the claim of miracles by revealed religion." And this means that there was already, as the "basis" of the response to revealed religion, a "primary skepticism about miracles" (*HCR* 95 / *GS–3* 348–49). This *skepticism* is, then, the basis of the critique of religion. And Strauss links this primary skepticism to the medieval critics of religion and hence to the ancients (*HCR* 95 / *GS–3* 349: "and antiquity"; "and classical"); he presents this "primary skepticism," or what he also calls "the horizon within which" arguments against miracles "first become possible" (*HCR* 95 / *GS–3* 349), as something earlier than modern science, pointing out that the evidence of this skepticism, that is, the thesis that knowledge of miracles is practically impossible, was already held by medieval critics of religion. The comparison and contrast with Descartes brings to the fore this "pre-modern basis of the critique of religion," and at the same time shows "what is indeed the presupposition preceding the foundation of modern science" (ibid.), that is, it shows the characteristically modern presupposition that *distinguishes* Hobbes's critique of religion from the medieval and ancient one. Both of these tasks, then, are achieved by examining Hobbes's published (1642) response to Descartes's *Meditations*.

I wish to note only two things about this final section of the manuscript. First, it clarifies the source of Hobbes's adoption of the argument that the world may be the work of an incomprehensible God; while that argument is in *agreement* with what Calvin came finally to argue, Hobbes did not learn the argument from Calvin, but from Descartes. Strauss shows that Hobbes acknowledges the Cartesian necessity of beginning philosophy with universal doubt, that is, that the "foundation of philosophy" is "the regression into consciousness, into the world of consciousness," begun with the "fiction of the annihilation of the world, with the retreat to the 'ideas'" (*HCR* 97 / *GS–3* 351). And, like Descartes, Hobbes makes this retreat in truth only on the basis of the possibility of a Deus deceptor. The "founding of science by means of a retreat into consciousness" is, Strauss clearly suggests, something that Hobbes *learns* from Descartes (*HCR* 98 / *GS–3* 352). Hobbes at the same time rejects Descartes's resolution of the Deus deceptor difficulty (found in Paragraphs 10 and 11 of Descartes's Sixth *Meditation*), that is, he rejects Descartes's claim that we can know through rational theology that God is not a deceiver; Hobbes *denies* that the createdness of the world follows from the positing of the existence of God as a first cause, and denies that God's truthfulness can be proven; God is, Hobbes argues, incomprehensible (*HCR* 98–99 / *GS–3* 352–53).[15]

This is so, Strauss stresses, even if "genuine natural science" operates on the basis of the existence of things, inquiring into their causes, or "does away with" the "fiction of the annihilation of the world" (*HCR* 101 / *GS–3* 354–55). For insofar as it deals with the *causes* of our sense perceptions—the causes of the "phenomena of nature" that are in our mind—natural science is dealing with things that are "not in our power and are accordingly not accessible to any absolutely certain knowledge." We can deduce these causes "only according to the principles of mechanics created by us ourselves" (*HCR* 101 / *GS–3* 355). That there *are* things in themselves, however—that they exist—is for Hobbes "certain, indisputable, self-evident." Unlike Descartes, Hobbes does not doubt that the world exists, but merely founds science on the *fiction* of its nonbeing or annihilation. Hobbes even presupposes, Strauss argues, that the corporeality of the things in themselves is "self-evident" (*HCR* 102 / *GS–3* 356). For what exists is known to be corporeal not through science but instead merely through the "refinement" of the prescientific view according to which bodies, as distinct from spirits, are beings that resist our force and are tangible or palpable. Science merely recognizes that spirits, too, if they exist, have resistance and palpability (*HCR* 102–103 / *GS–3* 356–57). Understanding being as resistance and palpability, Hobbes, unlike Descartes, holds the existence of things in themselves to be self-evident; we "experience the world in the resistance that it offers us, because we feel we experience it as independent of our thoughts" (*HCR* 104 / *GS–3* 359). Not a full blown Cartesian retreat into consciousness, then, nor any denial that man is a rational animal, part of and bound up with the world, but instead an *abstraction from* the existence of the corporeal world, or a retreat into an independent consciousness "*only* in the context of considering the faculty of *knowledge*," characterizes Hobbes's phenomenalism (*HCR* 105 / *GS–3* 360, first emphasis added). Our consciousness, an accident of a living body, is itself subject to "the irresistibly greater power of the resistant world," of undoubtedly existing bodies (*HCR* 106 / *GS–3* 361).

What all of this suggests is that Hobbes was, or was "originally," a metaphysical materialist, as Strauss discerns through the extraction of various passages in *The Elements of Law* and *Leviathan*, including claims about the corporeality of God. Hobbes's confidence in this original metaphysical materialism was shaken, however, according to Strauss, "above all by Descartes, and he was forced into 'phenomenalism'" (*HCR* 107 / *GS–3* 362).[16] Hobbes understands the Deus deceptor argument *only* as a pointed expression of "the possibility of a fully incomprehensible God," and merely a "symbolization of that possibility" (*HCR* 108 / *GS–3* 363).[17] It is, in short, only the *comprehensibility* of the world, and not its existence, that is a genuine problem for Hobbes. Hence, in his assent to the Deus deceptor argument, "Hobbes... confronts, not the possibility of a *Deus deceptor*, but the... much more threatening, and much *more credible* possibility that the world is the incomprehensible work of a simply incomprehensible God" (*HCR* 109 / *GS–3* 365).

Second, Strauss concludes by saying that "the retreat into consciousness is not the foundation of philosophy" for Hobbes (though it appears to be the "founding of science"). The reason is this: the retreat, as much as it may rescue a certain kind of science from the possible incomprehensibility of the world, "cannot... help me in a positive way with an orientation in a world that is completely incomprehensible" (*HCR* 109 / *GS–3* 364). It cannot tell one whether that science should be practiced, since the "orientation" at issue is that of philosophic/scientific reasoning, on one hand, and faith in an omnipotent, incomprehensible God (the God of Calvin), on the other. How then does Hobbes secure himself against such a God, and thereby secure philosophy? Strauss has already provided an answer: the consciousness of progress over and against the prescientific mind. What he does next, in what happens to be the last section of the (incomplete) work, titled "The Basis of Hobbes's Critique of Religion," (*HCR* 109–14 / *GS–3* 364–69) is show what guidance Hobbes found or provided toward this orientation rather than the other. The guidance proves to be "memory of art," understood in a new way, a way that emerges out of understanding the world as "resistance," or understanding man as the "resistor."[18]

IV

"Hobbes's fundamental critique of religion consists in his confrontation, carried out on the basis of this presupposition, with the possibility that the world is the work of a simply incomprehensible God and is therefore not only resistant and overpowering but also fully incomprehensible" (*HCR* 110 / *GS–3* 365). But "[a] s a consequence of this possibility, every orientation in the world becomes radically problematic. In what fact does Hobbes find protection against this threat, protection against the God of revelation?" (ibid.) Hobbes orients himself, Strauss argues, not by the "fact of nature" but by the "fact of art," since the works of art are comprehensible in principle." Withdrawal in defense against the possibility that the world is the work of an incomprehensible God is withdrawal to "the fact of art." And, Strauss now repeats, Hobbes's philosophy "is a philosophy of civilization: it wants to contribute to the securing and the advancement of civilization through knowledge of the conditions of civilization" (*HCR* 110–11 / *GS–3* 366). What characterizes civilization is that it has "at its disposal incomparably more and more highly developed arts" than does barbarism. So the "orientation" is "toward civilization and therefore toward the arts," understood not as imitation of nature but as the means by which self-interested human beings[19] repel or overcome nature (*HCR* 111 / *GS–3* 366). Hobbes's "ultimate division of being" is, then, "what is by nature and what is by art." But "art" understood as "the human capacity to bring about useful effects on the basis of reflection" (ibid.).

> The center of the critique of religion is the critique of miracles. The ultimate presupposition of the assertion of miracles is the belief that God can simply do anything, that the works of God are hence simply incomprehensible. Over and against the threat emanating from this belief to the original security of his orientation in the world, man finds his first protection in remembering that he understands that which he himself produces, i.e., in remembering art. When man has secured his orientation in the world by remembering art, he is in a position to take steps against the claim of belief that there are miracles. (*HCR* 112 / *GS–3* 367)

V

When we turn to the discussion of Hobbes in *Natural Right and History*, we seem to find Strauss making a new argument: the skepticism about the knowability of the world, and the modern scientific solution to it, is now presented as arising out of a problem that attends any "materialist-mechanistic physics," rather than out of an acceptance of the possibility of an unknowable God who has created the universe and who makes impossible any notion of "cause." But there is reason to think that this difference between the two accounts is less significant than it might seem.

Strauss quickly establishes that while Hobbes was indebted to the tradition of political philosophy for the view that political philosophy or political science is possible or necessary, and that Hobbes sided with the apparently "idealistic" tradition of political philosophy that public-spiritedly sought the "simply just social order," Hobbes attempted to combine this "political idealism with a materialistic and atheistic view of the whole" (*NRH* 167, 170). The novel result is that his political science can be characterized as "political atheism" (*NRH* 169). It is by way of justifying this claim that Strauss turns to his account of Hobbes's natural philosophy, telling us that we must keep that philosophy in mind when trying to understand Hobbes's political philosophy (ibid.). Hobbes's "natural philosophy is as atheistic as Epicurean physics," he states; it represents an attempt to combine that "materialist-mechanistic" physics with a "Platonic physics" that is "mathematical" (*NRH* 170). And this synthesis, this mathematical physics, is one that Strauss represents as occurring through "the abandonment of the plane on which 'Platonism' and 'Epicureanism' had carried on their secular struggle" (ibid.). What Strauss appears to mean by this is the struggle between materialistic atheism, on one hand, and those that would claim there are incorporeal substances (ideas), on the other (idealism). He later speaks of this as the "secular conflict between materialism and spiritualism" (*NRH* 174). "Platonism," in other words, means the positing of an incorporeal mind (cf. *NRH* 172), which for Hobbes was "out of the question."

Before addressing the manner in which Hobbes conceived of the new physics, Strauss first turns to the problem to which the new physics was a solution: the problem of "skepticism," over and against the "actualization of wisdom." "Skeptical philosophy" had always accompanied dogmatic philosophy, he argues, "as by its shadow" (*NRH* 171), and was to be eradicated by Hobbes by "doing justice to the truth embodied in skepticism." And this was to be achieved by first giving "free reign to skepticism" and erecting a new edifice on the "foundation of extreme skepticism." In a note to this argument, which pithily summarizes the section on Descartes from *Hobbes's Critique of Religion*, Strauss invites us to "[c]ompare Hobbes's agreement with the thesis of Descartes's first *Meditation*." The skepticism to which Strauss is referring here is, then, explicitly tied to the Cartesian argument of the Deus deceptor, even though the problem is now being called the shadow of "skeptical philosophy." And Strauss has dropped the entire argument showing disagreement between Hobbes and Descartes.

He then offers the reason—in Hobbes's mind—for the persistence of the skepticism that Hobbes set out to end. That reason is that the "predominant philosophic tradition" was one of "teleological physics" (*NRH* 172) and "the difficulty with which every" such physics "is beset." Strauss does not state what that difficulty is, but it seems safe to assume that he has in mind the lack of evidence concerning a naturally ordered whole. Still, this difficulty for a teleological physics does not itself give rise to skepticism; to the contrary, it opens the way to a "mechanistic physics," one that had "never been given a fair chance to show its virtues" owing to "social pressures of various kinds" (ibid.). Skepticism arises out of, is "engendered by," that materialist-mechanistic physics that Hobbes wished now to make victorious. Strauss explains Hobbes's understanding of that skepticism as follows: Hobbes had "learned from Plato or Aristotle that if the universe has the character ascribed to it by the Democritean-Epicurean physics, it excludes the possibility of any physics, of any science, or, in other words, that consistent materialism necessarily culminates in skepticism." Skepticism arises out of the difficulty attending all materialist-mechanistic physics, namely, that by understanding the mind as enslaved to the flux of mechanistic causation, materialists in fact make the world unintelligible. In *Hobbes's Critique of Religion* the problem of the intelligibility of the world had been presented as arising from the need to grant the premise of revelation according to which the world is the work of a mysterious, omnipotent, willing God. Here, however, the problem of the intelligibility of the world is presented as arising out of a mechanistic physics, and as something that Hobbes has "learned" from Plato and Aristotle.

But does this change represent a substantial or only a rhetorical difference? And if the former, what precisely is its significance? It may help to note that in the Aristotle chapter of *The City and Man*, where we receive Strauss's final presentation of the Deus deceptor argument, he indicates that the problem for philosophy that attends a mechanistic physics is the same problem as that of a willful, omnipotent God.

> We must reckon with the possibility that the world is the work of an evil demon bent on deceiving us about himself, the world, and ourselves by means of the

> faculties with which he has supplied us or, which amounts to the same thing, that the world is the work of a blind necessity which is utterly indifferent as to whether it and its product ever becomes known.[20]

While this formulation raises what appears to be a new concern—that is, of whether the fundamental cause that has produced the world cares or is *indifferent* to "whether it and its product ever becomes known"—it also conflates, as "amounting to the same thing," the problem for philosophy posed by the Deus deceptor and by mechanistic or blind necessity, that is, the problem of the knowability of the world.[21] In other words, the important challenge posed to philosophy by the biblical God of revelation seems to represent only a version, if one that is both more public and may have had other effects on the moderns' solution—of the problem already recognized by Plato and Aristotle.[22] Not Strauss's understanding of Hobbes, but instead his understanding of Descartes, has undergone a change. Strauss now reads Descartes's theological arguments as exoteric, and reads the Deus deceptor argument as having for its genuine intention the posing of the problem of the intelligibility of a world ruled by mechanistic-materialistic causation.

Still, it was indeed, historically, biblical revelation that had posed the problem for Hobbes and Descartes, and in *Natural Right and History* Strauss considerably mutes this fact. To be sure, he is not altogether silent about it: the discussion in *Natural Right and History* of the turn to the new physics is begun, after all, as an explanation of the claim that Hobbes's politics is "atheistic." And its description of the mind's activity in consciously constructing the world as an act of our "arbitrary will" or as "creation in the strict sense" (*NRH* 173) sounds much closer to the activity of the biblical God than had been even the description of that activity given in *Hobbes's Critique of Religion*. Finally, the account in *Natural Right and History* all but concludes with the striking statement that "the building of the City of Man on the ruins of the City of God rests on an unfounded hope" (*NRH* 175). Yet precisely as indications or suggestions, these are considerably less forcefully presented than was the thesis in *Hobbes's Critique of Religion*. What, if anything, beyond the changed understanding of Descartes, is the cause and significance of this change?

An explanation begins to suggest itself in the way in which Strauss describes, in *Natural Right and History*, the relation between Hobbes, on one hand, and Plato and Aristotle, on the other. He appears intent on framing the argument on Hobbes's physics in such a way as to draw our attention to what Hobbes "learned" and "did not learn" from Plato and Aristotle.[23] To consider only the first instance of these: Strauss claims (in a perhaps deliberately clumsy sentence, or at least one with three negatives in it) that what Hobbes "learned from Plato's natural philosophy was not that the universe cannot be understood if it is not ruled by a divine intelligence." But since Plato's dialogues may well lead readers, and indeed did lead many Platonists, to the conclusion to which Hobbes was *not* led, we might wonder why Hobbes did not learn it from Plato. And given Hobbes's published doubt of Aristotle's own belief in the Aristotelian doctrine of incorporeal or separate substances,[24] it could well be that Hobbes did not accept the doctrine of a divine, ruling intelligence as Plato's serious teaching. Strauss, from whom more than anyone we might expect such a hypothesis, appears to immediately rule it out: Hobbes failed to learn this, he implies, because "[w]hatever may have been Hobbes's private thoughts, his natural philosophy is as atheistic as Epicurean physics." Given his atheism, Hobbes considered an incorporeal mind to be "out of the question," as Strauss says a little later on the same page. In other words, Hobbes was simply closed to this as a possibility—not as a serious possibility for Plato but rather in itself.

With the stress Strauss puts on what Hobbes learned and did not learn from Plato and Aristotle, we are led to wonder whether there were not other aspects of their natural philosophy that Hobbes overlooked or too readily dismissed, and to which Strauss is inviting our attention. That there were indeed such aspects, and that they were even behind the Socratic turn to dialectics, that is, to the founding of political philosophy and hence of the "tradition" of political philosophy that Hobbes took for granted or overlooked (*NRH* 170), is made clear in Strauss's much more frank discussion of the matter found in the remarkable final chapter of *The Political Philosophy of Hobbes.* There he states in the following way the problem with a mechanistic physics that drove Socrates to found political philosophy as dialectics:

> Anaxagoras and others had tried to understand the things and processes in the world by their causes, by tracing them back to other things and processes in the world. However, this procedure affords no possibility of true understanding. [The accompanying note 3 here refers us to *Phaedo* 97b ff., where Socrates says that he no longer thinks it possible to know if "2" is by division or by addition, or how anything is.] Against this explanation of nature by the physiologists there is not only the objection that it is an insufficient explanation or no explanation at all; physics of the type of the Anaxagorean, "Epimethean" physics, which as such takes—whether expressly and intentionally or implicitly and unintentionally is of no importance—not the ordering power of reason, but disorder and irrationality as the principle of nature, necessarily leads to the destruction of all certain and independent standards, to finding everything in man's world very well as it is, and to subjection to "what the Athenians *believe*." Confronted with this absurd conclusion, Plato does not without further ado oppose to materialist-mechanistic physics a spiritualist-teleological physics [the accompanying note 4 is to *Phaedo* 99c–e], but keeps to what can be understood without any far-fetched "tragic" apparatus, to what the "Athenians" *say*. (*PPH* 142–43)

As Strauss goes on to argue in the same place, Hobbes misunderstood this Socratic turn to speeches.

In Chapter 4 of *Natural Right and History*, Strauss likewise presents Socrates as both founding political philosophy and as having never ceased his investigation into the nature of the beings. And the passage I have just quoted from *The Political Philosophy of Hobbes* helps us notice that in the section of *Natural Right and History* immediately preceding the account of the Socratic founding of political philosophy, that is, the conclusion of Chapter 3, Strauss had likewise referred to the Protagorean "Epimethean" doctrine:

> Epimetheus, the being in whom thought follows production, represents nature in the sense of materialism, according to which thought comes later than thoughtless bodies and their thoughtless motions. The subterraneous work of the gods is work without light, without understanding, and has therefore fundamentally the same meaning as the work of Epimetheus. Art is represented by Prometheus, by Prometheus' theft, by his rebellion against the will of the gods above. (*NRH* 117)

Protagoras, whom Plato presents as ascribing to the Epimethean doctrine, is therefore unable to do away with the possibility that what is held about the gods by pious human beings is true. The Epimethean, materialist doctrine of an unintelligible world and hence of the possibility that what religious believers say concerning revelations of gods's actions and intentions could be true, holds precisely the difficulty to which the Socratic turn to political philosophy had been addressed. Hobbes's founding of the new, modern phenomenalist physics, and of its necessary task of enlightenment or civilizing the world,[25] was undertaken in ignorance (see *NRH* 172: "as matters stood") of this fact. Strauss's own rediscovery of the original purpose of the Socratic turn rectifies this situation, and hence opens up the possibility of grounding the philosophic or rational life in a way that does not suffer from the difficulty to which the Hobbesian grounding (the progress of consciousness) has been shown to suffer.

Strauss's intention in framing the argument of the Hobbes section of *Natural Right and History* in such a way as to draw our thoughts to what Hobbes learned and did not learn from Plato and Aristotle has to be understood in light of the intention of the work as a whole. From the first chapter, that intention appears to be at its deepest level to address the argument raised by Heidegger against the very possibility of philosophy. The fullest reason for the change that we have traced might therefore best be sought in the digression (*NRH* 175–76) that appears in the Hobbes section that we have been examining. That digression concludes with the first reference to Heidegger's thesis about *Dasein* to be made since Chapter 1. Strauss leads up to it as follows. After the statement concerning Hobbes's "unfounded hope" to build the City of Man on the ruins of the City of God, Strauss speaks of how we, looking back on this attempt, find it difficult to know how Hobbes could have been so hopeful about the overcoming of human misery by means of the conquest of nature. The deepest reason for Hobbes's hope-filled error, and hence of the whole modern atheistic project, Strauss argues, is that the "experience, as well as the legitimate anticipation, of unheard of progress within the sphere which is subject to human control must have made him insensitive to 'the eternal silence of those infinite spaces' or to the crackings of the *moenia mundi*" (*NRH* 175). That is, Strauss reminds us that the premodern materialists, the Epicureans, were atheists of an apolitical sort *not* because they had never thought of combining mathematics and physics, but rather because, unlike Hobbes, they allowed nothing to obscure from them the ultimate futility of all human endeavors, nor to obscure the lack of significance of human things. And as Strauss next argues, the hopes Hobbes and his contemporaries kindled for overcoming human misery through human "construction" have not been extinguished by the "long series of disappointments that subsequent generations experienced." The persistence of these hopes has relied, Strauss argues, on repetitions of Hobbes's obscuring of the vision of the cracking of nature's walls, and on a corresponding false estimate of the significance of human life. The first instance of such post-Hobbesian obscuring, Strauss argues, is "the unplanned workings of 'History,'" which had the effect of "enhancing the status of man and of his 'world' by making him oblivious of the whole or of eternity" (*NRH* 175–76). As this statement implies, what Strauss means by awareness of the whole or of eternity—at least in part—is an (Epicurean) awareness of the cracking of the walls of the world, that is, the ultimate destruction of what is.[26] This awareness was, moreover, as he points out a little later, *also* part of the Socratic or "idealistic" tradition prior to Hobbes.[27] Strauss then concludes this brief digression by referring to a doctrine of Heidegger as another manifestation of the hopeful, post-Hobbesian obscuring of the whole, that is, of its ultimate destruction (*NRH* 176):

> In its final stage the typically modern limitation expresses itself in the suggestion that the highest principle, which, as such, has no relation to any possible cause or causes of the whole, is the mysterious ground of "History" and, being wedded to man and to man alone, is so far from being eternal that it is coeval with human history.

Dasein, by this account, is an expression of the turning away from eternity and hence entails an artificial "enhancing the status of man and his 'world.'" Despite the fact that Heidegger, in *Being and Time*, speaks much about death and being toward death, the atheism of Heidegger, Strauss had concluded, is an atheism achieved by the turning *away* from the ultimate decay of all things.[28] It carries within it the forgetting of eternity that had been begun by Hobbes. Strauss's new account of Hobbes's founding of modern science is designed to highlight, therefore, the manner in which Hobbes, unlike the classical political philosophers, turned away from the eventual destruction of the world, and how this was continued in various forms right through to Heidegger, who had himself undertaken a certain return to the ancients. The immediately preceding chapter, on classic natural right, shows the ancient approach to the problem that Hobbes confronted, an approach that begins with a concern for justice as our primary stance or orientation in the world.[29] That Strauss already speaks, at the time he was composing *Hobbes's Critique of Religion*, of writing a book on natural right, suggests that had he completed the manuscript of *Hobbes's Critique of Religion*, its conclusion would have moved in the direction of the argument that we find in *Natural Right and History*.

Notes

1. See Heinrich Meier, *GS–3* IX–XII.
2. Hereafter referred to as *HCR*. All translations are from this Bartlett-Minkov translation. Page numbers in parentheses refer to this translation, followed by the corresponding page numbers to the German original in *GS–3*.

3. *SCR*, "Preface," 19, and "Comments on *Der Begriff Des Politischen* by Carl Schmitt," 344–45. The original of this work was published as *Die Religionskritik Spinozas als Grundlage seiner Bibelwissenschaft Untersuchungen zu Spinozas Theologisch-Politischem Traktat* (Berlin: Akademie-Verlag, 1930).
4. An English translation of this preface is available in *JPCM* 453–56.
5. Thomas L. Pangle, "On the Strauss/Krüger Correspondence," chapter 4 of the present volume. I have relied on the translations of the Strauss-Krüger correspondence made by Pangle in his chapter.
6. Both the influence of Heidegger and the critique of Heidegger are manifest in the following passage, *SCR* 214: "Just as the assertion of miracles is called in question by the positive mind, positive critique of miracles is called in question by the mind that waits in faith or in doubt for the coming of the miracles. The weapon which the positive mind believes it has discovered in the fact that the assertion of miracles is *relative to the pre-scientific stage of mankind*, is taken away from the positive mind by the observation that this fact permits the *opposite* interpretation. Is the *will* to 'establish,' which needs only to have become victorious for experience of miracles to become impossible, itself something to be taken for granted? Does not man come to his most weighty and impelling insight when he is *startled out* of the composure of observation by which facts are 'established,' when he finds himself in the condition of *excitation*, in which alone miracles become perceptible at all?"

   One sees here the raising of Heideggerian arguments, not only in the denial of the depth of the everydayness of facts but in the reference to the agitated zone between life and death in which there is an intensification of experience that permits an "event" to happen. But as Strauss here suggests, the atheism that one sees in Spinoza, and that Strauss understands to have reached its culmination in Heidegger's *Dasein* interpretation of the call of conscience, the atheism of the positive or scientific mind, is something that Strauss understood to rest on a "will," not on an establishable progress of consciousness.
7. A work that, as *HCR* 75n11 makes clear, Strauss had already completed as he continued composing *HCR*.
8. See *SCR* 90: "He does not contend against religion, but against unmethodical seeking after causes. The anti-religious implication is not primarily intended. His critique of religion is not the object, but only the subsidiary result of analyzing and defining science."
9. Strauss goes through the features of this outlook at *HCR* 65–67 / *GS–3* 316–17: Fear of gods and of death prevent man's happiness and can be banished by the science of nature alone, which demonstrates that the fear is based on ignorance of nature. Science comprehends all of nature as necessitated or determined, not arbitrary or chaotic, and hence nature is not in need of gods. Nature is without riddle or secret in principle. "Thus only corporeal substances could be acknowledged as substances, and only local motions as alterations: the Epicurean outlook demands a mechanistic-corporealistic physics" (*HCR* 66–67 / *GS–3* 317). This is followed by an account of Socianism as the outward, exoteric version of Epicureanism.
10. *HCR* 67ff. / *GS–3* 317ff. This "modification" is according to Strauss prepared by Epicurus himself, who argues for following the myth of a beneficent God rather than "to be a slave to the fate of which the physicists speak" (*HCR* 67 / *GS–3* 318). This "slavery" seems to be what, in Chapter 5 of *NRH*, Strauss concentrates on as the problem that led Hobbes to phenomenalist science.

While Hobbes outwardly adopts all kinds of things from the Socinians, his "critique of the tradition... is based on... an Epicureanism that ventures into the light only under the cover of Socinianism" (*HCR* 72 / *GS–3* 322). Nevertheless, Strauss indicates that Hobbes did take something of importance away from Socianism (*HCR* 70 / *GS–3* 320): "From Socianism, accordingly, Hobbes came to understand the hope for immortality in the true Epicurean way of thinking as a simple guarantee against the fear of death, and not primarily as the reproachful reminder of man's duty and guilt. The presupposition for this conception of immortality is that the significance of God's punitive justice, if it is not denied in general, at any rate recedes behind his mercy." That is, the link between justice and the moral life and the longing for immortality was severed.

11. The footnote reads "Cf., in this connection, *Spinoza's Critique of Religion*, 144f., 204ff. [in the English translation]." *SCR* 144f. is the conclusion of Chapter 5, "The Critique of Orthodoxy." Here Strauss states that the "positive mind" (moved by empirical and positive science) can be said to lack an organ, to see less, than the believer. It succeeds only by mockery of belief, not by successfully defeating the believer in argument. At *SCR* 204ff., part of the section called "The Critique of Calvin," Strauss presents it as impossible for the positive mind to offer a sufficient critique of the unfathomable God.
12. The footnote directs us to *SCR* 212ff. There, in Section E of "The Critique of Calvin" chapter, Strauss states the following: "[T]he basically problematic character of [Spinoza's critique of revealed religion]... becomes most plainly manifest when brought face to face with the position upheld by Calvin." That position, the position of "revealed religion," has as its "central assumption" that "God is unfathomable will." Strauss's claim is that "[p]ositive critique finds itself face to face with this central assumption in particular when it contests the reality of miracles." The faith of the one who makes the assumption that God is unfathomable will is characterized by "Trust in God, obedience to him," and this trust discerns "in each cosmic process (not only in the stirrings of the human heart), the hand of God at work," and does not distinguish between miracles and nature (*SCR* 213). Strauss includes as part of "positive critique" of miracles the argument concerning a progressive development of consciousness, and indicates that that argument dooms the positive critique, in the end. He initially suggests, at *SCR* 212, that this attempt of positive critique, as opposed to "systematic critique," cannot refute the possibility of miracles. But then, at *SCR* 213, he argues that in fact positive critique has been the most effective critique:

> Positive critique does not merely prove that miracles are not knowable for the unbelieving understanding. It simultaneously detects, by virtue of the self-consciousness of the positive mind, the relativity of the accounts of miracles to the pre-scientific "vulgar" stage of mankind. *But is the assertion of miracles not more completely undermined by this than by any fruitless demonstrations that miracles are not possible?* When one considers the final result from all the efforts made in the course of seventeenth and eighteenth-century critique of miracles, one cannot but conclude that positive critique of miracles, which at first sight appears to be so inconspicuous and which does no more than inquire how miracles are to be recognized, is of more enduring significance than the attempt, at first sight so attractive, made in the metaphysics of the Enlightenment, to prove the impossibility of miracles. Positive critique demonstrates that the positive mind, applying precise observation and stringent analysis, is incapable of perceiving

> miracles. Previous to this, positive critique establishes that miracles must be accessible to that mind if they are to be indubitably established.

But then Strauss pivots, and shows that positive critique ultimately fails in this historicizing effort. He first raises an objection that Spinoza seems able to answer, concerning the disposition of the positive mind as one that matches a disposition described in Scripture (*SCR* 214):

> But are miracles—understood as primarily meant—"established"? Are not miracles looked forward to, implored in prayer and supplication? In Spinoza's sense, one may say against this, that according to the testimony of Scripture miracles were experienced also by those who did not await them in trust and faith.

Strauss then points out that the apparent parallel adduced by Spinoza does not in fact obtain: the unbelieving spectators in the contest between Jahweh and Baal, cited by Spinoza, experienced "doubt," but this is quite different from the disposition or moral attitude of the positivist mind (ibid.):

> These unbelieving "spectators" were however not convinced by merely seeing the miracle, but by a form of seeing that had a peculiar presupposition. They see—after waiting, not in faith, but in doubt, in uncertainty, to see whether the *event* announced will occur, by which the question, "Jahweh or Baal" will be decided. Can the man who has understood the meaning of this question even wish to "establish" anything?

What Strauss appears to be pointing out is that the positive mind does not have uncertainty or *doubt* at all; the Biblical doubter is one who has presented prayer and supplication to Baal, after all. The doubter waits for the "event"; his disposition is altogether different from that of the positive mind. The believer or even the *doubter* will therefore eventually turn the argument concerning the alleged development of the "self conscious mind" against the enlightenment (ibid.):

> Just as the assertion of miracles is called in question by the positive mind, positive critique of miracles is called in question by the mind that waits in faith or in doubt for the coming of the miracles. The weapon which the positive mind believes it has discovered in the fact that the assertion of miracles is relative to the pre-scientific stage of mankind, is taken away from the positive mind by the observation that this fact permits the opposite interpretation. Is the will to "establish," which needs only to have become victorious for experience of miracles to become impossible, itself something to be taken for granted? Does not man come to his most weighty and impelling insight when he is startled out of the composure of observation by which facts are "established," when he finds himself in the condition of excitation, in which alone miracles become perceptible at all?

13. In response to a point made by Krüger in his review of *SCR*, Strauss here explains in a footnote that what he had presented as "Calvin's teaching on miracles" is only the "final outcome" of Calvin's argument, and that it is only "as to *this result*" that "Hobbes agrees with Calvin."
14. The notes to this paragraph of *HCR* (¶¶ 236 and 237, with reference also ahead to notes 238 and 283, and thence also back to note 265) quote sections of *De Corpore* and *De Homine* and *De Cive* and *Elements of Law*. *Elements of Law* was published in 1640, *De Cive* in 1642; *De Corpore* was begun in 1642, even if it was not published until 1665. *Leviathan* was published in 1651. *Questions Concerning Liberty, Necessity, and Chance* was published in 1656. *De Homine* was not published until 1657. Later, Strauss will make reference to Hobbes's objections to Descartes's

Meditations. Those objections (and Descartes's replies), along with objections of and replies to six other prominent philosophers, were published in the first edition of the *Meditations*, published in Paris in 1641. (His objections and Descartes's replies are the third set.)

15. Following the argument of Tönnies, Strauss initially and tentatively (see Note 263) makes the case that Hobbes is a more radical "phenomenalist" than Descartes: Hobbes in some places argues that only the objects of our mind's representations, and not the existence of corporeal things, can be known with any certainty. That is, for Hobbes, "body" appears to be only a "positing of consciousness, of thinking"; even body characterized by extension is a "mere name," or something that "appears to" (but may not in fact) exist. If this is so, then while Hobbes appears repeatedly to equate substance and body, that is, to be a "metaphysical materialist," in fact his materialism would be only "methodical," that is, it would be a materialism that leaves open the question of whether sensibly perceived bodies exist in themselves.
16. Only in his confrontation with Descartes, Strauss points out, does Hobbes prove the existence of God by reasoning back from the "ideas" (in our minds) to their ultimate cause; in all other places he reasons from "observed corporeal effects to their ultimate cause," that is, God. Strauss takes this as decisive evidence that "materialism," not phenomenalism, is Hobbes's "fundamental conviction" (362).
17. Reckoning with the possibility of a God who actually wastes his time and energy, as it were, deceiving human beings is not something Hobbes considered worthwhile; for God (understood as body), he thought, treats men with "complete indifference." And as we have seen, the world's resistance vouches for its genuine existence rather than its simulation.
18. Strauss opens this final section by declaring that the basis of the critique of religion "is not 'phenomenalism'; the 'phenomenalist' thesis hardly appears in the writings of Hobbes devoted to a critique of religion; it is in any case, of no significance for his critique of religion" (*HCR* 109 / *GS–3* 364). For the "presupposition that Hobbes steadily makes use of in his critique of religion is rather 'materialism,' the monism of substances (see [*HCR* 64 / *GS–3* 314)." Strauss then argues that the "materialism" is also *not* the "basis," since "materialism," as he had already argued, is "the product of the scientific elaboration of the pre-scientific concept of body" (*HCR* 109–10 / *GS–3* 364). And that elaboration depends on "the articulation of being into resistant and nonresistant (into 'bodies' and 'spirits')." Materialism, to be sure, does away with this "articulation of being," by eliminating from being the nonresistant, or "spirits" (*HCR* 110 / *GS–3* 365). Materialism cannot completely overcome the presupposition of this articulation of being: the articulation into the resistant world, on one hand, and "we... who assert ourselves against the world by acting" on it, on the other, or into the two classes, "man and nature." (There is no resistance without man there to do it.) So, we can finally say, the presupposition of the critique of religion is the articulation of being as man and nature, which permits materialism to be established.

    Yet "'phenomenalism' is also present in Hobbes's original presupposition" (ibid.). For while being is articulated into man and nature, one part of that articulation, "man," is understood as a being with images or representations of being in himself, or an inner world into which he can retreat. This means that phenomenalism, just like materialism, has its "origin in" the "original presupposition" that being is man and nature, or rather, that "*we men are in the power of a resistant world, but in such a way that we can withdraw from this world into our inner world*." (ibid.) Strauss is now calling this "Hobbes's fundamental presupposition."

19. Strauss not only includes consciousness of self-interestedness ("sound common sense") and hence suspicion of alleged prophets, as part of Hobbes's understanding of "remembering art," but points out a certain agreement on this score between Hobbes, on one hand, and Socrates and the sophists, on the other (*HCR* 111–13 / *GS-3* 367–68).
20. *CM* 43. In the full argument (*CM* 42–43), which concerns Aristotle's defense of his view of the possibility of a happiness that is according to nature from the assertion of the poets that the divine is envious of man's happiness, Strauss begins with the suggestion that the assertion that the whole is the work of an evil demon or god—an assertion that he calls a modified version of the poetic assertion that the gods bear malice toward us—relies upon an understanding of the human good that lacks cogency: we allegedly cannot know what the good is, yet we know that the end toward which we are by nature inclined (i.e., knowledge) is bad. Strauss "therefore" examines the modern argument more carefully, that is, because of the argument's lack of cogency, Strauss does not think that this first version can possibly be what the moderns were really saying. The second version he arrives at in the following way. He first examines "the modern criticism of Aristotle's principle." To say that they criticized it because they rejected final causes is not sufficient, Strauss argues, since the ancient *materialists* had rejected final causes as well but had not denied that the good life is life according to nature, and they had claimed that nature provides the necessary things easily. In place of this unsatisfactory argument concerning the moderns' rejection of final causes, Strauss therefore offers a somewhat surprising alternative: the moderns' rejection of Aristotle's principle begins by pondering what *Aristotle himself* suggests when he declares that our nature is enslaved in many ways: nature is a harsh step-mother, or "the true mother of man is not nature." This is something that Aristotle and the moderns agree upon; it is not "peculiar to modern thought." What *is* peculiar to modern thought is, instead, "the *consequent* resolve to liberate man from that enslavement by his own sustained effort." The argument to this point has nothing to do with the problem of knowledge of the whole, or the need to refute revelation or miracles.

   But then how did this "resolve" to liberate man arise as a "consequence" of the enslavement-to-nature argument, when it *hadn't* arisen for Aristotle from that same argument? Strauss's suggestion is again somewhat surprising. The resolve shows itself, he states, in the "demand for the 'conquest' of nature: nature is understood and treated as an enemy who must be subjugated." And this "resolve," Strauss now suggests, is bound up with a Christian understanding of virtue: "Accordingly science ceases to be contemplation and becomes the humble and charitable handmaid devoted to the relief of man's estate." (Not just humble but also charitable, and a "handmaid," as science was to theology in the Christian Middle Ages.) Strauss here describes the moderns as if they were runaway slaves bent on the destruction of their former masters, the Christian theologians, still possessed of the virtues inculcated by their masters but working now for the good of all mankind, that is, for a different master. In any event, by this new telling, the moderns did not begin by rejecting the notion that our natural end is good because they accepted the possibility that the world is the work of an evil demon. To the contrary: the moderns are now said to understand science as being "for the sake of power, i.e., for putting at our disposal the means to achieving our natural ends." The notion of natural ends was still present, at this point, then, but the whole business seems to be a project with a moral component ("*our* disposal"). We still do not quite know, however, how this project acquired its motivation. "Those ends can no longer include knowledge for its own sake; they are reduced to comfortable self-preservation." Strauss next explains why not, and in explaining it, both spells out another or alternative manner in which Christianity/the battle with Christianity was bound up in the motives behind the moderns' "resolve" to liberate man:

> Man as the potential conqueror of nature stands outside of nature. This presupposes that there is no natural harmony between the human mind and the whole. The belief in such harmony appears now as a wishful or good-natured assumption. We must reckon with the possibility that the world is the work of an evil demon bent on deceiving us about himself, the world, and ourselves by means of the faculties he has supplied us with or, which amounts to the same thing, that the world is the work of a blind necessity which is utterly indifferent as to whether it and its product ever becomes known.

So now the presupposition of the conquest of nature is the *Deus deceptor*, presented as the equivalent of the argument of a mechanistic materialism, a world of "blind necessity." A certain disappointment in a world whose cause is fundamentally indifferent to whether we achieve the knowledge that appears to be our natural end, a disappointment that would only be possible if there were an original hope that the cause behind the world somehow *cares* about our coming to know it, seems in this account to have been behind the resolve to "liberate" man. And to those affected by this disappointment, the ancients' apparent assumption that there is a "harmony between the human mind and the whole . . . appears now as a wishful or good-natured assumption."

But did the ancients even hold the assumption in question concerning the "natural harmony between the human mind and the whole"? The appearance here that Strauss thought that they did is somewhat misleading. That harmony was something Strauss had indeed presented, on 41, to be an Aristotelian doctrine: "There is a natural harmony between the whole and the human mind. Man would not be capable of happiness if the whole of which he is a part were not friendly to him." Yet he gives two versions of this optimistic doctrine. He first suggests that it means that nature purposefully "supplies" man with food and his other wants. But he soon after affirms that in truth, according to Aristotle, "the nature of man is enslaved in many ways" (and, as we have seen, this includes the fact, disclosed on 42, that according to Aristotle nature does *not* supply our wants or is "not a kind mother but a harsh stepmother"). Between these two statements on 41 is his claim that according to Aristotle, the world is the best possible world; that is, the world could not be a better one because the evils with which it abounds could not be removed without greater evils, so that "man has no right to complain and to rebel." The rosy version of the world as the best possible world is that nature provides, the city is natural, and there is a harmony between the whole and the human mind. In the less rosy version, "only a rare few, and even these not always, achieve happiness or the highest freedom of which man is by nature capable." If even this version implies some kind of harmony between the human mind and the whole, it does not seem to be a "wishful or good-natured assumption." It is, rather, one that entails resignation, especially to mortality, a resignation that may well be needed precisely for theorizing, or seeing what we can see of the world as it is but as it may well not be forever. The modern "resolve" to liberate man may, then, in fact have been driven by a failure of resignation, a confused sense of a "right to rebel" (against whom?) even though that resolve *appears* to be less naive than the ancient position. On the Platonic-Aristotelian disposition toward our "enslavement" to nature, or our being "playthings of the gods," see also below, note 27.

21. Strauss's conflating of the two appears to follow the argument of the last four paragraphs of Descartes's first *Meditation*, where Descartes presents as alternative to creation by an omnipotent God "fate or chance or a continuous chain of events, or by some other means." "Fate" seems to mean mechanistic determinism; and "a continuous chain of events," especially if one guided by nothing but chance, would also suggest mechanism. Already in his 1959 lectures on Nietzsche's *Zarathustra* (6 of the transcript) Strauss had stated that Descartes did not believe in the possibility of a *Deus deceptor*, but was describing the problem of the knowability of a world caused by mechanistic-material causes.

22. Strauss's claim that these "amount to the same thing" is puzzling in that the unknowabilty is in each case quite different. The difficulty in the case of a materialist-mechanistic physics is that its own account of causation is self-defeating. If all human thinking is understood to be caused by a chain of blind material causes, this very understanding is caused by such a chain, in the person who makes it. And no mind would be moved to agree with the arguments of such a person by the principle of noncontradiction or rules of logic, but would instead be moved strictly by material causes. The doctrine itself would be the product of a series of blind material causes, rather than a doctrine that could be true or could convince another. The difficulty in the case of an omnipotent creative god, on the other hand, is that there are no causes at all; all that is comes to be out of nothing, and an oak tree may very well turn instantly into a jellyfish.

But there is this relation between the two doctrines: the unintelligibility resulting from the materialist-mechanistic physics—that is, from the claim that mechanistic determinism is the universal and sole cause of change in the universe—must if true undermine the trust we have in our minds to discover the truth. And it is this that drives Protagoras to declare that what any and all Athenians believe, is; or more generally, that "[each] man is the measure of all things," so that those who believe themselves to have had a revelation of gods overturning necessities are as correct, their statements about the world as true, as Protagoras's materialism.

23. The first statement appears at *NRH* 169–70:

> [Hobbes's] natural philosophy is of the type classically represented by Democritean-Epicurean physics. Yet he regarded, not Epicurus or Democritus, but Plato, as "The best of the ancient philosophers." What he learned from Plato's natural philosophy was not that the universe cannot be understood if it is not ruled by divine intelligence. Whatever may have been Hobbes's private thoughts, his natural philosophy is as atheistic as Epicurean physics. What he learned from Plato's natural philosophy was that mathematics is "the mother of all natural science."

The next two appear at *NRH* 172:

> For he had learned from Plato or Aristotle that if the universe has the character ascribed to it by Democritean-Epicurean physics, it excludes the possibility of any physics, of any science, or, in other words, that consistent materialism necessarily culminates in skepticism.... On the other hand,

what he had learned from Plato and Aristotle made him realize somehow that the corporeal mind, composed of very smooth and round particles with which Epicurus remained satisfied, was an inadequate solution.

24. See *Leviathan*, Ch. 46, Section 18, end.
25. "This implies that the whole scheme suggested by Hobbes requires for its operation the weakening or, rather, the elimination of the fear of invisible powers. It requires such a radical change of orientation as can be brought about only by the disenchantment of the world, by the diffusion of scientific knowledge, or by popular enlightenment. Hobbes's is the first doctrine that necessarily and unmistakably point to a thoroughly 'enlightened,' i.e., a-religious or atheistic society as the solution of the social or political problem" (*NRH* 198).
26. The footnote to this sentence brings out the point still more clearly. It includes quotations from Friedrich Engels and from J. J. Bachofen. Here is a translation of the Engels quotation:

    [N]othing exists in the eyes [of dialectical philosophy] but the unbroken process of becoming and passing away, the *endless* ascent from the lower to the higher.... We need not here go into the question of whether this way of looking at things agrees completely with the current state of natural science, which predicts a possible end of the earth's existence but *a quite certain end* of its habitability, which therefore also confers on human history not only an ascending but also a descending. We find ourselves *in any case quite far from the turning point.*

    And the Bachofen quotation:

    The East pays homage to the natural standpoint, the West replaces it with the historical.... One could feel oneself tempted to recognize, in this *subordination of the divine idea to the human*, the final stage of the falling away from an earlier, more elevated standpoint.... And yet this relapse contains the seeds for a very important progress [*Fortschritt*]. For we have to regard as such that freeing of our mind from the crippling shackles of a cosmic-physical view of life.... If the anxious Etruscan believes in the finiteness of his race, the Roman takes pleasure in the eternity of his state, *which he is not even capable of doubting.*

    (The emphases in both quotations are Strauss's.)
27. See *NRH* 177 "No Scipionic dream illuminated by a true vision of the whole reminds his readers of the ultimate futility of all that men can do." Not only in the Epicurean tradition, then, but likewise in what Strauss has been calling the "idealistic" tradition of political philosophy, one finds a "vision of the whole" as one of man's ultimate destruction. On this point, and the resigned moderation that results from such a vision of the whole, see also "The Problem of Socrates," Second Lecture, in *RCPR* 133, concerning the "false estimate of human things" as a "fundamental and primary error," and the subsequent discussion of spiritedness in the Fourth Lecture (*RCPR* 167). Consider also the following statement from TWM 85–86:

    Man has a place within the whole: man's power is limited; man cannot overcome the limitations of his nature. Our nature is enslaved in many ways (Aristotle) or we are the playthings of the gods (Plato). This limitation shows itself in particular in the ineluctable power of chance. The good life is the life according to nature, which means to stay within certain limits; virtue is essentially moderation. There is no difference in this respect between classical political philosophy and classical hedonism which is unpolitical: not the maximum of pleasures but the purest pleasures are desirable; happiness depends decisively on the limitation of our desires.

(The Plato statement can be found at *Laws* 709a1–3; cf. 644d7–e4 and 803c4–5.)

28. Consider in this light the very helpful remarks of Christopher Bruell, "Death in the Perspective of Philosophy," lecture delivered at the Carl Friedrich von Siemens Stiftung, Munich, July 17, 2003, 12–16: Heidegger calls not those who might be capable of it but rather "one and all" from the flight away from death, from absorption in the every day; he is a "prophet of doom," but one who also holds out the promise of a *Daseinsganzheit*, that is, of achieving a wholeness of being or *fully* existing in and through the proper stance toward death, and who also concedes no legitimacy to our natural if unfulfillable concern with immortality, to the point of tracing the belief in a prospect or image of an unending time and of the wish to bring time to an halt, to the outlook of "decadent Being." And his account of death as "individualizing" us misses what genuinely does so, and hence holds out the promise of a "Being-together" in a fated struggle with others as some kind of authentic being. And, most importantly, while Heidegger distinguishes empirical certainty of death from apodictic, theoretical certainty of it, he shows little interest in attempting to acquire such apodictic, theoretical certainty of it.
29. See note 10, above.

CHAPTER 8

LEO STRAUSS ON FARABI, MAIMONIDES, ET AL. IN THE 1930S

Joshua Parens

The end of the 1930s marked a turning point in Strauss's thought that Daniel Tanguay has aptly called his "Farabian Turn."[1] Although Strauss's most extended work on Farabi, Maimonides, et al. in the 1930s is *Philosophy and Law* (1935),[2] the turn Tanguay identifies is more evident in the smaller pieces that came out in the wake of *Philosophy and Law*—including "Some Remarks on the Political Science of Maimonides and Farabi" (1936)[3] but especially "The Place of the Doctrine of Providence according to Maimonides" (1937).[4] In these two pieces, Strauss evinces a growing awareness of the depth of Maimonides's debt to Farabi. Tanguay identifies two main features of the Farabian Turn: the focus on the political in Maimonides and a growing awareness of the centrality of esotericism. Prior to the Turn, in *Philosophy and Law*, Strauss elevated two features in his interpretation of Maimonides that fade into the background as early as the two pieces written in 1936 and 1937: the importance of Avicenna's account of prophecy and Maimonides's apparent reliance on supernatural resources for knowledge of things beyond the limit of natural human knowledge. Beginning in 1936, Strauss avoids any suggestion that the supernatural plays such a role.[5]

Our initial focus in this chapter will be on how "Place of Providence" provides a missing piece in Strauss's effort to show that political science is central in Maimonides's *Guide*. Before the Farabian Turn, Strauss was bold in declaring this centrality. And with the beginning of the Farabian Turn in 1936 and 1937, he remains bold in declaring its centrality and Maimonides's debt to Farabi regarding its centrality. Subsequently, however, and as early as his (1941) "Literary Character of the *Guide for the Perplexed*,"[6] Strauss speaks far more cautiously about the role of political science in Maimonides's thought. Indeed in "Literary Character," his main reference to political science in the *Guide* is to how "there is practically complete agreement among the students of Maimonides" that the *Guide* does not concern it (*PAW* 44). Indeed, there are moments in the *Guide* (end of II 39) as well as in

Maimonides's *Logic* (Chapter 14, end) that appear to exclude any concern with political science or philosophy.[7] Strauss moves from boldly underlining the importance of political science in and for the *Guide* in the 1930s to downplaying direct reference to political science in connection with Maimonides. As Tanguay notes, after the Farabian turn Strauss decided more and more to emulate premodern esotericism.[8] That emulation includes writing in an increasingly esoteric manner about the character and objectives of the *Guide*. Because of Strauss's greater frankness in his writings in the 1930s, they provide an indispensable window into understanding Strauss's lifelong interest in Maimonides and especially his *Guide*. Although his insights into Maimonides deepened even into the last decade of his life, his earliest, at times ambiguous, insights were often proffered with the greatest frankness.

After our initial focus on the pieces on Farabi and Maimonides, we will turn to consider Strauss's writings from the 1930s on Isaac Abravanel. Strauss came to see that Maimonides had been too readily assimilated to medieval Christian philosophy.[9] Because Abravanel's approach to political philosophy was deeply indebted to medieval Christian thought, Strauss came to see that Abravanel's own thought as well as his interpretations of Maimonides followed Christian patterns. We will add Strauss's understanding of Abravanel to our prior focus on his Farabian reading of Maimonides to paint a picture of Strauss's emerging understanding of Maimonides in the 1930s.

Arguably, the most striking insight overall in Strauss's writings on Maimonides, Farabi, et al. of the 1930s is also the broadest structural insight: In *Philosophy and Law*, Strauss shows that the prophetology (*Guide* II 32–48) is part of Maimonides's political science, and in the "Place of Providence" Strauss shows that his teaching on particular providence (*Guide* III 8–24) is also part of his political science. In other words, Strauss argues that the central chapters of the *Guide* are part of political science.[10] A potential source of confusion is worth nipping in the bud: Maimonides states that after *Guide* III 7 (the culmination of what every reader of the *Guide* readily acknowledges is the most elusive discussion in this most elusive of books, the biblical Account of the Chariot [*Guide* III 1–7]), "after this chapter, you will not hear from me even a single word about this subject." Strauss interprets this as Maimonides's establishment of the end of his discussion of divine science or metaphysics in the *Guide*. Maimonides implies thereby that *Guide* III 8–24 is not a metaphysical discussion. Now if one overinterprets Strauss, one could suppose that this implies that everything preceding *Guide* III 7 concerns metaphysics. This would obviously undercut the claim that the prophetology is part of political science. It is one thing to say that henceforth I will not say anything more about *x*, and quite another thing to say that all I discussed previously was about *x*. And it is obviously false to suggest that everything prior to *Guide* III 7 concerns metaphysics or divine science. In short, it is at least conceivable that both the prophetology and the teaching on particular providence are part of Maimonides's political science.

Aside from the bold insinuation that the central arguments of the *Guide* are political, what is the significance of Strauss's claim that these two sections are part of political science? To answer this question, we begin by considering why one might have assumed that these two sections were a part of metaphysics or divine science. Throughout the *Guide*, the exact content of divine science is in contention.

After all, the Introduction to the First Part opens with the riddle that equates the biblical or rabbinic mysteries, the Account of the Beginning and the Account of the Chariot, with natural science or physics and divine science or metaphysics. There is little agreement among scholars about what this means. It could mean that (*a*) the secret teachings of the Torah are these philosophic theoretical sciences (cf. *Guide* I 71), (*b*) the secret teachings of the Torah are some revealed equivalent to these philosophic sciences, or (*c*) the secret teachings of the Torah are a blend or synthesis of philosophic and revealed teachings. Perhaps the most widely prevailing interpretation is some version of (*c*). Strauss seems to have adopted some version of (*c*) in *Philosophy and Law*.

In keeping with some version of (*c*), one would think that the prophetology would be a part of the Account of the Chariot or divine science because the central role that the Active Intellect, the lowest of the separate intellects, plays in the reception of prophecy by the prophet. To say that the prophetology is part of political science is to discount the centrality of the theoretical psychology of prophecy.[11] Strauss does not discount completely that psychology in *Philosophy and Law*, but he does begin a process of shifting more and more emphasis from the psychology to political science. Similarly, one would think that Maimonides's teaching on particular providence would be part of his divine science. After all, who but God is responsible for particular providence? At this point, we may venture the conjecture that Strauss's break from his earlier stress on the role of the supernatural in prophetic action and human knowledge of the metaphysical and his turn to this unexpected approach to particular providence in "Place of Providence" are connected. As we will see, Strauss's analyses of prophecy and particular providence lead Strauss step by step back to Plato by way of Farabi, not only in *Philosophy and Law*, Chapter 3, and "Place of Providence," but perhaps especially in "Some Remarks."

In *Philosophy and Law*, Strauss begins the shift in orientation away from more theoretical inquiries toward political science in his analysis of Maimonides's *Guide* well before he gets to Chapter 3. In the Introduction, Strauss shows that what makes Maimonides's medieval enlightenment distinctive is that it, unlike the modern Enlightenment, takes as its "leading idea ...the idea of Law" (*PLA* 39). Because the modern Enlightenment is oriented elsewhere, namely, the autonomous individual or the subjective consciousness, interpreters like Julius Guttmann, whom Strauss devotes so much attention to criticizing in Chapter 1, treat "philosophy of religion" or "religious consciousness" as the central phenomena of all Jewish thinkers, including Maimonides (*PLA* 73). Since at least Spinoza, political philosophers have made every effort to transform religion into a part of man's private or social, as opposed to political, experience. Strauss discovers in Maimonides's concern with Law or the divine Law a different focus upon something both public and total. The Law, unlike contemporary religion, covers every aspect of life. Consequently, the Law proves to be the natural counterpoint to philosophy as a total way of life (*PLA* 73). The more partial or less encompassing a religion's demands become, the less relevant they are as a counterpoint to philosophy.

In Chapter 1, Strauss identifies in reverse order the two main steps of his argument: (Chapter 3) the philosophic foundation of the law and (Chapter 2) the legal foundation of philosophy (*PLA* 60). Already in Chapter 2's focus on the legal foundation, we can see the centrality of Law—and in a light that anticipates the focus of

Strauss's subsequent studies of Platonic political philosophy. Any reader of Strauss's writings on not only Plato but also Aristophanes will be reminded by Chapter 2 of the fate of Socrates in Aristophanes's *Clouds* and Plato's *Apology* and *Phaedo*. Through the lens of the city, the philosopher appears to be a renegade. The Law is the highest expression of the city's way of life.

The main focus of the legal foundation of philosophy (Chapter 2) is sufficiently difficult to detect in Maimonides that Strauss devotes little attention to it (cf. *PLA* 89–92, approximately three pages in Adler's translation). Figuring prominently in the middle of it is a declaration that we will not find after *Philosophy and Law*: "[H]uman intellect has a limit which it cannot cross; for this reason man is obliged for the glory of the Lord, to halt at this limit and not to reject the teachings of revelation that he cannot comprehend and demonstrate. Philosophy is free—in its own sphere. Its sphere is nature, not super-nature" (*PLA* 90–91).[12] In every other respect, Strauss associates Maimonides's position with that of Averroes.

Strauss presents Maimonides's legal foundation of philosophy as a mean between Averroes's defense of philosophy before the bar of the law in his *Decisive Treatise* and Gersonides's oddly proto-modern claims to pursue philosophy in his *Wars of the Lord*.[13] Averroes, unlike Strauss's Maimonides in *Philosophy and Law* (*PLA* 66–67), defends philosophy before the law by tacitly assuming that all of the relevant dogmas in the philosopher's confrontation with the law are "accessible to the unaided reason of man" (*PLA* 88). Yet Averroes is notoriously circumspect about how much of the truth the philosopher should make available to the multitude. Rather than the public teaching of the truth, he argues for the philosopher's bondage to the public teaching of scripture (ibid.)—a bondage that, by the way, Strauss identifies as the main source of intellectual freedom in the premodern enlightenment. In contrast, though Gersonides appears oddly proto-modern in his calls for "the *freedom of public communication*...of philosophic truths" (*PLA* 96), his understanding of the preexistence of the Torah undercuts any possibility of discovering truths at odds with it (*PLA* 100). Here, in *Philosophy and Law*, we already see hints of Strauss's teaching regarding esotericism. Although his argument regarding philosophy's bondage as the source of its freedom (*PLA* 88) clearly anticipates his more fully developed arguments about esotericism in *Persecution and the Art of Writing*,[14] Strauss's understanding of esotericism in *Philosophy and Law* (*PLA* 102–3) has mixed in it another more widely recognized sense of esotericism, the esotericism of incommunicable mysteries (*PLA* 66–67 and 95)—a sense that Strauss deemphasizes in his subsequent writings. Once again, Strauss's stress in *Philosophy and Law* on the supernatural element and the putative limitedness of human understanding of Maimonides's teaching undercuts his full embrace of esotericism.

We must renew our question as we turn to Chapter 3 of *Philosophy and Law*: How and why does Strauss shift the emphasis in his account of the philosophic foundation of the Law (i.e., the prophetology) from psychology to Law? Strauss answered this question in outline in his critique of Guttmann's approach to Maimonides in Chapter 1:

> [T]he philosophic foundation of the law, in spite of outward appearances, is not *a* teaching among others but is the place in the system of the Islamic Aristotelians and

> their Jewish pupils where the presupposition of their philosophizing comes under discussion. Now if they are following Plato in the philosophic foundation of the law, this means that these philosophers are Platonists not because they follow this or that Platonic theorem, however important—in this sense they are Aristotelians rather than Platonists—but because in the foundation of philosophizing itself, they are guided by Plato to answer a Platonic question within a framework laid out by Plato. Ultimately, they differ from Plato only in this, though decisively in this: for them the founder of the ideal state is not a possible philosopher-king to be awaited in the future, but an actual prophet who existed in the past. (*PLA* 75)

The prophet is understood in the light of Plato's philosopher-king. Even though Strauss in *Philosophy and Law* insists on the supernatural superiority of the prophet vis-à-vis the philosopher-king (*PLA* 66), his analysis of the prophetology leads him eventually to the striking admission that all or nearly all of Maimonides's account of the prophetology is natural rather than supernatural. And the remainder that is not natural is merely the possibility that God might withhold prophecy.[15] Maimonides so likens the revealed understanding of prophecy to the philosophic understanding developed by the Islamic *falāsifa* (esp. in *Guide* II 32) that Strauss is compelled to acknowledge that for Maimonides "prophecy as such is natural" (*PLA* 104). Wary of the possible implications of this, Strauss presses Maimonides's teaching, noting, for example, that in *Guide* 2.38 he comes close to siding with Avicenna in insinuating that the difference between the prophet and the philosopher-king is that the prophet possesses "direct" knowledge of "the upper world" whereas the philosopher possesses only "indirect" knowledge, that is, through the study of nature (*PLA* 109 and 116). This account of the difference between philosopher and prophet is a far cry from the earlier insistence on the supernatural insight provided by revelation. One of the most striking features of Strauss's account of Maimonides's prophetology is the way he finds again and again that apparent differences between Maimonides and the Islamic *falāsifa* prove ultimately to be just that, merely apparent.

In the last two sections of *Philosophy and Law*, Strauss focuses intensely on the exact sense in which prophecy is political rather than psychological. He frames this opposition by reference to the opposition between the mantic role and the political role of the prophet (*PLA* 120). Starting from the political center of the *Guide* (II 40), Strauss shows that Maimonides, by way of Avicenna and Farabi, characterizes politics in a manner that cannot but remind the reader of Aristotle's *Politics* (*Guide* III 6).[16] Although Strauss no longer appeals to the modern Enlightenment here, it is not difficult to see that the understanding of politics that he finds in Maimonides[17] is one that emphasizes not only the well-being of the body but also of the soul, that is, of the intellect (*PLA* 124). In other words, Maimonides's prophetology culminates in a political science that stresses the perfection of the individual intellect—which, of course, can be achieved only by the philosopher (cf. *PLA* 126 with *Guide* III 34). In the final section, Strauss famously argues that the Law so conceived enables those who live under it to "aristotelize" (*PLA* 133). Because they are no longer beset as were Plato and Aristotle by the task of discovering the "ideal state," believers in revealed laws may now turn their efforts to philosophy. It is as if the Jew under the Law lives in the end of days as described by Maimonides in his

Mishneh Torah. One wonders though whether discovering philosophy in the Law or among its aims means that the Law has divined the insights of the philosophers. Even though the perfect Law has been given, its perfection may not be fully apparent without proper interpretation. Perhaps due to some residual influence of the supernatural, direct knowledge and neo-Pythagorean mantic elements that Strauss finds in Maimonides in *Philosophy and Law* (*PLA* 129), he is prevented from fully plumbing the depths of the Platonic political philosophy he has begun to uncover in *Philosophy and Law*. Indeed, a certain overemphasis on a traditional understanding of theoretical philosophy obscures the full depth of Strauss's insight even into the 1940s.[18]

We turn now to the "Place of Providence" to consider the political supplement to the prophetology, Maimonides's teaching on particular providence. In comparison with his account of prophecy, Maimonides's teaching on particular providence is extremely secretive. He is untroubled by stating openly that the true account of prophecy is equivalent to the philosophic view with the sole exception of divine withholding. In contrast, Maimonides's own views on particular providence are, according to Strauss, revealed elusively under the guise of his interpretation of Job (cf. PoP 544n20 with *Guide* III 23 and III 17). Although all scholars acknowledge the surprising proximity of Maimonides's views on prophecy to that of the Islamic *falāsifa*, far fewer would assent to Strauss's claim that even with respect to particular providence Maimonides proves to be a "rationalist" (PoP 544n20). It is likely that it was the very secretiveness of Maimonides's position on particular providence that makes "Place of Providence" and "Some Remarks" such fruitful ground in the development of Strauss's views on premodern esotericism.

Scholars have sometimes complained about Strauss's characterization of Maimonides in the "Literary Character" as a *mutakallim* or dialectical theologian.[19] As has already been mentioned, "Literary Character" is itself far more elusive about the character and objectives of the *Guide* than his writings of the 1930s—apparently the closer Strauss got to the nerve of Maimonides's argument, the more uneasy he became about revealing it to his audience.[20] In "Literary Character" Strauss's point is neither that the *Guide* is devoid of philosophic content nor that Maimonides never adopts the viewpoint of the philosopher therein but that its *exoteric* surface is *kalām* (dialectical theology). Those who characterize the *Guide* as "Jewish philosophy" blend together the exoteric with the esoteric layers of this multilayered work—thus obscuring each of the layers and their relation to one another. In resisting the label "Jewish philosophy,"[21] however, Strauss was deepening the insights of some of his predecessors. In "Place of Providence," he underlines his agreement with Jacob Guttmann and Shlomo Pines in observing similarities in the structure of the *Guide* with the Mu'tazilite *kalām* (PoP 542n16). Now Saadya Gaon's (892–942 CE) debt to this *kalām* is well documented.[22] Yet Maimonides is so critical of the dialectical theologians as a group (though somewhat more sparingly regarding the Mu'tazilites) that we cannot but be somewhat surprised to see that the structure of the *Guide* is highly similar to what he criticizes. Unlike Guttmann and Pines, however, Strauss underlines a crucial Maimonidean departure. The Mu'tazilites are famous as proponents of the unity and justice of God.

Consequently, they divide their theological treatises into a first part on God's unity and a second part on God's justice. The unity section covers God and the angels; the justice section covers prophecy, the Law, and (particular) providence. Strauss's key insight is that Maimonides's philosophic or political approach to the prophetology severs the connection between his account of particular providence and God's justice. In other words, Maimonides's account of particular providence falls within the ambit of political science rather than the Mu'tazilite *kalām* teaching on God's justice (PoP 542). Although Maimonides imitates the Mu'tazilite *kalām* in his exoteric teaching, even that imitation is superficial. The surface structure of the *Guide* is similar to that of the theologians, but its meaning and intention are opposed to theirs. As Maimonides explains in *Guide* I 71, albeit somewhat indirectly, he will pursue a defense of Judaism that avoids the pitfalls of traditional *kalām*: Its main pitfall was to defend a given faith using any means fair or foul.[23] Above all, the *mutakallimūn* were willing to violate the "nature of existence," which nature was discovered by the philosophers. Indeed, according to Maimonides, *kalām* originated less as defense of one revealed religion against others than as defense of revelation against philosophy (*Guide* I 71).

Although Strauss highlights the opposition between the exoteric surface of the *Guide* and its esoteric depths in "Place of Providence" (PoP 545), he does not yet insist as he does in "Literary Character" that Maimonides is a practitioner of "enlightened *kalām*." Rather, in "Place of Providence" Strauss speaks more boldly perhaps than anywhere else in his oeuvre about the subject matter of the *Guide*. He takes far more literally than most interpreters the significance of what Maimonides identifies in the Introduction to the First Part as its subject matter, namely, the "true science of the Law." According to Strauss, the theme of the *Guide* is the Law, and the Law is analyzed from within the philosophic discipline of political science (PoP 548).[24] Most interpreters view the true science of the Law as the study of the theological foundations of the Law or of the fundamental articles of faith (cf. *Pereq Heleq*). In contrast, Strauss views the true science of the Law as the political-philosophic study of the aims of the Law. As we saw in *Philosophy and Law*, the highest aim of the Law studied by political science or philosophy is the philosophic aspiration to intellectual perfection. It would appear then that the theological foundations stressed so heavily by other interpreters reappear in Strauss as the enlightened theological surface of the *Guide*.

We need to turn back momentarily to Strauss's main focus in "Place of Providence": particular providence. According to Strauss, from *Guide* I 1 to III 7, at the end of which Maimonides announces his intention to cease theoretical discussions of the Account of the Chariot, Maimonides at times discusses providence but only or for the most part general providence (PoP 539n9). The discussion of particular providence then is limited to nontheoretical or practical philosophy (PoP 540). A crucial consequence of this is that discussions such as of the "doctrine of divine reward and punishment" are part of Maimonides's "exoteric doctrine" (PoP 545– 46)—or his "edifying doctrine[s]," as opposed to his "fundamental doctrine" treated in the prophetology. One must be careful then not to leap to the conclusion that Strauss's stress on the political character of Maimonides's teaching implies that there is nothing but edifying surface without any depth. The political (as well as super-political) end(s) of the Law is (are), according to Strauss,"a true and demonstrable fundamental doctrine" (PoP 548–49).

It may seem odd that we turn back briefly now to Strauss's earlier "Some Remarks." After all, Strauss underlines an important development from "Some Remarks" (1936) to "Place of Providence" (1937).[25] Yet we do so because "Some Remarks" reveals more clearly than "Place of Providence" the interrelation of particular and general providence in the thought of Maimonides. Ultimately, Strauss argues for a shocking convergence of Maimonides's teaching on particular providence with *Laws* 10: A convergence emerges even though Plato moves from a more philosophic teaching toward a teaching oddly anticipatory of the revealed teaching, and Maimonides moves in the opposite direction. In both cases, the teaching on particular providence proves ultimately to be the exoteric face of a philosophic teaching on general providence. Their different contexts, however, demand opposite rhetorical strategies. We cannot consider the details of Strauss's investigation of Maimonides's possible sources for the development of his position on particular providence here. Let it suffice to say that he shows that Maimonides either knew of or divined by himself the teaching of Plato's *Laws* 10 with the help of intermediaries such as Alexander of Aphrodisias (SR 22–24). Strauss sets the stage for this linking of Maimonides to Plato by offering what may be the first glimpse of the thesis of *Persecution and the Art of Writing*. Although Strauss refers in *Philosophy and Law* to esotericism and even differences between modern and medieval types of esotericism (*PLA* 102–3),"Some Remarks" hints at the likelihood that the philosopher, like the prophet, is subject to persecution. Protecting oneself from persecution seems to be on the tip of Strauss's tongue here. Over the course of several pages (SR 18–21), Strauss shows the striking similarities between the prophetic call to Israel to change its ways and return to God and the perfection of Zion, that is, the idea of the perfect city, on the one hand, and Socrates's divining of a perfect city in the *Republic* as well as his philosophic call to his fellow citizens to strive for virtue, on the other. How ironic that the one who demands justice should be persecuted. Most notable of all, however, may be that the return to Zion in the end of days is reimagined by Maimonides. Contrary to Jewish tradition regarding the Messianic age, the lion does not lie down with the lamb—in other words, nature is not controverted. On the contrary, the key natural divide among men is not undermined; it is in a sense reinforced or deepened:"Only [when the Messiah has come will] ...the privileges of the philosophers be fully recognized" (SR 20).

With Strauss's subtle adumbration of the differences between the prophetic, biblical view and the philosophic view still before our eyes, we turn to his analysis of the political teaching of Isaac Abravanel (1437–1508 CE), which includes Abravanel's transformation of Maimonides's political science. Because Abravanel is deeply indebted to Christian political thinkers, including most notably Thomas Aquinas, Strauss's "On Abravanel's Philosophical Tendency and Political Teaching" (1937)[26] enables us to deepen our understanding of the key differences between Maimonides and the main line of Christian political thought. Should the reader wish to have a more nuanced understanding of Strauss's interpretation of different trends in medieval Christian political thought s/he will have to wait for his "Law of Reason in the *Kuzari*" (1943).[27] Be that as it may, two clear and striking oppositions characterize the lines between Abravanel and Maimonides in Strauss's 1937 piece: On the one hand, Maimonides is a "thoroughgoing rationalis[t]" (APT 104); on the other, Abravanel sides with the "'mythical' or 'mystical' tendencies of the Midrash" (128). And, on the one hand, Maimonides adopts not only a pro-monarchical interpretation of the Bible but also a political interpretation of it; on the other, Abravanel adopts not only an antimonarchical interpretation but also an antipolitical one. The former opposition is evidently simpler and more straightforward. The character of Abravanel's mysticism is connected with what Strauss describes as "the fact that for him political philosophy loses its central importance" (APT 104).[28] It has a "much more restricted field than it had for Maimonides" (APT 105)—a field reminiscent of Aristotelian political thought, which, of course, takes the lead in medieval Christian thought in general (cf. APT 105 with 96–99).[29] As we saw in *Philosophy and Law*, the characteristically modern view of philosophy of religion as concerned with subjective religious consciousness is more closely linked to this restricted view of political philosophy than the total teaching of the Islamic *falāsifa* and Maimonides. Rationalism, then, is closely linked to (Platonic) political philosophy broadly understood.

The former opposition between Abravanel and Maimonides regarding the status of monarchy and politics is a bit more complicated than the opposition regarding rationalism and mysticism—though they are intimately connected, as is already evident from our inability to avoid referring to *political* philosophy to characterize that rationalism. The former opposition is more complicated because Maimonides's positive view of monarchy is characteristic of the vast majority of the rabbinic tradition (APT 112, 119). Yet the biblical attitude toward politics and the founding of the city is far closer to Abravanel's view than Maimonides's (APT 129).[30] Ultimately, Maimonides's positive attitude toward monarchy and politics is more deeply rooted in his philosophic orientation than the rabbinic attitude toward monarchy. He, like Farabi and other Islamic *falāsifa*, favors monarchy because it squares with his conception of Moses and prophets more generally as philosopher-kings. In contrast, not only does human kingship fill Abravanel with "disgust" (APT 117)—indeed, so deeply that he can be found speaking somewhat favorably of a "'mixed' constitution"—but also Abravanel prefers the rule of judge and prophet or priest to that of philosopher-king (APT 118, 126). In other words, Abravanel's animosity toward monarchy and politics is rooted in the view that "man's 'natural' state" is most analogous to Israel's life "in the desert, where Israel had to rely entirely for everything on miraculous providence" (APT 110–11). Here we arrive at the opposite pole to the convergence of Maimonides and Plato regarding particular providence we saw in "Some Remarks." Maimonides's rationalism places roughly as much stress on human self-reliance, as Abravanel's mysticism places upon faith in divine support.

In the 1940s, Strauss began to write about Maimonides in such a way that his debt to Farabi in political philosophy became more difficult, not easier, to detect. I do not mean that Strauss did not consistently acknowledge this debt, but he did little in writing to explain that debt, especially from the side of Maimonides. In "Literary Character," Strauss moved away from the emphasis in his 1930s writings on the political character of Maimonides's teaching to an emphasis on the enlightened *kalām* surface of the *Guide*. At the same time, of course, Strauss began to make the difference between exoteric surface and esoteric depth a central theme of his writing. For those sympathetic to Strauss's insights, then, it is not difficult to see that he eventually argued that the *Guide* consists in an enlightened *kalām* surface and a political philosophic depth. To the unsympathetic, he appears to be making Maimonides into a mere dialectical theologian. That is because of the unsympathetic tend to overstate the importance of the theological aspect of Maimonides's writings—thinking of him primarily as a "Jewish philosopher." Strauss insisted rightly that interpreters would never understand Maimonides properly until they understood the surface of the *Guide* for what it was, namely, enlightened *kalām*. It must be underlined that Maimonides learned from Farabi how to make and use a *kalām* surface.[31]

Fortunately, among the many useful appendices included in this volume is a translation of "A Lost Writing of Farâbî's" (1936).[32] This often dry explanation—of how Strauss discovered that what were thought to be parts of Farabi's *Enumeration of the Sciences* were in fact parts of the first part (the *Attainment of Happiness*) of a lost Farabian trilogy, *The Philosophy of Plato and Aristotle* (consisting of the *Attainment of Happiness*, *The Philosophy of Plato*, and *The Philosophy of Aristotle*)—contains one of Strauss's frankest statements of the depth and significance of Maimonides's debt to Farabi. Strauss concludes this piece by arguing that now that we know the outlines of this lost trilogy, we are finally in possession of the "central writings" of Farabi—because we can add this writing to the *Enumeration* (or *Encyclopedia*), the *Virtuous City*, and his *Political Regime*.[33] In explaining the importance of this discovery, Strauss cites the letter Maimonides wrote to Samuel ibn Tibbon explaining the unparalleled importance of Farabi's writings and especially his *Political Regime*. Strauss concludes this piece by stating that at last we are in a position to assess properly "the Islamic and Jewish philosophy of the Middle Ages: At the beginning of this epoch of the history of philosophy there stands not just any 'predecessor,' but the towering spirit [Farabi] who laid the ground for the later development and set down its limits by making his task the revival of the Platonic-Aristotelian philosophy as philosophy proper." The Farabian Turn set Strauss on the course to a Plato who was far less metaphysical than had been previously believed. In effect, it was through his study of Farabi and Maimonides that Strauss came to understand that Plato's "political philosophy broadly understood...[is] first philosophy.'"[34]

This chapter has explored the more explicit declarations of Strauss's writings in the 1930s about the centrality of political science or philosophy in Maimonides's writings to facilitate a recovery of the distinctiveness of the "Islamic and Jewish philosophy of the Middle Ages," especially that of Farabi and Maimonides. The Farabian Turn in Strauss's thought, though often elusive in the written word is there for anyone who can see and attend to Strauss's actions. Even while he grows quieter about the centrality of political philosophy in Maimonides's writings, Strauss's exploration of Maimonides's enlightened *kalām* demonstrates a key, oft-forgotten aspect of political philosophy.

Notes

1. Daniel Tanguay, *Leo Strauss: An Intellectual Biography*, trans. Christopher Nadon (New Haven: Yale University Press, 2007), 80.
2. Originally published as *Philosophie und Gesetz: Beiträge zum Verständnis Maimunis und seiner Vorläufer* (Berlin: Schocken Verlag, 1935). Translated by Eve Adler (Albany: SUNY Press, 1995); henceforth referred to as *PLA*.
3. Originally published as "Quelques remarques sur la science politique de Maïmonide et Farabi," *Revue des Études Juives* 100 (1936): 1–37. Translated by Robert Bartlett in *Interpretation* 18, no. 1 (1990): 3–30; henceforth SR.
4. Originally published as "Der Ort der Vorsehungslehre nach der Ansicht Maimunis," *Monatschrift für Geschichte und Wissenschaft des Judentums* 81, no. 1 (1937): 93–105. Translated by Gabriel Bartlett and Svetozar Minkov in *Review of Metaphysics* 57 (2004): 537–49; henceforth PoP.
5. Tanguay, *Leo Strauss*, cf. 55, 57, 61 with 65, 66, 67, and 97.
6. Originally published in *Essays on Maimonides*, 37–91, ed. Salo Baron (New York: Columbia University Press, 1941), it was eventually included in *PAW* 38–94.
7. Parens, "Strauss on Maimonides's Secretive Political Science," in *Leo Strauss's Defense of the Philosophic Life: Reading "What Is Political Philosophy?"* ed. Rafael Major (Chicago: University of Chicago Press, 2012), 116–36.
8. As Tanguay argues (Tanguay, *Leo Strauss*, 84), Farabi is the thinker who made Strauss aware of a different, more political and less metaphysical understanding of Plato. All the while that Maimonides's debt to Farabi became more apparent to Strauss, however, he seems to have grown increasingly uneasy about underlining the political character of Maimonides's teaching.
9. See Tanguay, *Leo Strauss*, 56, and Joshua Parens, "Escaping the Scholastic Paradigm," in *Encountering the Medieval in Modern Jewish Thought*, ed. Aaron Hughes and James Diamond (New York and Leiden: Brill, 2012), 207–27.
10. Why do I call these "central chapters"? (After all, the numerically central chapter in the *Guide* is II 13, the first of two crucial chapters on eternity versus creation.) First, these chapters surround what Maimonides seems to be setting up as the holy of holies, III 1–7. Second, the prophetology is of the essence of the theme of the *Guide*, the true science of the (divine) Law. Third, these two sections identified by Strauss consist of 17 chapters each. As Nasser Behnegar has noted, according to Strauss, the number 17 stands numerologically for "nature"—in a sense, the true center of all philosophizing ("Reading 'What is Political Philosophy?'" in *Leo Strauss's Defense of the Philosophic Life*, 41n5).
11. In the Aristotelian tradition to which Maimonides adheres at least in this, psychology is a theoretical science containing elements of natural science and divine science. Cf. *On the Soul* 402a5–7, 403a3–b18.
12. This stress on supernaturalism and the limits of human knowledge should be compared with the approach to Maimonides developed by Shlomo Pines and his students after Pines published his "Limits" article. Compare my *Maimonides and Spinoza* (Chicago: University of Chicago Press, 2012), Chapter 1 for evidence that Maimonides's arguments regarding the limits of knowledge are anything but straightforward, or as Strauss states immediately before the above quotation from *PLA*, "beyond doubt."
13. Averroes or Ibn Rushd (1126–1198 CE), *Decisive Treatise and Epistle Dedicatory*, trans. Charles E. Butterworth (Provo, UT: Brigham Young University Press, 2001). Gersonides or Levi ben Gershom (1288–1344 CE), *The Wars of the Lord*, trans. Seymour Feldman (3 vols.; Philadelphia: Jewish Publication Society, 1987, 1999).

14. *PAW* was published in 1952. Cf. note 6, above.
15. Cf. Parens, *Maimonides and Spinoza*, 112–15, on withholding and whether it is natural or supernatural.
16. And this despite Strauss's insistence that the Islamic Aristotelians did not possess the *Politics*. Cf. Shlomo Pines, "Aristotle's *Politics* in Arabic Philosophy," *Israel Oriental Studies* 5 (1975): 150–60.
17. And in Avicenna's *Healing: Metaphysics* 10, *Division of the Rational Sciences* (in *MPP–2* 74–88), and Farabi, *The Virtuous City* (in *Al-Farabi on the Perfect State*, ed. Richard Walzer [Oxford: Clarendon, 1985]).
18. Parens, "Strauss on Maimonides's Secretive Political Science," in *Leo Strauss's Defense of the Philosophic Life* (Chicago: University of Chicago Press, 2012), 116–36.
19. See W. Z. Harvey, "Why Maimonides Was Not a Mutakallim," in *Perspectives on Maimonides*, ed. Joel L. Kraemer (Oxford: Oxford University Press, 1991), 105–14, cited in Sarah Stroumsa, *Maimonides in His World: Portrait of a Mediterranean Thinker* (Princeton: Princeton University Press, 2009), 37n47.
20. See Heinrich Meier, *Leo Strauss and the Theologico-Political Problem* (New York: Cambridge University Press, 2006).
21. See *PAW* 19.
22. See Haggai Ben Shammai, "Kalam in Medieval Jewish Philosophy," in *History of Jewish Philosophy*, ed. Daniel H. Frank and Oliver Leaman (London: Routledge, 1997), 127–32.
23. See Farabi, *Enumeration of the Sciences*, Chap. 5 in *MPP–2* 21–23.
24. I believe that Strauss's scholarly understanding of political science or political philosophy in Maimonides developed in the direction of what he would refer to in the Platonic context as "political philosophy broadly understood" (*CM* 20). The view that political science or political philosophy is a mere discipline, still expressed here in "Place of Providence," is due in part to the continued influence of medieval Christian views of the division of the sciences on Strauss. I say that despite Strauss's evidently growing awareness of the divide between Maimonides and the Islamic *falāsifa*, on the one hand, and medieval Christian thought of the Thomistic school, on the other (e.g., PoP 541, 543n18; *PLA* 73n25). For more on medieval Christian views on the status of political science, see the discussion of Abravanel below.
25. See esp. PoP 542–43n17. It appears that in SR Strauss did not understand fully that the political center of the *Guide* was in the prophetology. In SR 12, he linked the articles or principles of faith that Maimonides enumerates in *Commentary on the Mishnah, Pereq Heleq*, with *Guide* III 25–50 rather than with II 39–40. He did so by referring to III 25–50 as Maimonides's discussion of "the divine law." In other words, in SR he had not fully grasped that the prophetology was the very heart of Maimonides's analysis of divine law. This might help to explain the extent of Strauss's focus on the psychology of prophecy in *Philosophy and Law*. (Then there's the problem of when these three pieces were actually written. Though they came out in 1935, 1936, and 1937, it was not necessarily the case that SR was not written before *Philosophy and Law*.) Perhaps not until PoP did Strauss come to understand fully the extent to which the core of the true science of the (divine) Law, the prophetology, was part of political philosophy.
26. Henceforth APT.
27. See esp. *PAW* 96–97.
28. Readers who have read widely in Strauss's thought will recognize here a phrasing that Strauss will use again, nearly verbatim, to describe the position of Martin Heidegger in "Philosophy as Rigorous Science and Political Philosophy," *SPPP* 30. See also Parens, "Strauss on Maimonides's Secretive Political Science," 118n5, 130.

29. See the general introduction to *MPP–2* 12–17, and Parens, "Escaping the Scholastic Paradigm."
30. In Appendix E of this volume, we have published for the first time a translation into English of "On Abravanel's Critique of Monarchy" (1937); first published as "Zu Abravanels Kritik des Königtums," in *GS–2* 233–34. In that piece, Strauss took H. Finkelscherer to task for arguing in a journal essay in *Monatsschrift für Geschichte und Wissenschaft des Judentums* (1937) that Ibn Caspi (1297–1340 CE) already maintained the kind of hostility toward monarchy expressed by Abravanel. (In APT 101n1, Strauss merely alludes to the divide between Abravanel and Ibn Caspi.) In "On Abravanel's Critique of Monarchy," Strauss notes that Ibn Caspi likens monarchy to sacrifices. Finkelscherer did not think through the significance of this reference to sacrifices, which in *Guide* III 32 are paradigmatic of legislation that expresses the second rather than the first intention of the legislator. They are merely conditionally rather than absolutely good. This kind of goodness is a far cry from Abravanel's rejection of monarchy as bad.
31. See *PAW* 40n9—and the *Book of Religion*, referred to below in note 33, a book that Strauss did not have the good fortune to see.
32. Originally published as "Eine vermisste Schrift Farâbîs," in *Monatsschrift für Geschichte und Wissenschaft des Judentums* 80 (1936): 96–106; translated in appendix D of the present volume.
33. Little did Strauss know that there was at least one more "central writing" by Farabi to be discovered, namely, his *Book of Religion*. See *Alfarabi's Political Writings: "Selected Aphorisms" and Other Texts*, trans. Charles E. Butterworth (Ithaca: Cornell University Press, 2001), and the critical Arabic edition by Muhsin Mahdi, *Abû Naṣr al-Fârâbî, Kitâb al-Milla wa Nuṣûṣ Ukhrâ* (Beirut: Dar al-Mashriq, 1968).
34. *CM* 20. See Strauss's observation in "A Lost Writing" in appendix E below that Ibn al-Qifti was wrong in thinking that the missing metaphysics at the end of *The Philosophy of Aristotle* was due to textual corruption.

CHAPTER 9

THE PROBLEM OF THE ENLIGHTENMENT: STRAUSS, JACOBI, AND THE PANTHEISM CONTROVERSY

David Janssens

> *Denn was die Philosophen sogar ein wenig nachsehend und parteiisch gegen Enthusiasten und Schwärmer macht, ist, dass sie, die Philosophen, am allermeisten dabei verlieren wurden, wenn es gar keine Enthusiasten and Schwärmer mehr gäbe.*
>
> —Lessing, "Über eine zeitige Aufgabe"

I

In his first book, Leo Strauss provides the reader with an interesting clue to one of the sources of his groundbreaking critical study of Spinoza's *Theologico-Political Treatise*. While identifying the guiding question of his undertaking, he also points out its pedigree:

> Even if all the reasoning adduced by Spinoza were compelling, nothing would have been proven. Only this much would have been proven: that on the basis of unbelieving science, one could not but arrive at Spinoza's results. But would this basis itself thus be justified? It was Friedrich Heinrich Jacobi who posed this question, and by so doing lifted the interpretation of Spinoza—or what amounts to the same thing—the criticism of Spinoza on to its proper plane.[1]

This statement is both literally and figuratively singular: the only reference to Jacobi in the whole book, unaccompanied by any mention of its source, it makes us wonder about the importance of this author for Strauss's endeavor. A renowned critic of the Enlightenment, Friedrich Heinrich Jacobi (1743–1819), singled out Spinoza as one of the main targets of his attacks.[2] Similarly, in *Spinoza's Critique of Religion*, Strauss casts doubt on the legitimacy of Spinoza's attack against revealed religion, thereby also questioning the foundations of the Enlightenment. In a discerning review of the book, his contemporary Gerhard Krüger noted that in *Spinoza's Critique of Religion* "there is concealed a fundamental philosophic discussion of the problem of the Enlightenment."[3] If this interpretation is sound, then from a merely formal point of view the procedure followed by Strauss closely resembles that of Jacobi: to address the problem of the Enlightenment by means of a critical assessment of Spinoza.[4]

However, even if Strauss's critique of Spinoza may be said to take its cue from Jacobi, it is not clear whether the latter's influence reaches beyond this initial impulse, nor is it clear to what extent. Recently it has been suggested not only that *Spinoza's Critique of Religion* is "by its own account, 'Jacobian' in orientation" but also that "the Jacobian dilemma and the critique of rationalism [remained] fundamental for Strauss's perspective" throughout his career.[5] Moreover, these assumptions carry an implicit criticism, to the extent that Strauss may be said to be heir to the irrationalism, conservatism, and authoritarianism attributed to the anti-Enlightenment with which Jacobi is commonly associated.[6] This chapter will attempt to show that such assessments are in need of qualification. It will be argued that even if a certain affinity between Strauss and Jacobi can be shown to exist, this affinity is far more complex than it seems.

In order to bring out this complexity, a closer look will be taken at those writings in which Strauss discusses Jacobi. To begin, there is his doctoral dissertation, which, although he later disparaged it as "a disgraceful performance," nevertheless merits closer investigation.[7] A comprehensive account, moreover, must broaden the inquiry. After the completion of *Spinoza's Critique of Religion*, Strauss worked as a coeditor of the Jubilee Edition of Moses Mendelssohn's collected works. As a part of this employment, he conducted research into the so-called Pantheism Controversy. This debate was launched by Jacobi, with Moses Mendelssohn as its principal addressee, and initially concerned the philosophical legacy of the thinker and writer Gotthold Ephraim Lessing. However, it soon developed into a fullblown debate concerning the foundations and the legitimacy of the Enlightenment, involving such prominent contemporaries as Johann Georg Hamann, Immanuel Kant, Karl Reinhold, and Johann Gottfried Herder.[8] The results of Strauss's research are published in the introductory commentaries he wrote to several of Mendelssohn's writings. Besides a thorough treatment of the latter's position in the controversy, these introductions contain an astute and well-documented investigation of its general background, particularly of the positions of Jacobi and Lessing.[9] In this respect, they enable us to come to a more exact determination of Strauss's own perspective. It will become apparent that, although Jacobi does play a very important role, this role differs considerably from what the current view has made it out to be.

II

Judged solely by its title and its structure, Strauss's doctoral dissertation is typical of the genre: an inconspicuous exhibition of academic proficiency. Yet his treatment of *The Problem of Knowledge in the Philosophical Doctrine of Fr. H. Jacobi* reveals some distinctive traits.[10] Thus, at the beginning of the work, Strauss expressly states his intention to treat Jacobi as a competent thinker in his own right, not as the romantic enthusiast and proponent of the *Sturm und Drang* he is often made out to be. Moreover, he cautions the reader that he intends to deal "not so much with

Jacobi himself, but rather with the problems or perspectives designated by the title 'Jacobi.'"[11] Near the end of the work, this approach is reaffirmed and put within a larger framework, when it is asserted that "the *eidos* 'Jacobi,' so rich in consequences for intellectual history,...corresponds to a distinct and autonomously coherent complex of problems on the level of timeless problems."[12]

For various reasons, these statements merit closer examination. To begin with, they are formulated in a language with unmistakable Platonic resonances, oddly prefiguring the interpretation of Platonic Ideas as timeless problems in Strauss's later works.[13] More important, they suggest that Strauss is more concerned with the philosophical problem brought to the fore by Jacobi than by the particular solution he propagated. This does not do away with the fact that the problem only becomes visible through the solution argued by Jacobi in his polemic against the Enlightenment. As Strauss shows in his analysis, this polemic is deployed on both the epistemological and on the ethical-political level although both dimensions are ultimately rooted in a single conviction characteristic of Jacobi's thought.

On the level of epistemology, the main target of Jacobi's critique is the Cartesian method of radical universal doubt at the heart of modern rationalism. As is well known, this method attempts to secure the reality of Being by reducing it to an indubitable condition of possibility, from which it then sets out to reconstruct Being according to the requirements of reason. In Jacobi's view, this amounts to a systematic reduction of Being or reality to non-Being or Nothingness—a procedure for which he coined the term "nihilism." All that remains is the pure thinking subject that thereby becomes the only source of reality and the sole warrant of genuine knowledge. Strauss rephrases this view of the Cartesian program as follows: "We can only know what we can produce. Thus, the philosopher who wants to understand the world must become the creator of the world."[14]

Moreover, according to Jacobi, the Cartesian procedure is deliberately selective: it filters out those aspects of its object that withstand reduction and rational control. In this way, it ignores or even destroys such vital elements of the object as it can never artificially replace or reconstruct. These elements point to what Jacobi calls "natural certainties" (*natürliche Gewissheiten*), which are known prior to any attempt at rational knowledge and therefore constitute the possibility of such knowledge. From his point of view, both the source of knowledge (human understanding) and its object (reality) are "irrational" or, to be more exact, "superrational" (*überrational*). They come to light in propositions that are grasped with intuitive immediacy and therefore cannot be made the object of subsequent rational proof, such as "I am" and "There is a world outside of me," but also the reality of God.[15] As a result, Jacobi rejects Kant's notion of God as a regulative idea of reason. The latter, he argues, reverses the original primacy of God with regard to reason, and thus is devoid of any content and hence both theoretically and ethically useless.[16]

Because of its deliberate disregard of these natural certainties as the limits of knowledge, Cartesian rationalism and the modern sciences based on it can be nothing more than the organization of ignorance, Jacobi holds.[17] For if the method of rational demonstration exerts its power within a domain limited by the irrational and transcendent certainties, a strict determinism can rule only within those bounds. Unable fully to justify the precedence of radical doubt over against natural certainty, rationalism can never attain the truth because it is based on an initial surrender of the truth.[18] Rationalism sacrifices theory or contemplation in order to radically exclude irrationality. In Strauss's words: "Doubt is the relinquishment of theoretical life (truth) for the sake of the theoretical evil (irrationality) which is necessarily related to it."[19]

On the level of ethics and politics, Jacobi's argument runs parallel to his epistemological critique. In this case, his polemic is directed against the idea of autonomy at the heart of the moral and political program of the Enlightenment. In his dissertation, Strauss summarizes the main contention as follows:

> Autonomism is the ethical form of general doubt, of the principle of modern culture, which invokes the autonomy of religious conscience, of scientific reason, and of moral legislation (*sola fides, sola ratio,* "only a good will"). In opposition, Jacobi emphasizes that, in ethical matters, it is simply unnecessary for the acting subject to understand the norm and to affirm it out of its own insight. It is not the case that insight precedes and obedience follows, but precisely the reverse: only out of obedience, as a result of following the norm, from the penetration of the norm into the center of our lives as a consequence of obedience, does moral insight emerge.[20]

Just as the principle of radical doubt and the belief in proof and demonstration express a refusal to submit to the transcendence of reality, so does the concept of autonomy disclose a rejection of the ethical norms inherent in this reality, incited by man's proud desire to be the sole source of morality. Correspondingly, just as it leads to organized ignorance and determinism on the level of knowledge, so does rationalism lead to atheism and fatalism on the level of morality and politics, Jacobi asserts. Contrary to its own claim, rationalism is incapable of replacing what is has destroyed; it is unable to establish morality on purely immanent grounds.

The intrinsic relationship among epistemology, ethics, and politics postulated by Jacobi explains why his opposition to the Enlightenment takes the form of a critical discussion of Spinoza. The latter, in Jacobi's view, exemplifies the defiance of Cartesian rationalism in the face of transcendence. In his introduction to Mendelssohn's contributions to the Pantheism Controversy, Strauss recalls how Jacobi locates the root of rationalism in "the tendency to prove everything and to accept nothing as given; if one follows this tendency honestly, i.e., without compunction, it leads to Spinozism, i.e., to atheism and fatalism...the origin of the tendency to prove everything is the will of man not to be dependent on a truth that transcends him, the will 'not to obey the truth, but to command it,' pride, vanity."[21] With unrivalled clarity, Jacobi argues, Spinoza's thought shows that the common root of the Enlightenment's philosophy and politics is a rebellious and revolutionary effort to liberate man from the authority of transcendence. As Strauss notes subsequently, Jacobi was "still too closely tied to the theistic tradition not to be compelled to see in atheism (and 'Spinozism is atheism') a result of anti-theism, of the revolt against God."[22]

According to Jacobi, however, the motive underlying this revolt proved to be at least as tyrannical as that of its putative opponent: Descartes and Spinoza heralded a new metaphysical despotism of autonomous demonstrative reason, which found its political complement in the new political despotism of Hobbes's *Leviathan*. His objections notwithstanding, Jacobi respected both Spinoza and Hobbes for the consistency and rigor of their thinking. In fact, he preferred these "classics of despotism" to the German *Aufklärer* of his time. What he perceived as the latter's half-hearted rationalism and readiness to compromise with autocratic regimes provoked his aversion to such an extent that he went so far as to defend the ideal of a liberal state.[23] Nevertheless, he remained intensely critical of rationalism because of the lack of justification and the "nihilism" characteristic of Cartesian doubt.

Claiming at least equal justice, Jacobi's own philosophic doctrine takes precisely this deficit as its point of departure. His procedure is first to pursue rationalism to its ultimate consequences, up to the point where its fatalism, atheism, and nihilism become apparent, as well as its rootedness in ignorance. The knowledge of this ignorance (*Wissen des Nicht-Wissens*) then becomes the basis for a *salto mortale*: a leap out of rationalism and nihilism into faith or *Glaube*, motivated by the willingness and the courage to take the risk of believing reality instead of doubting it. As Strauss emphasizes, the concept of *Glaube* at the heart of Jacobi's doctrine is not primarily religious: it comprises both "faith" and "belief" in the Humean sense, according to which human knowledge is ultimately based on indemonstrable beliefs. In this respect it proved to be a most powerful weapon in Jacobi's polemic against the Enlightenment, for it enabled him to argue that even the choice for rationalism and demonstration rests upon a primary belief, an initial act of faith.[24]

In Jacobi's view, *Glaube* is not only an epistemological but also and even primarily an ethical category: affirmation of the transcendence of reality is the basic prerequisite for true virtue (*Tugend*), which in its turn is the necessary condition for true knowledge. Without the recognition of his heteronomy and of the necessity of loving obedience to God's commands, man can never hope to attain true knowledge. In fact, Jacobi goes so far as to equate virtue and knowledge: the Platonic character of this identification, far from being accidental, actually points to the foundations of his thought, Strauss emphasizes. According to Jacobi, the history of philosophy is determined by the predominance of one of two typical theoretical attitudes, whereby each type is rooted in a more general type of intellectual and moral attitude. The first, which Jacobi dubs "Platonic," is characterized by nobility, audacity, confidence, faith, and love and is therefore able to gain access to truth and virtue.[25]

The other type, called "non-Platonic," displays the opposite qualities: baseness, apprehension, diffidence, distrust, disbelief, doubt, and pride, and accordingly the inability to attain truth and virtue. According to Jacobi, the non-Platonic attitude has become dominant in modern philosophy, and this decline has reached its nadir in the age of the Enlightenment. The latter, in spite of its earthly accomplishments, is animated by a Cartesian fear of the immediacy of transcendent reality and characterized by the subsequent attempt to circumvent its claims. Faced with what he perceives to be the dire consequences of this refusal, Jacobi's doctrine of *Glaube* is an emphatic attempt to restore the Platonic attitude. Through a change in morality, it seeks to reaffirm the transcendence of reality with a view to reinstating what has been lost and thus accomplishing a renewal of philosophy.[26]

Because of the largely analytic and descriptive nature of Strauss's account, it is difficult to assess the impact the *eidos* "Jacobi" may have had on his own thinking.

Looking ahead at his ulterior writings, it is nevertheless possible to highlight a few aspects. The first of these concerns the critique of Cartesian methodical doubt. Very likely, Jacobi's challenging the legitimacy of radical doubt informs Strauss's question in *Spinoza's Critique of Religion*, mentioned at the beginning, whether "the basis of unbelieving science" underlying Spinoza's philosophy is justified. For, as Strauss argues in the same book, it is precisely with an appeal to Cartesian doubt that Spinoza excludes both the possibility of miracles in general and of prophecy in particular (as a miraculous collaboration of reason and imagination).[27] In the same context, Jacobi's comment on the selective character of methodical doubt may very well have provided the background for a basic question, raised by the later Strauss, concerning the *Ethics*: "But is Spinoza's account clear and distinct?...Is its clarity and distinctness not due to the fact that Spinoza abstracts from those elements of the whole which are not clear and distinct and which can never be rendered clear and distinct?"[28] In *Natural Right and History*, he seems to answer this question in the affirmative when criticizing modern philosophy's "dogmatic disregard of everything that cannot become an object, that is, an object for the knowing subject, or the dogmatic disregard of everything that cannot be mastered by the subject."[29]

Second, among the elements of transcendent reality that are not and cannot be rendered clear and distinct under the auspices of rational demonstration, Jacobi gives pride of place to the existence of God. Against Kant, he argues that, as Strauss puts it in his dissertation, "The [philosophical] system must accommodate itself to the existence and meaning (*Sinn*) of God; the fundamental religious phenomenon may not be diverted (*umgebogen*) for the sake of the system."[30] Interestingly enough, we see Strauss himself making frequent use of a similar argument during the 1920s and 1930s, in various discussions involving the main currents within contemporary Judaism, such as political Zionism, cultural Zionism, Jewish orthodoxy, and the so-called return movement or neo-orthodoxy. Since it would lead us too far to discuss each of these debates in detail, a few examples must suffice.[31]

In his very first publication, a contribution to a Zionist debate written in 1923, Strauss argues against those Zionists who advocate a qualified acceptance of religious contents for purely political reasons, mainly with a view to the needs of the human soul: "Wholly inseparable from the essence of religion is a minimum of doctrinal content, which minimum is the existence of God, wholly independent of human existence and human need."[32] Two years later, the same criticism is directed against Jewish orthodoxy when Strauss reproaches its adherents for "obeying the law for the sake of their people or for the sake of all peoples, and not—or not primarily—for the sake of God."[33] In like manner, finally, Strauss addresses cultural Zionism and the "return movement," through representatives like Hermann Cohen, Franz Rosenzweig, Martin Buber, and Julius Guttmann.[34] In his view, the attempts of each of these thinkers to return to the Jewish tradition remained partial and qualified by reservations because of their failure to consider "the original, non-'internalized' meaning of the basic tenets of tradition."[35] In sum, Strauss criticizes contemporary Jewish thought for reducing one of the fundamental tenets of Judaism, the radical transcendence of a personal God, either to a postulate of reason or consciousness, to a product of religious experience, to a psychological need, to a cultural or even a natural phenomenon. An adequate philosophical understanding of the condition of modern Judaism, he argues, requires that this transcendence—with regard to the Jewish nation, to human consciousness, and to reason—somehow be accounted for in its original radicalness.

What makes these criticisms particularly puzzling and perplexing is that they are leveled by someone who presents himself not only as an adherent of "simple, straightforward political Zionism" but also as an admitted nonbeliever.[36] As becomes apparent from recently published material, the young Strauss was a political Zionist in the strict sense of the term, advocating the political self-organization of Jews on a purely secular, unbelieving basis. In his early publications, he systematically argues that modern science and politics have destroyed the closed world of the tradition, that the requirements of modern politics and those of the tradition are mutually exclusive, and that "political Zionism which wants to found itself radically must found itself as unbelieving."[37]

At the same time, however, Strauss never ceases to stress that the fundamental claims of the tradition somehow continue to exert their power and hence cannot be dismissed forthwith. Regarding this quandary, he admits there is no obvious way out. Precisely for this reason, unbelieving political Zionism is compelled to acquire full clarity regarding its own position. This, however, can only succeed on the condition that it rejects attempts to secure a middle ground and approaches "the question of God" with at least as much seriousness as "the question of politics."[38] As Strauss has already perceived at this initial stage, doing justice to both requires a renewed understanding of the old quarrel between belief and unbelief and thus of its latest installment, Spinoza's critique of religion.

Although he is never mentioned by name in these early writings, it is hard to disregard the impression that Strauss's perception of this fundamental issue and of the road to be taken is partially indebted to Jacobi.[39] This is borne out most clearly by what might be called the "theologico-political" aspect of Jacobi's polemic. As we have seen, Jacobi subordinates the epistemological question to the ethical-political question and focuses on the specific motive underlying modern rationalism. A similar approach may be said to be one of the distinctive characteristics of Strauss's study of Spinoza. In an article written in preparation of the book, he points out that Spinoza's theoretical critique, according to its own view of religion as based on obedience and faith, necessarily presupposes disobedience and unbelief. As a result, a critical reading of Spinoza must concentrate on "the 'Why' of theory as the 'Why' of disobedience and unbelief. This 'Why' precedes every theory; it is no theoretical insight or conviction, but a motive."[40] Subsequently, in the book Strauss traces this motive to the Epicurean tradition and its attempt to relieve the human condition by liberating man from fear of the gods, the cause of the greatest unrest and the gravest crimes. On the basis of this connection, he argues, "the concern for safeguarding and alleviating life may be designated as the characteristic concern of the Enlightenment."[41] As such, it animates Spinoza's construction of a world in which there is no place for an inscrutable God or for a revealed law teaching man what is good and what is evil.

At the same time, this concern reveals the limits and flaws of Spinoza's critique. As Strauss argues at various points in the book, Spinoza's neo-Epicurean motive caused him to disregard the fundamental distinction between superstitious or profane fear and genuine fear of God, which is the traditional prerequisite for true love of God and true obedience to the revealed law. This shows that Spinoza did not even attempt to understand or to take seriously his opponent. Driven by a Cartesian "will to immediacy," he was incapable of understanding the "will to mediacy," which, as a response to the original revelation, is the basis of obedience and loyalty to the tradition of revelation. Instead, he urged the legitimacy of his position to the point of committing a fatal *petitio principii* by presupposing the freedom of philosophizing that he set out to argue against revealed religion. While this precluded any offensive tactics and only allowed for a defensive position, it left his opponent essentially intact. The defensive critique, however, could only uphold itself and its freedom by permanently turning revealed religion into ridicule, thereby concealing its own questionableness.[42] In the final analysis, there is at "the basis of unbelieving science" a moral motive that is no more or no less problematic than that of revealed religion, Strauss concludes. This motive, furthermore, differs from its Epicurean precursor on a crucial point: its probity and its conscientiousness, which reveal it to be a descendant of biblical morality.[43]

Both the approach and the results of Strauss's investigation seem to be closely akin to those of Jacobi. For both, the inquest into the motive of the Enlightenment points to a revolutionary antitheism animated by proud human reason, self-postulating and therefore deeply problematic. In his dissertation, Strauss even goes so far as to subscribe to Jacobi's typological characterization of modernity as an age of fear, distrust, and pride:

> In any case, it seems to us that a specific moment of modern culture is viewed here for the first time in such a comprehensive manner. How little one has reason to regard—and to disregard—this expression as a mere circumstance of Jacobian sentiment, is made evident most clearly by the fundamental agreement in which it finds itself with the results of the research of contemporary sociologists (such as Troeltsch, Sombart, Max Weber, Scheler).[44]

However, Strauss immediately goes on to qualify his assent by adding that this does not mean he also shares the strong evaluative judgment (*Bewertung*) Jacobi appends to it. At this stage, Strauss is less dismissive regarding the claims of modern rationalism, even if in many ways he shares Jacobi's insight into its flaws. Thus, he makes the critical remark that although Jacobi is fundamentally aware of the scope of Cartesianism as "a general philosophic principle of method," he fails to do justice to "its profound practical legitimacy (*tiefes sachliches Recht*)."[45] As a critical response to Cartesian doubt, the foundation of Jacobi's doctrine of *Glaube* seems to be at least as questionable as that of its opponent. Accordingly, in *Spinoza's Critique of Religion*, though viewed with an increasingly critical eye, rationalism is still treated with more impartiality than is meted out by Jacobi.[46]

In a different form, this reservation is also visible on the ethical-political level. Commenting on Jacobi's defense of heteronomy, Strauss notes that it is basically the expression of the principle of traditionalism or, to be more exact, conservatism: "The principle of tradition—which doesn't mean the recognition of a particular tradition. Rather, one should say: principle of conservatism."[47] To the extent that the "leap of faith" implies the espousal of the principle of traditionalism, it leaves undetermined what particular tradition is embraced. Nevertheless, Jacobi insists that "the leap of faith" necessarily requires an espousal of the Christian tradition. Even though he justifies this view by equating the principle of Christianity with the absolute principle of religion as such, this cannot hide the fact that, as Strauss puts it, "the difficult problem of the specification (*Besonderung*) of the highest moral norm does not exist as a theoretical problem for Jacobi."[48] As a result, the leap of faith bears the mark of decisionism, in its attempt to affirm what, according to Jacobi's own doctrine, is in no need of affirmation. In exposing the act of faith at the basis of rationalism, the Jacobian option against Cartesian doubt succeeds in restoring the balance, but it fails to do better than its opponent.

These and other considerations suggest that Jacobi's influence on Strauss's early thinking, although certainly not negligible, is not as univocal as it appears to be. At the same time, they indicate that, as a result of his investigations into Spinoza's critique, Strauss had more or less reached a quandary. On the one hand, his youthful allegiance had become deeply problematic: modern rationalism was seen to be based on a questionable moral motive with biblical roots. On the other hand, the Jacobian alternative turned out to be equally flawed and unacceptable. In order to see how Strauss found his bearings in this dilemma, we must take a further look at the introductions to Moses Mendelssohn's collected works. Written between 1931 and 1937, these writings are of particular interest, not only because they reveal a profound knowledge of Mendelssohn's thought but also because they focus on the latter's dispute with Jacobi, which came to be known as the Pantheism Controversy. Above all, they suggest that Strauss had begun to find a way out of the quandary in which he found himself. Since both the Pantheism Controversy and its aftermath have been amply and excellently documented from a variety of perspectives by different authors, the discussion will be limited to such aspects and features as are salient in Strauss's analysis.[49]

III

The beginning of the Pantheism Controversy is well known: in 1783, Jacobi informed Mendelssohn, by way of a mutual acquaintance, that "in his last days, Lessing had been a committed Spinozist."[50] For Mendelssohn, this disclosure amounted to nothing less than a slanderous degradation of the highest to the lowest. At that time, the German intelligentsia revered Lessing as a champion of the Enlightenment while it denounced Spinozism as a heretical, atheistic, and anarchistic doctrine. By the same token, Jacobi cast a shadow over Mendelssohn's long-standing friendship with Lessing.

With his declaration, Jacobi wanted to buttress his contention that the Enlightenment and its rationalism as such ultimately led to atheism and fatalism. Lessing, he claimed, had reached the same conclusion and had consistently embraced its radical consequences. By making this publicly known, Jacobi intended to force upon the Aufklärer the dilemma of either following in the footsteps of Lessing and accepting the destructive effects of rationalism or rejecting rationalism in favor of his own doctrine of *Glaube*. As a result, Mendelssohn was compelled to defend not only the memory of his friend but also his own position as a protagonist of the moderate Enlightenment.

As Strauss argues, Jacobi's attack struck home because he and Mendelssohn found themselves on common ground. Both faced the same problem: "the final crisis of modern metaphysics of Cartesian-Leibnizian stamp."[51] More particularly, they both grappled with "the knowledge that the attempt of modern metaphysics to found the concept of God particular to faith by means of unbelieving speculation had failed."[52] The result of this attempt, generally known as natural theology or natural religion, had become increasingly problematic as the radical premises of "unbelieving speculation" had come to the surface and demanded a hearing. As we have seen, Jacobi responded to this crisis by a wholesale repudiation of modern metaphysics and the attempt to return to traditional faith. For Mendelssohn, this solution was out of the question. Refusing to abandon the moderate wing of the Enlightenment, he held on to the idea of a natural religion and to the possibility of harmonizing religion and reason, not least because it provided the cornerstone of his defense of Judaism as a religion of reason.[53]

In the course of his introductions, Strauss critically discusses several key elements of Mendelssohn's natural theology, showing how it became increasingly embattled by the atheism of radical Enlightenment, on the one hand, and by the Jacobian return to faith, on the other. For the present inquiry, these are relevant only to the extent that they enable Strauss to single out general characteristics and general problems. In this perspective, the most important point in his treatment is his observation that Mendelssohn systematically privileges goodness as the primary attribute of God. This, Strauss holds, is a central characteristic of the Enlightenment:

> The whole of the Enlightenment, insofar as it implicitly or explicitly preserves a relationship with the tradition rooted in the Bible, is characterized by the fact that it combats the traditional doctrines and convictions by having recourse to the goodness of God. More precisely, proper to the Enlightenment is the unequivocal priority it accords to God's goodness over His power, His honor and His punishing wrath; for the Enlightenment, God is not primarily the demanding, summoning God, but rather the benevolent God.[54]

The priority of goodness over the other divine attributes determines almost all of the distinctive tenets of Mendelssohn's natural theology, Strauss maintains. It provides the basis for his demonstration of the immortality of the soul, of human perfectibility and freedom, his concomitant rejection of eternal punishment and his denial of revelation. A good and benevolent God, Mendelssohn holds, does not need to make himself known by revelation but enables man to acquire knowledge of his design by studying the perfect order of creation. Moreover, a benevolent God could not have created man but with a view to happiness, so that man must be infinitely perfectible. As a consequence, Mendelssohn rejects the ceaseless suffering of eternal damnation, for it contradicts human perfectibility as well as the perfection of creation. In addition, human perfectibility also implies that every individual possesses both an irreducible existence and certain inalienable rights that not even God can violate. This can never lead to difficulties, Mendelssohn assures, for any conflict between the rights of man and those of God is excluded.[55]

According to Strauss, however, giving priority to divine goodness does not express "a theological concern of any kind, but instead the concern for the substantiality, the independence, the autonomy, and the proper right of the Ego (*das Ich*): the unconditional goodness of God is given priority because it is in accord with the claims of the autonomous Ego."[56] In other words, Mendelssohn's natural theology proves to be ultimately guided by and accommodated to interests particular to modern philosophy.[57] This is rendered manifest by several observations. Thus, for Mendelssohn, one of the principal tasks of modern metaphysics consists in securing human happiness and individual progress by liberating man from the fear of death and divine wrath. Not surprisingly, he once referred to his natural theology as to a "rather Epicurean" theism.[58]

This modern character also becomes apparent in Mendelssohn's attempts to "correct" the doctrines concerning the immortality of the soul of two of his revered predecessors, Plato and Leibniz. As Strauss shows, *Phädon*, Mendelssohn's translation of Plato's *Phaedo*, contains many alterations and emendations to the effect that the original teaching and its exigencies are mitigated and moderated. In a typical manner, for example, Mendelssohn's Socrates emphasizes the consoling effect of the idea of immortality of the soul, whereas Plato's Socrates does not regard this as a valid argument but instead considers it an obstacle to philosophizing. A similar approach marks Mendelssohn's *Sache Gottes, oder die gerettete Vorsehung*, ostensibly an elaboration of Leibniz's *Causa Dei*. Whereas Leibniz argues divine providence by asserting that God's justice is his goodness guided and limited by his wisdom, Mendelssohn reverses the order of wisdom and goodness. As a result, he must reject eternal punishment and suffering, which Leibniz could still justify as a necessary component of the best of all possible worlds.

However, although it was intended as a defense of the orthodox religious view of providence, Leibniz's concept of divine justice implied a radical break with the tradition since it no longer allowed divine justice to be distinguished from divine goodness and divine wisdom. In this way, Strauss argues, Leibniz prepared the momentous transition from the old notion of law to the modern notion of right: "[B]y dissolving the classical concept of justice which had preserved the original meaning of justice as obedience with regard to the law, he had considerably precipitated the process that aimed at the eradication of law understood as obligation in favor of right understood as claim."[59]

Mendelssohn, a self-confessed follower of Leibniz, could not but accept this result and adapt his natural theology in accordance with it. However, his edifice started to topple when his faith in the power and the authority of demonstration was decisively shaken in acrimonious disputes with critics who attacked his natural theology: "Compelled to defend his Judaism and his rationalism at the same time, he had to present Judaism as a purely rational religion. In any case, however, the teaching of the Bible is not demonstrative....Saving Judaism was only possible for him in this way, that he severely restricted the right and the significance of demonstration."[60] This restriction found its expression in Mendelssohn's introduction of the notion of "common sense" or "plain human understanding" (*gesundes Menschenverstand*), a specific human capacity to grasp intuitively and with full clarity certain essential truths that speculative reason alone cannot demonstrate. In

Mendelssohn's view, since common sense alone could provide a basis for agreement among men, it had to guide and to supplement reason, which he had come to regard as insufficient.

Not surprisingly, Strauss is critical of this move. In the first place, he notes that this new configuration of reason and common sense is merely a reiteration of the traditional religious notion of revelation as a necessary guide for insufficient reason. Confronted with the failure of Cartesian-Leibnizian metaphysics as a substitute for traditional faith, natural theology could do no more than to seek refuge on "the neutral isle of common sense," while the realm of speculation was invaded by the radical atheist metaphysics of Spinozism.[61] As Mendelssohn himself admitted, this move did not differ essentially from Jacobi's leap of faith out of speculation and demonstration. In both cases, the appeal to a faculty beyond speculation proved to be the only way of saving teleology.

Second, Strauss challenges Mendelssohn's judgment—foreshadowing the current view—that Jacobi's doctrine of *Glaube* threatens philosophical speculation and leads to irrational "enthusiasm" (*Schwärmerey*). On the contrary, he argues, it is precisely common sense that endangers speculation: "For common sense lets the animating conviction appear as self-evident, whereas [Jacobi's] admission that this conviction is merely believed, implies or may imply the knowledge of ignorance and therewith an impulse to speculation."[62] Differently stated, Jacobi's teaching preserves an unexplored latitude for philosophical speculation, which is altogether excluded by Mendelssohn's notion of common sense.

Third, Strauss argues that the notion of common sense merely compounds the predicament it seeks to escape from. Cartesian philosophy, he explains, was motivated by the view that traditional philosophy had relied too much on everyday language. As a result, it called for a distinct and purely scientific language. This demand, however, could not be brought into agreement with the equally important requirement that the new philosophy enlighten humanity in general by supplanting the old popular beliefs, for:

> especially in its "language," this philosophy was further removed from the language of common sense than the earlier philosophy; it tended to extreme unpopularity. However, it thus became entirely incapable of replacing the "popular system," and therewith of fulfilling one of its most important functions, that of "Enlightenment." Small wonder, then, that "enthusiasm" reared its head anew. However, small wonder, as well, that common sense, which had allowed itself to be enlightened to the best of its abilities by modern metaphysics, when it perceived that it could expect a new "obscurantism" from the "subtleties" of this metaphysics, dismissed its nurse without further ado and declared itself mature.[63]

It did so, however, in the illusion that it could now freely marshal clear and distinct metaphysical truths since it regarded the latter as having been assimilated within everyday language. Hence, although it was introduced to remedy the shortcomings of Cartesian philosophy, the notion of common sense remained within the horizon established by modern philosophy's estrangement from everyday language. As a result, it did not lead to a serious reconsideration of "earlier philosophy" in relation to premodern, "nonenlightened" common sense. As Strauss points out,

Mendelssohn was convinced that premodern metaphysics had been definitely surpassed by modern metaphysics. He therefore persistently identified metaphysics with modern metaphysics and thus proved incapable of understanding premodern thought as it understood itself. One example of this failure is his distorting appropriation of the Platonic teaching concerning immortality.[64]

According to Strauss, however, this general critique applies with equal force to Jacobi. The latter, in spite of his sweeping repudiation of modern metaphysics, also remains decisively bound to its presuppositions and exhibits a similar blindness to premodern thought. This becomes apparent in a central ambiguity of his critique of Spinoza. One of Jacobi's main objections against Spinozism is that it gives priority to action over thinking, whereby the latter is regarded as the mere continuation of action (*die Handlung im Fortgang*). However, he himself adopts precisely this proposition in his polemic against the Enlightenment when he asks, rhetorically and polemically: "Can philosophy ever be anything more than history?" and when he asserts that "every age has its own truth, just as it has its own living philosophy, which describes the predominant manner of acting of the age in question in its continuation (*in ihrem Fortgange*)."[65] These assertions show that Jacobi's irrationalism and traditionalism, according to which true knowledge can only result from virtuous action motivated by obedience to transcendent reality, are actually rooted in historicism. This accounts for the decisionism characteristic of his "leap of faith," as well as for his attempt to bring about a renewal of philosophy through a change in morality.

In spite of his efforts, Jacobi remained equally captive to the horizon of modern historical thought. Strauss concludes: "Persisting in his critique of Spinoza to the end, he would not have been able to appeal to history against the Enlightenment, nor to faith (*Glaube*) understood within the horizon of the concept of history."[66] The implications of this terse remark deserve our attention: a sustained critique of Spinoza, it seems, would have called into question "the concept of history" and, perhaps, opened the possibility of a nonhistorical approach to both the Enlightenment and faith. It is hard to disregard the impression that, in this remark, Strauss is thinking of his own undertaking. For, as his principal writings of the 1930s show, this is precisely the path his research has taken. Between *Spinoza's Critique of Religion* (1930) and *Philosophy and Law* (1935), he has radically questioned the universal claim underlying historical consciousness by tracing its origin to the concept of "prejudice" introduced by Descartes and adopted by Spinoza. By the same token, he has begun to reopen the quarrel of the ancients and the moderns and to recover the nonhistorical horizon of premodern thought, the horizon of "the old concept of law" shared and disputed by "earlier philosophy" and revealed religion. Guided by the medieval Enlightenment of Islamic and Jewish philosophers such as Farabi, Avicenna, Averroes, and Maimonides, he is led back to Plato and, ultimately, to the enigmatic figure of Socrates.[67]

IV

If Jacobi's thought was certainly influential in the development of Strauss's early thought, it was by no means decisive. Generally speaking, Jacobi made Strauss aware of the problem of the Enlightenment in two different ways: by means of his trenchant critique of the epistemological, theological, ethical, and political characteristics of modern rationalism, but equally by the shortcomings of the solution he proposed. On the first account, Strauss adopted several of Jacobi's criticisms and insights in his own study of Spinoza as well as in his discussions with contemporary thinkers. On the second account, he expressed a number of fundamental reservations as to Jacobi's doctrine. The most important of these pertains to Jacobi's failure to sustain his critique of Spinoza and his subsequent failure to question radically the horizon of modern thought. Although this constitutes a crucial and, in a certain respect, decisive point of divergence between Strauss and Jacobi, it is by no means the occasion for a critical farewell, nor does it fully express Strauss's final appreciation. Throughout his analyses, he repeatedly suggests that the many ambiguities and contradictions in Jacobi's position may have been deliberate. In his campaign against the *Aufklärung*, Jacobi constantly changed tactics and continually moved the line of battle. Depending on the conduct of his opponent, he would alternately take the side of radical atheists such as Spinoza and Hobbes against the prudent dogmatism of the Aufklärer or launch a spirited defense of Christianity and tradition against the antitheistic dogmatism of radical Enlightenment. For Strauss, this agility suggests that Jacobi may have been neither a dogmatic atheist nor a religious enthusiast. Commenting on Mendelssohn's bewilderment regarding the position of his opponent, he writes:

> It has been noted that he lacked Jacobi's spiritual freedom, and that, as a result, Jacobi's vacillating between atheism and Christianity remained incomprehensible to him: at times, he really did not know whether he encountered in Jacobi an atheist or a Christian; only for a brief instant did he prove capable of rising to the insight that Jacobi was a philosopher.[68]

According to Strauss, Jacobi's great example in this particular modus operandi was none other than Lessing himself. In various debates that had established his reputation as a writer and thinker, Lessing had alternately defended radical orthodoxy and radical Enlightenment without paying allegiance to either camp. He was unable to adhere to any doctrine, and his loyalty only regarded an elusive truth that lies between and beyond. The search for this truth enabled him to experiment with conflicting opinions without accepting any of them as final. This philosophical independence found its expression in his well-known love of paradox as well as in his preference for conversation over doctrine. For Mendelssohn, who disapproved of his friend's "theater logic" (*Theaterlogik*), this vital aspect of Lessing's thought was inaccessible: he could not accept a paradoxical truth but dismissed every philosophical dispute as "mere verbal disagreement" against the fixed background of the certainties perceived by common sense understanding. Identifying philosophy with ontology, he was unable to appreciate Lessing's dialectical style of thinking, which Jacobi had partly emulated:

> If one pays attention to the How rather than to the What—and for Jacobi and Lessing alike, the great manner of thinking held more weight than the recognition of this

> or that opinion—one will be inclined to reckon with the possibility that Jacobi was the most intelligent follower Lessing found among his contemporaries....Jacobi felt himself to be, not entirely without justification, the legitimate heir of Lessing and of the latter's radical, i.e., undogmatic way of thinking.[69]

To be sure, the praise implicit in this assessment is qualified. In the first place, it does not detract from the pertinence of Strauss's objections to Jacobi's historicism and his failure to pursue his critique of modern rationalism to the end. Furthermore, Strauss elsewhere suggests that even Jacobi did not fully fathom the extent of Lessing's irony and may have become its dupe.[70] In any case, it suggests that any influence Jacobi may have exercised over Strauss's thinking is secondary to the impact of Lessing and is even conditioned and mediated by the latter. Although an adequate assessment of this impact would exceed the limits of this chapter, it is not amiss to give two examples in support of this contention.

First, there is some evidence that Lessing played an important role in Strauss's rediscovery of the art of writing of ancient and early modern thinkers. This may be inferred from the introduction to Mendelssohn's *Sache Gottes*. Discussing the difference between Mendelssohn and Leibniz regarding the defense of eternal punishment, he makes the following noteworthy remark:

> Leibniz, however, did not believe in eternal damnation as it was understood by the Christian tradition....The fact that he was nevertheless able to defend the ecclesiastical doctrine is ultimately rooted in the conviction that determines the content of his defense: in the conviction of the unconditional priority of the beauty and order of the whole over the happiness of the parts, hence also of human beings, and in the conviction, inseparable from the former, that beatitude consists in the contemplation of the universal order. For the ideal of contemplation carries with it the division of mankind into the "wise" and the "many," and therewith the recognition of a twofold way of communicating truths, an esoteric and an exoteric.[71]

Although Strauss does not mention it in his commentary, he is well aware that the source of this view is none other than Lessing. This is borne out by "Exoteric Teaching," a text he wrote three years later in 1939 but chose not to publish at the time. There he refers to "*Leibniz von den ewigen Strafen*," in which Lessing comments as follows on Leibniz's defense of the orthodox view of eternal punishment:

> He did no more and no less than what all of the ancient philosophers used to do in their exoteric speech. He observed a sort of prudence for which, it is true, our most recent philosophers have become much too wise....I admit that Leibniz treated the doctrine of eternal damnation very exoterically, and that esoterically he would have expressed himself altogether differently on the subject.[72]

At the end of the same text, Lessing indicates that one ancient philosopher who observed this sort of prudence was Socrates, who "believed in eternal punishment in all seriousness, or at least believed in it to the extent that he considered it expedient (*zuträglich*) to teach it in words that are least susceptible of arousing suspicion and most explicit."[73] That this remark did not escape Strauss is evinced by the fact that he reproduced it in its entirety in *Persecution and the Art of Writing*.[74] As he indicates in "Exoteric Teaching," "Lessing was the last writer who revealed, while hiding, the reasons compelling wise men to hide the truth: he wrote between the lines about writing between the lines."[75] By the same token, Lessing may well have been the first writer from whom Strauss began to learn how to read between the lines.

Second, as an assiduous student of his undogmatic way of thinking and of his art of writing, Strauss knew that Lessing was familiar with medieval Jewish and Islamic theology and philosophy.[76] It is not unlikely that this had some bearing on his own investigations. Thus, in 1946 he sketched the plan of a book tentatively titled *Philosophy and the Law*, the final chapter of which was to be devoted to Lessing's *Nathan the Wise*. Although this celebrated play is generally regarded as a tribute to Mendelssohn, the symbol of enlightened tolerance, Strauss hints at a strikingly different interpretation: "The recollection of the man Maimonides was probably one of the motives underlying Lessing's *Nathan the Wise*, the outstanding poetic monument erected in honor of Jewish medieval philosophy."[77] It is still far from clear whether and to what extent Lessing guided Strauss to Maimonides's art of writing and perhaps also to the theater logic of Plato's dialogues, that poetic monument erected in honor of Socratic classical philosophy.[78] Nonetheless, if there is some foundation for the view that Strauss was a Jacobian, there is all the more reason to explore the possibility that he was a committed Lessingian.[79]

Notes

1. *SCR* 240.
2. Friedrich Heinrich Jacobi, *Uber die Lehre des Spinoza in Briefen an den Herrn Moses Mendelssohn* (Breslau: Löwe, 1785). Abridged English translation in: F. H. Jacobi, *The Main Philosophical Writings and The Novel 'Alwill*, trans. George Di Giovanni (Montreal: McGill–Queen's University Press 1994).
3. Gerhard Krüger, "Review of Leo Strauss' *Die Religionskritik Spinozas als Grundlage seiner Bibelwissenschaft*," trans. George Elliot Tucker, *Independent Journal of Philosophy* 5/6 (1988): 173. Very likely, Krüger's use of the word "concealed" is deliberate. As becomes apparent from his correspondence with Strauss, the latter encountered objections from Julius Guttmann, his superior at the Akademie fur die Wissenschaft des Judentums. Guttmann demanded that certain passages in the book be altered or even omitted. Though Strauss deferred to Guttmann, he asked Krüger to criticize the opaqueness of his work so as to guide his readers to his true intentions. See the Strauss–Krüger correspondence, in *GS–3* 379, 393.
4. See Frederick C. Beiser, *The Fate of Reason: German Philosophy from Kant to Fichte* (Cambridge, MA: Harvard University Press, 1987), 448.
5. See, respectively, Susan Shell, "Taking Evil Seriously: Schmitt's 'Concept of the Political' and Strauss's 'True Politics,'" and John G. Gunnell, "Strauss Before Straussianism: Reason, Revelation and Nature," in *Leo Strauss, Political Philosopher and Jewish Thinker*, ed. Kenneth L. Deutsch and Walter Nicgorski (Lanham, MD: Rowman & Littlefield, 1994), 183 and 171.
6. Compare Stephen Holmes, *The Anatomy of Antiliberalism* (Cambridge, MA: Harvard University Press, 1996).
7. Leo Strauss (with Jacob Klein), GA–*JPCM* 460.
8. As Strauss notes, the Pantheism Controversy marked the "formal reception of Spinoza." This reception was followed by a wave of "Spinoza enthusiasm" that lasted

into the twentieth century, until the spell was broken by Hermann Cohen's renewed excommunication. Cohen's attack formed the occasion for Strauss's reassessment of Spinoza's critique. Leo Strauss, "Preface to Spinoza's Critique of Religion," in *JPCM* 154–58. See also Leo Strauss, "*Das Testament Spinozas*," in *GS–1* 415–22; English translation in *LSEW* 216–23.

9. Both the dissertation and the introductions to Mendelssohn were published in *GS–2*. Henceforth, all references to those writings are to this volume, as *EPLJ* and EMFL, respectively. All translations of them in the present chapter are my own, D.J.
10. *EPLJ* 237–92. The dissertation, defended on September 17, 1920, was written under the direction of Ernst Cassirer, who conducted a large-scale research project on the problem of knowledge in modern philosophy. See Ernst Cassirer, *Das Erkenntnisproblem in der Philosophie und Wissenschaft der neueren Zeit* (Berlin: Verlag Bruno Cassirer, 1906). A French translation of the dissertation is available in *Revue de métaphysique et de morale* 99 (1994): 291–311 and 505–32.
11. *EPLJ* 243. In a handwritten note appended to a summary of his dissertation, Strauss calls his work "a non-Jacobian approach to Jacobian problems," adding the remark that "I have not presented 'Jacobi as such', but only insofar as I needed him"; *EPLJ* 297.
12. *EPLJ* 283.
13. In a similar vein, Strauss asserts in the introduction to the dissertation: "Certainly, a philosophy that understands itself and refuses to surrender to relativism, must conceive the truth it pursues as an independent and coherent condition, which it does not create but rather seeks, discovers and recognizes." *EPLJ* 244. Compare *WIPP* 39; *NRH* 123–24, 150n4; *CM* 119–21; *RCPR* 174–76.
14. *EPLJ* 249. Cf. *NRH* 173–74, 174n9, 201; *RCPR* 243–44; *LAM* 212.
15. *EPLJ* 249. Cf. Beiser, *The Fate of Reason*, 46.
16. *EPLJ* 285. Cf. Beiser, *The Fate of Reason*, 81, 89–91.
17. *EPLJ* 258. In this light, Beiser's assertion that "natural science is the source of nihilism" (*The Fate of Reason*, 85) must be supplemented: with equal justification, one might say that, for Jacobi, nihilism is the source of the natural sciences.
18. *EPLJ* 258–59.
19. *EPLJ* 252.
20. *EPLJ* 281.
21. EMFL 537–38; cf. *LSMM* 71. Compare *EPLJ* 278.
22. EMFL 549; cf. *LSMM* 85.
23. EMFL 533–35; cf. *LSMM* 65–68. Compare Frederick C. Beiser, *Enlightenment, Revolution, and Romanticism: The Genesis of Modern Political Thought, 1790–1800* (Cambridge, MA: Harvard University Press, 1992).
24. Cf. Beiser, *The Fate of Reason*, 89.
25. *EPLJ* 242–43, 270, 274–75, 277, 279–80, 282.
26. *EPLJ* 245–47, 252.
27. *Die Religionskritik Spinozas als Grundlage seiner Bibelwissenschaft*, *GS–1* 235–47.
28. "Progress or Return? The Contemporary Crisis of Western Civilization," in *JPCM* 117. Compare "Preface to Spinoza's Critique of Religion," in *JPCM* 253–54: "The *Ethics* thus begs the decisive question-the question as to whether the clear and distinct account is as such true and not merely a plausible hypothesis.... [T]he clear and distinct account of everything which it presents remains fundamentally hypothetical."
29. *NRH* 30. Cf. David R. Lachterman, "Laying Down the Law: The Theologico-Political Matrix of Spinoza's Physics," in *Leo Strauss's Thought: Toward a Critical Engagement*, ed. Alan Udoff (Boulder, CO: Lynne Rienner Publishers, 1991), 123–53.
30. *EPLJ* 251–52.

31. For a more extensive account, see David Janssens, "Weimar Revisited: Judaism, Zionism, and Enlightenment in Leo Strauss's Early Thought" (in Hebrew), *Iyyun* 50 (2001): 407–18.
32. "*Antwort auf das 'Prinzipielle Wort' der Frankfurter*," *GS–2* 305 (cf. "Response to Frankfurt's 'Word of Principle,'" *LSEW* 69).
33. "*Ecclesia Militans*," *GS–2* 353 (cf. "Ecclesia Militans," *LSEW* 126). See also "*Biblische Geschichte and Wissenschaft*," *GS–2* 357–59 (cf. "Biblical History and Science," *LSEW* 131–33).
34. "Preface to Spinoza's Critique of Religion," in *JPCM* 144–55.
35. *PLA* 136n3. Compare "*Bemerkungen zu der Weinbergschen Kritik*," *GS–1* 429 (cf. "Comments on Weinberg's Critique," *LSEW* 119); "Die Zukunft einer Illusion," *GS–1* 433 (cf. "Sigmund Freud, *The Future of an Illusion*," *LSEW* 203); "Zur Ideologie des politischen Zionismus," *GS–1* 447.
36. GA–*JPCM* 460.
37. "*Die Zukunft einer Illusion*," *GS–1* 433 (cf. *LSEW* 204). Cf. "Zur Ideologie des politischen Zionismus," *GS–1* 445: "Political Zionism is the organization of unbelief in Judaism; it is the attempt to organize the Jewish people on the basis of unbelief."
38. According to his closest friend Jacob Klein, these two problems were at the center of the young Strauss's attention. Compare Strauss, GA–*JPCM* 458.
39. Another indication is the fact that in his early writings Strauss frequently acknowledges his indebtedness to Rudolf Otto's *The Holy*. This seminal work initiated a renewal of theology by restoring the transcendence of God as its primary object and by identifying the irrational as the core of the divine. Already in his dissertation Strauss appeals to The Holy, pointing out that Otto's thought is substantially connected to Jacobi by way of the German philosopher Jacob F. Fries. See, respectively, "*Das Heilige*," "*Biblische Geschichte und Wissenschaft*," and "*Zur Auseinandersetzung mit der europäischen Wissenschaft*," *GS–2* 307–10, 357–62, and 341–50.
40. "Zur Bibelwissenschaft Spinozas and seiner Vorlaufer," *GS–1* 404.
41. *Die Religionskritik Spinozas*, *GS–1* 265.
42. *Die Religionskritik Spinozas*, *GS–1* 166, 193–94, 225, 247. Cf. *PLA* 28–30.
43. *Die Religionskritik Spinozas*, *GS–1* 266n276. Regarding the "free spirit" that animates modern theory, Strauss remarks: "it presupposes itself, like faith presupposes itself"; *GS–1* 214. See also *PLA* 37; "Preface to Spinoza's Critique of Religion," *JPCM* 151 and 172.
44. *EPLJ* 247. Consider also the later Strauss's well-known elaboration on Plato's simile of the cave, to the extent that modern thought has become trapped within a second cave beneath the first. As he suggests, fear may have been at the origin of this event: "People *may become so frightened* of the ascent to the light of the sun, and so desirous of making that ascent utterly impossible to any of their descendants, that they dig a deep pit beneath the cave in which they were born, and withdraw into that pit"; *PAW* 155 (emphasis added).
45. *EPLJ* 247–48.
46. *Die Religionskritik Spinozas*, *GS–1* 229–46.
47. *EPLJ* 282n135.
48. *EPLJ* 282.
49. See Chapters 2, 3, and 4 of Beiser, *The Fate of Reason*. In his account, Beiser names Strauss's introduction among the best treatments of the controversy. Compare Beiser, The *Fate of Reason*, 335n12. See also Alexander Altmann, *Moses Mendelssohn: A Biographical Study* (London: Routledge and Kegan Paul, 1974) and Hermann Timm, *Gott und die Freiheit: Studien zur Religionsphilosophie der Goethezeit* (Frankfurt: Klostermann, 1974). The main

documents of the controversy were edited and published in *Die Hauptschriften zum Pantheismusstreit zwischen Jacobi und Mendelssohn*, ed. Heinrich Scholz (Berlin: Reuther and Reichard, 1916; reprint, Waltrop: Hartmut Spenner, 2004). A concise discussion of Mendelssohn's position in the controversy, critical of Strauss's account, can be found in Allan Arkush, *Moses Mendelssohn and the Enlightenment* (Albany: State University of New York Press, 1994).

50. EMFL 531; cf. *LSMM* 64. Cf. Beiser, *The Fate of Reason*, 61.
51. EMFL 572; cf. *LSMM* 110.
52. EMFL 587; cf. *LSMM* 126.
53. Cf. Moses Mendelssohn, *Jerusalem, or On Religious Power and Judaism*, trans. Allan Arkush, with a commentary by Alexander Altmann (Hanover, NH: University Press of New England, 1984).
54. EP 491; cf. *LSMM* 35–36. Cf. *PLA* 44.
55. EMFL 583–86; cf. *LSMM* 122–25.
56. EMFL 585; cf. *LSMM* 125.
57. In *PLA* 78n28, Strauss renders this criticism more explicit by pointing out the Hobbesian pedigree of Mendelssohn's "surrender of the ancient natural right of duty in favor of the modern natural right of claim."
58. EMFL 573–74; cf. *LSMM* 110f.
59. ESG 527; cf. *LSMM* 160–61.
60. EMFL 578; cf. *LSMM* 116–17. Challenging Strauss's thesis, Arkush argues that Mendelssohn "could have defended Judaism without downplaying the importance or denying the possibility of philosophical knowledge of religious truths," because he never did "place such an absolute value on philosophical knowledge" in the first place. Rather, Mendelssohn regarded the balance between reason and common sense he tried to strike as a temporary settlement in anticipation of an ultimate demonstrative proof of God's existence. See Arkush, *Moses Mendelssohn and the Enlightenment*, 88–93.
61. EMFL 581; cf. *LSMM* 120.
62. EMFL 587; cf. *LSMM* 127.
63. EMFL 575–76; cf. *LSMM* 113–14.
64. EMFL 573; cf. *LSMM* 110. At EMFL 577 (cf. *LSMM* 115n304), Strauss comments on Mendelssohn's "pride in this progress [of metaphysics] and, at the same time, the concomitant inability to understand the character of Aristotelian ethics, which had been adopted by Maimonides."
65. EMFL 588; cf. *LSMM* 127. With slight alterations, I reproduce Beiser's translation of both quotations in *The Fate of Reason*, 88–89. On 88, Beiser aptly dubs Jacobi's doctrine an "epistemology of action."
66. EMFL 588; cf. *LSMM* 128.
67. For an account of this stage in Strauss's development, see David Janssens, *Between Athens and Jerusalem: Philosophy, Prophecy, and Politics in Leo Strauss's Early Thought* (NY: State University of New York Press, 2008), 77–108.
68. EMFL 570; cf. *LSMM* 107.
69. EMFL 542; cf. *LSMM* 76–77. Compare the characterization of Mendelssohn's position in ESL 474 (*LSMM* 15–16), with EMFL 556 (*LSMM* 92–93). Cf. *EPLJ* 282. Cf. *PPH* 145.
70. As Strauss observes, before admitting to Jacobi that for him "there is no other philosophy than Spinoza's," Lessing had already qualified his commitment by saying, "If I were to name myself after anyone, then I know no one better." In a similar vein, to Jacobi's avowal that "my creed is not in Spinoza," he had rejoined ironically: "I

hope it is in no book," that is, not even in Spinoza. See EMFL 546; cf. *LSMM* 80–81. Referring to Jacobi's conversation with Lessing in "A Giving of Accounts," Strauss praises the latter as "the author of the only improvised live dialogue on a philosophic subject known to me." In the same context, looking back on *SCR*, he states: "In this study, I was greatly assisted by Lessing," that is, not Jacobi. See Strauss, GA–*JPCM* 462.

71. ESG 522; cf. *LSMM* 155.
72. Gotthold Ephraim Lessing, "Leibniz von den ewigen Strafen," in *Werke in acht Bänden* (München: Carl Hanser Verlag, 1979), 7: 180–83. Cf. Strauss, "Exoteric Teaching," in *RCPR* 65; or appendix F in the present volume, p. 278. In his quotation, Strauss does not reproduce the final sentence.
73. Lessing, "Leibniz von den ewigen Strafen," *Werke* 7:196.
74. *PAW* 182.
75. Strauss, "Exoteric Teaching," in *RCPR* 64; or appendix F in the present volume, p. 276. Cf. Clemens Kauffmann, *Strauss und Rawls. Das philosophische Dilemma der Politik* (Berlin: Duncker & Humblot, 2000), 129–41.
76. In 1747, Lessing completed a comedy entitled *Der junge Gelehrte*. At the beginning of the play, the protagonist, a young scholar, is reading Maimonides's *Mishneh Torah*. See Lessing, *Werke* 1:282. In the famous *Fragments* purposely published by Lessing, Hermann Reimarus praises Maimonides as "the wisest (*verstandigste*) of all Jews." See Lessing, "Von Duldung der Deisten. Fragment eines Ungenannten," *Werke* 7:322. Compare Friedrich Niewohner, "Vernunft als innigste Ergebenheit in Gott. Lessing and der Islam," *Neue Zürcher Zeitung*, no. 262 (2001): 83.
77. Strauss, "Plan of a Book Tentatively Titled Philosophy and the Law," in *JPCM* 470. In the same context, Strauss announces: "While preparing the edition of Mendelssohn's metaphysical writings for the Jubilee-Edition of Mendelssohn's works, I discovered some unknown material which throws new light on that controversy." However, it is not clear from the text, nor does it become clear in the introductions what this material consists of. Although the book was never published, there is fragmentary evidence in Strauss's *Nachlass* in the University of Chicago Library that he worked on an interpretation of *Nathan the Wise*. Cf. Leo Strauss Papers, box 11, folder 7.
78. EMFL 535; cf. *LSMM* 68f. Consider also Strauss's comment on Mendelssohn's art of writing in casting *Morgenstunden*, as a dialogue: "A dialogue is a kind of drama; a drama, being a product of poetry, is an ideal presentation of nature, in specific cases an ideal presentation of real occurrences; and art is playful, whereas life is serious"; EMFL 590; cf. *LSMM* 129.
79. In a letter to Alexander Altmann, written in 1971, Strauss acknowledges his great debt to Lessing. Cf. Heinrich Meier, "How Strauss Became Strauss," chapter 1 of the present volume, p. 23. In 1937, Strauss wrote "Eine Erinnerung an Lessing," a short note in which he recorded that he did not find among his contemporaries "a single man of Lessing's spiritual freedom"; *GS–2* 607–8; cf. *LSMM* 162.

CHAPTER 10

"THROUGH THE KEYHOLE": LEO STRAUSS'S REDISCOVERY OF CLASSICAL POLITICAL PHILOSOPHY IN XENOPHON'S *CONSTITUTION OF THE LACEDAEMONIANS*

Richard S. Ruderman

The decade of the 1930s was, for much of the civilized world, a dark and darkening period. Not only was the West in the grips of a Great Depression, but its self-confidence was at perhaps its lowest ebb. After all, European liberalism (and the individualism that was thought to be its most beautiful flower) was being abandoned for Marxism and fascism; science—which was not a little implicated in the deaths of millions in the Great War—was increasingly seen as both evil and as a merely parochial Western view; and political science, having once been viewed as the queen of the social sciences, was increasingly viewed as impotent, at least with regard to generating the most needful thing of all, values. Collectivism in politics, irrationalism for the spirit, and a tired recounting of a tradition of political thought that no longer could speak to the age—such was the "spirit of the age" that, already a generation earlier, Spengler had dubbed the "Going-Under of the West."

Toward the end of that decade, Leo Strauss, a then little-known German émigré scholar to America, published his first article on classical political philosophy, an interpretation of Xenophon's *Constitution of the Lacedaemonians.* The immediate impression of scholarly abstractedness, unaware of the gathering storms just outside his study, seems redoubled when we look back from the vantage point of the later Strauss, who was anything but shy about openly invoking the "crisis of the West" and "the crisis of political philosophy"—usually in the opening paragraphs of his writings—as grounds for returning to the thought of classical antiquity.[1] In this essay, however, he appears to be silent about the state of the world in which he lives and writes. Moreover, in selecting Xenophon's *Constitution of the Lacedaemonians* as his subject, Strauss seems to be making every effort to evade, rather than to engage, the pressing issues of political philosophy as then understood. After all, the greatest thinkers of the period,

Nietzsche and Heidegger, had pronounced Socratic philosophy to be the decisive wrong turn taken by mankind. And Xenophon was hardly viewed as a Socratic worthy of *Dekonstruktion*: whatever his charms may be, the ability to grasp the intricacies of Socrates's most subtle teaching was not thought to be among them. Even if, in some perverse way, that failing could be turned to Xenophon's advantage—that is, if he could be shown to represent the poetic tradition of heroic overreaching that Socrates had undermined or destroyed—Strauss's choice of the *Constitution* fails to capitalize on it: far from there being a commanding Cyrus in its pages, the Spartan citizens (and even, to a considerable extent, its rulers) we meet there prove to be more or less interchangeable and unheroic.

In contrast to the high drama associated with Nietzsche and Heidegger, then, Strauss's first effort at a recovery of classical political philosophy seems modest to a fault. And yet, toward the end of his essay, Strauss does briefly indicate what it is about the contemporary political and philosophical situations that require overcoming if, indeed, a return to the classics is to be viable. First, in the midst of explaining the necessity and purpose of esoteric writing, Strauss observes that esoteric writing disappeared "at a rather recent date" and that "its reappearance is simultaneous with the reappearance of persecution" (535).[2] This quiet allusion to the persecution then rearing its ugly head in Soviet Russia and Nazi Germany is Strauss's sole reference to the contemporary situation. Second, Strauss proposes that insofar as "the restitution of a sound approach is bound up with the elimination of Rousseau's influence," the writings of "men like Xenophon" are precisely the "antidote" we need. Now, Strauss does not attempt to delineate the scope and meaning of the "influence of Rousseau." But, as the topic of the essay leads us to recall, Rousseau was the most vocal and impassioned defender of "Sparta" in modern times. Nor was Rousseau merely engaged in historical romanticism. Rousseau's defense of "Sparta" in the midst of the advance of enlightenment liberalism was closely connected to his promotion of the "citizen" who was fully dedicated to his fatherland over the "bourgeois individual" who combined the selfish exploitation of his fellow citizens with a craven deference to popular tastes and public opinion. Insofar, then, as Rousseau's preference for Sparta had paved the way for both the Communist and the Fascist efforts to subordinate the individual to the state, or the we-species, or the *Volk*, it could not have been more timely to reexamine the original meaning of Sparta, or the allure of the "spirit of Sparta."

What then is at issue in "The Spirit of Sparta or the Taste of Xenophon"? The title, at a glance, would seem to consist of two ideas linked by a conjunctive "or": we need to recover something of the "taste of Xenophon" that ran toward "the spirit of Sparta." But the "spirit of Sparta" alludes not so much to the "actual Sparta of the present or of the past" as to "the conviction that man belongs, or ought to belong, entirely to the city": "the incarnation of the political spirit was Sparta" (531). The spirit of Sparta, then, was alive and well, so to speak, in the "taste" of Stalin and of Hitler (not to mention Marx and Heidegger).[3] Indeed, insofar as modern liberalism encourages a certain broad tolerance—tending to official indifference—toward morality, contemporary critics of liberalism cannot but be attracted to a Sparta that was, as Xenophon writes, "on the watch for those who are easy-going toward what was believed to be the noble" (*Const. Lac.* 4.4).[4] Furthermore, as Strauss makes clear in the course of his interpretation of the satirical nature of Xenophon's encomium of Sparta, the "true name of that taste which permeates Xenophon's writings" is "philosophy" (531). The "or" in the title is disjunctive: "Sparta and philosophy are incompatible." As a call for a return to "Spartan virtue," Strauss's essay fails—though it succeeds in undermining Rousseau's parallel call. But it succeeds in pointing to the reasons why philosophy is the only available alternative to politics and life so understood.

Strauss announces a preference for the inconspicuousness of Xenophon at the start. This is not to say, however, that Strauss took Xenophon to be a lesser exemplar of the classical approach. As he wrote concerning his later book on Xenophon's *Hiero* in a letter to his friend Alexandre Kojève, he prefers to enter a room "through a keyhole."[5] Xenophon, more than his more openly theoretical and seemingly doctrinaire fellow classics Plato and Aristotle, compels his readers to think for themselves. Or rather, he is happy to present them with this simple alternative: take me at face value (and thus be charmed or even repelled by my apparent simplemindedness) or make the effort to connect the dots, and cross the T's in order to understand the truth behind the surface, but misleading presentation. Now this, in itself, stands opposed to Rousseau and his cult of sincerity. For Xenophon is ironic through and through. Strauss's admiration for such irony—and for esoteric writing more broadly—has led more than a few contemporary critics to accuse him of harboring a hidden and fiercely political agenda (namely, promoting the secret rule of the few). On the basis of this article, however, it is difficult to see how this could be so. For Xenophon's irony here is revealed to be, among other things, a political strategy whereby he is able to mount a criticism of the Spartan regime—a regime that turns out to be nothing other than the hidden rule of the few. Strauss shows through his analysis that Xenophon chose to imitate in his writing the manner in which Sparta—or rather its founder, Lycurgus—exercised and accomplished political rule. To put it another way: Xenophon could have openly denounced the various hypocrisies with which the Spartan regime was riddled. But this procedure would suffer from at least two serious defects. First, it would deny to readers the experience of uncovering those hypocrisies themselves. Since no regime or structure of authority has ever openly announced that it was being hypocritical, Xenophon wrote so that we might learn how to think through the various claims of authority to uncover their hypocrisies. (The extent to which people must reconsider the world they think they "know" is indicated by Xenophon in a comment he makes about the general view regarding the complexity of the Spartan infantry formation: "what most people imagine ... is the exact opposite of the truth [lit. of what is]"; 11.5.) Second, unless one first feels the attraction of politics at its most alluring, one cannot learn from the subsequent discovery of hypocrisies within it. When one is taught something directly, textbook-style, there is no sense of what is missing; but when one is attracted to a positive goal (here, the life of political virtue), one will be like the Ephors described by Xenophon when outfitting the Spartans for war: "anything missing is not at all likely to be overlooked" (11.2).

In order to uncover Xenophon's teaching, Strauss pays particular attention to the plan of his work. The *Constitution* consists of 15 chapters: the first ten chapters outline the way of life that Lycurgus attempted to design for the Spartans; the next three turn to war; and the final two to the institution of monarchy at Sparta. From this design alone, the reader is tempted to draw the conclusions that the Spartan regime was designed to prepare the citizens for war; that the successful prosecution of war is and ought to be the highest purpose of political life; and that the Spartan king, as war-leader or general, is the ultimate ruler and even hero of Spartan life. As Strauss shows, however, Xenophon quietly indicates problems with each of these three theses by marring certain aspects of the plan of the work and by utilizing ambiguous expressions and references.

The most striking "flaw" in the book's plan, Strauss argues, is the appearance of Chapter 14, a chapter devoted to a harsh critique of contemporary Lacedaemonia. For, it seems, Lacedaemonia has so fallen away from Lycurgus's original institutions and laws that other Greeks, who used to "beg" her to lead them in the past, now band together to prevent Lacedaemonian hegemony (14.6). However effective Lycurgus's enactments were at the start—or were on paper—they have failed over time to accomplish their task. Let us examine with some care what Lycurgus sought to accomplish and the manner in which he sought to do it.

Lycurgus's Founding

As mentioned above, Lycurgus wanted a city devoted to virtue—or what he and perhaps most others "believed" to be the noble. Rather than permit the myriad ways in which "all other cities" slacken in their pursuit of nobility, Lycurgus legislated from cradle to grave—nay, from prior to birth to beyond even death—with an eye toward developing the most "hardy" citizens, whose resourcefulness and physical toughness would always be available to the city whenever it needed to be at war. To produce the hardiest soldiers, Lycurgus promoted a unique and unrestricted diet for young girls with respect to food and drink. Spartan girls, that is, were encouraged to indulge their pleasures—their "animal natures" as Strauss says (505)—and, as a result, their manners, especially in sexual matters, were lax. Now, Xenophon does not state any of this openly: he merely speaks of the strict and opposed general Greek practices. Moreover, while he speaks of the moral education of Spartan men (which made them continent), he says not a word about the moral education of the women. And he prepared not just the womb, but even the sperm so as to produce the strongest offspring. For while he accepted a certain moral looseness in the women in order to produce robust mothers, he required a painful degree of self-control from the men to produce robust fathers: by making it shameful for husbands to be seen entering or leaving their wives's rooms, he made sexual intercourse rarer and, he believed, more likely to produce vigorous children. Lycurgus—and not only Lycurgus—believed that to deny ourselves pleasure is the first step toward the noble.

Thus Xenophon introduces the Lycurgan approach toward what we today call "gender differentiation." The men, but not the women, are required to develop a strong sense of shame with respect to pleasure (especially sexual pleasure) resulting, as Strauss notes, in the odd fact that Spartan men are "stronger" (or "better") at modesty than the women. Now, insofar as modesty is typically considered a female virtue (Strauss draws our attention to Plato, *Laws* 802e8–10), Xenophon thereby quietly raises the striking possibility that Spartan men, frequently regarded as the most manly, were in fact quite womanly in important ways. So complete was Lycurgus's desire for robust offspring that he was willing to denature both male and female Spartans—and so eager was he to produce many such young Spartans that he permitted both men and their wives a "surprisingly large freedom to indulge in adultery" (506). The denaturing, that is, was not completely successful, and Lycurgus's concessions to human nature led to a weakening of the family. (When Xenophon goes on to note that sexual intercourse with boys was refrained from "no less" than was incest, we cannot be too reassured, for the likelihood of incest rises with the increased obscurity of familial relations.)

Strauss next turns to "Spartan education." This education turns out to be entirely "physical education"—there was apparently no liberal education in Sparta. Indeed, unlike the Persian education outlined at the beginning of the *Education of Cyrus*, the Spartan education did not even include an education in speech. One might say that Sparta extended her teaching regarding continence even to the act of speech. Xenophon's apparent praise of this practice—which extends to his adopting a certain reticence in speech himself when discussing Sparta—cannot be viewed as sincere until we determine his attitude toward the importance of speech. Now Sparta, as Strauss shows throughout his essay, ranked deeds (especially actions in war) as higher than speech. Was this Xenophon's view? Not only was Xenophon, of course, a student of Socrates, that master of speech, but he himself, in the course of leading the retreat of the Ten Thousand Greeks from Persia, utilized speech often and with exceptional success. From the point of view of action or war itself, then, speech appears to be insufficiently appreciated at Sparta. More than that, however, Xenophon raises the question of whether not speaking of certain things is the best method by which to minimize their presence or influence within the hearts and minds of the citizens.

Just as Xenophon suggests that speech (or thinking) may be superior to deed (or action), so too he holds that the soul is superior to the body (10.3). But while Xenophon does mention the ways in which Lycurgus strove to improve the bodies of the Spartans, he says next to nothing about how he sought to improve their souls. Xenophon notes that Lycurgus felt "toil" was "an employment of the soul" (7.4), but this suggests that keeping the soul distracted or exhausted (presumably by keeping the body hard at work) is the safest way to handle its natural inclinations toward "big ideas," a certain "insolence," and the pursuit of "pleasure" (3.2).[6] (One might note here that enlightenment liberalism's promotion of equality, the private sphere, and a generally instrumental view of politics is no less hostile to these erotic longings of the soul than are its modern alternatives noted at the outset.) Strauss notes that Xenophon's sole reference to this undertaking consists of his "emphatic statement" (512) that Lycurgus "compelled all [the Spartans] to practice all virtues publicly" (10.4). He immediately goes on to note Xenophon's silence regarding any Spartan practice of the virtues of wisdom, justice, or moderation. And this should have been apparent from the start: insofar as the Spartan education in virtue consists of shaming and discipline alone, it cannot be expected to produce virtue, especially those virtues that cannot be compelled.

The use of political authority, then, to produce virtue can, at best, produce only "political virtue." Such virtue is to genuine virtue as compulsion is to freedom.

This means that Sparta produces only such virtues as are valuable to the political community, not virtues that perfect or fulfill the individuals in that community. Rather than practice wisdom, moderation, and justice, the Spartans practice merely continence, bashfulness, and obedience (514). Now, even where these virtues seem similar, their differences are decisive. Continence might seem to share an "affinity" with moderation, for example. But continence (or self-control) is less an actual virtue than the foundation of virtues—and even, to be honest, of vices: thieves must exercise self-control in order successfully to carry out their tasks. Moderation, on the other hand, shapes the whole soul, as it were. It is practiced in the dark (when unobserved) no less than in the light. And the Spartans, Strauss shows, cannot be said to practice moderation, at least with respect to food, drink, and sex. The best that Xenophon seems able to say of them in this regard is that they practice it with respect to wealth. But here too there is a gap between Lycurgus's legal intention and actual Spartan practice. Lycurgus made every effort to limit the acquisition of wealth. He made it a shameful practice and he even required that Spartan money be so heavy as to make its private possession all but impossible. That he still had to institute searches for gold and silver suggests that many Spartans could not be compelled to give up their natural desire for wealth, but merely to seek natural substitutes for the useless conventional money Lycurgus issued. In fact, Xenophon quietly indicates not only the presence of wealthy men in Sparta but even their ability and readiness to contribute purchased food to the common store in place of the missing contributions of "those who are idle" (5.3). And while such generosity might appear to compensate for their having amassed wealth against the spirit and letter of the law (see 7.2–3), their capacity to purchase their contribution rather than hunt for it means that they are able to buy their way out of hunting, which Lycurgus wished to establish as the "noblest occupation" (4.7). This would seem to supply a standing and devastating critique of Spartan nobility: not only does its hold over the citizens weaken when the necessity for it is removed, but its status as the poor man's substitute for wealth is all but broadcast.

The "spirit of Sparta," it now becomes clear, consists in a suspicion of—or even hostility toward—self-concern and a corresponding effort to channel that self-concern toward a more self-sacrificing nobility. That spirit, as we noted, was alive in the 1930s and, in such movements as communitarianism, not to speak of religious fundamentalism, is alive today. It becomes of pressing concern, then, to determine whether Xenophon viewed Lycurgus as a failed attempt at carrying out an essentially admirable project, or whether he viewed the project itself as somehow flawed.

The Problem of the Noble

Lycurgus, to repeat, wished to keep a watch out for those who were "easygoing toward what is believed to be the noble" (4.4). That is to say, he wished to inculcate what today is known as "moral seriousness." But perhaps there is a gap between "what is believed to be the noble" and genuine nobility. Let us reconsider Lycurgus's view of nobility. So important to him was nobility that, despite the general Laconic opposition to speech, Lycurgus designed mixed generational mess tables to encourage the kind of conversation that would turn on recounting "noble deeds performed in the city" (5.6). Even Lycurgus, then, concedes that speech is needed to identify, praise, and even exhort to the performance of noble deeds. But while Xenophon concludes the parallel passage that explains Lycurgus's efforts at developing the "legs, arms, and necks" of the citizens with the remark that "he succeeded" in doing so, he is silent with regard to the "success" of mess-table conversations about the noble (cf. 5.9 and 5.6). Were no such deeds performed that could be recounted? Or is the recital of noble deeds exclusively doomed to fail? That is, must not the "shameful" deeds (apparently buried in silence by Lycurgus) also be recounted, not least to help distinguish what it is that nobility consists in? Moreover, must not noble speeches (or at least reasoned speeches about the noble deeds) also be offered if nobility is to be properly understood and perforce performed? Strauss summarizes Lycurgus's accomplishments as follows:

> By educating the Spartans in bashfulness only, while withholding from them true education—education in letters and speech, education in wisdom and moderation and justice—in other words, by frightening them into submissiveness with the menace of severe and dishonoring punishments, he compelled them to do forbidden things in utter secrecy. (517)

This means, Strauss concludes, that the "famous Spartan sense of shame is...simply hypocrisy." The decline in Sparta is not then, strictly speaking, a decline in Spartan virtue: it is merely a decline in their willingness or ability to dissimulate or to hide their deviations from the publicly permissible virtues.

There remains to be considered one final potential virtue of the Spartans, namely the most vaunted of their virtues, manliness or courage. Oddly, Xenophon mentions this word only once in the entire treatise—and there in so "exceedingly ambiguous" a usage (520) that most editors amend it (with no manuscript authority whatsoever) to its opposite (9.5; cf. 4.2 for a word whose root is "manly")! The one appearance of "manliness" comes in a passage devoted to explaining the endless shaming that must be faced by those Spartans who fail to live up to the noble standard of life in Sparta, above all to face willingly a "noble death" (9.1). Such losers are left out when teams pick sides; must give way in the street even to their juniors; and "must support their spinster relatives at home and must suffer the blame for [or supply the cause of] manliness" (9.5). Now, unraveling the meaning of this exceedingly odd phrase is not easy. How would one explain the "cause of manliness"? We learn at the start of this brief chapter that manliness is caused by a readiness to "choose a noble death over a dishonorable life" (9.1). And that readiness is secured, as the end of the previous chapter suggests, by Lycurgus's having secured the Delphic Oracle's support for his laws. By doing this, Xenophon tells us, Lycurgus ensured that refusing obedience to the laws would henceforth not only be illegal, but "impious" (8.5). Thus, Spartan manliness, the willingness to accept or even seek out a noble death, is connected to religious belief. Indeed, the most Xenophon can say in defense of the willingness to die is that "more" people survive when soldiers are animated by it (not all or even the most brave are guaranteed survival) and glory (as well as political followers) will attend those who do survive. Manliness "accuses" in the same sense that the gods "accuse" those who fail to live up to their demands. Lycurgus wanted fear of the gods, no less than fear of the regime, to help make men "willingly" obedient.

The final theme of Strauss's essay, accordingly, is the connection between "political life" and "belief in the gods of the city" (532). While Lycurgus taught the Spartans to believe that the Delphic god had given them their laws, Strauss observes that Xenophon "distinguishes between the Spartans' obedience to Lycurgus' laws and their obedience to the god" (532).[7] For, Strauss continues, Xenophon raises the question of whether and in what manner the gods can interact or communicate with humans. Through the use of a simple trope, Xenophon compares the Spartans' feeding of their children with, first, their feeding of "the king and those with him" and, finally, their offering of "sacrifices to Zeus and to those with him" (533). In suggesting that the Spartan sacrifices amounted to a "feeding" of the gods for their own political purposes, Xenophon delivers his ultimate criticism of the Spartan constitution: the Spartans wish, through their sacrifices, to "seize beforehand [*prolambanein*]" the gods' goodwill just as they learned as children to "steal [*kleptein*]" something to alleviate their hunger (Strauss encourages us to compare 13.3 with 2.7). The Spartans' understanding of the noble, it appears, is fundamentally self-contradictory: the sacrifices they make in an effort to appear worthy of the gods' aid are, in truth, nothing but an underhanded effort to seek their own advantage.

The Meaning of Lycurgus's Authority

As we have seen, the place of the missing speeches about the noble is taken by the rich men's act of buying their way out of the noble activity of hunting, that is, by a silent or implicit critique of nobility. Now, their very act of becoming rich suggests a flaw in Lycurgus's basic teaching of obedience to authority. Accordingly, Xenophon next turns to an examination of how authority was constituted at Sparta and in what it consists. We here learn that Lycurgus did not attempt to introduce discipline until he had first secured "like-mindedness" among the best (or strongest) men in the city (8.1). Now, like-mindedness is a highly ambiguous term. For, as the case of the proverbial band of robbers reveals, a group can be "like-minded" about base ends no less than noble ones. Obedience to rulers, as well as like-mindedness within the ruling class, is a virtue only insofar as those rulers understand and properly enact wise laws. And, as we have seen, Xenophon raises doubts about the wisdom of many of Lycurgus's laws. But Strauss here raises an important objection. Did not Xenophon's Socrates teach that obedience as such, obedience to any laws, is identical to justice (*Memorabilia* 4.4.15)? And, we might add, did not Xenophon leave ambiguous at the very start of his treatise whether the Spartans owed their happiness to the quality or wisdom of Lycurgus's laws—or merely to their obedience to them (1.2)? Strauss responds to this objection with a digression explaining Xenophon's purpose and procedure in the *Memorabilia*. After noting that its purpose was to reveal only Socrates's speeches and deeds (and not his thoughts), Strauss goes on to suggest that Socrates's stated thesis about obedience to (any) law was, at best, a political teaching and not a philosophical one. Moreover, he demonstrates, Socrates himself includes in his discussion of obedience the relevant information that would enable his interlocutor to refute that thesis: there exist "natural" or "unwritten" laws that function as standards by which to judge (and to find wanting) any existing, written laws.

In what way, then, were the leading citizens "like-minded"? Xenophon explains they were not only of one mind with one another, they were like (in their fear of authority) the rest of the Spartans. Whom, then, did they fear? It is at this point in the discussion that Xenophon quietly introduces the office of the Ephors (8.3) who turn out to be the hidden rulers of Sparta. For the Ephors have more or less unlimited authority—they can even fine or imprison the magistrates, meaning that they (and they alone) are superior to the laws in Sparta. They behave, says Xenophon, like "tyrants" (8.4). The so-called wisdom of the Spartan laws, then, amounts to nothing more than a recognition that those laws are so inadequate to their task (of training citizens to prefer the city to themselves) that they must be supplemented with a tyrannical admixture of fear and shame. And finally, we should resist the all-too-natural conclusion that "like-mindedness" among the citizens is tantamount to "unity" or "harmony" among them. For insofar as they are like-minded about Lycurgus's teachings (e.g., that "stealing is good," that wealth enables one to escape from some of the onerous demands of nobility, that surviving until old age brings honor), the Spartan citizens are in fact prone to be in an endless contest with one another. There is, we learn, rampant dissension, rivalry, and even spying on one another. As Strauss observes, the classics taught that "one cannot assert that war against other cities is the aim of the life of the city without being driven to assert that war of individual against individual is the aim of the life of the individual" (524–25).

Xenophon concludes the section on Lycurgus's institutions (Chapters 1–10) with the summary praise of Lycurgus for laying an "irresistible necessity to practice the whole of political virtue" on the citizens (10.7). This praise, we can now see, is less enthusiastic than it may at first seem. For not only is "public virtue" (i.e., the virtue that one practices in public and for the sake of the public; 10.4) a rather poor cousin to genuine virtue, but it is hard to see what virtue—other than obedience—can arise as a result of compulsion.[8] Moreover, the irresistible necessity is apparently not utterly irresistible: Xenophon immediately goes on to speak of the different fates of those who comply with it and those who do not. And while those who do not comply are made unhappy, those who do are merely given an equal share (with the others who do). It should come as no surprise that, while all "praise" such institutions, no city chooses to imitate them (10.8).

Strauss, in his concluding remarks on this section, focuses on the identity of the "leading citizens" and of "Lycurgus" himself. Not only, as we have already noted, do the Ephors secretly rule (and rule like tyrants), but there were apparently various "like-minded" powerful men from the city who accompanied Lycurgus on his trip to Delphi. Who, Strauss asks, were these men? It seems, he suggests, that they were the group that became the Ephors. And it is not clear how or to what extent Lycurgus can be distinguished from this group. Lycurgus, Strauss proposes, "did not exist at all": he was a "mere name covering something much less solemn than an almost divine lawgiver belonging to a remote and venerable past" (527). (Strauss finds further textual proof of this at 13.10, where, according to the un-amended good manuscripts, "the Lycurgus with regard to [pitching the tents] is the king." "'Lycurgus' is, then, a name designating authority or the men in authority"; 527.) Finally, Strauss indicates that Xenophon leaves it to the reader to conclude that the Ephors themselves either are or are in the sway of the wealthy Spartan few. This would-be aristocracy of virtue turns out to be a hypocritical or hidden oligarchy.

The second section, on war (Chapters 11–13), follows. In this section, Xenophon tries to make the case that the Spartans "have omitted least what is necessary in military things" (12.7). Of course, this silently implies that they may have omitted quite a lot of what is necessary in the nonmilitary things. Furthermore, in noting the extraordinary power of the Ephors to oversee the others (even the king), Xenophon suggests "only the Lacedaemonians possessed the art of war" (13.5). Now, despite giving a relatively detailed account of how the Lacedaemonians prepare for war, Xenophon offers not a word on any successful, heroic, or noble military deeds by any Spartans (and this despite their recent victory in the Peloponnesian War). Readers of Thucydides will not be so surprised by this, insofar as he relates very few distinguished Spartan actions in that war (Brasidas, the least characteristic Spartan, being the sole exception), and suggests that, to no small degree, Athens defeated herself.

The final section, on the Spartan institution of kingship, is surprising for several reasons. First, we discover that there are two kings, not one. Second, and more important, it is here (in Chapter 14) that Xenophon unleashes his harsh criticism of present-day Sparta, thereby ruining the effect, carefully nurtured from the beginning, of an impassioned praise of Sparta. Regarding the king, we learn that they are not quite the true power in Sparta—they remain subordinate to the Ephors. Moreover, the Spartan constitution itself "incentivizes" the kings to go to war: while they have "power and honor" in wartime, they have only "honor" in peacetime (cf. 13.1 and 15.8).

Strauss ends with a consideration of why Xenophon would hide his criticism of Sparta—and why he would hide it somewhat ineptly. First, an open criticism of Sparta would easily be mistaken for praise of Athens—and this, Strauss notes, is something that Xenophon, in the aftermath of Socrates having been put to death by Athens, would be hesitant to do. More than the particular praise of Athens that he wishes to withhold, however, Xenophon does not wish to praise any other political system in comparison with Sparta. For, in the final analysis, Xenophon wishes to critique political life *tout court* from the point of view of the contemplative life. And this means that, beneath his hidden critique or satire of Spartan "education" lies a still more hidden defense or promotion of true, philosophic education. Now, as we recall from the start, this apparently antiquarian essay is, in fact, of no little relevance for the age in which Strauss wrote it. For enlightenment liberalism as well as its contemporary political enemies thwart the "natural" taste for "big ideas" or philosophy. Moreover, his later reputation notwithstanding, Strauss clearly taught that war must be for the sake of peace and not vice versa. Would not the times then call for an open account of Xenophon's philosophic teaching? Strauss, of course, does not address or even raise this question. But he is clearly no fool. Germany was in no mood—not even its leading philosopher was in the mood—to hear about the primacy of the contemplative life over the life of war and deadly decision-making.

And England and America needed at this time to hear, not of the ultimately superior value of peacetime, but of the grim necessity of fighting the given war that was about to be foisted on them.

What Strauss does see fit to share with his readers are a few brief comments about the character of a philosophic education. Such education is premised on the understanding that man does not belong "entirely" to the city.[9] This was, to repeat, a somewhat controversial if not fantastic assertion to make in 1939. For it was denied not only by the various illiberal politics of the day, but by the leading philosophical school of the day, namely historicism. Man, it taught, was wholly a creature of his society, of his times, of the (temporary) world-view whose creature he inevitably had to be. Even at the end of the twentieth century, leading American postmodernist Richard Rorty could still assert man is "socialized all the way down."[10] Twentieth-century man, Strauss implied, needs to begin to relearn, in an almost humble fashion, the elementary truths about human nature, insofar as his understanding of such truths is "directly opposite to…what is" (11.5). And, because the authors most conversant with those truths insisted on writing esoterically, he needs to relearn how to read such literature. I close by simply quoting Strauss's wonderful tribute to Xenophon's own peculiar type of esotericism:

> [S]uch a man was he that he preferred to go through the centuries in the disguise of a beggar rather than sell the precious secrets of Socrates' quiet and sober wisdom to a multitude which let him escape to immortality only after he had intoxicated it by his artful stories of the swift and dazzling actions of an Agesilaus or a Cyrus, or a Xenophon. (536)

Notes

1. See, for example, *NRH* 7–8.
2. All page references are to SSTX.
3. Sparta had its less extreme, and thus perhaps more influential, champions as well, such as William Mitford, whose popular *History of Greece* (1836) had a strongly pro-Spartan and anti-Athenian bias.
4. All chapter and paragraph references are to Xenophon, "The Constitution of the Lacedaemonians" in *Scripta Minora*, trans. E. C. Marchant (Cambridge, MA: Harvard University Press, 1968). I have occasionally altered the translation for greater adherence to the literal meaning of the text.
5. Letter to Kojève, August 22, 1948, in *OT* 236.
6. Note also that 8.4 suggests the Spartans understand by "soul" nothing more than the life-giving force in the body.
7. Rousseau concedes that legislators (such as Lycurgus), who are "unable to use either force or reasoning" to form a people, must always have "recourse to the intervention of heaven" in order to have the people abide by laws prior to their having been formed by them (*Social Contract*, 2.7).
8. For a similar critique of "political virtue," see Plato, *Republic* 430c.
9. Cf. *NRH* 5: "there is something in man that is not altogether in slavery to his society."
10. Richard Rorty, *Contingency, Irony, and Solidarity* (Cambridge, UK: Cambridge University Press 1989), 185.

CHAPTER 11

STRAUSS AND SCHLEIERMACHER ON HOW TO READ PLATO: AN INTRODUCTION TO "EXOTERIC TEACHING"

Hannes Kerber

> *What philosophy is seems to be inseparable from the question of how to read Plato.*
>
> —Seth Benardete

"Exoteric Teaching" is arguably one of the most important finds among the Leo Strauss papers. As his first attempt at an explanation of the concept of "exotericism" in general terms, the fragment enables the reader to cast a unique glance at the genesis of Strauss's hermeneutics. Its peculiar approach distinguishes the essay, which was written in December 1939, not only from its next of kin, "Persecution and the Art of Writing," but from most other studies, written and published mainly during the 1940s, in which Strauss applied his thesis of exoteric writing: While the main subjects of these articles are writers from the Jewish and Islamic Middle Ages, "Exoteric Teaching" takes a different route by presenting the issue exclusively from what may loosely be called a Western perspective.[1]

"Exoteric Teaching" discusses the German philosopher Gotthold Ephraim Lessing and the Protestant theologian Friedrich Daniel Ernst Schleiermacher, while mentioning such writers as Aristotle, Leibniz, Zeller, Kant, Ferguson, Rousseau, and Jacobi. The essay avoids naming or citing any non-Western thinker. This silence is particularly puzzling in the case of Moses Maimonides, who played a crucial role in Strauss's discovery of exotericism well before he wrote "Exoteric Teaching." Even more perplexing is the fact that, while Maimonides is left out of the typescript, he is mentioned in an early handwritten plan of the essay. In this plan, the title for the penultimate section of the essay's first part is: "Lessing—Leibniz—Hobbes (vera—pia dogmata)—Spinoza—RMbM—" (p. 287.)[2] In the corresponding section of the manuscript, which was written before the typescript, Strauss replaces Thomas Hobbes with René Descartes but does mention Maimonides at the end of the sequence of exoteric writers: "Leibniz is [...] that link in the chain of the tradition of exotericism which is nearest to Lessing. Leibniz, however, was not the only 17th century thinker who was initiated. Not to mention the prudent Descartes, even so bold a writer as Spinoza had admitted the necessity of 'pia dogmata, hoc est, talia quae animum ad obedientiam movent' as distinguished from 'vera dogmata.' Despite, or because of, that admission Spinoza rejected Maimonides's allegorical interpretation of the Bible as 'harmful, useless and absurd.' Thus, he cannot be considered a genuine spokesman of the tradition." (p. 286n117.)[3] The last two sentences—with the ambiguous personal pronoun that could refer either to Maimonides or to Spinoza[4]—were not transcribed by the typist and were also not reinserted later by hand. Whether this omission was a deliberate and, hence, authoritative decision or one of the many blunders of the typist overlooked by Strauss, cannot be determined with certainty since "Exoteric Teaching" was never prepared for publication. Another and more detailed plan of the essay slightly changes the title for the passage in question but does not resolve the problem: "Lessing—Leibniz—Spinoza (—RMbM)" (p. 292). How should one interpret the fact that here Strauss has put Maimonides's name in parentheses? Do the parentheses indicate that Strauss wanted to include the ambiguous suggestion about Spinoza's critique? Or do they show that Strauss decided to drop the reference to Maimonides altogether after writing the manuscript? However these questions might be answered, the textual difficulties highlight the fact that non-Western thinkers would have played only a minor role, if any, in "Exoteric Teaching."

The peculiar approach of "Exoteric Teaching" is reflected not only in the essay's silence about Maimonides, but first of all in its focus on Lessing and Schleiermacher. These two thinkers seem to have been important for Strauss during the 1930s, but are not prominently featured in his published works. Recalling his early studies of Spinoza, Strauss remarked decades later that at this time "Lessing was always at my elbow." The influence of Lessing's writings, according to Strauss's own account, was subtle and initially unrecognized: "I learned more from him than I knew at that time. As I came to see later Lessing had said everything I had found out about the distinction between exoteric and esoteric speech and its grounds."[5] This later reconsideration of Lessing, which took place probably around 1936–37,[6] shows that the young Strauss's thought was ripe for the discovery of exotericism long before he began to write "Exoteric Teaching."[7] However, this essay for the first time combines a general discussion of philosophico-political reasons for exoteric communication with a sketch of the fate of exotericism in ancient times and in modernity.

The essay's most substantive part is a discussion of Schleiermacher's way of reading Plato and his refusal to interpret Plato as an exoteric writer. The fine introduction, which Schleiermacher wrote for the first volume of his pathbreaking translation of the Platonic dialogues into German, shows that he, like many earlier writers but unlike many of his successors,[8] was very much aware of exoteric writing.[9] While doing away with what he sees as the most common misconceptions of earlier interpretations, Schleiermacher reports in rather baroque German that past interpreters of Plato "have formed the opinion, partly from individual statements of Plato himself [and] partly from a widespread tradition, which has preserved itself since antiquity, of an esoteric and exoteric [dimension] in philosophy, as if his proper wisdom were either not at all contained in Plato's writings or only in secret allusions, which are difficult to locate."[10] Schleiermacher's attempt to refute the opinion that Plato wrote exoterically is complex because, according to his account, the concept is "utterly vague" and "has cultivated itself in the most manifold forms (*hat sich in die mannigfaltigsten Gestalten ausgebildet*)."[11] Yet, two views of exotericism stand out for Schleiermacher: The pre-Platonic "Pythagorean" view, on the one hand, declared certain *subjects* to be "esoteric," such as the political teaching that the Pythagoreans did not wish to discuss in public.[12] In the view of those post-Platonic thinkers who mixed Socratic philosophy with sophistry, on the other hand, the distinction between exoteric and esoteric concerned not so much specific subjects as a *manner of presentation*: What could not be explained in a popular lecture, but could very well be explained in a lecture for an expert audience, was called "esoteric."[13] Schleiermacher strongly denies that either of these views is correct in the case of Plato: "in whichever of the two senses one would want to apply these concepts to the Platonic writings and philosophy in order thereby to divide both into two parts, one will get caught up everywhere."[14] In Schleiermacher's eyes, the latter view—according to which there is one genre of philosophic writings that is easy to understand, that is, popular or "exoteric," and another genre of philosophic writings that is hard to understand, that is, scientific or "esoteric"[15]—is futile with regard to Plato, because all of Plato's writings are hard to understand and therefore he "could have confided his most difficult and most mysterious wisdom [to these writings] just as well."[16] The Pythagorean view, on the other hand, which implies that Plato spoke about certain issues only within the confines of the Academy and on principle never in writing, almost refutes itself because "in the field of philosophy nothing might be found on which a judgment could not be encountered in [Plato's] writings, [expressed] either directly and clearly or at least according to the reasons (*den Gründen nach*)."[17]

Setting aside other differences for the moment, one cannot fail to notice that Strauss, who does not explicitly mention Schleiermacher's critique of these two versions of exotericism in "Exoteric Teaching," agrees with him in rejecting both of them. Like Schleiermacher, Strauss would object to those interpreters of Plato who follow (to use Schleiermacher's *façon de parler*) either the "Pythagoreans" or the "Socratic sophists." While Strauss and Schleiermacher are convinced that the dialogues are the sole basis for understanding Plato's teaching, the two groups in question give up this *material completeness of the dialogues*: The Pythagoreans do not rely on the dialogues but have recourse to an oral tradition. Orality, while being the original form of philosophic communication and therefore a conceivable option for the transmission of the esoteric teaching,[18] has major defects: Not only does oral communication require permanent political stability[19] and perfect comprehension on the part of each successor, it also limits the potential audience to those who happen to be a link in the chain of the tradition.[20] In a word, oral *traditio* is very unlikely to achieve the goal of preserving over time an undistorted *traditum* for the intended audience.[21] While the Pythagoreans tear apart the material completeness of the dialogues by assuming the existence of an oral tradition that communicates certain "esoteric" subjects independently of the writings, the Socratic sophists make the very same mistake in a different manner. According to their view, "exoteric" books are intended for nonspecialists outside the school, while other writings are "esoteric," that is, intended only for the students within the school. The main task for the interpreter is therefore to distinguish between the two genres and to disregard[22] all books that belong to the former since they contain exclusively "exoteric" matters that are philosophically well-nigh worthless.[23] This rather crude way of dividing the twofold audience by membership cards is problematic, not only because every successful school has to include a variety of disciples[24] but also because it is to be expected that all writings become public eventually. Its political precariousness alone renders this "exotericism" unusable. Hence, Strauss was aware that if there is any need at all for exotericism, "no written exposition can be strictly speaking esoteric."[25]

After debunking these two views of exotericism in the introduction to his translation of Plato's dialogues, Schleiermacher mentions a third view that he does not ascribe to a specific group and that for him is not even worth discussing in detail: "And those indeed who trace back the distinction between the esoteric [and the exoteric] merely to the quarrel with polytheism and with the popular religion, in fact overturn (*aufheben*) [the distinction] completely and either make it into a legal safe-keeping (*rechtliche Verwahrung*)—which would be highly insufficient because Plato's principles on that topic are clear enough to read in his writings, so that one can scarcely believe that his pupils might have needed further instruction, the publication of which he shied away from—or into a childish performance (*kindische Veranstaltung*), which delights itself in saying in a loud voice behind closed doors what in fact may also be said publicly but only in a low voice."[26] This provides the first weak point for Strauss's attack on Schleiermacher's argument in "Exoteric Teaching"—only because Schleiermacher refrains from calling a spade a spade is he able to lend credibility to the view that Plato abstained from practicing "legal safe-keeping," that is, that Plato abstained from drawing a veil over his denial of the gods of the city even though such impiety was forbidden in Athens under penalty of death.[27] The ambiguity of the expression "polytheism and the popular religion" enables Schleiermacher, according to Strauss, to claim that Plato's principles on the topic are easily recognizable in his writings. If, however, "Schleiermacher had used the less ambiguous expression 'belief in the existence of the gods worshipped by the city of Athens,' he could not have said that Plato's opposition to that belief is clearly expressed in his writings." (p. 280) Thus, Strauss not only calls into question Schleiermacher's criticism of exotericism for reasons of political caution, but he also provides a toehold for that argument in favor of exotericism that he would later elaborate most prominently in "Persecution and the Art of Writing": If a writer wants to conceal an opinion from the censor for fear of persecution but nevertheless wants to communicate his true thoughts to the reader, he must write in a way that achieves both ends.[28]

However, Strauss's most important objection to Schleiermacher's criticism is a different one. In "Persecution and the Art of Writing," Strauss makes clear that Schleiermacher's major point against those interpretations that distinguish between Plato's exoteric and esoteric teachings is his "unusually able argument [...] that there is only *one* Platonic teaching."[29] In his writings on Plato, Schleiermacher time and again emphasizes the unity of Plato's thought, which is reflected in the unity of his teaching.[30] Those who distinguish between exoteric and esoteric teachings, in his view, are to be blamed because they are tearing this unity apart.[31] At the same time, Schleiermacher does not simply brush aside the difficulties of interpreting Plato, which have led some scholars to deny the unity of Plato's philosophy or presentation. According to "Exoteric Teaching," Schleiermacher explains the impression of multiplicity in Plato that has misled many scholars by asserting that while there is only *one* Platonic teaching, "there is, so to speak, *an infinite number of degrees of the understanding of that teaching*: it is the same teaching which the beginner understands inadequately, and which only the perfectly trained student of Plato understands adequately." (p. 280)[32] The seeming multiplicity that overshadows the underlying unity is then due to the process of understanding. In this process, the reader starts out with an imperfect and therefore fragmentary understanding of the teaching that will then improve ad infinitum gradually and continuously. While the understanding thus changes, the teaching that is understood remains the same. Plato ensures, according to Schleiermacher, that this ongoing enhancement of the reader's understanding has the character of a "self-activity (*Selbsttätigkeit*)."[33] Plato forces the reader to think for himself by writing in the literary form of a dialogue, that is, by not teaching directly what the reader is searching for in a treatise but by "exposing the [reader's] soul to the necessity to search for [the end of the investigation] and to guide [the soul] to the way on which it can be found."[34] For this purpose, Plato, in Schleiermacher's presentation, first brings the reader to realize his state of ignorance and then relays the actual thought to the reader indirectly in two ways. This indirect communication is achieved either 1) by "weaving contradictions into a riddle to which the intended thought is the only possible solution" and giving "in a seemingly strange and accidental manner such allusions which will be found and understood only by him who searches genuinely and independently,"[35] or 2) by dressing up "the actual investigation with another [investigation], not as if with a veil but as if with a grown-on skin (*angewachsenen Haut*), which conceals from the inattentive [reader] (*dem Unaufmerksamen*) but only from him that which actually ought to be observed or found, but which for the attentive [reader] (*dem Aufmerksamen*) sharpens and chastens the sense for the internal coherence."[36] At first sight, Schleiermacher's remarks about Plato's two sets of literary devices—on the one hand, teaching through riddles, contradictions, and brief indications, and on the other, a meaningful differentiation of fore- and background of the text—seem to be very close to Strauss's own way of reading Plato. This proximity shows above all that, unlike many other interpreters, both Schleiermacher and Strauss believe that the literary form of the dialogue, which merges the advantages of spoken and written communication, is Plato's answer to Socrates's critique of writing in the final exchanges of the *Phaedrus*.[37] Closer consideration reveals, however, a deep disagreement between Schleiermacher and Strauss, which manifests itself in two ways. First, while Schleiermacher stresses the continuous character of the process of understanding, according to Strauss, understanding is characterized not by continuity but by discontinuity. Second, what Schleiermacher takes as an indefinite multiplicity of degrees of understanding in Strauss's view turns out to be a strict duplicity of the Platonic teaching.

The continuity of understanding is that premise that in Strauss's eyes has caused Schleiermacher to misinterpret Plato: "Schleiermacher tacitly assumes that the way from the beginning [of the process of understanding] to the end is continuous, whereas, according to Plato, philosophy presupposes a real conversion, *i.e.* a total break with the attitude of the beginner" (p. 281).[38] Against Plato, Schleiermacher describes the structure of understanding not as a *periagōgē* but as continuous. While Schleiermacher could argue that he was forced to depart from Plato's view (since Plato was wrong about the structure of understanding), Strauss shows the price Schleiermacher had to pay for understanding Plato supposedly better than Plato understood himself. Schleiermacher's assumption of continuity made him not only blind to "the difference between the morality of the beginner and the morality of the philosopher [...] which is at the bottom of the difference between exoteric and esoteric teaching" (p. 282),[39] but also to the very form of exotericism that, in Strauss's eyes, is employed by Plato. This form of exotericism, to come to the second point of disagreement between Schleiermacher and Strauss, is compatible with both the material completeness of the dialogues and the unity of the author's thought, because it comprises in one and the same text two kinds of teaching, each of which addresses a different audience.[40] One teaching is conveyed by the explicit statements that the author deposits in plain view on the surface of the text while the other teaching is indicated only "between the lines." This duplicity of presentation is the reason why the process of coming to understand such a text is characterized by discontinuity rather than continuity. The advance from the surface teaching to the hidden teaching is something like a turnaround. This metaphorical description of the hermeneutical experience is itself in need of interpretation and may be best elucidated by using an example.[41]

In "Persecution and the Art of Writing," Strauss lists several concrete disagreements between modern historians and their predecessors rooted in the principles of modern scholarship.[42] One of these examples is the gulf between the older and the more recent understandings of Thomas Hobbes's attitude toward religion: Strauss asserts that while many earlier "philosophers and theologians believed that Hobbes was an atheist," many contemporary historians "tacitly or explicitly reject that view."[43] In a footnote to this statement, Strauss refers to the studies of five contemporary scholars who oppose the older opinion that Hobbes was an atheist. Among these studies is Strauss's own book *Die Religionskritik Spinozas als Grundlage seiner Bibelwissenschaft*, which was published more than a decade earlier, and in which Strauss asserts that Hobbes, while coming very close to atheism, was not "an atheist in the theoretical sense of the term."[44] With the reference to his own book in the footnote of "Persecution and the Art of Writing" Strauss merely alludes to his earlier misinterpretation and recent reassessment of Hobbes's attitude toward religion, which he would later lay out in detail.[45] This self-criticism is made in order to illustrate the typical consequence of the rejection of exotericism. The assumption that there is only one doctrine for all practical purposes amounts to taking the author's words at face value. By doing so, the reader closes his eyes to the fact that authors in the past did hide their thoughts for political, philosophical, and didactic reasons, or that not everybody has come into the world to bear witness unto the truth in front of everyone.[46] Thinking through the reasons that induced a writer to present his thought in a twofold manner for a twofold audience can be tantamount to a complete turnaround of the understanding of that writer, as Strauss knew by first-hand experience. While the young Strauss's Hobbes was an agnostic, the mature Strauss understood him as a philosopher who "expressed himself with great caution in writings which he published with his name on their title pages" but who anticipated in his thought the infamous heretical work by Hermann Samuel Reimarus, which was published by Lessing a century later.[47]

Even more impressive than the revaluation of Hobbes is, however, the revolution in Strauss's understanding of Maimonides. While Strauss referred to him in *Die Religionskritik Spinozas* as a "believing Jew,"[48] a series of careful studies written during the 1930s brought to light the philosopher Maimonides.[49] According to Strauss's own account, this new interpretation of Maimonides that was sparked by an *aperçu* on Plato was crucial for the development of his own understanding of exotericism.[50] The fact that neither Maimonides nor Hobbes played a decisive role in the essay "Exoteric Teaching," whereas Lessing did, shows not so much that the essay should be understood as an autobiographical supplement that informs the reader of a further source of Strauss's insight, but rather that the *periagōgē*, which we associate with the name of Plato, can be experienced when studying philosophers from any time or place.

Notes

1. A version of this essay has been delivered as the Joe R. Long Lecture at the University of Texas at Austin on April 5, 2013. I wish to thank Thomas L. Pangle, Devin Stauffer, and Erik Dempsey for a challenging discussion of the talk as well as Tom van Malssen, Alexander Orwin, Karl Dahlquist, Jeremy Bell, Heinrich Meier, and Ralph Lerner for their friendly critique of an earlier version of the essay.
2. All references in brackets in the body of the text refer to my edition of "Exoteric Teaching" or "Lecture Notes for 'Persecution and the Art of Writing'" in this volume.
3. For the most detailed critique of Maimonidean hermeneutics, cf. Benedict de Spinoza, *Tractatus theologico-politicus* in *Opera quae supersunt omnia*, ed. Carl H. Bruder (3 vols.; Leipzig: Tauchnitz, 1843–46), vol. III, 120–23 (cap. 7, §75–87); Spinoza, *Theologico-Political Treatise*, trans. Martin D. Yaffe (Newburyport, MA: Focus Philosophical Library, 2004), 97–100. On this question, see *SCR* 173f. and *Die Religionskritik Spinozas*, in *GS–1* 224–26.
4. The fact that Strauss left unclear whether it was "despite, or because of" this admission that Spinoza rejected Maimonides's allegorical reading of the Scripture, lends further support to the supposition that the ambiguity of the personal pronoun was not a slip of the pen.
5. GA 3.
6. See, above all, EMFL 528–605. Cf. ESG 522 and "Eine Erinnerung an Lessing," *GS–2* 607–8 (English translations in *LSMM* 59–145, 155, 162).
7. The distinction is already present in *Philosophie und Gesetz* (1935). Cf., for example, *GS–2* 47, 82–83, 88–89, and 123 with 612. (English translation in *PLA* 59, 95–96, 102–3 and 132.)
8. Cf. Arthur M. Melzer, "Esotericism and the Critique of Historicism," *American Political Science Review* 100, no. 2 (2006): 280: "it is difficult to find a single major

philosopher writing before 1800 who did *not* somewhere make open and approving reference to the practice of esotericism, regarding either his own writings or (more commonly) those of others." See also his "On the Pedagogical Motive for Esoteric Writing," *The Journal of Politics* 69, no. 4 (2007): 1015–31.

9. Cf. Friedrich Schleiermacher, "Einleitung," in *Platons Werke* (second edition; Berlin: G.A. Reimer/Realschulbuchhandlung, 1817), vol. I.1, 11–26. Reprinted in id., *Über die Philosophie Platons*, ed. Peter M. Steiner (Hamburg: Felix Meiner, 1996), 33–47. The introduction was published for the first time in 1804 in the first edition of *Platons Werke* (A) but Schleiermacher's revisions in the second edition (B) reflect his mature understanding of the matter.
10. Friedrich Schleiermacher, *Über die Philosophie Platons*, 33 (B 11/A 11). All translations from German are my own, H.K.
11. Ibid., 33–34 (B 11/A 11).
12. "Nämlich bei den ersten Pythagoreern ging dieser Unterschied so unmittelbar auf den Inhalt, daß Gegenstände als esoterische bezeichnet wurden, über welche sie sich außerhalb der Grenzen ihrer innigsten Verbindung nicht mitteilen wollten; und es ist zu vermuten, daß weit mehr ihr politisches System die Stelle des esoterischen ausfüllte, als ihre eben so unvollkommenen als unverdächtigen metaphysischen Spekulationen. Damals aber war auch die Philosophie mit politischen Absichten und die Schule mit einer praktischen Verbrüderung auf eine Art verbunden, die hernach unter den Hellenen gar nicht wieder Statt gefunden hat." Ibid., 34 (B 12/A 12).
13. "Später hingegen nannte man vornehmlich das esoterisch, was in dem populären Vortrage, zu dem sich nach der Vermischung der Sophisten mit den sokratischen Philosophen Einige herabließen, nicht konnte mitgeteilt werden, und der Unterschied ging also unmittelbar auf den Vortrag, und nur mittelbar und um jenes willen erst auf den Inhalt." Ibid., 34–35 (B 12–13/A 12–13)
14. Ibid., 35 (B 13/A 13).
15. Ever since Jacob Bernays's *Die Dialoge des Aristoteles in ihrem Verhältniss zu seinen übrigen Werken* (Berlin: W. Hertz/Bessersche Buchhandlung, 1863), German scholars have debated the question of exotericism intensively by the example of Aristotle's enigmatic references to *exōterikoi logoi*. They seem to have settled for the view that the term primarily refers to a genre. Cf. Michael Erler, "Philosophische Literaturformen," in *Der Neue Pauly. Enzyklopädie der Antike* (Stuttgart/Weimar: J. B. Metzler, 2000), vol. IX, 874: "In Aristotle, but probably already in Plato, one can distinguish three areas in which philosophical texts were used: literary works ('dialogues') for the public; 'exoteric' exercises or public courses of instruction; and strictly academic lectures and discussions within the school." See Konrad Gaiser, "Exoterisch/esoterisch," in *Historisches Wörterbuch der Philosophie* (Darmstadt: Wissenschaftliche Buchgesellschaft, 1972), vol. II, 865–67.
16. Friedrich Schleiermacher, *Über die Philosophie Platons*, 35 (B 13/A 13).—Schleiermacher's critique of this version of exotericism is also directed against Wilhelm Gottlieb Tennemann, one of the most important interpreters of Plato at the time. According to Tennemann, Plato investigated subjects "about which most confused and most erroneous notions (*Vorstellungsarten*) prevailed, but which had acquired such a reputation by virtue of their age, by virtue of their connection to holy truths, [as well as] by virtue of the protection of priests and the state, that they were considered to be an inviolable property of humankind (*ein unverletzbares Eigenthum der Menschheit*)." Plato therefore "chose the dialogical form by which he could say truths without being responsible for them." Based on these considerations, Tennemann asserts that it is likely that "the writings of his esoteric philosophy were written in a

different form [than the dialogical form]." Wilhelm Gottlieb Tennemann, *System der Platonischen Philosophie* (Leipzig: J.A. Barth, 1792), vol. I, 128. On the esoteric writings, cf. also 114, 137, 141, 149, 162–64 and 264–66. See also Tennemann, *Geschichte der Philosophie* (Leipzig: J.A. Barth, 1799), vol. II, 205–22.

17. Friedrich Schleiermacher, *Über die Philosophie Platons*, 36 (B 14/A 13–14).
18. In "Persecution and the Art of Writing," Strauss makes clear that those ancient philosophers who had become convinced of the essential difference between philosophers and nonphilosophers had to choose one of two ways but then only discusses the latter: "They must conceal their opinions from all but philosophers, *either* by limiting themselves to oral instruction of a carefully selected group of pupils, *or* by writing about the most important subject by means of 'brief indication.'" *PAW* 34–35. My italics, H.K.
19. Cf. *PAW* 50.
20. The observation that "writings are naturally accessible to all who can read" (*PAW* 35 with *Phaedrus* 275d9–e3) should be understood as a promise as well as a warning.
21. Cf. Plato, *Phaedrus* 277a2 and 276d4.—In the manuscript, Strauss crossed out a sentence that seems to turn this line of argument against Schleiermacher himself: "[Schleiermacher] forgets the fact that Plato has not written his dialogues for his pupils only, but rather as a possession for all times, or that not all readers of Plato are pupils of Plato." See below p. 280n50. For κτῆμα ἐς αἰεί, see Thucydides, *Historiae* 1.22.4.
22. According to a widespread, though apparently spurious tradition, Andronicus of Rhodes, Aristotle's eleventh successor as head of the peripatetic school, did not include the "exoteric" writings in his edition of Aristotle's works.—As I have indicated in note 15, above, Aristotle's usage of *exōterikoi logoi* has led many scholars to believe that the term always refers to a genre of writings. This view, which entirely ignores the crucial fact that there is no consistent antonym to "exoteric" throughout the *corpus Aristotelicum*, can easily be refuted on the basis of *Physics* Δ 10 (217b29ff.)
23. Hegel's critique of Tennemann's notion of exotericism (cf., above, footnote 16) in his *Lectures on the History of Philosophy* emphasizes the absurdity of a *material* division of exoteric and esoteric teaching: "How simpleminded! This looks as if the philosopher is in possession of his thoughts in the same way as of external things. But the thoughts are something utterly different. Instead of the reverse, the philosophic idea is in possession of the human being. When philosophers elaborate on philosophic subjects, they have to follow [the course of] their ideas; they cannot keep them in their pocket. Even when speaking externally (*äußerlich*) to some people, the idea must be contained [in this speech], if the matter (*Sache*) has any content at all. It does not take much to hand over an external item (*Sache*), but the communication of an idea requires skill. The idea always remains something esoteric; hence, one does not merely have the exoteric (*das Exoterische*) of the philosophers. These notions are superficial." *Werke*, ed. Eva Moldenhauer and Karl Markus Michel (Frankfurt am Main: Suhrkamp, 1986), vol. XIX, 21–22. See also ibid., 76–77: "One does not have to make the distinction [of the esoteric and the exoteric] as if Plato had two such philosophies: one for the world, for the people; the other, the internal, saved for the confidants. The esoteric is the speculative that is written and printed and nevertheless remains hidden for those who have little interest in straining themselves. It is not a secret but still hidden." Cf. Strauss's reference to Hegel, below, p. 291.
24. With one eye to the centrifugal forces within the philosophical school Strauss himself founded, Heinrich Meier writes in his "Preface to the American Edition," in *Leo Strauss and the Theologico-Political Problem*, trans. Marcus Brainard (Cambridge:

Cambridge University Press, 2006), xix: "For the school, no less than for the commonwealth, it holds true that different addressees have to be addressed differently, that they grasp the teaching differently and pass it on differently." Cf. ibid., 15 with xvii–xx.—For Strauss's own critique of philosophical schools, see his "Restatement on Xenophon's *Hiero*," in *OT* 194–96.

25. *PAW* 187. Cf. ONI 349: "according to the *Seventh Letter*, as well as according to the *Phaedrus*, no writing composed by a serious man can be quite serious." Cf. Plato, *Seventh Letter* 344c1–d2 and *Phaedrus* 276d1–e3 and 277e5–278b4.
26. Friedrich Schleiermacher, *Über die Philosophie Platons*, 36 (B 14/A 14).
27. "Socrates was executed for not believing in the gods of Athens, in the gods of the city. By considering and reconsidering this fact, we grasp the ultimate reason why political life and philosophic life, even if compatible for almost all practical purposes, are incompatible in the last analysis: political life, if taken seriously, meant belief in the gods of the city, and philosophy is the denial of the gods of the city" (SSTX 531–32); "In the time of Xenophon, impiety constituted a criminal offence. Thus philosophy, which is essentially incompatible with acceptance of the gods of the city, was as such subject to persecution. Philosophers had therefore to conceal if not the fact that they were philosophers, at least the fact that they were unbelievers" (SSTX 534).
28. For the first elaborate version of this argument, cf. SSTX 534. It should be noted that Strauss immediately indicates the limitations of this argument: "It would, however, betray too low a view of the philosophic writers of the past if one assumed that they concealed their thoughts *merely* for fear of persecution or of violent death" (SSTX 535, my italics, H.K.). Cf. also *PAW* 17.
29. *PAW* 28. My italics, H.K.
30. Cf. especially Friedrich Schleiermacher, *Über die Philosophie Platons*, 31–32 (B 9–10/A 9–10).
31. Cf., once again, ibid., 34–35 (B 12–13/A 12–13).
32. My italics, H.K. I here quote the wording of the manuscript and the alternative reading of the typewritten versions because "degrees of understanding" shows more clearly than "levels of understanding" the connection of this statement to the one that occurs later in the essay: "The difference between the beginner and the philosopher (for the perfectly trained student of Plato is no one else but the genuine philosopher) is a difference not of degree, but of kind" (p. 281).
33. Friedrich Schleiermacher, *Über die Philosophie Platons*, 40 (B 19/A 19). Cf. also 39, 41–42, 60, and 110. On the self-motion of the soul, see, for example, Plato, *Phaedrus* 245c5–246a1.
34. *Über die Philosophie Platons*, 41 (B 20/A 20). On rhetoric as *psychagōgia*, see Plato, *Phaedrus* 261a7ff. and 271c10ff. Cf. Plato, *Gorgias* 452e9–453a5 and Gorgias, *Encomium of Helen*, in Gorgias von Leontinoi, *Reden, Fragmente und Testimonien*, ed. Thomas Buchheim (second edition; Hamburg: Felix Meiner, 2012), 2–16.
35. *Über die Philosophie Platons*, 41 (B 20/A 20).
36. Ibid., 41–42 (B 20/A 20). See below p. 281.
37. Cf., for example, *Über die Philosophie Platons*, 40 (B 18–19/A 18–19) with *CM* 52. It should be noted that in the *Phaedrus* (258d1–2) Plato's Socrates does *not* consider writing speeches as something shameful (*aischron*) in itself. Cf. 277d1–278b4.
38. Seth Benardete emphasizes this structure of understanding when he writes in "Strauss on Plato," in *The Argument of the Action: Essays on Greek Poetry and Philosophy*, ed. Ronna Burger and Michael Davis (Chicago: University of Chicago Press, 2000), 409: "Something happens in a Platonic dialogue that in its revolutionary unexpectedness is the equivalent to the *periagōgē*, as Socrates calls it, of philosophy itself."

39. Strauss's most radical discussion of this problem, which in Plato comes up as the difference between *aretai politikai* and genuine virtue (e.g., *Phaedo* 82a10–b3), can be found in "The Law of Reason in the *Kuzari*," in *PAW* 139: "It is hardly necessary to add that it is precisely this view of the non-categoric character of the rules of social conduct which permits the philosopher to hold that a man who has become a philosopher, may adhere in his deeds and speeches to a religion to which he does not adhere in his thoughts; *it is this view, I say, which is underlying the exotericism of the philosophers*" (My italics, H.K.).
40. In his review of Schleiermacher's *Platons Werke*, the classical scholar August Boeckh criticizes Schleiermacher's rejection of exotericism and suggests, in passing, an alternative. According to Boeckh, Plato's true teaching, which he communicated straightforwardly in the Academy, can also be found in some "dark corners" of his writings: "Accordingly, the difference of the esoteric and the exoteric is based neither on the subjects nor on the external form of the presentation alone, but on the higher or lower degree of the unveiled scientific explanation, in such a way, that the exoteric, like the myth, has an externally manifest side, which the uninitiated accept, but [it] also has an internal meaning, which is intelligible only for the initiated. [...] Plato would have acted coyly in a curious fashion if he would have had no exoteric [teaching] (*nichts Esoterisches*)." August Boeckh, *Kritik der Uebersetzung des Platon von Schleiermacher* (1808), in *Gesammelte kleine Schriften*, ed. Ferdinand Ascherson and Paul Eichholtz (Leipzig: B. G. Teubner, 1872), vol. 7, 7, cf. 4–9.
41. Cf. Seth Benardete, "Strauss on Plato," 409: "There cannot be a method (*methodos*) of thought in the thoughtful going after (*metienai*) of thought."
42. In the central paragraph of the essay, Strauss lists seven items: 1) the distinction of ancients and moderns, 2) Averroes' attitude toward religion, 3) the Greek physicians' attitude toward religion, 4) the distinction between exoteric and esoteric teaching, 5) Eusebius of Caesarea's attitude toward religion, 6) Thomas Hobbes's attitude toward religion, and 7) the lucidity of the plan of Montesquieu's *De l'esprit des lois*. Cf. *PAW* 27–29.
43. *PAW* 28.
44. *GS–1* 145 and *SCR* 100–1.
45. "On the Basis of Hobbes's Political Philosophy," in *WIPP* 182–89. Cf. *NRH* 199n43.—On Strauss's and Hobbes's approach, see footnote 77 in Heinrich Meier's "Die Erneuerung der Philosophie und die Herausforderung der Offenbarungsreligion," in id., *Politische Philosophie und die Herausforderung der Offenbarungsreligion* (München: C.H. Beck, 2013), 86f.
46. At all times, Christian authors have used "milk," instead of "solid food," in order to communicate the One Truth. Using the examples of Augustine and Thomas Aquinas, Frederick J. Crosson makes this point very clear, but also underlines the differences between the philosophical tradition of exotericism and the Christian tradition of "latent" teaching: "A central difference is that in the Christian tradition the manifest teaching expressed in similitudes and metaphors and parables aims at communicating the truth, at bearing witness to the truth, in a form in which it is able to be understood (at least partially) by all. There is only one doctrine, presented in different depths of meaning to the two audiences" ("Esoteric versus Latent Teaching," *Review of Metaphysics* 59, no. 1 (2005): 86).
47. *WIPP* 189.
48. *GS–1* 238, 254 and *SCR* 185, 199.
49. See, above all, the article "The Literary Character of the *Guide of the Perplexed*," which was written in 1938 but published for the first time in *Essays on Maimonides: An Octocentennial Volume*, ed. Salo Wittmayer Baron (New York: Columbia University

Press, 1941), 37–91 (= *PAW* 38–94). For the role Maimonides played in Strauss's understanding of exotericism, cf. also "Der Ort der Vorsehungslehre nach der Ansicht Maimunis," in *GS–2* 183–87 and "Quelques remarques sur la science politique de Maïmonide et de Fârâbî," in *GS–2* 137–38, 144–45, 148, 152–56; see *GS–2* 134n28 with Strauss's marginal note (*GS–2* 160), and SR 11–12, 15–16, 18, 21–24.

50. Cf. GA 3: "Maimonides was, to begin with, wholly unintelligible to me. I got the first glimmer of light when I concentrated on his prophetology and, therefore, the prophetology of the Islamic philosophers who preceded him. One day when reading in a Latin translation Avicenna's treatise *On the Division of the Sciences*, I came across this sentence (I quote from memory): the standard work on prophecy and revelation is Plato's *Laws*. Then I began to understand Maimonides's prophetology and eventually, as I believe, the whole *Guide of the Perplexed*. Maimonides never calls himself a philosopher; he presents himself as an opponent of the philosophers. He used a kind of writing which is in the precise sense of the term, exoteric." See Avicenna: *On the Divisions of the Rational Sciences*, in *Medieval Political Philosophy: A Sourcebook*, ed. Joshua Parens and Joseph C. Macfarland (second edition; Ithaca, NY: Cornell University Press, 2011), 75.

APPENDICES: SEVEN WRITINGS BY LEO STRAUSS

PRELIMINARY NOTE TO APPENDICES

Our appendices include seven writings by Strauss himself. Five may be found in their German originals in *GS–2* and are now translated into English for the first time. Four of these were left unpublished: a review of Karl Mannheim's *Ideologie und Utopie* (our appendix A);[1] lecture notes for two talks to young Zionist groups (our appendices B and C);[2] and a brief reply to an article by Herbert Finkelscherer on the medieval Jewish biblical exegete Isaac Abravanel's conception of politics and society, as regards Abravanel's critique of monarchy (appendix E).[3] The fifth, on a lost writing by the medieval recoverer of Platonic and Aristotelian philosophy Abu Naṣr al-Fârâbî, originally appeared in *Monatsschrift für Geschichte und Wissenschaft des Judentums* 80 (1936): 96–106 (our appendix D).[4] The sixth is a newly edited and annotated version of Strauss's manuscript in English on "Exoteric Teaching"[5] with supplementary materials gathered and introduced by Hannes Kerber (our appendix F). And the seventh is Strauss's notes for a lecture in English on "Persecution and the Art of Writing," also newly edited and annotated by Hannes Kerber (our appendix G).

Unless otherwise indicated, all footnotes in appendices A to E are the translators'. Footnotes followed by {LS} are Strauss's own.[6] Footnotes followed by {HM} are

[1]"Der Konspektivismus," *GS–2* 365–76, 620–21.

[2]"Religiöse Lage der Gegenwart," *GS–2* 377–92, 621; "Die geistige Lage der Gegenwart," *GS–2* 441–64, 623.

[3]"Zu Abravanels Kritik des Königtums," *GS–2* 233–34, 615.

[4]"Eine vermißte Schrift Farâbîs," *GS–2* 167–77, 614.

[5]A previous version, edited by Kenneth Hart Green, has appeared in *Interpretation* 14 (1986): 51–59; reprinted in *RCPR* 63–71.

[6]These are found mostly in "Eine vermißte Schrift Fârâbîs" and "Zu Abravanels Kritik des Königtums." In our translations of these (in appendices D and E), Strauss's original footnote numbers have been freely altered to accommodate the addition of translators' (and editor's) footnotes.

Heinrich Meier's as editor of *GS–2*. All footnotes designated by Arabic numerals in appendices F and G are Hannes Kerber's. Those designated by Roman numerals in appendix F are Strauss's. About the editorial apparatus to appendix F in particular, see Hannes Kerber's Editorial Note.

Interpolations in square brackets are the translators'. Interpolations in parentheses inside titles or quotations from other authors are Strauss's. All emphases, whether inside or outside quotations, are Strauss's.

Page numbers that have been inserted into the translated texts of appendices A–E, inside curly brackets and in boldface, are to *GS–2*.

APPENDIX A

LEO STRAUSS: "CONSPECTIVISM" (1929)[1]

Translated by Anna Schmidt and Martin D. Yaffe

Conspectivism, the greatest power within present-day philosophy, is not a "direction [of thought],"[2] as materialism, positivism, idealism, etc., are "directions [of thought]." It is, rather, a method or a style. In the previous century, the effort arose to dissolve philosophy into the history of philosophy. This effort is continued by conspectivism and transformed into a new effort. Both efforts presuppose that a naive, head-on attack on the problems has been overcome. This overcoming has its basis in the consciousness "that man...after a development so long, full of sacrifice and heroic, has reached the highest stage of consciousness."[3] At this high stage, the attempt to solve the problems is out of the question. But while in the previous century one was still so naively reflective as to deny the problems altogether, conspectivism is full of the reflectively reflective knowledge that there are problems—hard, perhaps insoluble problems; it sees its very task in awakening and sharpening the sense of the problematic; but it does not itself solve the problems;

[1] [Leo Strauss, "*Konspektivismus*," *GS–2* 365–75, 620–21.] Unpublished. Typescript of 13 pages with autograph entries and corrections in ink and pencil. Page 1 dated by Strauss in handwriting: "1929." Leo Strauss Papers, Box 8, Folder 3, Department of Special Collections, University of Chicago Library {HM}.

Strauss's essay is a book review (unpublished) of Karl Mannheim, *Ideologie und Utopie* (Bonn: F. Cohen, 1929). All page numbers in parentheses in Strauss's text are to this volume (see note 4). Emphases in Strauss's quotations from Mannheim are Strauss's own.

The English translation, *Ideology and Utopia*, by Louis Wirth and Edward Shils (New York: Harcourt, Brace and World, 1936) is inexact and hence useless for helping readers understand Strauss's criticism of Mannheim.

Strauss himself coins the term *Konspektivismus* with a polemical intention. In "Religious Situation of the Present" (appendix B), which appropriates words and phrases and even a full sentence from "*Konspektivismus*," Strauss associates this coinage with three synonyms: the German *Zusammenschau* ("synopsis," "overview"), the Greek σύνοψις, and the Latin *conspectio* (*GS–2* 382, with page 428, below).

[2] Strauss writes "*Richtung*" ("direction"). The German word "*Denkrichtung*" ("direction of thought" or "school of thought") seems to be implied.

[3] [Handwritten note in the upper margin of the typescript:] All citations derive from Mannheim's *Ideologie und Utopie*. {HM}

it does not even attempt to solve them; but it keeps the option open to solve them in the future, perhaps in the near future, the next time, so to speak; in short, it replaces the solution of the problems and the denial of the problems by the wrestling with the problems.

The progress from naive reflectiveness to reflective reflectiveness has the result that philosophy creates for itself a new subject matter. Naively reflective philosophy dissolved into the history of philosophy; it dismembered the philosophies of the past; reflectively reflective philosophy occupies itself exclusively with the **{366}** philosophy of the present. Now the return to earlier standpoints is at times still indispensable even today; but the admirable division of labor that corresponds to the high stage now reached allows the thinker of the present to entrust to the historians the providing of access to the past. Let us take the example that a conspectivist spirit[4] finds itself prompted to deal with the problem of utopia; it learns that Thomas Münzer is of very great significance for the history of utopia; the conspectivist spirit will then take up the pertinent literature, especially Holl's essay on Luther and the visionaries,[5] and obtain from it an exhaustive knowledge of the facts of the case. This procedure is unobjectionable. For even if the limitedness of the historian compels us to be greatly suspicious about his *value judgments*, the historian's objectivity allows the user to gain a reliable overview of the *facts* from the documents drawn on by the historian. Meanwhile, as already indicated, the conspectivist thinker is only occasionally dependent on the historian; usually he occupies himself with present-day phenomena that need not be imparted by a third party. We can now attempt a first definition of conspectivism: conspectivism does not deal directly with the problems, as naive philosophy does; nor with the history of philosophy, as does naively reflective philosophy; but exclusively with the philosophy of the present.

The moment conspectivism constitutes itself, new horizons open up that were completely unknown to earlier generations. We point here only to the bottomless problematic that lies in conspectivism itself. We said that it concerned itself only with present-day philosophy. What happens if *all* present-day philosophers are conspectivist thinkers? This possibility does not bear contemplating; but that its realization is imminent is not to be doubted. If we see correctly, then the encounter and dialogue of conspectivist thinkers will become the theme and method of philosophy. But, as has been said, for now we are not there yet. For now, there are still a number of more naive spirits who deal with the problems directly. That is why for now the conspectivist thinker still has the possibility of concerning himself with naive philosophers, of moving back and forth among these philosophers. This movement is called dialectics. Dialectics is the preliminary stage of the encounter and dialogue, thus the preliminary stage to the stage at which the **{367}** conspectivist thinkers will be completely among themselves. Having reached this stage, the

[4]The German is *Geist*, which can mean either "spirit," "mind," or "intellect." As an adjective, *geistig* can mean "intellectual" or "referring to the intellect," as in Strauss's lecture title "The Intellectual [*geistige*] Situation of the Present" (appendix C).

[5]Karl Holl, "*Luther und die Schwärmer*," *Gesammelte Aufsätze zur Kirchengeschichte* (3 vols.; Tübingen: J. C. B. Mohr, 1927), 420ff.

spirit will have reached its being in-and-for-itself; the truth of the spirit in itself will unveil itself in the conspectivist spirit. In the Socratic dialogue taking place among Graf Keyserlingk, Peter Wust, Arthur Liebert, Margarete Susmann et al., philosophy's initial situation is being recreated at a higher stage.

The victory parade of conspectivism is not to be slowed by reactionary spirits repeatedly shouting slogans like "To the things themselves!" "Back to the sources!" etc. Imbued with the consciousness that everything effective at present is of equal value, conspectivism incorporates thoroughness dialectically into its own position; it transforms the naive thoroughness into a thoroughness of a higher order. The fact that even the conspectivist thinkers raise the demand for philological precision and methodological exactness shows clearly how comfortably thoroughness can be integrated into conspectivist thinking.

Since these remarks have the purpose of introducing the reader to conspectivism, this may be the right moment for some brief information about the most natural mode of access to the conspectivist writings. The novice should not be deterred by all the talk about wrestling in these writings; he must keep in mind that wrestling can be a beautiful, indeed a graceful, gesture. He best begins by reading the literary and entertainment supplements included in the widely distributed democratic newspapers. Here he becomes acquainted effortlessly with the first concepts; he thus spares himself the time-consuming detour via the naive problems and via the history of philosophy; he learns how positions that took a decade or longer to establish are overturned or even dispensed with within a few minutes by a few clever moves, using dashes, question marks, and exclamation points; in this manner he understands from the start the powerful progress in technical thinking that the conspectivist methods have brought; he learns to apply these methods himself without difficulty. Trained in this way, he advances to the reading of conspectivist periodicals, pamphlets, and books; these writings he easily recognizes by titles such as: "Currents of Present-Day Thought"; "New Ways of (or to) Philosophy"; "Spirit and World of Dialectics"; "The Resurrection of Metaphysics"; "Thinkers of the Time"; etc. Once he has educated himself with the help of these classic works, he can then turn to the preconspectivist writings and gradually apply himself to **{368}** processing them dialectically by writing essays, pamphlets, and books.

If a naif has, with strenuous labor, gained a concept for himself, has thought it through to the end "with unsparing ruthlessness even toward himself," has put his thoughts on paper, and, finally, published them for whatever reasons, then anyone is free to read his book. How someone reads it depends on what kind of human being he is. If he is narrowminded and has a "categorial apparatus" at hand, then he will cast the book aside: as "metaphysical," if he is a positivist; as "psychological," if he is a Neo-Kantian; as "un-existential," if he is an adherent of the religious-metaphysical renewal movement. But if he is open to everything new, if he is hence predestined for conspectivism, then he notices that the book contains a word of the future. In this case—and this case alone is of public interest—the following will then happen: the attentive reader incorporates the new word into his vocabulary; he reads other books, of which one or the other may be as significant as the first book taken as our example; in these books he also encounters new words that he incorporates; his philosophy becomes more and more universal; effortlessly he overcomes the onesidedness of the various naifs. Of course he reflects on the various keywords and catchwords; he notices connections; he sits down and writes; the result of such a wrestling is a synthesis, that is, an essay or a pamphlet or a book in which the various words are combined dialectically. The dialectical combination of the keywords and catchwords of present-day philosophy—this and nothing else is conspectivism. That is why conspectivism is no standpoint, but rather a method; more exactly, it is a literary genre. Those books are conspectivist in which validity, value, Gestalt, stream of life, dialectics, the existing thinker, the conditions of production, Weltanschauung, structure, ontology, etc., etc., move in a bacchantic whirl.[6]

In order to write such books, one needs a peculiar style. Characteristic of the conspectivist style are, for instance, sentences containing a "without"; one would write, say: "without underestimating the great significance of Hegelianism, one will have enough of a critical conscience to concede that this philosophy does not fully satisfy the demands of an existential worldview." Also, adjectives ending in *-haft* are necessary in conspectivist prose; while the naif uses the **{369}** adjectives ending in *-haft* only in words like *fabelhaft* or *grauenhaft*,[7] etc., it is the concern of the conspectivist author to develop "*gestalthaft*," "*bildhaft*," "*raumhaft*,"[8] etc., for everyday use. These indications may suffice for now. Let me just add that the conspectivist style has exercised a fruitful effect on the language of the educated. If a merchant, judge, or physician because of his attitude somehow finds himself incapable of opting for a certain worldview, or if he somehow finds a metaphysical grounding in absolute values to be required, then he owes the possibility for this to the conspectivist authors.

Only now, "*ex post*," has Karl Mannheim developed the program of conspectivism long dominating the practice of philosophic authorship.[9] What is better called conspectivism, he calls "dynamic synthesis." One would do Mannheim an injustice if one were to describe him without qualification as a conspectivist thinker. In his book *Ideology and Utopia* (here being reviewed) one finds a whole number of naive remarks stemming from direct contact with the problems that still await conspectivist reworking. Mannheim's book is to be counted among the conspectivist literature not so much because it is itself conspectivist in form, but because, as already said, it develops the program of conspectivism for the first time. That is why we have to take a different position toward it than toward the properly conspectivist literature; we shall therefore review it not on the basis of conspectivism, but on the basis of naive thinking and in naive seriousness.

Mannheim's book, which beckons the reader with its interesting subjects—the three treatises of which it consists are titled "Ideology and Utopia," "Is Politics as a Science Possible? (The Problem of Theory and Practice)," "The Utopian Consciousness"—is daunting at first for its wealth of technical expressions, arousing

[6] Strauss's German sentence reads: *Konspektiv sind jene Bücher, in denen die Geltung, der Wert, die Gestalt, der Lebensstrom, die Dialektik, der existierende Denker, die Produktionsverhältnisse, die Weltanschauung, die Struktur, die Ontologie usw. usw. in bacchantischem Taumel sich bewegen.*

[7] *Fabelhaft* means "fabulous"; *grauenhaft* means "dreadful."

[8] These terms mean something like "Gestalt-like," "image-like," and "space-like."

[9] The German is *Schriftstellerei*, which can have the pejorative meaning of "scribbling" (in the sense of "hack writing").

admiration and fear. It just teems with "structural," "categorial apparatus," "outlook," "situation," "synthesis," "deliberation," "ontology," etc. This expenditure of technical terms would be tolerable, perhaps even necessary, if it were in the service of conceptual precision. But an expression such as "categorial apparatus" is precisely *not* possible strictly speaking. Why Mannheim embellishes the word "decision," which has long been recognized and accepted as a technical term **{370}**, with the epithet "ontological," why he says "lived ontic" instead of "life," remains unintelligible so long as one has not yet noticed how little precision there is in Mannheim's writing in general. He speaks of a sociological—that is, social-*scientific*—link (137) when he should speak about a social link at most. He speaks of the solution of a synthesis (122) when he means the solution of the task to produce a synthesis. Ellipses of this sort do not become more tolerable by being counterbalanced with pleonasms such as "in the truly ultimate end" and "unsparing relentlessness." When Mannheim says, "It could not...be our task *this time* to solve problems once and for all," one would like to call out to him: "but next time, please." But in doing so one has to be prepared that what will matter to him next time is being right; for he declares programmatically that he does "not" want "to conceal" the "contradictions, for being right does not matter *for now*" (5). A sentence such as the following highlights his syntax: "For magical times one would of course not be so intellectualist as to assume that on account of epistemological considerations the magical 'system of order' has disappeared..." (57). "*on a completely new manner*" (124)[10] is also not quite impeccable grammar. "*Chairos*" (201) is presumably formed from *Kairos* by analogy with *Chaos–Kaos*; the fact that the word is emphasized in print, and therefore could not easily be overlooked on a proof-page, speaks decisively against the hypothesis that we are dealing with a printer's error. The enumeration of the formal shortcomings of Mannheim's book could be continued indefinitely; the examples cited will suffice to justify the assertion that reflects one's first impression: that this book has not been written with the requisite care. Yet this is, if you will, the author's business only. It is the reader's task to keep to what is worthy of attention, something that can be found in the book nonetheless. Worthy of special attention are *the* thoughts of Mannheim's, which may be summarized as follows.

The fact that there are various, opposing philosophical and political parties incapable of convincing one another was also known previously, under quite different conditions than today. But previously this fact was interpreted differently than it is today. Previously one drew from it, for instance, *the* consequence that prior generations had chosen a wrong approach, that it was therefore necessary to take a new path to *the* **{371}** truth, the truth valid for all human beings and times. One put a new system in place of the existing systems, which might have fundamentally differed as to method and form from the previous systems but which was for that reason no less—a system. This possibility no longer exists today. The lasting insight of the 19th century is the insight into the historical and social conditionality of all systems: there is no free-floating thought, all thought is bound to *its* historical and social place. But

[10] Strauss's point is that this phrase is grammatically incorrect. Mannheim writes "*auf einer ganz neuartigen Weise*," which is in the dative, whereas the preposition *auf* in this idiom should take the accusative: "*auf eine ganz neuartige Weise*."

does not knowing thereby lose its meaning? No—it merely fundamentally changes its meaning. It gives up chasing the chimera of timeless truths; it understands that its meaning lies in understanding the present, present-day life, the social situation from which it stems. The place of metaphysics is taken over by the "sociological diagnosis of the time," the "analysis of the situation," the "report on the situation." This science grows out of the understanding of ourselves and our world that is given with our life itself; it unfolds when we question the particular and narrowminded viewpoint that we hold initially with the other, equally partial and narrowminded viewpoints that are effective in the same social and historical space. In carrying out this confrontation we are on the way to the only possible totality, to the total understanding of our situation. At every moment, we must guard ourselves against the previously gained insight's positing itself as absolute, against our fleeing into a system that reassures us by blocking the horizon from us. The inclination to such absolutizing is admittedly given with human nature, with our thinking and acting. "But this is precisely the function of historical research...in our epoch, to keep rescinding these inevitable...self-hypostasizings and to keep relativizing the self-deification in a constant countermovement, thereby forcing us to be open to the addition" (40).

At this point the question becomes urgent to the reader: how indeed is the addition supposed to happen? Mannheim answers: through the other *present-day* viewpoints. But who says that an adequate understanding of the present situation is indeed achieved through the "dynamic synthesis" of viewpoints, however successful, which exist at present? Can the possibility be ruled out from the start that all these interpretations may be blind to the same fundamental facts; that one thus never even encounters these fundamental facts if one orients oneself from the beginning only by these viewpoints? **{372}** Mannheim presupposes further that the various present-day viewpoints are *equivalent* (40: "now there are too many equivalent positions, even intellectually equally powerful ones, which mutually relativize themselves..."). His proof of this equivalence is that from each of these positions one sees facts that one does not see, or at least does not see *in that way*, from the other positions. But are all facts equally important? Are all aspects equally radical? What determines importance and radicality? The totality! Now Mannheim assumes that only that viewpoint is total that as a "synthesis" does justice to all the others. But can it be ruled out from the start that the total viewpoint might be supremely "unjust"? In order to know which facts must be at the center of a total viewpoint, one must know which facts *are* central; but one does not come to know this by pitting the viewpoints dominant at present against one another. Here Mannheim's premature judgment of Ranke's "obliviousness"[11] (63) comes back to haunt him; Ranke said: "All the heresies of the world will not teach you what Christianity is—one can come to know it only by reading the Gospel." This sentence is neither naive nor ominous, but simply true. If one understands that thought is conditioned by the situation, it does not follow that one cannot come to see the situation originally, free of the dominant viewpoints. This freedom does not fall into anyone's lap; it must be won by understanding the tradition as such in which we are caught up. Admittedly, this tradition cannot be seen clearly

[11] Ger.: *Ahnungslosigkeit*. In Strauss's next sentence, "oblivious" is *ahnungslos* and "ominous" is *ahnungsvoll*.

if—as Mannheim does throughout—one orients oneself only by the more recent centuries. When Mannheim takes premodern developments into consideration, then only "traditionalism" in contrast to modern "rationalism," the "medieval-Christian objective unity of the world" in contrast to the "Enlightenment's absolutized unity of the subject," or at the most the "magical system" and "the prophets": in Mannheim's book, which poses the question of the meaning of science, specifically of the possibility of politics as a science, the foundations of our scientific tradition which lie in Greek antiquity are forgotten! Of all people it is *Mannheim*, who desires and hopes that the history of word meanings "will be researched at the level of methodological exactness possible at present" (38), who is guilty of this omission. **{373}**

But let us disregard the lack of "methodical exactness," of "philological precision" (1), this failure to answer demands that Mannheim himself makes; let us further suppose that in fact every analysis of a situation that is possible in that situation is "somehow" a "synthesis" of the extreme positions effective in this situation: is it permissible therefore to make this *fate* of all research into the *principle* of research? Mannheim speaks of the danger that lies in the "false contemplation of the researching stance" vis-à-vis political practice. Well—the same danger exists vis-à-vis scientific practice. Mannheim, who at many points is brushing the outer limits of liberalism—by incorporating illiberal elements into the liberalism that in fact has a hold on him by means of a "dynamic synthesis"—does not in truth overstep these limits. (Particularly interesting in this respect is Mannheim's interpretation of fascism, which we cannot enter into here.) We say: liberalism has a hold on Mannheim, and we are justified inasmuch as it is the essence of liberalism to elevate insights gained in a contemplative attitude to principles of practice.

The "analysis of situation" sought by Mannheim does not want to be "value free." It is aware that the will to know *what is*, this will that forbids every escape and every lie, contains a "value judgment"; that given with our life already, from which this situation analysis arises, are valuing, taking a stance, praising and blaming; that it is possible only on the basis of a "decision" guiding the eye, illuminating the horizon. This "decision" stands at the beginning; not, however, as an axiom from which anything one likes can be inferred, but as an implicit drive to question, which becomes explicit, understood, tested, and doubted in carrying out the confrontation. Thus, the analysis of situation that is always grounded in a "decision," succeeds in the unveiling of ideologies by showing for what they are "outdated and outlived norms and forms of thought, but also worldviews" that do not clarify the present situation but conceal it (51). A "decision" underlies the "sociological diagnosis of the time" that seeks a "dynamic synthesis," and in particular underlies the "politics as science in the form of a political sociology" (143) also demanded by Mannheim, namely, the decision for a politics of the center, whose support is to be the "socially free-floating intelligence." The **{374}** stratum of intellectuals that is—according to Mannheim's thesis—the support of the "spirit" is the "predestined advocate of the intellectual interests of the whole." This stratum is not a class; it owes its unity not to its economic situation but to "education." The intellectuals, who as individuals are conditioned by class and always remain within certain limits, have in their education "a homogeneous medium" in which the heterogeneous class tendencies can confront each other; the intellectual struggle made possible by education is a "downsized image" of the class struggles. The result of this confrontation is expected to be a "total orientation" about the social situation, as it cannot be reached from the extreme standpoints of classes and parties; but not a "politics peculiar to intellectuals," which would hardly be possible in the time of mass movements. The stratum of intellectuals has the possibility and the "mission" of anticipating intellectually and thus beginning a "dynamic mediation" between the classes opposed to each other, between the "ruthless representatives of yesterday's principles" and the "one-sided emphasis on the day to come" (121–34). We leave undecided whether this type of influence on politics is possible at all in the present situation; we only point out an allusion that Mannheim makes in the context of his treatise on politics as a science,[12] an allusion whose momentousness is deplorably at odds with how little it is developed. We recall the significance of the distinction between an ethics of intention and an ethics of responsibility for Max Weber.[13] Unless we are mistaken, the insight into this distinction was the deepest and strongest motive for his conviction that it is impossible to decide scientifically between opposing moral principles; for here two irreducible, unjustifiable, unconditional possibilities of human behavior seemed to face each other, compelling each human being to face an either/or. There is no doubt: Max Weber faced *this* choice. Are we still facing it today? If we comprehend correctly the remark that Mannheim makes at the conclusion of his second treatise,[14] then he is of the opinion that the ethics of intention is no eternal possibility, but *one* stage in the history of humanity, destined to be overcome by the ethics of responsibility that Max Weber professed. But if that is the case, is not the meaning of "decision" fundamentally changed? Do not then the questions that Mannheim asks himself have to be asked entirely differently? This question leads back to the **{375}** more fundamental question of how the world in which science emerged looked before the incursion of the biblical consciousness. Only by orienting ourselves by this world can we gain the horizon in which alone we can radically question and answer henceforth. In orienting ourselves by this world we would also see that, under Mannheim's implicit presuppositions, one would have to inquire not into the possibility and necessity of utopia, but into the possibility and necessity of planning. But Mannheim utterly lacks precisely this orientation.

[12] I.e., in "Is Politics as a Science Possible? (The Problem of Theory and Practice)."

[13] See Max Weber, "Politics as a Vocation," in *From Max Weber: Essays in Sociology*, trans. H. H. Gerth and C. Wright Mills (New York: Oxford University Press, 1946), 120: "We must be clear about the fact that all ethically oriented conduct may be guided by one of two fundamentally differing and irreconcilably opposed maxims: conduct can be oriented to an 'ethics of intention' or to an 'ethics of responsibility' [*'gesinnungsethisch' oder 'verantwortungsethisch' orientiert*]. This is not to say that an ethics of intention [*Gesinnungsethik*] is identical with irresponsibility, or that an ethics of responsibility [*Verantwortungsethik*] is identical with unprincipled opportunism. Naturally, nobody says that. However, there is a gaping contrast between conduct that follows the maxim of an ethics of intention—that is, in religious terms, 'The Christian does rightly and leaves the results with the Lord'—and conduct that follows the maxim of an ethics of responsibility, in which case one has to give an account of the foreseeable results of one's action." Translation modified. See Weber, *Politik als Beruf*, in *Gesammelte Politische Schriften*, ed. Johannes Winckelmann (Tübingen: J.C.B. Mohr, 1971), 551–52. Cf. also *NRH* 69ff.

[14] I.e., of "Is Politics as A Science Possible? (The Problem of Theory and Practice)."

APPENDIX B

LEO STRAUSS: "RELIGIOUS SITUATION OF THE PRESENT" (1930)[1]

Translated by Anna Schmidt and Martin D. Yaffe

I would be facing an insoluble task if I had to report to you all that is being *written* about religion today; for *infinitely much* is being written: each day a new book, a new pamphlet, a new essay comes out concerning our question. The task would be simplified—and the simplification in our case amounts not so much to the temptation to give in to laziness as to an imperative of reason—if I limited myself to reporting what was being *thought* today, being thought *thoroughly*. For while there are many who write, there are few who think, who think thoroughly. I do not mean to claim that a necessary opposition exists between thinking and writing, although that claim might not be all that indefensible. I am happy to admit that there are a number of men who write after they have thought, have thought thoroughly. We need to concern ourselves with these men only.

Meanwhile a further restriction recommends itself. Most of even the thorough authors are apostles of a master. And here we keep to the proverb: "One does not go to the apprentice, but to the blacksmith." It is indisputable that the kind of literature that advances the understanding of a great and deep mind, commentary, has a value that should not be disparaged. But the commentator is not the author. And in concerning ourselves with the religious situation of the present we do not want to become confused by the multitude of commentators, but to stick to the very few authors, to the *auctores* of the situation. **{378}**

We are interested in the religious situation of the present as *Jews*. For that reason we take a stronger interest in those authors who, being Jews, determine the present

[1] ["*Religiöse Lage der Gegenwart*," in *GS–2* 377–91, 621.] Unpublished. Manuscript with 13 handwritten pages and inscribed cover, in ink with penciled supplements and corrections. On the cover Strauss has noted under the title: "Paper to be read on 21 December 1930 in the Kadimah Federation Camp in Brieslang near Berlin." Leo Strauss Papers, Box 8, Folder 4, Department of Special Collections, University of Chicago Library. {HM}

Kadimah was a national student Zionist organization founded in Vienna in 1882 (and disbanded by the Nazis in 1938). Its Hebrew name means "Forward."

situation. Of the Jewish writers of the present who are of interest in our context, the most important one by far is without any doubt Franz Rosenzweig.[2] I will therefore confine myself to a presentation of Franz Rosenzweig's doctrine. In the short time that I have, I would only cause confusion by giving a survey of the various theories. The thorough treatment of a work that is indicative of and peculiar to the present situation is much more suitable for our purpose.

However, I cannot even turn to my task limited in this limited way, I cannot begin my thus limited task in the right manner, so long as I have not clarified the topic itself. In this clarification it will turn out, however, that the topic is *not a serious* topic. That is why I divide my presentation into 2 parts:

1. Clarification of the topic;
2. Rosenzweig's doctrine and its difficulty.

The title of my presentation consists of four words—rather, since we can safely disregard the article "the," of three: "Religious," "Situation," "Present." We want to look at these three words in sequence in their context as determined by the topic.

1. *Religious* Situation of the Present. Obviously this does not mean in one particular respect: in the way that we can consider the situation of the present as conditioned by the Versailles Treaty, by the crisis of the world economy, by the Balfour Declaration, etc.; nor that the religious situation of the present is of the same order as the political, social, economic, technical, scientific, artistic situation. Instead what is meant is: the situation of the present in the *most important* respect. It is, for instance, unthinkable that the topic of your study group, the validity of norms, values, and laws, would *not* belong to our topic; rather, it essentially belongs to it. For that reason, for example, the philosophic situation should not be distinguished and excluded from the religious situation; but certainly the only reason why you did *not* say "*philosophic* situation of the present" was because otherwise there would have been the danger of letting loose a flood of incomprehensible technical terms. Avoiding this will be my most pressing concern. But the matter prohibits disregarding philosophy, **{379}** prohibits distinguishing between religion and philosophy in looking at the present religious situation. I therefore replace "religious situation of the present" with "*intellectual*[3] situation of the present."

2. Intellectual *Situation* of the Present. The expression is intelligible but inappropriate:[4] the intellect is not a thing that is situated, or that could have a situation. The intellect is actual[5] in seeing and searching, in believing, wishing and hoping, in demanding and giving an account, in responsibility, in questioning and answering. Now, questioning has priority over answering. God does not *question*,

[2] Franz Rosenzweig (1886–1929), German-Jewish theologian, originator of the "new thinking" and leading advocate of the "movement of return" to Judaism; see Strauss, Preface to *SCR*, in *JPCM* 146–48 with 151–53, 453, 460.

[3] Ger.: *geistige*. (The emphasis is Strauss's.)

[4] Ger.: *uneigentlich*. Or: inauthentic. Likewise five sentences later in this paragraph. In that same sentence, "proper" is *eigentlich*, whose range of meanings includes "real," "actual," "true," "appropriate," and "authentic."

[5] Ger.: *wirklich*. Or: real.

although he does answer. Questioning is more characteristic of the human intellect than is answering. There is no answer without questioning,[6] although there is questioning without answer. It may be that questioning is not the sufficient definition of the intellect—in any case, questioning is proper to the intellect and not, like the situation, inappropriate. We therefore now say: the intellectual *questioning* of the present. This expression has a pleonastic effect: although we speak of "the social question," we do not speak of social questioning, etc. We therefore say: *the* questioning of the present. The questioning asks something; it asks a question;[7] we grasp the questioning of others—in this case, of the present—from their question. We therefore say: *the* question of the present.

3. The Question of the *Present*. Let us imagine, in a fanciful manner, a Kadimah camp assembly in the twelfth century, in the century of R[abbi] M[oses] b[en] M[aimon],[8] and that you had asked a student of the RMbM to speak to you so that he might help you, by means of what he has learned from his teacher, to free yourselves from your confusion and perplexity. What would he have spoken to you about? Creation, providence, the unity of reason and revelation. Hence, about *substantive* questions. In another age, one would probably have spoken about *other* questions, but always about substantive questions. Nobody would have minded whether or not they were questions of the *present*. At the time, they *were* questions of the *present* that were being dealt with, but they were not being dealt with *as* questions of the present. When we question, seriously question, we then *by that very fact* ask questions of the present. And if we pose *the* question that we are certain is *the* question, then we are asking *the* question of the present. We will therefore cross out "of the present" and say: *The* question. There can, however, be no doubt about what *the* question is that is and must be the most important one for us: it is the question, what is the *right* life? how *should* I **{380}** live? what matters?[9] what is needful?[10] Thus, our modern topic of the "religious situation of the present" boils down to the old, eternal question, *the* primordial question.

There is no doubt that this is the question for the sake of which you have posed the question concerning the religious situation of the present. For in order to learn the latest from the realm of intellect and wit, you did not need to travel from noisy Berlin to quiet Brieselang. But how does it come about, then, that the simple question poses itself not only to you but also to the present as such, as the question of the religious or intellectual situation of the present? This automatic alteration of the question takes place on account of an implicit or explicit, but in any case tyrannical, conviction: the conviction that the answer to the question could be gained solely or essentially from the knowledge and understanding of the present as it exists in the present. This conviction and its causes we have to consider first.

[6] Or: questions.

[7] Ger.: *Das Fragen fragt etwas, es fragt eine Frage.* Strauss's sentence has a Heideggerian formulation.

[8] "RMbM" is the traditional Hebrew acronym for Rabbi Moshe ben Maimon (i.e., Moses Maimonides). We have retained it here, along with Meier's bracketed interpolations. The acronym recurs in Strauss's next clause and later on.

[9] Ger.: *worauf kommt es an?*

[10] Ger.: *was tut not?*

If we pose the question concerning the right life unselfconsciously and naively, convinced that we can answer it if we make an honest effort and do not let ourselves be put off by any detour, then the present,[11] attired in the most splendid robes, confronts us with the raised eyebrows of a haughtily knowing, exalted personage and calls out to us:

> Stop! You unsuspecting ones! Do you not know that the inexhaustible earth brings forth new generations year after year, which, barely having reached maturity, are all destined to charge with all the fire of youth directly at the truth, at *the* truth? This has now been happening for thousands of years. For thousands of years the attempt has been made, and time and again it has failed. At one time, later generations did not let themselves be confused by the failure of earlier ones; full of delusion they said to themselves, if they failed—perhaps they approached the issue the wrong way; let's just begin from the beginning; let's begin completely from the beginning. And they began from the beginning, and they also failed. The unhappy ones did not know—what I, the Present, the powerful goddess, know—that they *had* to fail. They had to fail since they were seeking *the* truth. For there is not *the one eternal* truth, but each age has *its* truth, and you, you 20-year-olds, you can reasonably seek only your truth, the truth of your age, my—the present's—truth. Being in full possession of *this* knowledge, which is **{381}** my greatest pride, I am allowed to smile at the past—at its naivety. I do not hide that my smile conceals a little *envy*: at the élan of youth, which, in the superiority that my knowledge gives me, I cannot permit myself: the long, magnificent robes that strike your eye would hinder me very much in an assault on the truth, which can only be dared in combat gear; I cannot go on the assault: I am stuck at the base; I do not hide that I am sometimes ashamed before the frontline soldiers; but then my good sense tells me: "You have no reason to be ashamed; the base is *your* virtue, *your* duty; you would be dishonest, you would be betraying yourself, if you, such an exalted, superior, refined personage, were to take on the dirt and hardship of the front lines. I have it much harder, since I, too, would rather go on the assault and cannot and must not."—So, while my smile is not a naive smile at their naïveté, and is indeed a smile that is not without grief and shame, it is, at the same time, also not a poisonous smile: My smile is benevolent: I exculpate, I *justify*: I exculpate the earlier generations since they did against their will what I prescribe to my children. To be sure, they did seek *the* truth, but they found the truth without time;[12] they failed—measured by *their* standard; measured by *my* standard, they reached the goal. So now, enthroned high above the entire past, I call out to you: It is befitting for thinking beings to know what they are doing and what they can reasonably want: therefore, know and be imbued with it once and for all, that you can find only your truth, the truth of the present, and therefore can reasonably seek only it.

In this way the present speaks a lot to us, not through the mouth of stubborn goats in Scotland[13] but through the mouth of the most agile, most progressive, most expert, most lively children of our time. So let us hear more closely what they are saying to us. We cannot seek *the* answer to our question, but only the answer for *us*, for the *present*. But where and how to find this answer? Surely not in the

[11] Or: the Present. Likewise in the following.

[12] Ger.: *ohne Zeit*.

[13] This expression seems proverbial, with no literary antecedent.

study. No—only through coming to know the *powers* of the present! Where do we encounter these powers? In the struggle of parties, groups, trends, currents, etc. But are we supposed to hear what the truth of the present is from the cacophonous noise of the public? No—these conflicting trends do not harmonize on their own; their harmony **{382}** must first be produced by us. In what manner, though? The thoughtful person cannot devote himself completely[14] to *one* trend; he sees all too clearly that in each of these trends are truth and untruth; hence he must try to do justice to all, to the truth in all. In short—what he needs is a "*synthesis*."

Now then: 1) since everything human is historical, there is not *the* question, but always only the question of the *present*. In order to answer this question, or even just to pose it, we must know the situation of the present. 2) The situation of the present—that is, the factual, effective answers of the present. 3) The answer is given by a synopsis, σύνοψις, *conspectio*—conspectivism.[15]

1. *Critique of Conspectivism.*

α. The Incredible Difficulty of a Synthesis. Conspectivism is possible only because of the complete absence of a concrete notion of the emergence of a "position." Every position that can at all be taken seriously is the work of an immense effort of an individual. When Kant—who already had achievements that by themselves would have made him immortal (Kant–Laplace theory), who was no inexperienced young man who yet had to acquire the necessary knowledge of facts—had accomplished the breakthrough to his position, he needed 11 years for the *Critique of Pure Reason*—not to write it, but just to think it. Let us assume that something similar goes for Marx or for Nietzsche. These men came to completely different results with their immense efforts. What an exponential effort it would take to find a position from which both positions were unified! How much deeper would someone have to descend in order to find the common point from which.... One need only imagine these difficulties in order to comprehend that the people who today talk of synthesis simply do not mean[16] anything by it. But they must mean something by it! As it seems to me, conspectivism comes about in the following manner.

β. The Genesis of Conspectivism from the reader turned writer. The originators of positions have laid down the results of their **{383}** immense effort in published books. Everyone can buy these books or have them given to him as a gift or borrow them and then read them. Now, there are two types of readers. Some are narrowminded; they have a fixed and ready opinion; they read only in order to confirm their opinion: should the book *not* be of their opinion, they have enough arguments ready-at-hand to dismiss the book. For, what aren't there arguments for; certain fundamental insights of Kant's, which today any jackass has or believes he has, were "refuted" with sovereign superiority by jackasses among Kant's contemporaries. This type of reader is harmless and innocuous. More harmful is the second type. To this type belong people who are stimulated by the books, who are open to everything new; these people are easily excited; they adopt one book's conclusions

[14] Ger.: *mit Haut und Haar.*

[15] Ger.: *Konspektivismus.* Compare the following with Strauss's unpublished review by this title, translated in appendix A, above.

[16] Lit.: think. Likewise in the next sentence.

and then again another's. Since they are precisely *not* narrow, they cannot resist the conflicting theories. The theories can be formulated in certain keywords; these keywords can easily be adopted. One reads and reflects while reading; it occurs to one how things are related; one sits down and writes. The result of this very entertaining activity is a synthesis, that is, a book or a pamphlet or an essay. That is the essence of the conspectivist spirit:[17] the conspectivist spirit is the lazy reader turned writer.

γ. Sham Understanding. In truth, one understands nothing conspectively, even if one is very bright. I want to give an example. In our time, somewhere there lives a philosopher in the full sense of the word.[18] Completely unknown just five years ago, today his name and work are talked of everywhere. This philosopher in his main work has, among other things, written a few pages about idle talk, what it means and what it inflicts.[19] That was meant as a, so to speak, purely factual statement, not as the author's appeal to spare him from idle talk. What happened? A woman[20]—the noble word "lady" obviously forbids itself—reads this philosopher, and before she can even have the slightest idea of what the man really means, she goes around in London and yaks and yaks. She found the paragraph on idle talk certainly "very fine"; she has understood him in *this* sense; but she did not understand him in such a way that she would finally, finally shut her unbearable trap.

Therefore: if one takes *seriously* the great men who dominate the present, then one will not wish to attempt a synthesis, which amounts to muddling and diluting what was important to them. It **{384}** is preferable to despair in light of their contradiction than to give in to a stale and cowardly mishmash.

2. *The Situation of the Present can be grasped*[21] *in the totality of the positions effective in the present.* Why *all* these positions? Because they are *equivalent.* Why are they equivalent? Because each one sees facts that the others do not see, or see indistinctly. But obviously it appears not to be important to see *everything* equally distinctly—but to see what is important distinctly and what is not important indistinctly. We must therefore already know beforehand what is important. One answers: what is important is the *total situation* of the present: what matters is the totality. The reason why individual positions cannot convince one another, cannot do justice to one another, is that they are not total.[22] But is "justice" what matters simply? Is not "injustice" vis-à-vis what is not true truly just? Cannot the total view be supremely unjust? In truth, *all* views are total.

But assuming that a synthesis were possible and that all the positions effective in the present were equivalent: would it therefore be necessarily so that the synthesis actually conceived *the* situation of the present? For is it necessary that *all* viewpoints, that the *true* viewpoint be contained in the present viewpoints in such a way that it results from their synthesis? Is it not possible that *all* present standpoints

[17] German: *Geistes.* Except where otherwise noted, *Geist* and its cognates are "intellect" and its cognates.

[18] The reference is to Martin Heidegger. See the following note.

[19] Heidegger, *Sein und Zeit* §35 (10th ed.; 167–70)

[20] Ger.: *Weib.* In the next clause, "lady" is *Frau.*

[21] Ger.: *ist fassbar.* Later in this subsection, "view" is *Auffassung,* and "viewpoint" is *Gesichtspunkt.*

[22] Ger.: *untotal.*

rest on a mistaking of the fundamental facts? Are not perhaps all these standpoints "ideologies"? This is in no way settled. If we want to come to know the present just as it *is*, free from the dominant views, which we must first examine, then we must first of all be free of the present. This freedom does not fall into our laps; we must win it for ourselves.

3. *Necessity of the Naivety of the Questioning.* But is it true at all that we have to come to know the situation of the present in the first place? From mankind's always having a present, it nevertheless does not follow that one need be concerned with it: our *fate* is *not* our *task*. This is the principal mistake to which today's man keeps succumbing: the attempt to determine the task from the fate. This attempt is absurd if there is *no* God: then fate is chance, and if God *is*, then fate is providence, and we are not allowed to want to play God. This error manifests itself also in the will to synthesis: even if each standpoint may *be* a synthesis *in fact*—it is nonetheless *never willed as* a synthesis; what has been willed is always the *truth*. **{385}** We have to look *ahead*; we *never* come to know what we have to do by being reflective.

We want to do justice to the matter, then.[23] We turn to the matter,[24] that is, the question concerning the right life, with the will to answering it. But in order not to suffer shipwreck as thousands have suffered shipwreck *before* us, we do want to hear the *warning* of the present, the call: watch out. We will not listen to the present if it turns this failure into a theory, if it asserts the *inevitability* of failure. In order to be able to get beyond the present, we must take the warning of the present seriously, we must be in a position to interpret more closely the experience on which the present insists. We therefore do not ask about the *present*, but about the *warning* of the present. But in this warning we let ourselves encounter the present. We thus admit: failure will certainly not have been accidental, due to individual inadequacy, to the stupidity of earlier generations; it will have its *serious* reasons. In order to understand these serious reasons, we must take seriously the question about them, we must not truncate this question by the dogmatic assertion that there are no eternal truths.

By the way, what about the historical *experience* of this failure?

The question was posed for the first time by Socrates. Whether and in what sense he himself gave an answer is obscure. In any case, his student Plato answered it: in the *Republic*.[25] In order to illustrate the difficulty of true understanding, Plato in this work compares the situation of human beings to the situation of cave dwellers: a cave with a long entry stretching upwards; the human beings from childhood on are bound inside the cave by chains around their thighs and necks; they thus always remain in the same place, and they are prevented by their neck chains from turning their heads around; from above a firelight shines from a distance; above, between the fire and the prisoners runs a walkway, alongside which runs a wall; along this wall human beings carry all sorts of artifacts, statues, etc.; it appears that the prisoners there can see only the shadows of those artifacts, which are cast by the fire's light

[23] Ger.: *Wir wollen also sachlich sein.*

[24] Ger.: *Sache.*

[25] See, for the following, *Republic* 514a–517a.

onto the cave's wall facing them; to them, therefore, the shadows would be the true things. Now, if one of them were unchained and put into a position to gaze freely up toward the light, which however could happen only under great pain **{386}**, he would, being blinded by the glow, be incapable of recognizing the things whose shadows he had seen before; he would be at a complete loss if he were told that now he was seeing the things whose shadows he had been seeing until now; above all, the very sight of the light would pain him so much that he would turn away and want again to retreat into the dark of the cave; and it would require a long habituation and effort, indeed the use of force, for him to be capable of seeing the true things, of living in the light of the truth. Brought back into the cave, he would retain the memory of his life in the light, but would be completely incomprehensible and laughable to his companions precisely because of this. Thus Plato presents the difficulties of philosophizing, the *natural* difficulties. If they are so extraordinary, is it any wonder that there are so many conflicting opinions? Bearing in mind the Platonic parable, we will not be misled by the anarchy of opinions, but will have to exert ourselves as much as possible to get out of the cave.

We said: Plato presents the *natural* difficulties of philosophizing. That is, those difficulties natural to man as man, as a sensitive-intellectual being, the difficulties that according to the Platonic view are given by his sensitivity.[26] We say "natural" because there are difficulties that are not "natural" but become effective only under certain presuppositions. RMbM in *Moreh Nebuchim*[27] (I 31) expands the enumeration of reasons given by a Greek philosopher for the differences of opinion in philosophy, and therefore for the difficulty of philosophy simply, by a fourth reason; about this he says, literally:

> *In our time* there exists a fourth reason, which he [*sc.*, Alexander of Aphrodisias] did not mention, since it did not exist among them; namely, *habituation* and *schooling*; for human beings by nature love what they are habituated to and incline to it;...thus it happens to man regarding the opinions with which he has grown up: he loves them and holds on to them and keeps away from deviant opinions. For this reason as well, then, man is prevented from coming to know the truth. Thus it happens to the multitude regarding God's corporeality...on account of habituation to *writings* in which they firmly believe and to which they are habituated, whose wording seems to indicate God's corporeality.

Let us sum up: by the fact that a tradition resting on revelation has entered the world of philosophy, the difficulty of philosophizing is fundamentally augmented **{387}**, the *freedom* of philosophizing fundamentally limited.

In RMbM's remark, the struggle of the entire last 3 centuries, the struggle of the Enlightenment, is in a sense sketched, outlined: in order to render possible philosophy in its natural difficulty, the artificial difficulty of philosophizing has to be eliminated;[28] there has to be a struggle against *prejudices*. In this, modern philosophy is fundamentally different from Greek philosophy: the latter struggles only against

[26] Ger.: *Sinnlichkeit*.

[27] That is, *Guide of the Perplexed*. Strauss uses the traditional Hebrew title.

[28] More or less lit.: removed from the world.

appearance and opinion; modern philosophy's struggle begins prior to that against prejudices. The Enlightenment thus wants to recover Greek philosophy. What does it achieve? It achieves: the freedom of *answering* but not the freedom of questioning, only the freedom of saying No instead of the traditional Yes. (Mortality vs. immortality, chance vs. providence, atheism vs. theism, passion vs. reason.[29]) But this liberation from the Yes of the tradition takes place by means of a commensurately deeper entanglement in the tradition. For instance, the Enlightenment conducts its struggle against the tradition in the name of tolerance, ultimately in the name of love of neighbor; thus religion is now being based entirely on love of neighbor, in such a way, however, that with the doubt of love of neighbor (as understood by the Enlightenment)[30] religion as such becomes altogether doubtful. Or to take an example from a later stage of the Enlightenment: when the Enlightenment becomes openly atheistic and believes it sees through "God" as being a construct of the human heart, the only way it does so is by internalizing the purposes of God into mankind: self-redemption of mankind, self-assurance of immortality (museum, etc.), assuming the role of providence. And if opponents of Enlightenment arise at every stage of it, then these opponents, for their part, take over the successes of the Enlightenment and reconstruct their position in accord with these. (E.g., revelation is understood as being a human product, as morals and as form, not as law; creation is understood not as being the creation of the world, but as what is binding in advance on human beings.)[31] In general: since the Enlightenment, each generation has *generally* reacted to the preceding generation without questioning the foundation. For example, the concept of the "irrational"—rationalism understood in the narrowest sense.[32] **{388}**

Example: The Problem of Creation

1. God has created the world in complete freedom, out of love; he rules over it in complete freedom—justly and wisely, but in such a way that we are not authorized and not able to know the ways of his justice and wisdom. In his freedom he can perform miracles. Miracles are not in themselves "more divine" than the usual course of the world; but there is no reason for saying that God could not and would not perform miracles.
2. The struggle against miracles in the name of metaphysics: miracles are unworthy of God as the perfect being.
3. Modern physics understands nature completely on its own terms: No scientific proof of God possible. God related to the humanity of human beings.
4. Nature a construct of human intellect.[33]
5. By analogy with this construct, the whole of "culture," and with it religion, is understood as a construct of the human mind.[34]

[29] Ger.: *Verstand.*

[30] Ger.: *aufgeklärt verstanden.*

[31] Ger.: *als Vorher-verbindlich über den Menschen verfügt sein.*

[32] [Note in margin:] Theory vs. Intuition
Mannheim's Ideology and Utopia {HM}

[33] Ger.: *Verstand.*

[34] Ger.: *Geistes.*

6. Novel understanding of the original religious attitude (in contrast to mysticism): the demanding God who summons before him.[35] The abandonment of creation remains.

The entanglement in the tradition is further intensified by a *theory* that *legitimizes* this entanglement. While the Enlightenment itself was wholly convinced that history was accidental, that the victorious party was not in the right just because it happened to be victorious, in the nineteenth century the belief that world history is the world's court of judgment becomes dominant. (A belief that can be justified in the natural sciences, where in fact an unequivocal progress, a building on the accomplishments of earlier generations, is possible but that is, at bottom, impossible.[36]

Thus: the question πως βιωτέον is hard to answer today not merely on account of the *natural* difficulties, not merely on account of the dominance of a tradition of which we are aware as being a tradition, but on account of our total entanglement in the tradition, which goes so far that we *can*not express ourselves purely and freely, that every attempt to express and determine what we have seen and experienced is impossible at first. But what then can we do now?)

The struggle against the tradition that leads to the complete entanglement in the tradition, also dissolves the tradition. In every subsequent **{389}** generation there is *in fact* ever less tradition. The struggle against the tradition was ever again forced to appeal to the *opponents* of the tradition, to those against whom the tradition had arisen and prevailed. Those elements that were supplanted by the tradition reappear (the pagans, Epicurus, vindication of heretics of all types, the sophists, idolatry). These elements became *understood*. The end of this struggle is the *complete rejection* of the tradition: not just of its answers, also not just of its questions, but of its possibilities: The pillars on which our tradition rested, prophets and Socrates-Plato, are torn down since Nietzsche. *Nietzsche's* siding with kings against prophets, with sophists against Socrates—Jesus not only no God, also no charlatan, also no genius, but a moron. Θεωρεῖν[37] *and* "good–evil" rejected—Nietzsche the *last* Enlightener.

The tradition has been shaken at its *roots* by Nietzsche. It has altogether forfeited its self-evidence. We stand in the world completely without authority, completely without orientation. Only now has the question πως βιωτέον regained its full sharpness. We *can* again pose it. We have the possibility of posing it in full seriousness. We can no longer read Plato's dialogues superficially, in order to notice admiringly that old Plato already knew this and that; we can no longer polemicize against him superficially. And the same with the Bible: we no longer think without evidence that the prophets were in the right; we ask ourselves seriously whether it was not the kings who were in the right. We really must begin *entirely* from the beginning.

We *can* begin entirely from the beginning: we lack any polemical passions against the tradition (we have, after all, nothing from where we could be polemical); and at

[35] Ger.: *der Fordernde, vor sich fordernde Gott.*

[36] This sentence and the entire next paragraph are enclosed in parentheses in Strauss's ms.

[37] Gk.: Contemplating.

the same time, the tradition has become completely estranged from us, completely questionable.

But we cannot answer immediately as we are; for we know that we are deeply entangled in a tradition; we are yet much further down than Plato's cave dwellers. We must raise ourselves to the *origin* of the tradition, to the level of *natural ignorance*. If we wanted to concern ourselves with the present situation, we would be doing nothing other than the cave dwellers who describe the interior of their cave.

We have the *possibility*, then, of understanding the origins of our tradition freely: if we make the greatest effort; that is, understanding freely what has always been handed **{390}** down as more or less *self-evident*. But what is "self-evident" is really[38] always *not understood*. This lack of understanding is the final reason why the struggle against the tradition has become possible and necessary. The final result; the *factual ignorance* of the origins (e.g., μεγαλοψυχία–nobility).[39]

The question concerning the religious situation of the present is no serious topic. The serious thing that is meant by this question is the question concerning the right life. The answer to this question requires not only no special attention to the present situation, but in fact the determined[40] return to our historical origins, the uncompromising scrutiny of the supposed "achievements" of history.

[38] Ger.: *im Grunde*.

[39] Ger.: *Vornehmheit*. The Greek *megalopsychia* means, lit., "greatness of soul."

[40] Ger.: *entschlossenen*.

APPENDIX C

LEO STRAUSS: "THE INTELLECTUAL SITUATION OF THE PRESENT" (1932)[1]

Translated by Anna Schmidt and Martin D. Yaffe

Introduction: *captatio benevolentiae*

The topic is *disreputable*. A proper scholar[2] adjusts his ambition to speaking only on topics he has expert knowledge of, that is, on topics whose material he knows and has adequately worked through intellectually. I do not have the reassuring awareness:[3] here no one can damage or hurt me, here I am knowledgeable, as regards this evening's topic. I am not a specialist in the present: I have neither climbed all its heights nor descended into all its nooks. The awareness that it is *impossible* to be a specialist in the present probably prompts people who care about their scholarly prestige to stay away from this topic.

If I nevertheless put up for discussion the intellectual situation of the present, it is because I feel emboldened by the following consideration. Certainly it is very fine and comfortable to be able to step forth as if clad in iron armor. But the armor of scholarship always clads a being scarcely made of iron—namely, a human being who questions. Now, there are questions that are hard to ask and even harder to answer, so that one would really prefer to deny they exist. But they force themselves onto us: we ask them and we answer them—even if with the worst conscience. Now, the precaution of not doing things in public that one does secretly with a bad conscience is certainly very prudent; but perhaps *too* prudent; is it not almost

[1] [Leo Strauss, "*Die geistige Lage der Gegenwart*," *GS–2* 441–64, 623.] Unpublished. Bound manuscript with 12 written pages (three of them loose) and inscribed cover, in ink, with additions and corrections in pencil. Two pages (two sides) with the draft of an alternative introduction under the title *Preliminary Remark* and a further sheet (two pages) attached with the plan of the lecture, all in pencil. On the cover and on the first page of the manuscript, Strauss has noted: 6.II.1932. Leo Strauss Papers, Box 8, Folder 6, Department of Special Collections, University of Chicago Library. {HM}

[2] Ger.: *Wissenschaftler*. Or: scientist (depending on the field of study).

[3] Ger.: *Bewusstsein*. Or: consciousness (henceforth depending on the context).

already *cowardice*?[4] Therefore, if we do not want to be cowards, we should admit that now and again we nevertheless think about the intellectual situation of the present and hence under certain conditions express these thoughts among ourselves **{442}**. They are not entirely absurd, after all—perhaps they will even be of some use for our respectable scholarly work as well. That being said, on to the subject-matter.

1. *What does the intellectual situation of the present matter to us Jews?* It matters to us insofar as the *present situation of Judaism* matters to us.

Both the dissolution process and the consolidation process determined in a European manner.[5]

That seems paradoxical: Does not the consolidation, in contradistinction to Jewish self-renunciation, have the character of Jewish self-reflection, of the return and retreat to Judaism? Does it not have the *restitutio in integrum* as its aim? Is not the integrity of Judaism the guiding thought of the Jewish movement?

In order to recognize the European determination of the consolidation process, one need only look at the 3 steps of this process in a row.

1. *Political Zionism*. People as a natural group of human beings, which is held together by a common enemy; national association as an imperative of *honor*. *Difference from the tradition*: Pinsker's[6] motive. Trust in oneself versus trust in God (not: power vs. spirit).
2. *Cultural Zionism*. Jewish tradition turns into the stuff of a European behavior: Jewish humanism. Ahad Ha'am[7] and Hegel. *Difference from the tradition*: not revelation but development.
3. *Return to the Law*. Rosenzweig[8] and Elective Affinities.[9] *Difference*: *the Law as such*. In principle: European *reservations* against the tradition (Cohen, The Social Ideal)[10]—or renunciation of European *prejudices*. In either case: the situation of the present matters to us.

[4] Ger.: *Duckmäuserei*. Or: hypocrisy.

[5] Ger.: *europäisch bedingt*.

[6] Leo Pinsker (1821–91). See his *Autoemancipation* (1882) in *The Zionist Idea: A Historical Analysis and Reader*, ed. Arthur Hertzberg (New York: Harper & Row, 1959), 181–98. Cf. *LSEW* 104.

[7] Ahad Ha'am, pen name of Asher Hirsch Ginsberg (1856–1927), the "founder of cultural Zionism" (Strauss, Preface to *SCR*, in *JPCM* 144–45 with 341, 355n41). See Ahad Ha'am's address to the First Zionist Congress (1897), in *JWM* 541–43. Cf. *LSEW* 81, 119, 131, 203–4.

[8] See note 3 of appendix B.

[9] Ger.: *die Wahlverwandtschaften*. That is, the title of Goethe's novel. Rosenzweig understands the term to mean "the maze of *feeling*" in contrast to "the maze of action" (the emphasis is Rosenzweig's); see *Franz Rosenzweig: His Life and Thought*, ed. Nahum N. Glatzer (2nd ed.; New York: Schocken Books, 1963), 13. Cf. Strauss, Preface to *SCR*, in *JPCM* 153.

[10] Hermann Cohen (1842–1919): "in the middle of World War I, the greatest representative of German Jewry and spokesman for it, the most powerful figure among the German professors of philosophy of his time, stated his view on Jerusalem and Athens in a lecture entitled 'The Social Ideal in Plato and the Prophets'" (Strauss, JA, in *JPCM* 398–99); see Cohen, "Das soziale Ideal bei Platon und den Propheten," *Hermann Cohens Jüdische Schriften* (3 vols.; Berlin: C. A. Schwetschke & Sohn, 1924), I, 306–30. Cf. *LSEW* 76, 107, 109–10, 112–14, 134, 139–73, 216, etc.; Strauss, Preface to *SCR*, in *JPCM* 154, 158–59, and "Introductory Essay to Hermann Cohen, *Religion of Reason Out of the Sources of Judaism*," in *JPCM* 267–82; and chapter 4 of the present volume.

What does the intellectual situation of the present matter to us Jews? It matters to us insofar as the present situation of Judaism matters to us; for the present situation of Judaism is at the same time determined by Judaism's past, by Jewish history *and* by the present world situation. The determination of the Jewish situation at any given time by two factors—by Judaism and by the world—has existed at least for as long as we have lived in the Galut.[11] Determination by the second factor has considerably *intensified*, so much that it has *changed* fundamentally since the beginning of the age of assimilation and the *dissolution* of the Jewish tradition dating from this age. Now, in the last decades, the **{443}** dissolution process has been countered by the attempt at a *consolidation* of the setting of Jewish life,[12] by Zionism in particular. But no one who knows this attempt from seeing for himself and does not judge it by its surface can fail to see that it is by dint of *European* thoughts and demands that the consolidation of Judaism is being attempted in our time. For example, it may be true—though in the end it is not as true as most people believe—that Jewish socialism has its origin in the demands and promises of the Prophets: this socialism would not have been able to receive its present form without the authoritative influence of European ideas. *The consolidation of the setting of Jewish life is no less determined in a European manner*[13] *than is the dissolution of Jewish tradition preceding it.* That seems paradoxical. Is not this consolidation precisely the consequence of Jewish self-reflection in contrast to Jewish self-renunciation in the age of assimilation?

Now this determination can be evaluated in various ways. One can say: we have *learned* many things from Europe in the last 150 years, much that is dubious, but nevertheless also a few things of undoubted value; that is, we have learned a few things that we could not have learned from the Jewish tradition; we thereby have certain *reservations* vis-à-vis the Jewish tradition, *European* reservations; what ensues accordingly is this demand: that the consolidation of the setting of Jewish life be carried out in a manner that takes into account these reservations that cannot be renounced; and for just that reason we must be concerned with Europe.

One thing about this view[14] cannot be disputed: it is *upright*; it does not make the task comfortable for itself; it does not smuggle in foreign elements under the cover of the Jewish flag, that is, by the use of biblical and talmudic passages torn out of context. But it causes a certain unease, since it is alarmingly reminiscent of the view of *Reform*[15] that wanted to renew Judaism by making it up-to-date and that thereby only rendered Judaism hollow and sentimental. Over and against all attempts at Reform, the argument of S. R. Hirsch[16] will always remain victorious—that it would be contradictory to measure the eternal by standards of time.

[11] Heb.: Exile.

[12] Ger.: *jüdischen Lebenszusammenhangs.*

[13] Ger.: *europäisch bedingt.*

[14] [Note in the margin:] Example Cohen's "The Social Ideal in Plato and the Prophets" {HM}

[15] That is, the "reformation of Judaism sought by enlightened Jews [comprising] not simply a diminution of the ritual burdens of the Jew but also an elimination or, at least, a blurring of the ethnic and national features of traditional Judaism" (*JWM* 156).

[16] Samson Raphael Hirsch (1808–88), German rabbi and intellectual founder of neo-Orthodoxy. See his "Religion Allied to Progress" (1854) and "A Sermon on the Science of Judaism" (1855) in *JMW* 197–202, 234–35. Cf. CaM 184n58–58, with APT n58 as supplemented in *LSMC* 603n58.

Let us make these facts a bit clearer to ourselves. The Jewish **{444}** problem, whose urgency in the age of National Socialism scarcely needs proof, forced out of Herzl[17] the idea of the Jewish national state, which then, simply for reasons of realistic politics, was altered into the idea of the Jewish national home in Palestine. Herzl imagined this state as being exactly like a European state. But whereas in European states the national state idea was indissolubly connected with the national culture—I recall the significance of the French Revolution for the original French nationalism, and of France's Catholic tradition for today's French nationalism—merely political Zionism lacked that sort of native soil: Herzl's Palestine was in Ahad Ha'am's opinion nothing else than a Jewish Liberia. Thus Zionism was led from being merely political Zionism to being cultural Zionism, the demand for national culture, and that means: the care and development of the Jewish tradition came to be accepted. Now, no one could overlook that things are different with Jewish culture than with the cultures of other peoples. Jewish culture is identical with learning and fulfilling the Law. Thus many cultural Zionists were led to acceptance of the Law and submission to the Law, and so Zionism was getting ever closer to Jewish tradition. There arose the possibility that European reservations vis-à-vis the Jewish tradition were no longer even possible and necessary: *the integrity of* Judaism seemed to become possible again.

Now there is something awkward about acceptance of the Law by cultural Zionism, since according to the view of Jewish tradition Jewish Law is a Law given by God. Were the Law to prescribe only actions and prohibitions, it could in the end be fulfilled also by unbelievers; but it also and especially prescribes prayers: how should he pray who does not believe in God? The atheistic Zionist is hence confronted with the question, *why* does he not believe in God? Since the unbelief of a Jew in our time is nothing else than the general unbelief, the atheistic Zionist, in any case, sees himself compelled to concern himself with the intellectual situation of the present.

But not only he. Those Jews of our time who took an active part in the consolidation process, who in this way came to **{445}** accept the Law and who have not been driven mad by the difficulty of believing in God, conceive of the Law differently than the Jewish tradition. I recall the outstanding man of this group, Franz Rosenzweig, who reproaches Jewish orthodoxy for de facto having granted priority to prohibitions over commands (e.g., with respect to שבת);[18] in contrast, he wants to regard prohibitions only as the other side of commands. In his struggle against the rigidity of the Law, he goes so far as to want to dissolve entirely the distinction between *minhag* and *din*.[19]

The question concerning the intellectual situation of the present is *ambiguous*: it can be understood in a way that is matter-of-fact or in a way that is vain; it can

[17]Theodor Herzl (1860–1904), father of political Zionism, founder of the World Zionist Organization, and author of *Der Judenstaat* (*The Jews' State*; 1896). See his "A Solution of the Jewish Question," in *JMW* 533–38. Cf. *LSEW* 81, 83–87, 102, 119, 128, 203, with the editor's note at 82n2.

[18]Heb.: *shabbos*. That is, "Sabbath," transliterated according to the Ashkenazic (Germanic) pronunciation.

[19]Heb.: custom ... law. See, for example, *Franz Rosenzweig*, ed. Glatzer, 233–47; cf. Strauss, Preface to *SCR*, in *JPCM* 153.

serve the seriousness of self-reflection or the frivolousness of self-satisfaction and self-assurance. We want to come to a rather drastic distinction between the serious and the vain question concerning the intellectual situation of the present. We begin *prior* to this distinction: we pretend as if the question were *not* ambiguous.

Let us suppose then that this question is straightforward—it is however *not natural*. In order to see this, one need only consider the following: at any time there existed an "intellectual situation of the present"; but no one concerned himself with it; no one ever knew *that* there was an "intellectual situation of the present." Thoughtful people concerned themselves with the eternal; and the temporal—the temporal that was important from [the point of view of] the eternal and for the sake of the eternal was never the present but rather the past, the *old*: what was founded in the past and has lasted for a long time has stood the test of time; and what has stood the test of time has the opinion going for it that it is true. In contrast, the present, the new, is held to be suspect; it is only for a brief while, it is brief, short-lived, a momentary ripple not worth one's attention. In recalling this earlier way of thinking one understands that interest in the intellectual situation of the present is not *natural* to man but is tied to certain *historical* conditions, that it really is something *of the present*. Thus we get our first answer to the question about the *intellectual situation of the present*: this situation *is characterized* **{446}** *by the question about it*. If, then, we wish to understand the intellectual situation of the present, we must ask: *why* does the whole world today ask about the intellectual situation of the present?

This question cannot be settled by the statement: well, we live *today*, and therefore what happens today is of greater importance for us than what happened in the past. This answer is justified regarding all practical tasks, small and large. If I want to buy myself a hat, then what matters to me are the present hat designs and the present hat prices only; if someone wants to get married, then what matters to him are the provisions of the German Civil Code only and he does not need to take an interest in Roman law or the Code of Hammurabi; what interests the statesman is only the present constellation of powers, etc., etc. But if one asks about the *principles* of action, about *the* right and good, then it is conceivable that here it would be extremely dubious to let oneself become involved with the present: namely, assuming that the present were an age of decline. Why then do we inquire today about the intellectual situation of the present *as a matter of principle*[20]—and not for instance about the intellectual situation of the biblical time or of the Greek golden age?

One need only ask the question in this form in order to already have the answer: were these ages for us still the classic ages, the authoritative ages, then *they* would be at the center of our interest. But precisely this is characteristic of our age: that the old *traditions*—the tradition of the Bible and the tradition of Greek philosophy—have lost their power. The 17th and 18th centuries, the Age of *Enlightenment*, has won *freedom from all tradition*. The fact that a particular doctrine or institution can invoke, be it the Bible, be it Plato or Aristotle, no longer compels us.

The Enlightenment won the freedom from traditions by fighting the traditions in the name of the *principles* of the tradition: it fought against Aristotelian-scholastic

[20] Ger.: *in prinzipieller Absicht*.

science in the name of the Greek principle of science; it fought against the intolerance of Judaism and Christianity in the name of the biblical principle of love of one's neighbor. The 19th century radicalized this fight of the Enlightenment: it challenged the *principles* of the tradition; it called into question science as such and love of neighbor as such; it tore down the *pillars* on which the European world is built. This decisive act, this *completion* **{447}** *of the Enlightenment*, is tied and will always remain tied to the name of Friedrich *Nietzsche*.

Not only the traditions but the principles of the tradition were called into question by Nietzsche. The freedom of thinking that had been won by the Enlightenment, the freedom to think the opposite of what the Middle Ages had thought has become infinitely exceeded; we are *completely free*. But free *for what*? Have the principles of the tradition been replaced by other binding principles? Not at all. We therefore do not *know* at all *what* we are free *for*, what we live for, what the right and good are according to which we can be at peace with ourselves. *Our freedom is the freedom of radical ignorance.* The intellectual situation of the present is characterized by our knowing nothing anymore, by our knowing nothing.

Out of the recognition and admission of this ignorance grows the necessity of *questioning*, questioning about the right and good. And here the following paradox presents itself: while the present is as *compelled to question as any age, it is less capable of questioning than any age*. We *must* question without being *capable* of questioning. From this embarrassment arises the question concerning the intellectual situation of the present.

If someone says today that the first and most urgent question is the question concerning the right life and that this question must be answered by reason, that is, scientifically, then the present confronts him with the verdict: this question cannot be answered by scientific means; the answer to this question can be only a *value judgment*, and value judgments cannot be justified and cannot be refuted by scientific means; they rest on will or on belief, on the free decision of the person. Since that is so, a universally binding knowledge about the right life is not possible—there exists at bottom a "polytheism of values." The *de facto anarchy* is thus *claimed* to be necessary and thereby consolidated.

I do not have the possibility here of proving with the requisite thoroughness the untenability of this utterly unphilosophical view, that is, a view that cuts off the real question. This proof would be identical with a radical critique of the life's work of Max Weber.[21] Here I would prefer only to recall two points. 1) The concept of "value judgment" presupposes that there are judgments that are not value judgments—hence properly scientific judgments; it is in this sense that value-free science mattered to Weber. Now it is not **{448}** that difficult to show that Weber's science, which he intended to be value-free, is wholly conditioned by his value judgments; these are the ultimate presuppositions of his scientific research. 2) Now Weber has in no way shirked the clarification of these presuppositions; on the contrary: his whole scientific life's work aims precisely at this clarification, that is, the understanding of its presuppositions from their history; thereby he provided himself with an altogether different basis than a merely personal decision.

[21] Cf. "Conspectivism" (appendix A), note 40.

In principle: the "free decision of the person" that does not want to depend on any justification "does not take place in a vacuum." It is conditioned by the *history* in which the person concerned stands. The knowledge of man's being conditioned by the history that is *his* history is called *historical consciousness*. The historical consciousness that develops into historical *science* is the closest counterauthority against the ruling anarchy: as science, historical science makes possible universal validity.

But as it happens, historical consciousness is just that factor that thwarts the question concerning the right life. For if man is essentially historical, then there is not *the* right life; but each age, each historical situation has *its* "right life," *its* ideal of life. *Therefore* we cannot ask about *the* right life, but only about *our* right life, about the ideal of life that is *up-to-date*,[22] the right life of the *present*. But how to know what ideal of life is the one suitable to the present? That is possible only if the *situation* of the present is known.

We began from the fact that the intellectual life of the present is characterized by the *question* concerning the intellectual situation of the present. We asked about the *reason*[23] for this question. The reason for this question is the necessity to ask about the right life. Under the presuppositions of historical consciousness the question concerning the right life *compels* us *to ask the question concerning the intellectual situation of the present.*

Because man is essentially historical, there are no eternal principles, no eternal ideal of life. One can thus not ask about *the* ideal of life, but only, at best, about the present ideal of life. In order to determine the present ideal of life, one must know the present *situation*. The present situation is known in the life of the present, which we grasp above all in the intellectual productions of the present. **{449}**

Now, these productions themselves, however, have the character—explicitly or implicitly—of answers to the question concerning *the*—or rather concerning the present—ideal of life. And these answers are all in contradiction with one another. The situation of the present—it consists in the *contradictions* of the present. That is why one can only extract a unified ideal of life from the situation of the present if these contradictions can be resolved in the form of a higher unity: the present ideal of life would be the *synthesis* of these actual answers that are effective today. But such a synthesis is impossible. What is the higher synthesis supposed to be in which Marx's and Nietzsche's ideal of life—the conviction that exploitation is bad in itself and the conviction that the abolition[24] of exploitation is the abolition of life—could be unified? Or how is a synthesis of capitalism and communism imaginable? Whoever proposes a synthesis here is confusing synthesis with compromise.

But even granted that a synthesis of the answers effective at present were possible, it is a question whether this synthesis would disclose for us the *real* situation of the present. For if all of today's positions *are mistaken about a basic character of the present situation*, then this fundamental defect cannot be disposed of by the synthesis of these positions: on the contrary, a synthesis would only reinforce this defect.

[22] Ger.: *zeitgemäß*.

[23] Ger.: *Grund*.

[24] Ger.: *Aufhebung*.

Allegedly, the situation of the present is knowable from the present positions. How does one recognize that a position is a present one? Surely not by its being represented in a writing published in 1932. Even now books still appear that are written from the standpoint of Thomas Aquinas, from a standpoint, that is, that no one will so easily describe as being a present one. In order to recognize a standpoint *as* a present one, one must already have a guiding idea of the present. And this guiding idea can be gained only from the knowledge of the entire historical process out of which the present comes. In any case, the situation of the present cannot be known *from* the present.

What is present may be said only on the basis of a knowledge of the entire course of history. Now, this course is open to extremely different interpretations. Which of these interpretations is the right one? There seem to be as many possibilities as there are present positions. If the anarchy of present positions is not **{450}** overcome,[25] then the question of which interpretation of the entire course of history is the right one cannot be answered. And since we can determine the situation of the present only if we can answer this question, *the situation of the present is not determinable, not knowable.*

Allegedly, the situation of the present is knowable from the entirety of positions effective in the present. Why from *all* these positions? Because they are equivalent. Why are they equivalent? Because each one sees facts that are not seen or seen only vaguely by the others. But obviously it is not seeing everything equally clearly that is important—but seeing clearly what is important and vaguely what is not important. For if one position looks at the world from the frog's perspective and another looks at it from the bird's perspective, there is surely no doubt which of these positions takes priority. I must therefore already know beforehand which facts are important. But this presupposes that I know what is important. But if I know this, then I know which life is the right one, and I do not need to ask about the situation of the present at all.

Now as it happens, the reason why we ask about the situation of the present is the fact that we do not know what is right. And it turns out that the question concerning the situation of the present cannot be answered. Thus the question concerning what is right cannot be answered at all. Thus the radical ignorance remains and must remain. We are thus condemned to live without orientation; that is, we cannot live at all. Let us attempt to determine this inability of ours to live more exactly.

The intellectual situation of the present is determined by the historical consciousness. This means that eternal, unconditional principles of living are not recognized: all that is left are conditional, precisely historically conditioned principles. Now, in our world, fundamentally different historical principles are effective, but these can now no longer be summed up in *one* universally binding, eternal order: the polytheism of values, *anarchy*, rules. Now the fact cannot be completely forgotten that in earlier times eternal, unconditional principles knowable to reason *itself*, and hence an order, were held to be possible and necessary.

[25] Ger.: *aufgehoben*. Cf. the previous note.

This belief is now considered *naive*: we know based on a radical *reflection* that rational knowledge about *the* right is not possible. Being more radically reflective, we are *superior* to the past. **{451}** Do we not *thus* have knowledge as an unconditional standard? No; for we merely say: *if* knowledge is the ideal of life, then the more radical knowledge is preferable to the more naive knowledge; but *that* knowledge is the ideal of life is itself historically conditioned. In fact, conditioned by the European tradition founded by the Greeks. In the non-European worlds there are completely different ideals of life, and it is impossible for us to hold these worlds to be inferior to us on account of their naivety. Hence the result: historical consciousness leads to the awareness of superiority over the European past and the awareness of the complete equality of non-European ideals; and in many cases: contempt for the European past and prostration before everything exotic. Now, it is natural to man to treasure and *cultivate* what is his own, what is handed down to him by his forebears, whereas he *confronts* what is foreign proudly, suspiciously, cautiously, at most with respect and admiration. Measured by this natural stance, the stance dominant in Europe today appears to be antinatural, *perverse*. Our inability to live, which manifests itself in our inability to question, is our unnaturalness, the unnaturalness of our world.

Nonetheless we, too, are still in a certain way natural beings. And even if, in this respect, we had to despair in the face of ourselves, the fact that even today children are generated naturally and born naturally could reassure us. And even if these children become corrupted soon enough by the dominant unnaturalness, there yet remains the hope, so long as there are human beings on the earth, that some day human beings will be able to be natural again.

We, too, are still natural beings. That we are still natural shows itself in the fact that we, confronted with the ignorance of what is right, escape into the *question* concerning what is right—escape from the unnaturalness of our situation. The *need* to know, and therefore the questioning, is the best guarantee that we are still natural beings, humans—but that we *are not capable of* questioning is the clear symptom of our being threatened in our humanity in a way that humans have never been threatened.

Under the presupposition of historical consciousness, the question concerning the right life compels us to ask the question concerning the intellectual situation of the present. Since *this* question cannot be answered, then the question concerning **{452}** the right life seems no longer answerable. Should it be answerable, this would be possible only by *calling historical consciousness into question*. But is this not a fantastic undertaking? *How* may historical consciousness be called into question? By recognizing basically this: historical consciousness is itself historically conditioned, therefore itself destined to give way to another consciousness. There is a world, that is, a real, historical world beyond historical consciousness. That this possibility exists *in principle* no one will dispute. But, it will be said, this world is the barbarism that awaits us no matter what; historical consciousness will go away if humanity unlearns what it has learned arduously enough over the past centuries; the renunciation of historical consciousness is identical with the relapse into a stage of lesser reflection.

Let us pause here for a moment. Historical consciousness is—one cannot emphasize this strongly enough—according to its own view a stage of higher awareness: we know *more* than the earlier generations; we know more deeply, more profoundly, than the earlier ones that everything human is historically conditioned. But as it happens historical consciousness is the reason why, although we are compelled to question, we are incapable of questioning. *Thus* we are more incapable of questioning than the earlier generations—since we know more, since we know too much. But we are compelled to question since at bottom we know *nothing*. Being fundamentally *ignorant we cannot come to knowledge since we know too much*. Since we *believe* we know too much. We will not be able to remove our radical ignorance until this belief that we know is abolished.

Historical consciousness includes in itself the conviction that we stand at a higher stage of reflection than earlier human beings: we regard ourselves as having *progressed*. Now there are without question many men especially today who are of the opinion that our age is an age of decline. But precisely such men are mostly of the opinion that the character of decline of our time has its reason in our being too conscious, that in our time knowledge plays a role not allotted to it in healthy times; precisely such men usually believe that there are opportunities for coming to knowledge as there have never been before (Spengler);[26] they are of the opinion that precisely *because* today it is twilight, the owl of Minerva could begin its flight. That we have progressed is quite the dominant opinion. **{453}**

But how do things really stand concerning our progressiveness? Our progressiveness could only be the result of the modern development. Let us therefore question the history of this development.

The modern centuries are dominated by the pathos of progress in knowledge and through knowledge. At the beginning of the modern development stands the fight against scholastic science. This science was stagnating; it essentially did nothing other than transmit and explain Aristotle. Regarding physics, within which the fight primarily took place, the founders of modern philosophy and physics were astonished at the fact that the Scholastic philosophers investigated not nature but—Aristotle. (Cremonini.)[27] This was possible only because Scholasticism presupposed explicitly or implicitly that science was essentially completed: one did not see a *possibility* of advancing; one did *not* have *the intention* of advancing; one *did not have confidence* in advancing. Modern philosophy begins with the completely opposite intention: plus ultra. One can illustrate this opposition in the following manner. Science emerged with the Greeks in an age of civic flourishing, as a concern of free citizens; it had its center in the city of Athens, of whose citizens Thucydides writes that they are always ready to *hope*, always anxious to discover something new—as opposed to the Lacedaemonians, who regard science with mistrust, who are *not* hopeful, little confident in their ability, holding on to the old. Scholastic science was (at least in Christendom) pursued by monks. The newer philosophy is once again

[26] Oswald Spengler (1880–1936), *Der Untergang des Abendlands* [*The Decline of the West*] (1918); cf. PoR 100.

[27] Cesare Cremonini (1550–1631). Prolific expositor of Aristotle; accused of Averroism.

the concern of free citizens, who, as once were the Athenians, were ready to hope and keen to do something new again. Full of self-confidence did one thus confront classical philosophy; it was not long until a dispute began about the superiority of the moderns over the ancients. In any case, the unimaginable revolutions in the natural sciences proved that a progress beyond classical science was possible and real. It is a question, however, whether this progress was a fundamental progress, a progress in the foundation. If one turns with this question to the modern *philosophers*, then all will answer that also in philosophy the moderns got further than the ancients. And this getting further is indeed quite evident; for assuming equal effort and equal seriousness, must not **{454}** science also progress with the progressing of time?

Certainly so, if one assumes in addition the same starting-point.

In contrast to this predominant awareness of progress and progressiveness in the more recent centuries, however, stands the fact that in these centuries the conviction of the *authoritative significance of the Greeks* keeps breaking through. From this point of view, the fight against the Middle Ages appears as an attempt to recover Greek freedom, Greek science. At the beginning of modern philosophy stands the Renaissance, the renaissance of *antiquity*. In fact, the fight against the Scholastics is in considerable part conducted in *the* manner of opposing *genuine* Greek science—whether it be Aristotle himself, or Plato, or Democritus and Epicurus—to the *corrupt* Greek science of Scholasticism.

Now, one can say: this *counter*-movement is always a misunderstanding or only a device or a subsequent corrective of the *real* movement, which is a movement of *progress*. This remark is surely justified within certain limits—namely, insofar as one keeps to the *explicit consciousness* of the newer centuries. But if one looks at what went on *in reality*, then one gets a different impression.

Even the fiercest opponents of the Greeks believed themselves able to put into effect the progress they had in mind only after they had laid the foundation for it by a *return*, namely, by a return to *nature*. Rousseau's call to *return* to nature, which has become part of our collective memory, is only *one* example of that and not even the best one. The reversionary character of modern philosophy shows itself much more fundamentally in the fact that is decisive for the whole span of the 17th and 18th centuries: in the *fight against prejudices* that fills these centuries. The word "prejudice" is indeed the Enlightenment's polemical keyword—it is met with so to speak on every page of every writing of the Enlightenment. One must *free* oneself from prejudices, and this freeing is accomplished by *retreating* to a plane, or even a point, from which one can finally free progress of prejudice once and for all.

Today's reader of a writing from the Age of Enlightenment **{455}** in which prejudices are fought so fiercely will often have to smile when he realizes just how strong were the prejudices of the supposedly prejudice-free gentlemen of the Enlightenment. One could even say: the century of the Enlightenment was the century of prejudices. We today are therefore very cautious in the use of the word "prejudice." *Historical consciousness* has corrected us in that it is not possible for man to live prejudice-free: every age has *its* prejudices; and the fight against prejudices *as such* always only means the fight against the prejudices of *others*—for with one's own prejudices there is the awkwardness of not being able to know them *as* prejudices. If then only historical consciousness has set us straight about the universal significance of the category of "prejudice," the *overcoming*[28] *of historical consciousness* would bring with it the *overcoming of the universal significance of "prejudice."*

With respect to questioning historical consciousness it was said: if everything human is historical, then historical consciousness is also historical; that is, destined at some time to be no more. This historical conditionality of historical consciousness can be demonstrated concretely by the category of "prejudice."

The *word* "prejudice" is older than modern philosophy—but only in the Age of Enlightenment does it achieve *authoritative* significance. What Greek philosophy fought against was opinion or appearance, not prejudice. (However, νόμωι φύσει.)[29] How did "prejudice" get this authoritative significance in the Age of the Enlightenment?

About this we receive a remarkable piece of information from a famous scholastic of the 12th century. This philosopher cites in an important context an enumeration by Alexander of Aphrodisias of the reasons for the differences of opinion in philosophy, for the difficulties of philosophizing. 3 reasons are dealt with there, which all express the *natural* difficulties of philosophizing, that is, such difficulties as exist *always*, at *all* times where human beings philosophize. Now, this scholar adds to this enumeration the following words:

> In our time there exists a fourth reason, which he (*sc.*, Alexander of Aphrodisias) did not mention, since it did not exist among them; namely, *habit* and *schooling*; for human beings by nature love what they are habituated to and incline to it...this happens to man regarding the opinions in **{456}** which he has grown up: he loves them and holds on to them and stays away from differing opinions. For this reason as well, therefore, man is prevented from knowing the truth. This happens to the multitude regarding God's corporeality...due to habituation in the *writings* in which one firmly believes and to which one is habituated, whose literal meaning seems to indicate God's corporeality.[30]

Now surely there were many Greek writings in which the gods were presented corporeally. Why did these writings not compromise Greek philosophy? It is therefore not being accustomed to writings in general, not having grown up in a tradition in general, but rather being accustomed to *very specific* writings, having grown up in a tradition of a *very specific* character: namely, in a tradition possessing an *authority* as *unconditional* as that of the *tradition of revealed religions*. The fact that a tradition based on revelation entered the world of philosophy increased the *natural* difficulties of philosophizing by adding the *historical* difficulty.

In other words: The natural difficulties of philosophizing have their classical depiction in Plato's allegory of the cave. The historical difficulty may be illustrated by saying: there *now* exists another cave *beneath* the Platonic cave.

The Enlightenment's whole fight against prejudices is in a sense sketched and thus anticipated in the cited statement from the 12th century. The statement sheds a

[28] Ger.: Aufhebung.

[29] Gk.: by convention, by nature.

[30] Maimonides, *Guide of the Perplexed* I 31.

new light on this fight: the Enlightenment's fight against prejudices did not have the absolute meaning that the Enlightenment itself attached to it; and not because man always has and must have prejudices, but precisely the reverse, because prejudices in the strict sense of the word are only the "prejudices" of the revealed religions. This implies that the fight against prejudices has reached its end only when revealed religion has been called into question in its foundation and in its consequences.

If then the Enlightenment's fight against prejudices is only the fight against *the* historical difficulty of philosophizing, then the true goal of this fight is only: the recovery of philosophizing in its natural difficulty, of natural philosophizing, that is, of Greek philosophy. **{457}**

[Draft of an Alternative Introduction]

Preliminary Remark

We are all convinced that there is an unambiguous distinction between good and bad; therefore also between virtue and vice. Hence we distinguish between virtuous and vicious actions with the confidence of sleepwalkers. We are so sure of this distinction that we are even able to distinguish between virtuous and vicious *topics*. It is virtuous, say, to examine the questions of the sources of the collected Hippocratic writings or the connection between Hellenistic philosophy and the formation of Islamic sects; it is *still* virtuous if one grasps how Plato presents his teacher Socrates, or if one reconstructs a whole philosophical system from meager relics. To speak about vicious topics in public is not unobjectionable. Let it only be said that among the vicious topics there is nothing more vicious than the one we want to talk about tonight: the intellectual situation of the present. The proof of this is that a true scholar[31] will never occupy himself with this question in his capacity as scholar; the scholar knows that making a conjecture or finding evidence of filiation is a much greater blessing than occupying himself with things that may be more interesting, but that can only be talked about vaguely. If scholars are the embodiment of virtue, then writers[32] are the embodiment of vice. What we are attempting tonight is thus writer-like. And that is so by necessity. Imagine, if you please, that someone wanted to speak about the intellectual situation in the 14th century. In order to do this in the right manner, he would have to have studied for years; he would have to have become a specialist in the 14th century. Since without a doubt infinitely *more* is being written today than in the 14th century, how many years would someone have to have studied the intellectual situation of the present in order to be capable of treating it in a scholarly way. I have to confess for my part that I am far from being a specialist in the present. I am not embarrassed to say that I have never read nor heard a word by either Graf Keyserlingk or Margarete Susmann.[33] Not only will my claims often lack a sufficient material foundation—the claims will also often appear to you as in themselves confused **{458}** or otherwise defective. I am herewith asking for your indulgence.

[31] See note 3.

[32] Ger.: *Literaten*.

[33] See "Conspectivism" (appendix A), p. 219.

But why talk about such a matter at all, a matter that appears not to allow for scholarly treatment? Well—even the most virtuous man occasionally has the need to take a break from his virtue. Or, to say it less frivolously: it is good for even the most respectable scholar to put the books aside for once and do some thinking like a simple man of the people. Whatever he comes up with then does not need to be right, it does not need to be more than a reasonable conjecture; but it may be useful for his respectable work nonetheless.

Presupposing historical consciousness, the question concerning what is right compels the question concerning the situation of the present. Is this path *really* necessary? If all human thinking is in itself historical, then it has been arranged that we—when *we*, that is, men of *this* present world asking about what is right *as such*, believe we have found what is right *as such*—have thereby eo ipso found the answer that corresponds to our world, the *present* ideal of life. We cannot escape the *fate* of historicity—but we need not be concerned about that in our thought.

Fate as Principle

Historical consciousness must no longer be the *principle*. In what sense must historical consciousness be called into question? Insofar as it leads to the question concerning the situation of the present. It leads to this question only insofar as it is made the *principle* of questioning, insofar as it wants to be more than knowledge of the conditions and the fates of questioning.

Now, this path is in no way necessary. If everything human is in itself historically conditioned, then, without our needing to concern ourselves about it, it has been arranged that in searching for *the* ideal of life we are bound to find only the one that corresponds to our world, to the present, the *present* ideal of life. If everything human is itself historical, then *for just that reason* we do not need to be concerned with the historicity of our question. It is not the knowledge of historicity as such that leads to the explicit question concerning the present ideal of life and therefore concerning the situation of the present, but *incorporating* the knowledge of historicity, [i.e.,] historical consciousness, into the **{459}** question, making it the element, the presupposition, the *principle* of the question—when this knowledge in fact pertains only to the conditions and fates of questioning. But if the primary question of the human being who does not live in a binding given order is the question concerning a binding reasonable order, it is this *question* alone that must primarily occupy him and not the fate and the condition of this question. And only if it turns out that he cannot answer this primary question of his without considering the conditions and fates—*then and only then* does his historicity matter to him. That he needs this *detour*, however, must be demonstrated; it is not at all self-evident. Of course, we cannot avoid this detour today. Why that is the case, I will attempt to show, by[34]

[34] Here Strauss's draft of an alternative introduction breaks off in mid-sentence.

[Plan of the Lecture in Draft]

1. The disreputability of the topic—the scholar adjusts his ambition to speaking only on topics with respect to which, as far as knowledge of the material and its intellectual penetration are concerned, he can step forth as if clad in iron armor. At least I for my part do not at all have the reassuring awareness—here no one can damage or hurt me, here I am a first-class expert—concerning the topic I am going to speak about tonight. Nevertheless it appears to me permissible to speak about it. For the iron armor of scholarship in each case clads a being scarcely made of iron, a human being who doubts. Not to voice these doubts because they themselves are unclear, as are the speculations that [come] from concerning oneself with these doubts[35]
2. Why does the situation of the present matter to us Jews? → Impossibility of understanding "Law." Reservations and prejudices.
3. a) Question *ambiguous*
   b) Question not *natural* but *historical.*
   c) Situation of the present characterized by the question concerning it. Why? Why not concerning situation in biblical time or Greek golden age?
   d) Destruction of the power of the tradition by the Enlightenment: **{460}** Enlightenment fights traditions in the name of the principles of the tradition.
   e) Nietzsche calls the principles into question: we are *totally* free. But for what?
   f) No binding principles any more. Radical ignorance, necessity of questioning.
   g) Being compelled to question as any age, we are less capable of questioning than any age.
   i) "Value judgments" not scientifically justifiable (according to Weber).—Free decision of the person, anarchy—does not take place in a vacuum, however, but is conditioned by *history. Historical consciousness*—seems to guarantee the overcoming[36] of anarchy.
   k) Meanwhile historical consciousness makes the question concerning the right life impossible—at best the *present* ideal of life → question concerning the intellectual situation of the present. Therefore: *situation of the present characterized by historical consciousness.*
   l) This question not capable of being answered. Hence no orientation, and consequently no life: we are incapable of living.
   m) Perversion and unnaturalness. But nevertheless we are *natural* beings—in that we *question.* Natural beings threatened in our naturalness by an unnatural world.

[35] [The text breaks off here in the middle of the line. LS has left blank a space of two lines to the next period and has noted in the left margin:] *Duckmäuserei in dem Nichtbehandeln des Themas* [cowardice/hypocrisy in the non-treatment of the topic] {HM}

[36] Ger.: *Überwindung.*

[37] Ger.: *aufgehoben.*

n) Our unnaturalness shows itself to us in [the form of] historical consciousness insofar as this is understood in the way that it leads to the question concerning the situation of the present. Therefore: division of historical consciousness.
o) Possibility of this division in principle: but not relapse into barbarism? Thus: historical consciousness has *progressed* when compared to *naive* consciousness. That is: *Being fundamentally ignorant we cannot come to knowledge since we know too much, believe* we know too much. If, then, we are therefore to come to *knowledge*, then this belief in knowing must be overcome.[37] *Historical consciousness must be overcome insofar as it means: it itself constitutes as such a* superior *manner of knowing.*
p) How do things really stand concerning our progressiveness? While the progressive tendency is primary, modern philosophy is always characterized by a countermovement—and not only as a condition independent of it, but as its condition proper.—State of *nature. Liberation from prejudices.* The meaning[38] of modern philosophy must be understood in light of this *fundamental* intention **{461}** of this philosophy.
q) "Prejudice" and historical consciousness.
   i) Historical consciousness can be interpreted by means of the category of "prejudice".
   ii) Prejudice a historical category.
   RMbM[39] citation
r) Natural and historical difficulties of philosophizing—the meaning of the fight against prejudices is liberation from the historical difficulties. First and second cave.
s) Modern philosophy's self-interpretation as progress hides this meaning completely. It leads to a continuous erosion of the tradition, in accordance with the intention of the reversionary tendency, while it leads at the same time to the consolidation of a new tradition—the modern tradition. A process of destruction that passes itself off as a process of construction.
t) *Finally* one stands at the foundation of the tradition—one stands at the starting-point of the questioning from which the tradition has arisen—without knowing it, or in any case, without drawing the consequences from it.
   Nietzsche's significance: Socratic question is not posed seriously, but is cut off by a dictate. Inner lack of clarity: Callicles[40] *and* intellect[41] (order of humanity).
u) In any case, Nietzsche has enabled us to understand the Socratic question again, to recognize it as *our* question. The Platonic dialogues are no longer *self-evident* for us—no longer self-evidently all right, no longer self-evidently wrong, surpassed, out of date, but we read them as if we were conducting them ourselves if we were capable of doing that.

[38] Ger.: *Sinn.* Likewise in subsections r) and s).
[39] That is, Maimonides. See note 8 of appendix B.
[40] Cf. Plato, *Gorgias* 481b–527e (esp. 482c–486d).
[41] Ger.: *Geist.*

But we are not capable of doing that, since all the concepts that we *are equipped with* derive from the modern tradition. *This is what* we have to know—*this is why* we have to concern ourselves with the intellectual situation of the present. The question betrays the awareness of the fact that the question concerning what is right can*not* be answered *without* being clear about our incapacity to question—but this question is fundamentally misguided if it is supposed to replace the real question.

The question concerning the intellectual situation of the present should serve **{462}** to awaken in us the willingness to come out of the cave of modernity—it is absurd if asked for its own sake: it would then amount to our describing the interior decor of the 2nd cave.

Historical consciousness has the function of leading us back to the natural questions. It is a self-misunderstanding of historical consciousness if it pretends to be a higher type of knowing.

v) *Plato and the Nomos and Revelation*

APPENDIX D

LEO STRAUSS: "A LOST WRITING OF FARÂBÎ'S" (1936)[1]

Translated by Gabriel Bartlett and Martin D. Yaffe

In an article that appeared in the last volume of JQR, I. Efros tries to show that "the second of the three parts of (Falaquera's) *Reshit hokmah*, entitled החלק השני במספר החכמות,[2] is a literal translation of the whole of Farâbî's important work known as the 'Encyclopedia'[3] or by its Arabic title as *Iḥṣâ al-'Ulûm*" (JQR, N.S., Vol. 25, p. 227).[4] This assertion is in need of considerable qualification, which Efros manifestly neglected to undertake only because the editions of *Iḥṣâ al-'ulûm* were not yet available to him.[5]

[1] ["Eine vermißte Schrift Farâbîs," *GS–2* 167–77, 614.] First published in *Monatsschrift für Geschichte und Wissenschaft des Judentums* (Breslau, 1936), 80th annum, volume 1 (January), 96–106. The essay came into being from a handwritten submission in November 1935. {HM}

The originally published edition uses "Farâbî" throughout, rather than the more accurate "Fârâbî." In a personal communication to the translators, Professor Heinrich Meier reports that Strauss did not correct the published spelling in the personal copy of the article in which he noted numerous remarks. For this reason, the translators have likewise retained "Farâbî" as Strauss's spelling throughout the article.

[2] Heb.: "The Second Part in the Enumeration of the Sciences."

[3] I.e., what is now known as his *The Enumeration of the Sciences*. For a brief description, see Charles Butterworth's introduction to the selection translated in Alfarabi, *The Political Writings: "Selected Aphorisms" and Other Texts*, trans. Butterworth (Ithaca, NY: Cornell University Press, 2001), 72f., or to that same selection as reprinted in *MPP–2* 18f. Strauss uses the then-received title *Encyclopedia* (or *Encyclopedia of the Sciences*) throughout.

[4] I.e., Israel Efros, "Palaquera's *Reshit Hokmah* and Alfarabi's *Iḥṣâ' al-'Ulum*," *Jewish Quarterly Review* n.s. 25 (London, 1934–35): 227–35.

[5] For the editions available to Strauss but not to Efros, see note 21.

Reshit Chokhmah II falls into nine chapters (more exactly, "parts"), *Iḥṣâ al-'ulûm* into an Introduction and five chapters. The correspondence is

Reshit Chokhmah II	*Iḥṣâ al-'ulûm*
Chap. 1	Introduction
Chap. 3	Chap. 1
Chap. 5	Chap. 2
Chap. 6	Chap. 3
Chap. 7–8	Chap. 4
Chap. 9	Chap. 5

As this list leads one to suspect and the examination of the texts themselves confirms, the second and fourth chapters of *R. Ch.* II are not borrowed from Farâbî's *Encyclopedia*. The same goes for not inconsiderable parts of all the remaining chapters. Not borrowed from Farâbî's *Encyclopedia* are:

in the 1st chapter: the 5th and 6th "uses" of the book (ed. David,[6] 21.2–19);

in the 3rd chapter: the explanation of שם, פעל and מדבק (24.8–27.20);[7] Falaquera himself says, in referring to this interpolation: וצריך שנבאר זה אע״פ שאין זה מכוונת זה הספר (24, 18–19);[8]

in the 5th chapter: the last part (39.25–41.10). Falaquera himself says, in referring to this interpolation: וכבר הארכתי וגו׳ (41.8);[9]

in the 6th chapter: the explanation of analysis and synthesis (43.14–28); **{168}**

in the 7th chapter: the last part (51.24–53.9). Falaquera himself says, in referring to this interpolation: ואלו הענפים לא זכרום מקצת הפילוסופים בזכרם מספר החכמות. ואני כדי שיהיה הספר שלם זכרתים (53.8–9);[10]

in the 8th chapter: the last part (54.19–55.30). The interpolation begins with the words: ויש מי שחלק זו החכמה וגו׳;[11]

in the 9th chapter: the last part of the paragraph on political science (58.19–59.5).

The parts of chapters 7, 8, and 9 not taken from Farâbî's *Encyclopedia* are a (more or less literal) translation of the corresponding sections in Ibn Sîna's *Encyclopedia* (*Iqsâm al-'ulûm*).[12] I indicate the passages from Ibn Sîna's writing according to the Latin translation by Alpagus (in: *Avicennae Compendium de anima etc.*, ab Andrea Alpago ...ex arabico in latinum versa, Venetiis 1546):

[6] Moritz David, ed., *Schemtov ben Josef ibn Falaqueras Propadeutik der Wissenschaften Reschith Chokmah* (Berlin: M. Poppelauer, 1902).

[7] Heb.: noun, verb ...preposition.

[8] Heb.: "And it is necessary that we explain this, although this is not part of the intention of this book."

[9] Heb.: "And I have already spoken at length, etc."

[10] Heb.: "And these are the branches. Some of the philosophers did not mention them when they mentioned the number of the sciences. But I have mentioned them so that the number would be complete." (Reading המספר for הספר. Otherwise: "so that the book [*sic*] would be complete.")

[11] Heb.: "And there is someone who has divided this science, etc."

[12] Ibn Sîna (Avicenna), *Fî aqsâm al-'ulûm al-'qliyyah* (Epistle on the Divisions of the Rational Sciences). Cf. Muhsin Mahdi's introduction to a selection from it in *MPP–1* 95f., or to that same selection in *MPP–2* 74f.

R. Ch. II, chap. 7 (51.24–53.9)	Avicenna, ed. Alpagus, fol. 141–42
chap. 8 (54.19–55.30)	fol. 143–44
chap. 9 (58.19–59.5)	fol. 140b.[13]

In order to identify the source of the part of the third chapter that is not taken from Farâbî's *Encyclopedia*, one must consider that this section (24.8–27.20) treats the same subject as the greater part of the thirteenth chapter of Maimonides's *Millot ha-higgayon*,[14] where, incidentally, a sentence is cited from Farâbî. The last section of the fifth chapter (39.25–41.10) is borrowed from Farâbî's writing on the purposes[15] of Plato and Aristotle (see below, n. 39).

The most important supplement of Falaquera is the fourth chapter, which treats the genesis of the sciences.[16] It cannot yet be proved at present that this chapter is a more or less literal translation of a section from a writing of Farâbî's. But it is indubitable that the same thoughts developed there go back to Farâbî. Let, for example, the conclusion of the chapter (30.28 ff.) be compared with the concluding part of *Iḥṣâ al-ʿulûm* (or with *Reshit Chokhmah* 59), or the immediately preceding passage (30.25–28)[17] with Farâbî's *k. taḥṣîl al-saʿâda*,[18] 39–42 (or with *Reshit Chokhmah* 70.17–19). Reminiscent of Farâbî **{169}** is, also and above all, the discussion occurring passim in this chapter pointing to the political function of science in that the

[13] For the last passage mentioned, cf. Strauss, *Philosophie und Gesetz* (Berlin: Schocken, 1935), 111 [= *GS–2* 112; *PLA* 122–23]. {LS}

[14] Heb.: *Logical Terms*. See Israel Efros, *Maimonides' Treatise on Logic* (New York: Academy for Jewish Research, 1938; reprint, Literary Licensing, LLC, 2011).

[15] The German *Tendenz* (*Tendenzen* in the plural) recurs frequently in Strauss's article and is rendered as either "purpose" or "tendency": when it refers to Fârâbî's writing on Plato and Aristotle whose existence Strauss is inferring from Falaquera et al., it is "purpose(s)"; when it refers to the distinctive characteristics of Falaquera's own writing, it is "tendency."

[16] Handwritten marginal note in Strauss's personal copy: cf. Farâbî. *De ortu scientiarum* (ed. Baeumker), *Revue néoscholastique de philosophie* 41 (1938): 84 ff. Cf. Farmer, *Al-Farabi's Arabic-Latin writings on music*, 1934. {HM}

[17] This passage is, incidentally, the best key to the understanding of Maimonides's prophetology. Falaquera says there that the art of lawgiving is the art of representing figuratively, by means of the imagination, speculative concepts that are difficult for the multitude, and the means of bringing about those political activities that serve the attainment of happiness, and the amphibolous speech concerning those speculative and practical matters that are accessible to the multitude only in an amphibolous manner. This suggests, among other things, that the prophets' dependence (asserted by Maimonides as by the Falâsifa) on the perfection of the imagination is to be understood only on the basis of the political, lawgiving function of prophecy. {LS}

Handwritten marginal note in Strauss's personal copy: cf. Arist[otle] *Metaph*[*ysics*] 1074a38 and Alex[ander of] Aphr[odisias] as well as Averroës ad loc. {HM}

Handwritten marginal note on "amphibolous speech" in Strauss's personal copy: perhaps translation of اقناع (cf. *Reshit Chokhmah* 70.19) = "persuasion" {HM}

[18] The *k. taḥṣîl al-saʿâda* or *kitâb al-saʿâda* (*kitâb* = book) is translated into English by Muhsin Mahdi as *The Attainment of Happiness*, the first part of the trilogy whose existence Strauss is inferring in the present essay and which also includes *The Philosophy of Plato* and *The Philosophy of Aristotle*. See *Alfarabi's Philosophy of Plato and Aristotle*, trans. Mahdi (Ithaca, NY: Cornell University Press, 1969; 2nd ed., 2001). Particularly as regards its second and third parts, Strauss refers to the trilogy in question usually as the "book" (or "writing") "on the purposes of Plato and Aristotle," and occasionally as "*The Two Philosophies*." His authorities here are Ibn al-Qifti (see notes 32–33) and Averroes (see notes 41–43), respectively.

sciences emerge in the *nation*, or rather in the nations. The same consideration also justifies the (provisional as well as hypothetical) attribution to Farâbî of the second chapter, which treats the genesis of language in the nations.

Falaquera's book is a decidedly Jewish book, whereas the model is not to the same degree an Islamic book. Thus there are no citations in Farâbî from the Qur'an or other Islamic sources corresponding to the Bible citations in *R. Ch.* II (54.4–5 and 54.15–17). The same difference shows itself perhaps most clearly in that, to the "uses" of an encyclopedia of the sciences enumerated by Farâbî, Falaquera adds the following two "uses" while remarking explicitly that both these "uses" would be of greater importance than the previous ones (*sc.*, borrowed from Farâbî):

1. a Hebrew encyclopedia of the sciences is necessary so that the loss of the "wisdom of our Sages," owing to the Galut, can be made up for again;[19]
2. "from this book it will become clear whether we are authorized by our Torah to learn these sciences (*sc.*, the ones about to be discussed) or not, or whether they contradict anything that is mentioned in our Torah....[20] This was the first intention in composing this book" (21.2–19).

Falaquera's determining interest, to prove the agreement between the doctrines of philosophy and the doctrines of the Law, is in no manner characteristic of Farâbî, as his **{170}** *Encyclopedia of the Sciences* shows in particular: according to Farâbî, the religious sciences (*fiqh* and *kalâm*) are no more than branches of political science. In this connection, let it be noted that Farâbî's explications of the *kalâm* are significantly shortened by Falaquera (cf. 59–60).

As interesting as this is in some respects, the fact that in the *second* part of *Reshit Chokhmah* the greatest part of Farâbî's *Encyclopedia* as well as significant parts of Ibn Sîna's *Encyclopedia* are preserved is of no special importance; for the originals have been edited and moreover are accessible in Latin translations that are more usable than Falaquera's Hebrew translation because they are more complete.[21] It is otherwise as regards the *third* part of the *Reshit Chokhmah*; for this part, which contains the translation of Farâbî's book on the purposes of Plato and Aristotle, must replace the original, the greatest part of which is regarded, at least for the time being, as

[19] Cf., in this connection, Maimonides, *Guide of the Perplexed* I 71, beginning. {LS}

[20] As regards this order of the questions—*a.* legal permissibility of philosophizing, *b.* contradiction or agreement between philosophy and law—cf. my discussion of Ibn Rushd's *Faṣl al-maqâl* in *Philosophie und Gesetz*, 71 [= of Averroes's *Decisive Treatise*, in *GS–2* 70f.; *PLA* 84]. {LS}

[21] *Iḥṣâ al-'ulûm* was edited by [Uthmân] Amin, Cairo 1350 [A.H.], and A. G. Palencia, Madrid 1931 (cf. P. Kraus's review of this edition in *Islam* XXII 82–85) [= Paul Kraus, "Kleine Mitteilungen und Anzeigen: Angel Gonzáles Palencia, *Alfârâbî Catálogo de las ciencias*," *Der Islam* 22 (1934): 82–85]. The Latin translation by Gerard of Cremona is reprinted in the Palencia edition.—*Iqsâm al-'ulûm* was edited in the collection of *Tis' rasâ'il*, Istanbul 1298 [A.H.]. The Latin translation by Alpagus can be found in the collection of Alpagus cited above. {LS}

lost.[22] Steinschneider has already suspected that the second and third parts of *Reshit Chokhmah* III might be taken from the aforementioned work of Farâbî's.[23] Now, after Farâbî's *k. taḥṣîl al-sa'âda* has been made available by the Hyderabad edition of 1345,[24] it can be proved that the entire third part of *Reshit Chokhmah* is a translation (albeit significantly abridged)[25] of Farâbî's book on the purposes of Plato and Aristotle.

The first part of *R. Ch.* III is a (incomplete) translation of Farâbî's *k. taḥṣîl al-sa'ada.* As proof, I first cite the beginnings of both works and then list the mutually corresponding passages.

> Farâbî: "*Book on the Attainment of Happiness.* The human things that must be realized among the nations and the inhabitants of the cities, by means of which earthly happiness in the initial life and the highest happiness in that life can be realized, (fall into) four kinds: the speculative virtues, the cogitative virtues, the moral virtues **{171}**, and the practical arts. The speculative virtues are those sciences whose ultimate intention is solely this, that the beings and what they encompass become intelligible (νοητά)." [26]

> Falaquera:[27] החלק הראשון בביאור הדברים ההכרחיים בהשיג ההצלחה: ואומר כי הפילוסופים זכרו שהדברים האנושיים אשר בהגיעם באומות ובאנשי המדינות תגיע להם עמהם הצלחת זה העולם בחיים הראשונים וההצלחה האחרונה בחיים האחרונים ארבעה סוגים והם השלמיות העיוניים (והשלמיות המחשביים) והשלמיות המעשיים (read: היציריים) והמלאכה המעשית. והשלמיות העיוניים הם החכמות אשר הכוונה האחרונה מהם שיגיעו עמהם הנמצאים מושכלים על אמיתתם בלבד.

[22] See now, however, *Alfarabius De Platonis Philosophia (Falsafat Aflâṭun)*, ed. Franz Rosenthal and Richard Walzer (London, 1943) and *Al-Fârâbî's "The Philosophy of Aristotle" (Falsafat Arisṭûṭâlîs)*, ed. Muhsin Mahdi (Beirut, 1961), with Mahdi's editorial remarks in his *Alfarabi's Philosophy of Plato and Aristotle*, 151–52. Cf. also note 51.

[23] *Alfarabi*, St. Petersburg, 1869, 176–178. [= Moritz Steinschneider, *Al-Fârâbî (Alpharabius), des arabischen Philosophen Leben und Schriften* (St. Petersburg, 1869).] {LS}

[24] See note 21.

[25] See notes 28 and 29.

[26] Cf. *Alfarabi's Philosophy of Plato and Aristotle*, 13. In Strauss's German text, "intelligible" is the plural noun *Verstandenen*: "intelligibles." We have rendered it as a printer's error for *verstandenen*.

[27] Heb.: "The first part in the explanation of the things necessary in the attainment of happiness: He says that the philosophers have mentioned that the human things by the attainment of which the nations and the people of the cities gain both happiness in the prior life of this world and final happiness in the afterlife are of four kinds: the theoretical virtues, (the deliberative virtues) the productive virtues, and the practical art. And the theoretical virtues are the sciences whose ultimate intention is that existing things thereby become intelligible by their truth alone."

Falaquera	Farâbî	Falaquera	Farâbî
62.2–4	(Falaquera's supplement)	67.1[28]–68.26	26.16–29.15
62.4–5	2.6–7	68.27–32	31.3–10
62.5–9	(Falaquera's supplement)	69.1–12	31.17–32.17
62.9–28	2.7–3.19	69.13–15	(Falaquera's supplement)
62.28–29[29]	4.2	69.16–26	36.12–37.5
62.31–63.10	4.16–5.10	69.26–27	37.16
63.10–14	(Falaquera's supplement)	69.27–28	38.5–6
63.15–31	5.11–6.19	69.28–70.8	38.9–39.8
63.32–64.1	8.10–13	70.8–10	(Falaquera's supplement)
64.1–12	10.7–11.3	70.10–14	39.8–12
64.12–20	11.6–18	70.14–23	42.5–16
64.20–65.23	12.14–14.9	70.23–29	42.19–43.8
65.23–66.8	15.3–16.5	70.29–71.10	44.13–45.11
66.8–9	16.15	71.11–13	(Falaquera's supplement)
66.10–30	20.8–22.8	71.14–72.4	45.12–47.5

The *Taḥṣîl* concludes with the words:[30]

> Philosophy, the description of which this (*sc.*, what was just explicated) is, has reached us from the Greeks as stemming from Plato and Aristotle. Neither of these **{172}** two has given us philosophy without at the same time giving the ways to it and the ways to its revival in case it has become tarnished or annihilated. We proceed in the following to present the philosophy of Plato and the ranks of order of his philosophy: We begin with the first part of the philosophy of Plato and thereupon follow the ranks of his philosophy, one after the other, until we have exhausted them altogether. We proceed likewise with the philosophy that Aristotle has given us: to wit, we begin to present his philosophy starting from its first part. From this it will become clear that the purpose they were both pursuing with what they have given is one and the same, and that they have both endeavored to give one and the same philosophy.[31]

The *Taḥṣîl* is therefore the introduction to a work that was devoted to the presentation of the philosophy of Plato and Aristotle. The same goes for the first part of *R. Ch.* III: the second part of *R. Ch.* III treats the philosophy of Plato, the third part the philosophy of Aristotle. It might even follow already from the conclusion of the *Taḥṣîl*, but above all from the report of Ibn al-Qifti

[28] Falaquera justifies the omission with the words: וכבר דברנו בשלמיות היציריים בחלק הראשון ["and we have already spoken of the productive virtues in the first part"] (66.31–67.1). {LS}

[29] Falaquera justifies the omission with the words: וכבר זכרתי בחלק השני וגו' ["and I have already mentioned in the second part, etc."] (62.29–30). {LS}

[30] Cf. the conclusion of *R. Ch.* III 1: הפילוסופיא שזה תארה הגיע מהיונים מאפלטון ומאריסטוטליס וכל אחד מהם נתן הפילוסופיא והדרכים לקנותה ולהדשם (read: ולחדשה) כשתאבד. ואני ראיתי לזכור ספרים בפרט ואע״פ שנזכר כל זה במה שקדם בכלל. ["And the philosophy of this description has come from the Greeks—from Plato and from Aristotle. And each of them has given philosophy and the ways to acquire it and to renew it when it is lost. And I have seen fit to mention their books individually, even though all this has been mentioned in general in what has preceded."] {LS}

[31] Cf. *Alfarabi's Philosophy of Plato and Aristotle*, 49–50.

(ed. Lippert, 278)[32] about Farâbî's book "*On the Purposes (of the Philosophy) of Plato and Aristotle*," that this book, just like *R. Ch.* III, was formally divided into three parts: into an introduction, in which "the secrets and the fruits of the sciences" were investigated and "the gradual ascent" from science to science was discussed; "*thereupon* he (Farâbî) begins with the philosophy of Plato by communicating the purpose that he (Plato) pursues with it, and his (Plato's) writings about it; *thereupon* he has the philosophy of Aristotle follow this."[33] This description corresponds completely with *R. Ch.* III. At the conclusion of the edition of the *Taḥṣîl*, the heading of the following part is given once more; it is: "The Philosophy of Plato, its Parts, and the Ranks of Order of its Parts, from First to Last."[34] The heading of the second part of *R. Ch.* III, בפילוסופית אפלטון וסדר חלקיה מראש ועד סוף,[35] is manifestly the translation of this.

As regards in particular Farâbî's presentation of the philosophy of Aristotle in the work so named, according to the report of Ibn al-Qifti it was structured as follows: Farâbî

> prefaces it (*The Philosophy of Aristotle*) with a significant introduction in which he **{173}** makes his (Aristotle's) gradual ascent to his philosophy known; thereupon he begins to describe his (Aristotle's) purposes with respect to his logical and physical writings, one book after the other, until his discussion about these things, in the manuscript we find, arrives at the beginning of theology (metaphysics) and the proof for this (*sc.*, for the necessity of metaphysics), resting as it does on physics.

The third part of *R. Ch.* III is structured exactly so: from an introduction that depicts Aristotle's path to his philosophy (78.6–80.9), there follows the presentation of logic (80.10–81.13) and physics (81.14–91.1), and finally the proof for the necessity of metaphysics, which rests on physics, and the beginning of metaphysics (91.1 to the end): metaphysics itself is absent in *R. Ch.* III also. This absence, incidentally, is not to be attributed to a corruption of the manuscripts, as Ibn al-Qifti seems to think, but it corresponds to Farâbî's plan:[36] whereas he characterizes his presentation of the philosophy of Plato with the words "We begin with the first part of the philosophy of Plato and follow the ranks of his philosophy, one after the other, until we have exhausted them altogether," he says with respect to his presentation of the philosophy of Aristotle only "We begin to present his philosophy

[32] Ibn al-Qifti, *Ta'rîkh al-ḥukamâ'*, ed. Julius Lippert (Leipzig: Dieterich'sche Verlagsbuchhandlung, 1903).

[33] The editor notes in connection with this: "That is all that we have found out about this book." {LS} The emphases in Strauss's quotation from Ibn al-Qifti in the text are Strauss's.

[34] Cf. *Alfarabi's Philosophy of Plato and Aristotle*, 53.

[35] Heb.: "On the Philosophy of Plato and the Order of its Parts from Beginning to End."

[36] Handwritten marginal notes in Strauss's personal copy:

cf. *Cuzari* V 1, Thomas *ad E.N* 1211; Efros' *RMbM* about Ab[raham] b[ar] Hiyya; Terminology s.v. חכמה ["Wisdom"]

cf. *Moreh* Introd.: Politics > Metaphysics > Physics.

See below, n. 54. {HM}

For "Efros' *RMbM*": see note 4.

from its first parts on."[37] A complete presentation of the philosophy of Aristotle, therefore, was not at all intended by Farâbî.[38] And that is why the third part of *R. Ch.* III is a (by and large) complete translation of the third part of Farâbî's book on the purposes of Plato and Aristotle. Even Falaquera's sole deviation from the structure attested to by Ibn al-Qifti of Farâbî's work speaks for this conclusion: Falaquera does not enumerate the individual logical writings of Aristotle. But that they had been enumerated in his model, that this model therefore corresponds completely to Ibn al-Qifti's statements about the book in question by Farâbî, is proved by the fact that Falaquera, true to his habit, **{174}** explicitly justifies the omission of this enumeration:[39] וכבר זכרתי בחלק השני הספרים השמונה שחבר בה (*sc.* בחכמת ההגיון) ארסטו' ונזכור אותה בכאן בקצרה (80.11–12).[40]

In Ibn Rushd's *Long Commentary on the Metaphysics*, a writing of Farâbî is cited, "*The Two Philosophies*,"[41] which is identical with the writing translated by Falaquera. The statement of Farâbî cited by Ibn Rushd from this writing can be identified in *R. Ch.* III.

> Ibn Rushd:[42] "*Una autem istarum opinionum est, quod agens creat formam, et ponit eam in materia.... Quidam dicunt quod illud agens invenitur duobus modis, aut abstractum a materia, aut non. Illud autem, quod est non abstractum apud eos, est sicut ignis, qui facit ignem, et homo generat hominem. Abstractum vero est illud quod generat animalia et plantas, quae fiunt non a simili. Et haec est sententia Themistii, et forte Alpharabii, secundum quod apparet ex suis verbis in duabus philosophiis: quamvis dubitet in ponendo hoc agens in animalibis generatis a patre et matre.*"[43]

[37] Cf. *Alfarabi's Philosophy of Plato and Aristotle*, 50.

[38] Cf. also the similar break in the presentation after pointing from physics to metaphysics in *Taḥṣîl* 12–14. Let it be pointed out at least in passing that, among other things, the conclusion of the Aristotle presentation in *R. Ch.* III 3 and the corresponding section in *Taḥṣîl* (or in *R. Ch.* III 1, 64–65) agree in part literally. {LS}

[39] I.e., in *R. Ch.* 39.25–41. Falaquera has therefore taken up the relevant section of the book on the purposes of Plato and Aristotle into his adaptation of Fârâbî's *Encyclopedia*. That *R. Ch.* 39.25–41.10 is borrowed from the book on the purposes shows up also in that this passage is composed in the same narrative style that characterizes the book on the purposes: note the constantly recurring expression here, as there: ואחר כך עיין ["And afterwards he examined"] (or חקר ["he investigated"] or the like). {LS}

[40] Heb.: "And I have already mentioned in the second part the eight books that Aristotle composed in it [*sc.*, in the science of logic], and we will recall it here in brief."

[41] Handwritten marginal note on "*The Two Philosophies*" in Strauss's personal copy: (*sc.*, the exoteric and the esoteric philosophy!) {HM}

[42] *ad Metaph.* XII (comm. 18, fol. 143, col. 2, l. 27–39). The passage is, incidentally, of importance also for demarcating Farâbî's teaching from Ibn Sîna's. {LS}

[43] Lat.: "One of these opinions, however, is that the agent creates the form and places it in matter....Certain people say that this agent is found in two modes, either remote from matter, or not. For them, however, the [agent] that is not remote is like fire that makes fire, and man generates man. In truth, the remote [agent] is the one that generates animals and plants, which are not made from [something] similar. And this is Themistius's view, and perhaps Fârâbî's according to what appears from his words in *The Two Philosophies*: in any case, he would hesitate to place this agent in animals generated by a father and mother."

Falaquera: ...ורבים מהנפשיים יתנו אל החמרים אשר יפגשום ואשר יכינם הטבע להם נפש כי האדם הוא אדם היה לפניו אדם והאדם מאדם וכמו כן בבעלי חיים (...) מה שאינו בבעלי חיים ומהצמחים מי שאינו מצמח והגופים המחצביים אינם נהוים מהדומים להם במין ועל כן צריך לחקור אותו אלו ויותר מזה לחקור מי שנתן האנושית על דרך כלל והדומה לזה משאר בעלי חיים וצורת מין ומין ... ועל כן צריך לחקור מי שנתן צורת אותו המין ועל דרך כלל מי שנתן צורות המינים אם הם הגופים השחקיים או השכל הפועל או יהיה השכל הפועל נותן הצורה והגופים השחקיים נתנו תנועות החמרים.[44] (90.22–31)

By this agreement, that *R. Ch.* III is a translation of Farâbî's writing on the purposes of Plato and Aristotle should be proved completely. **{175}**

This writing can therefore be reconstructed to some extent if a rule is first secured for the use of those parts of it that are preserved only in Falaquera's translation.[45] This rule can be obtained by observing Falaquera's tendency and technique in his adaptation of *k. taḥṣîl al-sa'âda* and *Iḥṣâ al-'ulûm*. Falaquera in general translates very literally. Often, however, he leaves out significant parts of the original, occasionally by making known his deviation from the original. The supplements are easy to recognize as such in general, without the comparison with the original being necessary (or even only possible).[46] Above all, if one considers the fact that most of Falaquera's supplements stem from the tendency characteristically distinguishing him from Farâbî, to prove the agreement between the doctrines of philosophy and those of the Law. This tendency was pointed out above in examples from his adaptation of the *Iḥṣâ al-'ulûm*. It shows itself also in his adaptation of the *Taḥṣîl*.[47] The fact that in the *Taḥṣîl* is found an explanation of "Imâm" (43.9–17) that Falaquera left untranslated merely appears to contradict this; for with this explanation Farâbî is pursuing the by no means believing, but philosophical intention of leading away from the Islamic givens and toward the Platonic doctrine of the

[44] Heb.: "And many of the animate [beings] give to the materials that they encounter, [provided] that nature has prepared them, a soul, as a man has been [originated] from another man before him, who has been [originated] from a man, and in like manner with the animals....Some among the animals, and plants that are not [originated] from a plant, and the mineral bodies, are not [originated] from what is similar to them in species, and therefore it is necessary to investigate these things, and moreover to investigate who gave the human [soul] in general, and similarly [the souls] of the rest of the animals and the form of each and every species....And therefore it is necessary to investigate who has given the form of this particular species and in general who has given the forms of the species, whether it is the heavenly bodies or the Active Intellect, or whether it has been the Active Intellect giving the form and the heavenly bodies have given the movements of the materials."

[45] That *R. Ch.* III 1 might be of use for establishing the text of the *Taḥṣîl* is to be noted in passing. {LS}

[46] 72.21–25: ומצאנו וגו׳ ["and we have found, etc."]; 75.22–26: ויראה לי וגו׳ ["and it has seemed to me, etc."]; 77.3–11: ראינו וגו׳ ונשוב למה שהיינו בו ["we have seen, etc., and let us return to where we were"]. The last example is especially important because, through this remark of Falaquera's, it is ascertained that the preceding report about Plato's *Republic* stems from his model. {LS}

[47] Cf. in particular the supplements at 68.13–15 and 71.11–13. {LS}

Handwritten marginal note in Strauss's personal copy: 65.32: האלוה יתה—cf., in contrast, *taḥṣîl* 15, par. 2, lines 1–2 {HM}

philosopher-king: "The meaning of Philosopher and First Leader and King and Lawgiver and Imâm is one and the same."[48]

Since, therefore, Farâbî's book on the purposes of Plato and Aristotle is able to be reconstructed, and since his *Encyclopedia of the Sciences*, his *Political Regime*,[49] and his book on the political regimes[50] have been edited,[51] his central writings are thus preserved and available. The interpretation of his doctrine is therefore possible. A sufficient proof that it is necessary, however, is the statement of *Maimonides's* about the "second teacher."[52] Maimonides writes to the translator of his *Moreh nebuchim*:[53] "Do not concern yourself with any books of logic other than those the wise Abû Naṣr al-Farâbî has composed. For **{176}** everything he has composed in general, and his *The Principles of Beings*[54] in particular—everything is pure flour." And he immediately adds that the books of Ibn Sîna, with all their merits, cannot compare with those of Farâbî. It is time that the conclusions from this authoritative

[48] Handwritten marginal note in Strauss's personal copy: cf. Razi on Socrates as his Imâm (Kraus in *Orientalia* 1935) [= Paul Kraus, "Raziana I," *Orientalia* N.S. 4 (1935), 300–34]. {HM}

[49] Lit.: *Perfect State*. Strauss uses the German title *Musterstaat*, in reference to the Arabic text edited by Friedrich Dieterici, *Alfarabi's Abhandlung der Musterstaat* (Leiden, 1895). See the following note and notes 53 and 54.

[50] On the apparent redundancy here, cf. Muhsin Mahdi's introduction to a selection from Alfarabi's *The Political Regime* in *MPP–1* 31: "[The *Political Regime*] is known by two titles: the *Principles of Beings* (or the *Six Principles*) and the *Political Regime*. The first title seems to have been extracted from the opening passage of the work, which gives the impression that it is a treatise on the principles of the natural world and their respective ranks of order: 1) the First Cause, 2) the Second Causes, 3) the Active Intellect, 4) the soul, 5) form, and 6) matter. The entire first part of the work consists of an account of these six principles and of how they constitute the bodies and their accidents. Only when one proceeds to the second part (the human and political part...) does one perceive that this account is an introduction to, and a preparation for, an account of political life and a classification of political regimes. Alfarabi wrote a parallel book, the *Principles of the Opinions of the Citizens of the Virtuous City*, which discusses the same themes in similar terms. As the titles indicate, however, the *Political Regime* is concerned more with regimes or constitutions, whereas the *Virtuous City* is concerned more with the opinions of the citizens in these regimes." See also note 54.

[51] As regards the edited texts of the *Encyclopedia [sc., Enumeration] of the Sciences* and the *Political Regime*, see notes 3 and 49; also, Muhsin S. Mahdi, *Alfarabi and the Foundation of Islamic Political Philosophy* (Chicago: University of Chicago Press, 2001), 241, 243. As regards the edited text of "the book on the political regimes" (*sc.*, the *Virtuous City*), see *idem*, 244.

[52] On this term, cf. Mahdi's Introduction to *Alfarabi's Philosophy of Plato and Aristotle*, 4f.: "Alfarabi's scientific or philosophic works proper—his commentaries, especially his large commentaries, on individual works by Plato and Aristotle ...established his reputation as the greatest philosophical authority next to Aristotle (Alfarabi was known as the 'Second Master')....Many of these works seem to be lost; the ones that have survived remain for the most part hardly ever studied; and the few that have been edited deal with specialized subjects whose relevance to the general character of Alfarabi's thought and of Islamic philosophy is not easy to establish."

[53] I.e., *Guide of the Perplexed*. The translator is Samuel ibn Tibbon. Cf. Joel L. Kraemer, *Maimonides* (New York: Doubleday, 2008), 438–43.

[54] The authentic title of this book is *The Political Regimes*. It consists of two parts, the first of which treats the hierarchy of the cosmos, the second of which treats the hierarchy of the city. Structured in the same manner is the book on the perfect state, which in the manuscripts of the British Museum and the Bodleian Library is described simply as a "political book." {LS}

explanation about the true proportions be drawn for the understanding of the Islamic and Jewish philosophy of the Middle Ages: At the beginning of this epoch of the history of philosophy there stands not just any "predecessor," but the towering spirit who laid the ground for the later development and set down its limits by making his task the revival of Platonic-Aristotelian philosophy as philosophy proper.

APPENDIX E

LEO STRAUSS: "ON ABRAVANEL'S CRITIQUE OF MONARCHY" (1937)[1]

Translated by Martin D. Yaffe

H. Finkelscherer, in an essay that appeared in the last annum of this journal,[2] has made the assertions that one of the most important antimonarchist arguments of Abravanel, and "a quite similar attitude" toward the Judean monarchy, are to be found "already in Joseph ibn Caspi." That the attitude of both authors is quite similar must be contested: Finkelscherer himself immediately notes the "difference in tone between Caspi's aristocratic-philosophical ideal and Abravanel's theocratic one" (81st annum, p. 506). On the other hand, the assertion that Abravanel's argumentation agrees with Caspi's requires more serious consideration.

For Abravanel in any case, the most important part of his antimonarchical argumentation, i.e., the one that is decisive for the whole question, is his explanation of Deut. 17:14f., according to which this passage expresses no command to appoint a king but merely a permission to do so. More precisely: he compares the provision regarding the appointment of the king with the provision regarding the אשת יפת־תאר.[3] Accordingly, the sense of the crucial biblical passage is: if you should have and express the wish, against the divine will, to appoint a king over yourselves, then you should not appoint as king over yourselves him whom you wish, but

[1] [Leo Strauss, "Zu Abravanels Kritik des Königtums," *GS–2* 233–34, 615.] Unpublished. Typescript with entries and corrections in Strauss's hand. 2 pages, in the possession of Jenny Strauss Clay. Strauss's annotations refer to the essay by Herbert Finkelscherer, "Quellen und Motive der Staats- und Gesellschaftsauffassung des Don Isaak Abravanel," in *Monatsschrift für Geschichte und Wissenschaft des Judentums* (Breslau, 1937), 81st annum, 496–508, and had evidently been intended as a brief review for publication in this journal. Whether Strauss in fact sent the contribution to the editorial office is not known. {HM}

[2] See the previous note.

[3] Heb.: "beautiful-looking woman" (Deut. 21:11).

him whom God will choose. Caspi says quite similarly (on Deut. 17:14): וצום שלא ישימוהו רק אשר יבחר י״י על פי נביא.[4] Is this statement of Caspi's necessarily saying, however, that the appointment of the king is not commanded but only permitted? He is certainly not in any way comparing the provision regarding the appointment of the king with the provision regarding the beautiful-looking woman, but with the provisions regarding sacrifice (on I Sam. 8:6). He is thus pointing, as Last[5] as well as **{234}** Finkelscherer rightly remarks, to Maimonides's explanation of the sacrificial legislation. The explanation given in *Moreh*[6] III 32, which both Last and Finkelscherer have in mind, says: sacrifices do not correspond to the first intention of the divine lawgiver, they are therefore not simply good, but they were ordained only with respect to the ignorance of the people at that time, they are therefore only conditionally good. This explanation by no means implies, however, that sacrifices, being ordained as only conditionally good, are not commanded but only permitted. And therefore Caspi is in no way asserting as Abravanel does, undoubtedly in the wake of Ibn Ezra, that the appointment of the king is not commanded but only permitted.

There is only one way to vindicate Finkelscherer's assertion: one would have to show that Caspi in fact considered the entire sacrificial legislation to be non-obligatory. In other words: one would have to show that his words למנות מלך מצוה ג״כ כענין הקרבן[7] contain a silent allusion not to *Moreh* III 32 but to *Moreh* III 46. For in the latter chapter (III 102a–b, Munk)[8] Maimonides says in plain words: "If we do not perform this mode of worship at all, I mean the sacrifices, then we commit no sin whatever." Caspi, the thoroughgoing connoisseur of the *Moreh*, may very well have been thinking of this somewhat more isolated remark, and not of the much more famous expositions of *Moreh* III 32, when he compared the law of the king with the sacrificial laws. But that he was actually thinking of that remark would need proof. Only if this proof were supplied would one be obliged to assert definitively that Caspi really has anticipated the decisive antimonarchical argument of Abravanel.

[4] Heb.: "And he commanded them not to appoint him, except one whom the Lord will choose by the say-so of a prophet." Quoted by Finkelscherer, 506.

[5] Finkelscherer, 506n58, quotes I. H. Last's edition of Caspi's commentary on the Prophets, *Adney Kesef* (2 vols.; London, 1911–12), vol. I, 15, on I Sam. 8:6: אין ראוי לפי התורה שיהיה לעמו מלך לשפטם ("It is not proper according to the Torah for our people to have a king to judge them"); Last's editorial footnote *ad loc.* notes Caspi's allusion to Maimonides's *Moreh*. At 506n57, Finkelscherer cites Last's edition of Caspi's commentary on the Torah *Matzref la-Kesef* (Krakow, 1906) on Deut. 17:14, i.e., as the source for Caspi's view expressed in the sentence translated in note 4. And at 506n60, Finkelscherer again cites Caspi's *Adney Kesef* on I Sam. 8:6, as the source for the sentence translated in note 7, which Finkelscherer, 506, quotes with Caspi's words כענין הקרבן ("like the matter of sacrifice") emphasized.

[6] I.e., *Guide* [*of the Perplexed*]. Strauss uses the traditional Hebrew title.

[7] Heb.: "And to appoint a king is a commandment, just like the matter of sacrifice." See note 5.

[8] Maïmonide, *Le Guide des égarés*, ed. and trans. S[alomon] Munk (3 vols.; Paris, 1856–66; nouv. éd., Paris, 1970).

APPENDIX E

SUPPLEMENTARY NOTE ON ARCHIVAL MATERIALS

Jeffrey A. Bernstein

In 1937, Leo Strauss wrote two essays on the thought of Don Isaac Abravanel (1437–1508 CE)—"On Abravanel's Philosophical Tendency and Political Teaching" and "Zu Abravanels Kritik des Königtums" (translated as "On Abravanel's Critique of Monarchy" in appendix E of the present volume).[1] These two essays present a lens through which one sees Strauss's engagement with later medieval Jewish thinkers as it displays a newfound emphasis (characteristic of his writings in the 1930s) on political philosophy and medieval rationalism. Further, as Joshua Parens shows in chapter 8 of our volume, Strauss's engagement with Abravanel also discloses his first significant treatment of "the main line of Christian political thought" as distinguished from the Jewish and Islamic variety (the exemplary instance of which is the thought of Maimonides).

Around one month before the present volume went to press, I came across a 43-page set of undated handwritten notes (in Box 20, Folder 14 of the Leo Strauss Archive, Special Collections, Regenstein Library, University of Chicago) the significance of which bears directly on both essays from 1937.[2] Five pages of the manuscript, divided into three distinct sections, deal with Abravanel's commentary on I Samuel (Chapter 1, Verses 4–35). The first section carries the heading "Abrabanels Kommentar zum Buche Samuël" while the next two sections simply state "Abrabanel ad Samuël". The remaining 38 pages deal with Abravanel's commentary on I Kings (Chapters 1 and 17–20). Given the degenerated state of some of the pages, it is difficult to provide definitive sections for the entire group; that said, the overwhelming majority of pages can be sectionalized according to the designations that occur as book number-scriptural book-chapter-subscript verse—for

[1] See *GS-2* 195–227 and 233–34, respectively.

[2] I would like to thank Nathan Tarcov and the Special Collections Department at the Regenstein Library for allowing me to conduct research there. I would also like to thank Martin D. Yaffe, Richard S. Ruderman, and Timothy W. Burns for inviting me to briefly present my findings in the present context.

example, $1Reg17_4$ ("Reg" being the abbreviation for "Regnum"—the conventional Latin designation for the scriptural book). The manuscript as a whole,[3] therefore, contains materials covered in both Abravanel essays.

One of the distinctive qualities about "On Abravanel's Philosophical Tendency" is its reference to many classical Jewish commentaries on the Hebrew Bible. These occur, in that essay, largely in the notes and in one paragraph.[4] "On Abravanel's Critique of Monarchy" (probably as a result of the scholarly focus and brevity of Strauss's treatment) makes no mention of these commentaries. From reading only those essays, one might question how substantive a role these commentaries play in Strauss's treatment of Abravanel. The handwritten notes provide the following information: At least with respect to I Samuel and I Kings (which texts figure directly in "On Abravanel's Philosophical Tendency" and, by implication, in "On Abravanel's Critique of Monarchy"), Strauss was working extremely closely with the rabbinic commentaries. The notes largely assume a form similar to that of the *Miqra'ot Gedolot*.[5] He provides a verse, notes certain significant Hebrew terms, provides Abravanel's commentary on said verse, and then provides commentary on the same verse from the *Midrash Tanhuma,* the *Targum* by Onkelos (ca. 35–120 CE), Solomon ben Isaac ("Rashi," 1040–1104 CE), David Kimchi/Qimchi ("Radak/Radaq," 1160–1235 CE), and Levi ben Gershom/Gersonides ("Ralbag," 1288–1304 CE). Strauss employs the conventional (German) shorthand for these commentators and texts, hence, "Tanchuma," "Raschi," "RDK"/"RDQ," and "RLBG."

Strauss's notes do not provide similar commentary from Maimonides; neither do they provide analogous commentary from Christian sources (some of whom Abravanel would have been familiar with), or philosophical analogues and/or divergences.[6] The question as to the occasion for which these notes were composed thus remains open.[7] Regardless of whether the notes were taken in specific preparation for the Abravanel essays or taken earlier and simply used in those essays, they offer an instructive glimpse into Strauss's workroom and show readers the scrupulous attention to detail that marked Strauss's philosophical practice before, during, and after the reorientation that he underwent in the 1930s.

[3] Listed on the Special Collections website as "Arabic Notebook 'Biblical Book of Kings.'"

[4] ¶26 in *Isaac Abravanel: Six Lectures*, ed. J. B. Trend and H. Lowe (Cambridge: Cambridge University Press, 1937), 123; ¶28 in *Leo Strauss On Maimonides: The Complete Writings*, ed. Kenneth Hart Green (Chicago: University Of Chicago Press, 2013), 607. Readers should note that Green's edition follows the *GS*.

[5] That is, the "large format Bible," which provides verse-by-verse commentary supplied by the *Targumim* (Aramaic translations of the Hebrew Bible) and *Rishonim* (medieval Jewish scriptural commentators).

[6] This is significant only insofar as "On Abravanel's Philosophical Tendency" deals with Abravanel's divergence from the medieval Jewish adoption of Platonic political philosophy in favor of a more explicitly Aristotelian standpoint characteristic of medieval Christian thought.

[7] Thomas Meyer (Wake Forest University) suggests that the handwriting in the notes dates from Strauss's early Berlin years (1926–27). If this is correct, it opens up research possibilities into the possible differences between his treatment of classical Jewish sources in 1) the 1920s, 2) his path through "Jewish Thomism" (*GS–3* 765) in *Philosophie und Gesetz*, and 3) the Abravanel essays.

EDITORIAL NOTE TO APPENDICES F AND G

Hannes Kerber

Strauss left among his papers three versions of the fragment[1] "Exoteric Teaching"—a four-page manuscript (M) written on both recto and verso in blue ink,[2] a 19-page typescript (TS),[3] and its carbon copy (CC).[4] The two typewritten versions are nearly identical[5] but bear many different handwritten corrections in pencil, red crayon, and black ink by Strauss and at least one other person.

An edition based on TS was published with some editorial revisions by Kenneth Hart Green in 1986.[6] M and CC, however, throw new light on the genesis of the essay. Further, a comparison of the typewritten versions with M strongly suggests that the typist was not Strauss himself. Nor can TS be considered authoritative since Strauss did not prepare the essay for publication. The deviations from M, most of which occur in the last part of the essay, can therefore not be regarded with certainty as Strauss's deliberate corrections but may be among the many errors made by the typist that were missed by Strauss when he looked over TS and CC. (For example, it is not clear whether Strauss wanted to leave out the second part of footnote XXXVI in the typewritten version or whether he simply did not notice the typist's failure to transcribe it.)

[1] In M, TS, and CC, the first paragraph is numbered "I." However, this numeral was later crossed out in both TS and CC. Likewise, the last line in M is the numeral "II," which was not copied by the typist.

[2] Leo Strauss Papers (Box 17, Folder 2), Special Collections Research Center, University of Chicago Library. M is written on paper of the Union College, Schenectady, NY. In the top right-hand corner of the first page of M, Strauss initially wrote in blue ink "Dec., 1, 1939—". Later he crossed this out and wrote, in pencil, "Dec., 1939: I."

[3] Leo Strauss Papers (Box 23, Folder 8).

[4] Leo Strauss Papers (Box 14, Folder 12). In the top right-hand corner of the first page of CC, "Carbon not corrected" was written in a hand other than Strauss's.

[5] The last two pages of TS were replaced by two pages written on a different typewriter. These pages take into account most of the corrections that appear in CC. Also, the text of footnote VI cannot be found in CC while the superscripted number is in the main text.

[6] *Interpretation* 14, no. 1 (1986): 51–59. A more heavily edited version was included in *RCPR* 63–71.

This edition takes TS, which Strauss corrected more carefully than CC, as the basis from which it notes deviations from M and CC. It notes as well any handwritten corrections in the body of the text in the three versions. In the text of Strauss's own footnotes, however, I have noted only obviously significant deviations and handwritten corrections in order to preserve readability. Typographical or reading errors that were later corrected, minor variations in comma placement, orthographical inconsistencies in German or French quotations, and discrepancies due to the fact that Strauss used British spelling while the typist nearly always used American spelling, have been corrected silently. Words underlined, by hand or by typewriter, have been italicized.

Editorial revisions are kept to a minimum. In a few cases, mainly in Strauss's footnotes, I have corrected errors made by the typist and overlooked by Strauss on the basis of the manuscript.[7] Only in a handful of cases did I find emendations of Strauss's text indispensable.[8]

All footnotes with Roman numerals are Strauss's; those with Arabic numerals as well as all additions in square brackets are my own. The great number of deviations and handwritten corrections in all three of the versions compelled resorting to abbreviations in the apparatus. Therefore, I have adopted a simple system: 1) The deviations from TS have been indicated by a reference to the source, followed by the deviation. For example, the note "M: has" to the word "had" in the body of the text is to be read as "the manuscript reads 'has' (whereas the typescript and the carbon copy read 'had')." 2) The handwritten corrections have been indicated with a reference to the source, followed by the original word, an arrow and the correction. For example, the note "M: popular → public" to the word "public" in the body of the text is to be read as "in the manuscript, 'popular' was replaced with 'public' (which was adopted by the typescript)." All corrections in M are Strauss's but it is not always clear whether the corrections in TS and CC were made by Strauss or by someone else. Therefore, I have only identified those handwritten corrections that can be attributed with certainty to Strauss.

The two plans for "Exoteric Teaching" (Supplements 1 and 2, below)[9] reveal that Strauss initially intended to write a much longer essay. They map out additions to the existing text as well as details of the second part of the essay, which Strauss never carried out. Even though the plans cannot be dated precisely, it seems fairly

[7] For example, TS has in footnote I "120ff." while M has "120f." In similar cases, I have restored the reading of M in fn II: edd. → eds. / fn III: Lessing' → Lessing's / fn VII: and "The ordinary distinction between offensive and defensive wars is quite empty." (*Loc. cit.*, §§ 60 and 276) → (*Philosophische Sittenlehre*, § 60) and "The ordinary distinction between offensive and defensive wars is quite empty." (*Loc. cit.*, § 276) / fn IX: 34ff. → 34f. / fn XIV: 153ff. → 153f. / fn XXXI: 44ff. → 44f. / fn XXXIII: bonds → bands / proportionately → proportionally.

[8] Cf. the editorial comments in fn 280n53, XXIII, XXIV, XXVI, and fn 283n82. In accordance with the original text, a few minor mistakes in the quotations in fn IV, XXXIII and XXXVII were corrected. Cf. Adam Ferguson, *An Essay on the History of Civil Society*, edited by Fania Oz-Salzberger (Cambridge, UK: Cambridge University Press, 1995), 24f., 29 and 177.

[9] Leo Strauss Papers (Box 17, Folder 2). The first paragraph of an earlier draft of the essay, also entitled "Exoteric Teaching" can be found on the back of the later plan. An even earlier version, entitled "Exoteric Literature," and a third plan, entitled "Exoteric teaching," can be found in the same folder.

clear that the second one was written at a later time since it is both more detailed and closer to the part of "Exoteric Teaching" that was finished.

A third supplementary document (appendix G) consists of a closely related set of notes. On December 6, 1939, while working on "Exoteric Teaching," Strauss gave a lecture titled "Persecution and the Art of Writing" at Union College, Schenectady, NY.[10] Among his papers, Strauss left a five-page manuscript (of which four pages have survived) with elaborate notes for a lecture of the same title.[11] These notes seem to be an *aide-mémoire* and some of the writing has been crossed out.[12] Like the two plans, the lecture notes are of an essentially private character and should therefore be read in the light of Strauss's published works. In the hope of making this task easier for the reader, I have annotated these documents extensively but by no means exhaustively, while I have kept the editorial notes for "Exoteric Teaching" to a minimum.

★ ★ ★

The bulk of this work was made possible by a generous grant provided by the German National Merit Foundation for the academic year 2010/2011. I am very grateful to Robert B. Pippin for inviting me to spend that year with the Committee on Social Thought at the University of Chicago. Nathan Tarcov, Leo Strauss's literary executor, has kindly given his permission for the publication and has supported me constantly. I am indebted to Wiebke Meier, Svetozar Minkov, and Devin Stauffer for help in deciphering some of Strauss's hieroglyphs, to Stuart D. Warner, William Wood, and especially to Jeremy Bell for friendly critique, as well as to Martin D. Yaffe and Richard S. Ruderman for giving me the opportunity to publish such a lengthy critical edition. To Heinrich Meier and Ralph Lerner, who have encouraged me from the very beginning with their insights and advice, I am deeply grateful.

[10] Cf. Leo Strauss to Jacob Klein, November 28, 1939, in *GS–3* 586. As Heinrich Meier has kindly informed me, Strauss noted in the margin of his own copy of the article "Persecution and the Art of Writing" that he gave lectures on the topic in October and December 1939 as well as in February, March, and April 1940.

[11] Leo Strauss Papers (Box 17, Folder 2).

[12] Deletions by LS are indicated by chevrons ("<…>") and additions by the editor in square brackets ("[…]").

APPENDIX F

LEO STRAUSS: EXOTERIC TEACHING (1939)

Edited by Hannes Kerber

Le partage du brave homme est d'expliquer librement ses pensées. Celui qui n'ose regarder fixément les deux pôles de la vie humaine, la religion et le gouvernement, n'est qu'un lâche.

—Voltaire.[1]

The distinction between exoteric (or public[2]) and esoteric (or secret) teaching is not at present considered to be of any significance for the understanding of the thought of the past: the leading encyclopedia of classical antiquity does not contain any article, however brief, on *exoteric* or *esoteric*. Since a considerable number of ancient writers had[3] not a little to say about the distinction in question, the silence of the leading encyclopedia cannot possibly be due to the silence of the sources; it must be due to the influence of modern philosophy on classical scholarship; it is that influence which prevents scholars from attaching significance to numerous[4], if not necessarily correct, statements of ancient writers. For while it is for classical scholars to decide whether and where[5] the distinction between exoteric and esoteric teaching occurs in the sources, it is for philosophers to decide whether that distinction is significant in itself. And modern philosophy is not favorable to an affirmative answer to this philosophic question. The classical scholar Zeller may have believed to have cogent reasons for rejecting the view that Aristotle "designedly chose for (his scientific publications) a style obscure and unintelligible to the lay mind"; but it must be doubted whether these reasons would have appeared to

[1]"It is the lot of the brave [or decent] man to explain his thoughts freely. He who does not dare to look directly at the two poles of human life, religion and government, is only a coward." Quoted with some alterations from Voltaire, *L'A, B, C, ou Dialogues entre A, B et C* (dixième entretien, sur la religion), in *Dialogues et Anecdotes Philosophiques*, edited by Raymond Naves (Paris: Garnier, 1939), 304.

[2]M: popular → public

[3]M: has

[4]M: important → numerous

[5]TS/CC: when → where

him equally cogent, if he had not been assured by the philosopher Zeller that the rejected view "attributes to the philosopher a very childish sort of mystification, wholly destitute of any reasonable motive."[I]

As late as the last third of the 18th century, the view that all the ancient philosophers had distinguished between their exoteric and their esoteric teaching was still maintained, and its essential implications were fully understood at least by one man. Gotthold Ephraim Lessing united in himself in a unique way the so divergent qualities of the philosopher and of the scholar. He discussed the question of exotericism clearly and fully in three [6]little[6] writings of his: in "Leibniz von den ewigen Strafen" (1773), in "Des Andreas Wissowatius' Einwürfe wider die Dreieinigkeit" (1773) and in "Ernst und Falk" (1777 and 1780).[II] He discussed it as clearly and as fully as could be done by someone who still accepted exotericism not merely as a strange fact of the past, but rather as an intelligible necessity for all times and, therefore, as a principle guiding his own literary activity.[III] In short, Lessing was the last writer who revealed, while hiding them, the reasons compelling wise men to hide the truth: he wrote between the lines about the art of writing between the lines.

In "Ernst und Falk," a character called[7] Falk, who expresses himself somewhat evasively and sometimes even enigmatically, tries to show that every political constitution, and even the best political constitution[8], is necessarily imperfect: the necessary imperfection of all political life makes necessary the existence of what he calls free-masonry, and he does not hesitate to assert that free-masonry, which is necessary, was always in existence and will always be. Falk himself is a free-mason, if a heretical[9] free-mason, and in order to be a free-mason, a man must know truths which ought better to be concealed.[IV] What[10] is then the concealed reason of his view that all political life is necessarily[11] imperfect?[V] The intention of the good

[I] *Aristotle and the Earlier Peripatetics* (translated by Costelloe and Muirhead), London 1897, I 120f.

[6]Added by LS in M between the lines or in the margins.

[II] See Lessing, *Werke*, eds. Petersen and von Olshausen,VI 21–60 ("Ernst und Falk") and XXI 138–189 (the two other treatises mentioned above). Compare also Lessing's "Über eine zeitige Aufgabe" (XXIV 146–153).

[III] Lessing's exotericism was recognized to a certain extent by Gottfried Fittbogen, *Die Religion Lessings*, Leipzig 1923, 60ff. and 79ff. Fittbogen does not however see the most important implications of his valuable remarks, since his interpretation of Lessing is based on a Kantian or post-Kantian view of the meaning of philosophy.

[7]TS: character, called → character called [correction not in CC]

[8]M: and even the absolutely best political constitution [This part of the sentence was not transcribed by the typist. LS reinserted it in TS and CC. However, he dropped the word "absolutely."]

[9]M: heretic → heretical

[IV]"*Falk*. Weißt du, Freund, daß du schon ein halber Freimäurer bist?...denn du erkennst ja schon Wahrheiten, die man besser verschweigt. *Ernst*. Aber sagen *könnte*. *Falk*. Der Weise *kann* nicht sagen, was er besser verschweigt." Second Dialogue, *loc. cit.*, p. 31. ["*Falk*: Do you know, friend, that you are already half a free-mason?...because you already realize truths which are better to be concealed. *Ernst*: But which *could* be said. *Falk*: The wise man *cannot* say what he would do better to conceal."]

[10]TS: Which → What [correction not in CC]

[11]M: necessarily is

[V]In the 3rd dialogue (p. 40), it is explicitly stated that only such shortcomings of even the best political constitution have been explicitly mentioned as are evident even to the most shortsighted eye. This implies that there are other shortcomings of political life as such which are not evident to "shortsighted eyes."

works of the free-masons is to make good works superfluous,[VI] and free-masonry came into being[VII] when[12] someone who originally had planned a scientific society which should make the speculative truths useful for practical and political life conceived[13] of a "society which should raise itself from the practice of civil life to speculation."[VIII] The concealed reasons[14] of the imperfection of political life as such are the facts[15] that all practical or political life is essentially inferior to contemplative life, or that all works, and therefore also all good works, are "superfluous" as far as the level of theoretical life, which is self-sufficient, is reached, and that the requirements of the lower are bound from time to time to conflict with, and to supersede in practice, the requirements of the higher. Consideration of that conflict is the ultimate reason why the "free-masons" (i.e. the wise or the men of contemplation[16]) must conceal certain fundamental truths. It may be added that Lessing points out in "Ernst und Falk" that the variety of religions is due to the variety of political constitutions[IX]: the religious problem (i.e. the problem of historical, positive religion) is considered by him as part and parcel of the political problem.[17]

In "Leibniz von den ewigen Strafen" and in "Wissowatius," Lessing applies these views to an explanation of Leibniz' attitude toward religion. The explicit purpose of these two little treatises is to discuss "the motives and reasons" which had induced Leibniz to defend certain orthodox beliefs (the belief in eternal damnation and the belief in trinity).[X] While defending Leibniz' defense of the belief in eternal damnation, Lessing states that Leibniz' peculiar way of assenting to received opinions is *identical*[18] with "what all the ancient philosophers used to do in their exoteric speech."[XI] By making that statement, he not only asserts that all the ancient philosophers made use of two manners of teaching, of an exoteric manner and an esoteric manner; he also bids us[19] *trace back*[18] all essential features of Leibniz' exotericism to the exotericism of the ancients. What, then,

[VI] 1st dialogue (at the end) and 3rd dialogue (p. 39).

[VII] The contradiction between the statement made at the beginning that free-masonry is always in existence, and the statement made toward the end that free-masonry came into being at the beginning of the eighteenth century enables us to see that free-masonry is an ambiguous term. [In M the sentence is concluded: "...18th century shall enable us to see that 'free-masonry' is an ambiguous term, and that the secret meaning of that term indicates what ought to be called in unmetaphoric language—philosophy." In TS/CC the conclusion reads differently ("...ambiguous term, and that the secret meaning of the term is 'philosophy.'") and was crossed out by LS.]

[12] TS: being, when → being when [correction not in CC]

[13] TS: life, conceived → life conceived [correction not in CC]

[VIII] 5th dialogue (toward the end).

[14] M: reason → reasons

[15] M: is the fact → are the facts

[16] M: speculation → contemplation

[IX] 2nd dialogue (p. 34f.).

[17] M: (i.e. the problem of positive religion) is a part of the political problem → (i.e. the problem of historical, positive religion) is considered by him as part and parcel of the political problem

[X] *Werke*, XXI 143 and 181.

[18] Italics added in TS (correction not in CC).

[XI] *Loc. cit.*, 147.

[19] TS: bids us to → bids us [correction not in CC]

[20] TS/CC: Which are, then, → What, then, are

are[20] the essential features of Leibniz' exotericism? Or, in other words, what[21] are the motives and reasons which guided Leibniz in his defense of the orthodox or received opinion?[XII] Lessing's first answer to this question is that Leibniz' peculiar way of assenting to received opinions is identical with "what all the ancient philosophers used to do in their exoteric speech. He observed a sort of prudence for which, it is true, our most recent philosophers have become much too wise."[XIII] The distinction between exoteric and esoteric speech has then so little to do with "mysticism" of any sort that it is an outcome of prudence. Somewhat later on Lessing indicates the difference between the esoteric reason enabling[22] Leibniz [6]to[6] defend[23] the orthodox doctrine of eternal damnation, and the exoteric reason expressed in[24] his defense[25] of that doctrine.[XIV] That exoteric reason, he asserts, is based on the mere possibility of eternally increasing wickedness of moral beings[26]. And then he goes on to say: "It is true, humanity shudders at this conception although it concerns the mere possibility. I should[27] not however for that reason raise the question: why frighten with a mere possibility? For I should[28] have to expect this counterquestion: why not frighten with it, since it can only be frightful to him who has never been earnest about the betterment of himself." This implies that a philosopher who makes an exoteric statement, asserts, not a fact, but what Lessing chooses to call "a mere possibility": he does not, strictly speaking, believe in the truth of that statement (e.g. of the statement that there is[29] such a thing as eternally increasing wickedness of human beings which would justify eternally increasing punishments). This is indicated by Lessing in the following remark introducing a quotation from the final part of Plato's *Gorgias*: "Socrates himself believed in such eternal punishments quite seriously, he believed in them at least to the extent[30] that he considered it expedient[31] to teach such punishments in terms which do not in any way arouse suspicion and which are most explicit."[XV]

Before proceeding any further, I must summarize Lessing's view of exoteric teaching. To avoid the danger of arbitrary interpretation, I shall omit all elements of that view which are not noticed[32] at a first glance even by the most superficial

[21]TS/CC: which → what

[XII]Cf. *loc. cit.*, 146.

[XIII]*Loc. cit.*, 147. Cf. Plato, *Theaetetus* 180c7–d5, with *Protagoras* 316c5–317c5 and 343b4–5.

[22]M: underlying → enabling

[23]M: defence of → defend

[24]M: underlying → expressed in

[25]M: explicit defence → defence

[XIV]*Loc. cit.*, 153f.

[26]M: a moral being → moral beings

[27]M: shall

[28]M: shall → should

[29]In M "is" is italicized.

[30]M: at least so far

[31]M: expedient (*zuträglich*)

[XV]*Loc. cit.*, 160. Cf. also the remarks about "believing" on pp. 184, 187, and 189. [In M this footnote begins: "Or: 'in terms which are least open to suspicion and most explicit' ('mit den unverdächtigsten und ausdrücklichsten Worten')."—For a different translation of the same passage, cf. *PAW* 183.]

[32]M: evident → noticed

reader of Lessing, although the obvious[33] part of his view, if taken by itself, is somewhat enigmatic. 1) Lessing asserts that all the ancient philosophers and Leibniz[XVI] made use of exoteric presentation of the truth, as distinguished from its esoteric presentation. 2) The exoteric presentation of the truth makes[34] use of statements which are considered by the philosopher himself statements, not of facts, but of mere possibilities. 3) Exoteric statements (i.e. such statements as would not [6]and could not[6] occur within the esoteric teaching) are made by the philosopher for reasons of prudence or expediency. 4) Some[35] exoteric statements are addressed to morally inferior people who ought to be frightened by such statements. 5) There are certain truths which must[36] be concealed. 6) Even the best political constitution is bound to be imperfect. 7) Theoretical life is superior to practical or political life. The impression created by this summary, that there is a close connection between exotericism and a peculiar attitude toward political and practical life, is not misleading: "free-masonry," which [6]as such[6] knows of secret truths, owes its existence to the necessary imperfection of all practical or political life.

Some readers might be inclined to dismiss Lessing's whole teaching at once, since it seems to be based on the obviously erroneous, or[37] merely traditional,[XVII] assumption that *all* the ancient philosophers have[38] made use of exoteric speeches. To warn such readers, one must point out that the incriminated sentence permits of a wholly unobjectionable interpretation: Lessing implicitly denies that writers on philosophical[39] topics who reject exotericism, deserve the name of philosophers.[XVIII] For he knew the passages in Plato in which it is indicated[40] that it was[41] the sophists who refused to conceal the truth.

After Lessing, who died in the year in which Kant published his *Critique of Pure Reason*, the question of exotericism seems to have[42] been lost sight of almost completely, at least among scholars and philosophers as distinguished from novelists. When Schleiermacher introduced that style of Platonic studies, in which classical scholarship is still engaged, and which is based on the identification of the natural order of Platonic dialogues with the sequence of their elaboration, he still had to discuss in detail the view that there are two kinds of Platonic teaching, an exoteric

[33] M: evident or obvious → obvious

[XVI] In a private conversation, published only after his death, Lessing said to F. H. Jacobi about Leibniz: "Es ist bei dem größten Scharfsinn oft sehr schwer, seine eigentliche Meinung zu entdecken." *Werke*, XXIV 173. ["With the greatest ingenuity it is often very difficult to discover his real opinion."]

[34] M: may make → makes

[35] M: At least some → Some

[36] M: ought better → must

[37] M: and → or

[XVII] Compare Clemens Alexandrinus, *Stromata*, V [ch. IX] 58 (365 Stählin).

[38] M: had → have

[39] M: philosophic

[XVIII] Cf. for a similar example of Lessing's way of expressing himself his *Briefe antiquarischen Inhalts* VII (*Werke*, XVII 97ff.).

[40] M: made clear → indicated

[41] M: were

[42] M: has → seems to have

kind and an esoteric one. In doing this, he makes five or six extremely[43] important and true remarks about Plato's literary devices,[XIX] remarks the subtlety of which has, to my knowledge, never been surpassed or even rivaled since. Yet he failed to see the crucial question. He asserts that there is only one Platonic *teaching*[18]—the teaching presented in the dialogues—although there is, so to speak, an infinite number of levels[44] of the understanding of that teaching[45]: it is the same teaching which the beginner understands inadequately, and which only the perfectly trained student of Plato understands adequately[46]. But is then the teaching which the beginner actually understands[47] identical with the *teaching*[18] which the perfectly trained student actually understands? The distinction between Plato's exoteric and esoteric teaching had sometimes been[48] traced back to Plato's opposition to "polytheism and popular religion" and to the necessity [6]in which he found himself[6] of hiding that opposition; Schleiermacher believes he has[49] refuted this view by asserting that "Plato's principles on that topic are clear enough to read in his writings, so that one can scarcely believe that his pupils might have needed still more information about them."[XX] Yet, "polytheism and popular religion" is an ambiguous expression:[50] if Schleiermacher had used the less ambiguous expression[51] "belief in the existence of the gods worshipped by the city of Athens," he could not have said that Plato's opposition to that belief is clearly expressed in his writings.[52] As a matter of fact, in his introduction to his translation of Plato's *Apology of Socrates*, he considers it a weak point of that writing that Plato has not made more energetic use of the argument taken from Socrates's service to Apollo, for refuting the charge that Socrates did not believe in "the[53] old gods."[XXI] If Plato's Socrates believed[54] in "the old gods," is not Plato himself likely to have believed in them as well? And how can one then say that Plato's opposition to "polytheism and popular religion"

[43] M: very → extremely

[XIX] F. Schleiermacher, *Platons Werke*, I 1, Berlin 1804, 20 (3. Auflage, Berlin 1855, 16). [The references to the third edition in footnotes XIX, XX, and XXI were added by LS between the lines in CC, but not in TS. In footnote XXII, LS made no reference to the third edition.]

[44] M: degrees [In TS and CC, LS inserted "degrees" between the lines without crossing out "levels."]

[45] TS/CC: understanding that teaching → the understanding of that teaching

[46] M: perfectly → adequately

[47] TS: understands, → understands [correction not in CC]

[48] M: be

[49] M: to have

[XX] *Loc. cit.*, 14 (3rd ed. Berlin 1855, 12).

[50] In M, one and a half sentences which originally preceded this sentence were crossed out: "But he forgets the fact that Plato has not written his dialogues for his pupils only, but rather as a possession for all times, or that not all readers of Plato are pupils of Plato. Yet this refutation is based on."

[51] Omitted in TS, but later inserted by LS. (Correction not in CC.)

[52] In M a sentence originally following this sentence was crossed out: "And is not that belief some sort of 'polytheism and popular religion'?"

[53] In TS and CC, but not in M, the opening quotation marks were placed in front of "a weak point . . ." because the typist wrongly took the opening quotation marks in the sentence that was crossed out (cf. n52) to indicate the beginning of the quotation in this sentence.

[XXI] *Platons Werke*, I 2, Berlin 1805, 185 (3. Aufl., Berlin 1855, 128).

[54] TS/CC: has believed → believed

as such is clearly expressed in his writings? Schleiermacher's strongest argument against the distinction of two teachings of Plato appears to be his assertion that Plato's [6]real[6] investigations are hidden, not absolutely, but only from the inattentive readers, or that attention[55] is the only prerequisite for a full understanding of his real investigations as distinguished from those investigations which are merely the "skin" of the former.[XXII] But did any man in his senses ever assert that Plato wished to hide his secret teaching from all readers or from all men? Did any man whose judgment can claim to carry any weight in this matter ever understand by Plato's esoteric[56] teaching anything other than that teaching of his dialogues which escapes the inattentive readers only? The only possible difference of opinion concerns exclusively the meaning of the distinction between inattentive and attentive readers: does a continuous way[57] lead from the extremely inattentive reader to the extremely attentive reader, or is the way between the two extremes interrupted by a chasm? Schleiermacher tacitly assumes that the way from the beginning to the end is continuous, whereas, according to Plato, philosophy presupposes a real conversion[58],[XXIII] *i.e.*[18] a total break with the attitude of the beginner: the beginner is a man who has not yet for one moment left the cave, and who has even never[59] turned his eyes away from the shadows of man-made things[60] toward the exit of the cave, whereas the philosopher is the man who has left the cave and who (if he is not compelled to do otherwise) lives[61] outside of the cave, on "the island of the blessed."[62] The difference between the beginner and the philosopher (for the perfectly trained student of Plato is no one else but the genuine philosopher) is a difference not of degree, but of kind. Now, it is well-known that, according to Plato, virtue is knowledge or science; therefore, the beginner is inferior to the perfectly trained student of Plato not only intellectually, but also morally. That is to say, the

[55] M: the attention → attention

[XXII] "Das geheime...(ist) nur beziehungsweise so..." I 1, 12.—"...die eigentliche Untersuchung wird mit einer anderen, nicht wie mit einem Schleier, sondern wie mit einer angewachsenen Haut überkleidet, welche dem Unaufmerksamen, *aber auch nur diesem*, dasjenige verdeckt, was eigentlich soll beobachtet oder gefunden werden, dem Aufmerksamen aber nur noch den Sinn für den inneren Zusammenhang schärft und läutert." *Loc. cit.*, 20. (The italics are mine.) ["The secretive...(is) only relatively so..."; "...the actual investigation is covered with another, not as if with a veil but as if with a grown-on skin, which conceals from the inattentive [reader] but only from him that which actually ought to be observed or found, but which for the attentive [reader] sharpens and chastens the sense for the internal coherence."]

[56] M: secret or esoteric → esoteric

[57] In TS, "path" was written (not by LS) between the lines, and a question mark in the margin.

[58] M: "conversion" → conversion

[XXIII] *Republic* 518c–e and 521e [recte: 521c]. Cf. also *Phaedo* 69a–c. [In TS and CC, LS added "and 619c–d" to the references to the *Republic*. However, in M he inserted the reference in footnote XXIV. Cf. FP 361n11 and *CM* 27n34.]

[59] M: not even → even never

[60] In M, Strauss added "of men and man-made things" in the margin. The typist dropped "men and."

[61] M: and prefers the life → and who lives → and who (if he is not compelled to do otherwise) lives

[62] M: cave, the life on "the island of the blessed" to the life in the cave → cave, on "the island of the blessed"

morality[63] of the beginners has a basis essentially different from the basis on which the morality of the philosopher rests: their virtue is not[64] genuine virtue, but vulgar or political virtue only,[65] a virtue based not on insight[66], but on customs or laws.[XXIV] We may say, the morality of the beginners is the morality of the "auxiliaries" of the *Republic*, but not yet the morality of the "guardians." Now, the "auxiliaries,"[67] the best among whom are the beginners, must believe[68] "noble lies,"[XXV] *i.e.*[69] statements which, while being useful for the political community, are nevertheless lies. And there is a difference not of degree but of kind[70] between truth and lie or untruth. And what holds true of the difference between truth and lies[71] holds equally true of the difference between esoteric and exoteric teaching; for Plato's exoteric teaching is identical with his "noble lies." This connection of considerations, which is more or less familiar to every reader of Plato, if not duly emphasized by all students of Plato, is not even mentioned[72] by Schleiermacher in his refutation of the [6]view that there is a[6] distinction between Plato's exoteric and esoteric teaching. Nor does he,[73] in that context, [6]as much as allude[6] to Lessing's dialogues ("Ernst und Falk" and Lessing's conversation with F. H. Jacobi) which probably come closer[74] to the spirit[75] of the Platonic dialogues and their technique than any other modern work in the German language[76]. Therefore Schleiermacher's refutation[77] of the view in question is not convincing. A comparison of his *Philosophic Ethics* with the *Nicomachean Ethics* would bring to light the reason[XXVI] why he failed to pay any attention to the difference between the morality of the beginner and the morality of the philosopher, *i.e.*[18] to the difference which is at the bottom of the difference between exoteric and esoteric teaching.

I return to Lessing. How was Lessing led to notice,[XXVII] and to understand, the information about the fact [6]that[6] "all the ancient philosophers" had distinguished

[63] M: basis of morality → morality

[64] M: is not, and cannot be, → is not

[65] Originally, footnote XXIV was placed after "only." LS made the correction in M in pencil.

[66] M: philosophy → insight

[XXIV] *Republic* 430c3–5, 619c–d and *Phaedo* 82a10–b8. [LS inserted in M, but not in TS/CC, "*Rep.* 619c–d." Cf. the comment to footnote XXIII.]

[67] M: "auxiliaries"

[68] TS/CC: believe in → believe

[XXV] *Republic* 414b4ff. Cf. *Laws* 663d6ff.

[69] TS/CC: i.e. in → *i.e.* [italics added in TS, correction not in CC]

[70] TS/CC: is no difference of degree, but of kind, → is a difference not of degree but of kind

[71] M: lie,

[72] M: as much as alluded to → even mentioned

[73] M: he pay any attention, → he,

[74] TS/CC: come probably nearer → probably come closer

[75] M: spirit of the technique → spirit

[76] TS/CC: in the German language does → in the German language [The five words were added between the lines in M.]

[77] M: refutation is not convincing → refutation

[XXVI] That reason can be discovered by an analysis of the following statements, *e.g.*: "Knowledge of the essence of reason is ethics" (*Philosophische Sittenlehre*, § 60) and "The ordinary distinction between offensive and defensive wars is quite empty." (*Loc. cit.*, § 276).

[XXVII] Cf. the remarks of the young Lessing on the relevant passage in Gellius (XX 5) in the tenth *Literaturbrief* (*Werke*, IV 38).

between their exoteric and their esoteric teaching? If I am not mistaken, he rediscovered the bearing of that distinction by his own exertion after having[78] undergone his conversion[79], *i.e.*[18] after having had[80] the experience of what philosophy is and what[81] sacrifices it requires. For it is that experience which leads in a straight way to the distinction between the two groups of men, the philosophic men and the unphilosophic men, and therewith to the distinction between the two ways of presenting the truth. In a famous letter to a friend,[XXVIII] he expresses his fear that "by throwing away certain prejudices, I have thrown away a little too much that I shall have to fetch back[82]."[XXIX] That passage has sometimes been understood to indicate that Lessing was about to return from the intransigent rationalism of his earlier period toward a more positive view of the Bible and the Biblical tradition. There is ample evidence to show that this interpretation is wrong.[XXX] The context of the passage makes it clear that the things which Lessing had "thrown away" before and which, he feels, he ought to "fetch back" were truths which he descried "from afar" in a book by Ferguson, as he believed on the basis of what he had seen in the table of contents of that book. He also descried "from afar" in Ferguson's book "truths in the continual contradiction of which we happen to live[83] and we have to go on living continually in the interest of our quietude." There may very well be a connection between the two kinds of truth[84]: the truths which Lessing[85] had thrown away formerly[86] may have been truths contradictory to the truths[87] generally accepted by the philosophy of enlightenment[88] and also accepted by

[78] CC: having had

[79] M: "conversion" → conversion

[80] TS: i.e. after having made → *i.e.* after having had [correction not in CC]

[81] TS/CC: which → what

[XXVIII] To Moses Mendelssohn, of January 9, 1771.

[82] LS inserted between the lines in M, without crossing out "to fetch back," the alternative translation "get back again" (which was adopted by TS/CC). In the margin of the manuscript he put an exclamation mark. My decision to retain the first translation is supported by LS's use of this translation a few lines later.

[XXIX] Another statement about the crisis which Lessing underwent when he was about forty, occurs in the *Briefe antiquarischen Inhalts*, LIV (*Werke*, XVII 250).

[XXX] See e.g. von Olshausen in his introduction to *Werke*, XXIV 41ff.—Compare also Jacobi's letter to Hamann of December 30th, 1784: "Als (Lessings) Erziehung des Menschengeschlechts ... von einigen für eine nicht unchristliche Schrift, beinahe für eine Palinodie angesehen wurde, stieg sein Ärger über die Albernheit des Volkes bis zum Ergrimmen." (F. H. Jacobi, *Werke*, I 398). ["When (Lessing's) *Education of the Human Race* ... was considered by some as a not un-Christian writing, [but] almost as a palinode, his anger about the absurdity of the people grew to the point of fury."]

[83] brM: actually live → happen to live [In M, a few sentences of this paragraph ("The context of the passage ... he ought to 'fetch back' are 'truth in the continual contradiction of which we have to live'; such truths he descried 'from afar' in a book by Ferguson as he believed on the basis of what he had seen in the table of content of that work.") were crossed out by LS. He inserted a red cross in crayon in the margin. The passage that is reproduced in TS and which differs slightly from M is to be found on a brown slip of paper (brM), which also has a red cross in crayon in the margin.]

[84] brM: truths

[85] brM: L.

[86] TS: formerly, → formerly [correction not in CC]

[87] brM: those → the truths

[88] brM: his enlightened contemporaries → the philosophy of enlightenment

Lessing throughout his life.[89] At any rate,[90] two years later he openly rebuked the more recent philosophers who had evaded the contradiction between wisdom and prudence by becoming much too wise to submit to the rule of prudence which had been observed by Leibniz and all the ancient philosophers. External evidence is[91] in favor of the view that the book referred to by Lessing[92] is Ferguson's *Essay on the History of Civil Society*.[XXXI] The "truths in the continual contradiction of which we have to live," which had been discussed by Ferguson and which are indicated to a certain extent in the table of contents of his *Essay*,[XXXII] concerned the ambiguous character of civilization, *i.e.*[18] the theme of the two famous early writings of Rousseau, which Lessing, as[93] he perhaps felt, had not considered in his youth carefully enough[94].[XXXIII] Lessing expressed his view of the ambiguous character of civilization [6]some years later[6] in these more precise terms: even the absolutely best civil constitution is necessarily imperfect. It seems then to have been[95] the political problem[96] which gave Lessing's thought a decisive turn away from the philosophy of enlightenment indeed, yet not toward romanticism of any sort—toward what is called a deeper, historical view of government and religion[97]—, but toward an older type of philosophy. How near he apparently came to certain romantic views on his way from the philosophy of enlightenment to that older type of philosophy[98] we may learn from what F. H. Jacobi tells us in an essay of his which is devoted to the explanation of a political remark made by Lessing. According to Jacobi, Lessing once said[99] that the arguments against Papal[100] despotism are either no

[89]LS inserted "and accepted also by Lessing throughout his life" in the margin of brM. However, "also" was dropped by the typist.

[90]brM: At any rate, he censured → At any rate,

[91]M: decides → is

[92]M: in question → referred to by L.

[XXXI]Cf. von Olshausen, *loc. cit.*, 44f., who however rejects this conclusion on the basis of "internal reasons."

[XXXII]Cf. e.g. the following headings of sections: "Of the separation of arts and professions" [part IV, sect. 1] and "Of the corruption incident to polished nations" [part VI, sect. 3].

[93]Inserted in TS/CC.

[94]M: dismissed in his youth somewhat too rashly → not considered in his youth carefully enough

[XXXIII]The influence of Ferguson's mitigated Rousseauism on Lessing can be seen from a comparison of the following quotations with what Lessing says in "Ernst und Falk" on the obvious reasons of the necessary imperfection of all civil societies. Ferguson says in Part I, section 3 and 4: "The mighty engine which we suppose to have formed society, only tends to set its members at variance, or to continue their intercourse after the bands of affection are broken." "The titles of *fellow-citizen* and *countryman*, unopposed to those of *alien* and *foreigner*, to which they refer, would fall into disuse, and lose their meaning." "...it is vain to expect that we can give to the multitude of a people a sense of union among themselves, without admitting hostility to those who oppose them." See also Part IV, section 2: "...if the lot of a slave among the ancients was really more wretched than that of the indigent labourer and the mechanic among the moderns, it may be doubted, whether the superior orders, who are in possession of consideration and honours, do not proportionally fail in the dignity which befits their condition."

[95]M: At any rate, it was → It seems then to have been

[96]M: question → problem

[97]M: society and religion → government and religion

[98]TS: philosophy, → philosophy [correction not in CC]

[99]M: had remarked → once said

[100]M: papal

arguments at all, or else they are two or three times as valid against the despotism of princes.[XXXIV] Could Lessing have held[101] the view that ecclesiastical despotism is two or three times better than secular despotism?[102] Jacobi elsewhere says in his own name[103] but certainly in the spirit of Lessing, that that despotism which is based "exclusively"[104] on superstition, is less bad than secular despotism.[XXXV] Now, secular despotism could easily be allied[105] with the philosophy of enlightenment, and therewith with the rejection of exotericism strictly speaking, as is shown above all by the teaching of the classic of enlightened despotism: the teaching of Hobbes. But "despotism based exclusively on superstition," *i.e.*[18] not at all on force, cannot be maintained if the non-superstitious minority does not voluntarily refrain from [6]openly[6] exposing and refuting the "superstitious" beliefs[106]. Lessing had then not to wait for the experience of Robespierre's despotism to realize the relative truth of what the romantics asserted against the principles of J.-J.[107] Rousseau who seems to have[108] believed in a political solution of the problem of civilization: Lessing realized that [6]relative[6] truth one generation earlier[109], and he rejected it in favor of the way leading to absolute truth, or of philosophy. The experience which he had[110] in that moment enabled him to understand the meaning of Leibniz'[111] "prudence" in a manner infinitely more adequate than the enlightened Leibnizians among his contemporaries did and could do. Leibniz is then that link in the chain of the tradition of exotericism which is nearest to Lessing. Leibniz, however, was not the only 17th century thinker who was initiated. Not to mention the prudent Descartes,[112] even so bold a writer as Spinoza had admitted the necessity of "pia dogmata, hoc est, talia quae animum ad obedientiam movent"[113] as distinguished from "vera

[XXXIV]Jacobi, *Werke*, II 334 ("Etwas das Lessing gesagt hat"). Jacobi quotes in that article Ferguson's *Essay* extensively. [Cf. Jacobi, "Something that Lessing Said," translated by Dale E. Snow, in *What is Enlightenment? Eighteenth-Century Answers and Twentieth-Century Questions*, edited by James Schmidt (Berkeley: University of California Press, 1991), 198.]

[101] M: Lessing held then → Should Lessing have held

[102] M: despotism. → despotism?

[103] M: name,

[104] M: exclusively ("einzig und allein")

[XXXV]Jacobi, *Werke*, III 469. Cf. Lessing's "Gespräch über die Soldaten und Mönche" (*Werke*, XXIV 159).

[105] M: reconciled → allied

[106] M: and attacking the increasing "superstitions" → and attacking "superstitions" → and refuting "superstitious" beliefs

[107]TS/CC: J.J. → J.-J.

[108]TS: who had → who seems to have

[109] M: before → earlier

[110]TS/CC: made → had

[111] M: Leibniz's

[112] Here a footnote was added in M by LS in pencil but not transcribed by the typist: "The early Cartesians distinguished the 'exoteric' *Discours de la méthode* from the 'acroamatic' *Meditationes*. Cf. É. Gilson's commentary on the *Discours* (Paris 1930, p. 79). Cf. e.g. *Discours de la méthode*, sixième partie, *in princ.*: writing, being an action, is subject to religious and political authority, but thought is not." See *Discourse on Method*, trans. Richard Kennington (Newburyport, MA: Focus Philosophical Library, 2007), 48.

[113] *Tractatus theologico-politicus*, cap. 14, § 20 (Bruder). The quotation is taken from a longer sentence: "Sequitur denique, fidem non tam requirere vera, quam pia dogmata, hoc est, talia, quae animum ad obedientiam movent; tametsi inter ea plurima sint, quae nec umbram veritatis habent, dummodo tamen

dogmata."[XXXVI] But Lessing did not have[114] to rely on any modern or[115] medieval representatives of the[116] tradition:[117] he was familiar with its sources. It was precisely his intransigent classicism—his considered view that close study of the classics is the only way in which a diligent and thinking man can become a philosopher[XXXVII]—which had led him, first, to notice the exotericism of some ancient[118] philosophers, and later on to understand the exotericism of all the ancient philosophers.

---

is, qui eadem amplectitur, eadem falsa esse ignoret; alias rebellis necessario esset." ("It follows, finally, that faith does not require true dogmas so much as pious ones, that is, such as move the spirit toward obedience—even though among them there may be very many that do not have even a shadow of truth, yet so long as he who embraces them is ignorant of their being false. Otherwise he would necessarily be rebellious." Spinoza, *Theologico-Political Treatise*, trans. Martin D. Yaffe (Newburyport, MA: Focus Philosophical Library, 2004), 164.) Cf. also *SCR* 171; *PAW* 180; *GS–2* 199.

[XXXVI] *Tractatus theologico-politicus*, cap. 14, § 20 (Bruder). [In M the footnote continues: "Cf. cap. 15 towards the end. See also *Tract. de int. emend.* § 17 and 14 and Hobbes, *Leviathan*, ch. 12 and 46."—The reference to the *Tractatus de Intellectus Emendatione* was inserted in M between the lines.—Cf. *PAW* 35n17.

[114] M: Lessing had not

[115] M: and → or

[116] M: that

[117] In M this sentence is preceded by two sentences: "Despite, or because of, that admission Spinoza rejected Maimonides' allegorical interpretation of the Bible as 'harmful, useless and absurd'. Thus, he cannot be considered a genuine spokesman of the tradition." Both sentences and the footnote to the Spinoza quotation ("*Tractatus theologico-politicus*, cap. 7, § 87 (Bruder).") were not transcribed by the typist. In M, LS made two little marks in black ink, one before and one after the last two sentences.

[XXXVII] He writes in the 71st *Literaturbrief* (*Werke*, IV 197), after having quoted a statement of Leibniz in praise of criticism and study of the classics: "Gewiß, die Kritik auf dieser Seite betrachtet, und das Studium der Alten bis zu dieser Bekanntschaft (with Plato, Aristotle, Archimedes and Apollonius) getrieben, ist keine Pedanterei, sondern vielmehr das Mittel, wodurch Leibniz der geworden ist, der er war, und *der einzige Weg*, durch welchen sich ein fleißiger und denkender Mann ihm nähern kann." (The italics are mine.) Ten years later (1769) he says in the *Briefe antiquarischen Inhalts* XLV (*Werke*, XVII 218): "Wir sehen mehr als die Alten, und doch dürften vielleicht unsere Augen schlechter sein als die Augen der Alten; die Alten sahen weniger als wir, aber ihre Augen...möchten leicht schärfer gewesen sein als unsere.—Ich fürchte, daß die ganze Vergleichung der Alten und Neuern hierauf hinauslaufen dürfte." ["Certainly, the criticism considered from this side, and the study of the ancients pushed to this familiarity (with Plato, Aristotle, Archimedes and Appolonius) is not pedantry, but in fact the means whereby Leibniz became who he was and *the only way* through which a diligent and thinking man can approach him." "We see more than the ancients, and yet perhaps our eyes might be worse than the eyes of the ancients; the ancients saw less [or, fewer things] than we, but their eyes...may easily have been sharper than ours.—I am afraid, that the entire comparison of ancients and moderns might come down to this."—Cf. "Notes on Philosophy and Revelation," in Heinrich Meier, *Leo Strauss and the Theologico-Political Problem*, translated by M. Brainard (Cambridge, UK: Cambridge University Press, 2006), 178f.]

[118] M: classical → ancient

APPENDIX F

SUPPLEMENT 1: EARLY PLAN OF "EXOTERIC TEACHING"

A

1) To-day the distinction between exoteric and esoteric teaching is wholly opposed—this opposition is due to the fact that modern philosophy has destroyed the possibility of understanding—and that class. scholarship has made a tremendous progress.[1]
2) At the end of the 18th century, that distinction was still understood: Lessing.
3) Schleiermacher's criticism: he does not see any more the moral problem involved. [Schleiermacher] to whom we are indebted for the deepest insights into the element of Plato's writings

3a) Lessing—Leibniz—Hobbes[2] (vera—pia dogmata)—Spinoza—RMbM[3]—

4) Post-Ciceronian authors.
5) Cicero—but he himself is an exoteric writer.[4]
6) Plato— a) Letters Ep. II, 314a–c.[5] Ep.VII, 341a–e, 344d.[6]
   b) Phaedrus, Rep (drama and writings); Timaeus
7) Xenophon Cynegeticus.[7]

[1] Cf. the following statements in *PAW*: "We are prevented from considering this possibility [i.e., the possibility of communication of crucial issues between the lines], and still more from considering the questions connected with it, by some habits produced by, or related to, a comparatively recent progress in historical research" (*PAW* 26). "Modern historical research [...] has counteracted or even destroyed an earlier tendency to read between the lines of the great writers" (*PAW* 31f.).

[2] LS first wrote "Spinoza—Hobbes" but crossed out "Spinoza."

[3] That is, Rabbi Moshe ben Maimon, the traditional acronym for Maimonides.

[4] Cf. *PAW* 34n16 and 185n85. See "Der Ort der Vorsehungslehre nach der Ansicht Maimunis," in *GS–2* 188n29; PoP 547n29.

[5] Cf. *OPS* 29.

[6] Cf. *PAW* 35n17 and 187n90.

[7] Cf. *PAW* 29n11: "[C]ertain contemporaries of the 'rhetor' Xenophon believed that 'what is beautifully and methodically written, is not beautifully and methodically written' (*Cynegeticus*, 13.6)." See also LS to Jacob Klein, August 7, 1939, in: *GS–3* 576 and SSTX 502.

8) Plato's remarks on Homer and especially on Hesiod.[8]
9) Hesiod on Muses....[9]
10) Herakleitus
11) The big exceptions: Epicurus and Sophists.[10]
    cf. Cic. *Rep.* III 16, 26,[11] N.D. I 41.[12]
    cf. Usener.[13]
    a) Epicurus
    b) Sophists.

[8] Cf. LS to Jacob Klein, October 10, 1939, in *GS–3* 582: "To cut the matter short, what Plato says in the *Theaetetus* on the poets of the past, namely that they had disguised philosophy as poetry, can really be *demonstrated* in the case of Hesiod (who occurs in the *Republic* somewhere in the middle of an enumeration). I am convinced that it is not different in the case of Homer. One day read the *Shield of Achilles*! And the self-identification with Odysseus in the *Odyssey* and the strange fact that Thersites *says* the truth."

[9] Cf. LS to Jacob Klein, October 10, 1939, in *GS–3* 581f., esp. 582: "The key to the book are—the Muses, who are explicitly referred to as the main issue. The Muses have a twofold genealogy: 1) exoterically they descend from Zeus and Mnemosyne; 2) esoterically they are offspring of Ocean. You will immediately guess how this is connected on the basis of the beginning of the *Odyssey* as well as the remarks in the *Theaetetus* and in the *Metaphysics* on the origin of Thales' dictum." Cf. *LAM* 36f.

[10] Cf., however, *PAW* 36.

[11] See *LAM* 90 with 136n21. Cf. Cicero, *Republic* 3.16.26: "Ad haec illa dici solent primum ab iis, qui minime sunt in disserendo mali, qui in ea causa eo plus auctoritatis habent, quia, cum *de viro bono queritur, quem apertum et simplicem volumus esse, non sunt in disputando vafri, non veteratores, non malitiosi*; negant enim sapientem idcirco virum bonum esse, quod eum sua sponte ac per se bonitas et iustitia delectet, sed quod vacua metu, cura, sollicitudine, periculo vita bonorum virorum sit, contra autem improbis semper aliqui scrupus in animis haereat, semper iis ante oculos iudicia et supplicia versentur; nullum autem emolumentum esse, nullum iniustitia partum praemium tantum, semper ut timeas, semper ut adesse, semper ut impendere aliquam poenam putes, damna...." (My italics, H.K.). ("To such arguments as these the following are usually the replies first given by those who are not unskilful in disputation, and whose discussions of this subject have all the greater weight because, in the search for the good man, whom we require to be open and frank, they do not themselves use crafty and rascally tricks of argument—these men say first of all that a wise man is not good because goodness and justice of or in themselves give him pleasure, but because the life of a good man is free from fear, anxiety, worry, and danger, while on the other hand the minds of the wicked are always troubled by one thing or another, and trial and punishment always stand before their eyes. They add, on the other hand, that no advantage or reward won by injustice is great enough to offset constant fear, or the ever-present thought that some punishment is near, or is threatening,.... losses ...." Cicero, *De Re Publica. De Legibus*, translated by Clinton Walker Keyes (Cambridge, MA: Harvard University Press, 1961), 205–07.)

[12] Cf. Cicero, *De natura deorum*, 1.41.115: "'At etiam de sanctitate, de pietate adversus deos libros scripsit Epicurus.' At quo modo in his loquitur? Ut T. Coruncanium aut P. Scaevolam pontifices maximos te audire dicas, non eum qui sustulerit omnem funditus religionem nec manibus ut Xerxes sed rationibus deorum inmortalium templa et aras everterit". ("'Yes, but Epicurus actually wrote books about holiness and piety.' But what is the language of these books? Such that you think you are listening to a Coruncanius or a Scaevola, high priests, not to the man who destroyed the very foundations of religion, and overthrew—not by main force like Xerxes, but by argument—the temples and the altars of the immortal gods." Cicero, *De Natura Deorum. Academica*, translated by H. Rackham (Cambridge, MA: Harvard University Press, 1961), 111.) Cf. also 1.44.122f.: "'At etiam liber est Epicuri de sanctitate.' Ludimur ab homine non tam faceto quam ad scribendi licentiam libero." ("'Why, but Epicurus (you tell me) actually wrote a treatise on holiness.' Epicurus is making fun of us, though he is not so much a humorist as a loose and careless writer." Cicero, *De Natura Deorum*, 119.)

[13] Hermann Usener published a collection of fragments called *Epicurea* in 1887. For the Cicero quotations from the previous footnote, cf. *Epicurea* (Stuttgart: Teubner, 1966), 100.

B. Explanation: Gellius XX 5:[14] res civiles—subtiliores

↓

(natura)

Exoteric philosophy is a Weltanschauung σῴζων political and moral life: makes man the center of the universe.[15]

Esoteric philosophy sees man in his insignificance.[16]

Disproportion of things political and things speculative—cf. Ar. on laws and τέχναι.[17]

Quieta movere and Quieta non movere[18]

Philosophy as essentially unrevolutionary and as interested only in truth.

Lessing had not to wait for the French Revolution in order to separate himself from the philosophy of Enlightenment.

Lie in the soul—lie in speech.[19]

[14] See Aulus Gellius, *The Attic Nights*, 20.5: "Commentationum suarum artiumque quas discipulis tradebat Aristoteles philosophus, regis Alexandri magister, duas species habuisse dicitur. Alia erant, quae nominabat ἐξωτερικά, alia, quae appellabat ἀκροατικά. Ἐξωτερικά dicebantur, quae ad rhetoricas meditationes facultatemque argutiarum *civilumque rerum* notitiam conducebant, ἀκροατικά autem vocabantur, in quibus philosophia remotior *subtiliorque* agitabatur quaeque ad *naturae* contemplationes disceptationesve dialecticas pertinebant" (My italics, H.K.). ("The philosopher Aristotle, the teacher of king Alexander, is said to have had two forms of the lectures and instructions which he delivered to his pupils. One of these was the kind called ἐξωτερικά, or 'exoteric,' the other ἀκροατικά, or 'acroatic.' Those were called 'exoteric' which he gave training in rhetorical exercises, logical subtlety, and acquaintance with politics; those were called 'acroatic' in which more profound and recondite philosophy was discussed, which related to the contemplation of nature or dialectic discussions." Aulus Gellius, *The Attic Nights*, translated by John C. Rolfe (Cambridge, MA: Harvard University Press, 1961), vol. 3, 431–33.)

[15] Cf. *LAM* 93; *NRH* 155 and 248.

[16] Cf. *GS–1* 244f.; *SCR* 190.

[17] Cf. *CM* 21f.: "[Aristotle] is much less sure than Hippodamus of the virtues of innovation. It seems that Hippodamus had not given thought to the difference between innovation in the arts and innovation in law, or to the possible tension between the need for political stability and what one might call technological change."

[18] LS is alluding to the legal maxim "stare decisis, et non quieta movere" ("to stand by decisions and not to move quietude") that calls for the adherence to precedents and warns against changes. In Germany, "quieta non movere" became well known after Bismarck mentioned the proverb in a speech in 1891: "There is an old, good political proverb: *Quieta non movere*, that means, do not disturb what rests quietly; and this is truly conservative: not to support a legislation which upsets something for which no need for change exists." Cf. Otto von Bismarck, *Werke in Auswahl*, edited by Rudolf Buchner and Georg Engel (Darmstadt: Wissenschaftliche Buchgesellschaft, 1983), vol. 8 (B), 73.

[19] Cf. Plato, *Republic* 382a–e and 535d–e. See *PAW* 35 and *WIPP* 136.

APPENDIX F

SUPPLEMENT 2: LATER PLAN OF "EXOTERIC TEACHING"

Plan.

I

1. Philosophy and class. scholarship; Zeller.
2. Husserl: Philos. als strenge Wiss. und Philos. als Weltanschauung.[1]
3. Lessing'[s] explanation of exotericism.
4. Schleiermacher'[s] criticism of exotericism. Hegel's criticism of exotericism.[2]
5. The basis of Lessing's rediscovery of exotericism: the political problem.

[1]The second point of the list was inserted in the margin. The numbers of the first part of the plan were changed accordingly.—Edmund Husserl's "Philosophie als strenge Wissenschaft" was first published in *Logos* 1, no. 3 (1911): 289–341. In his late essay "Philosophy as Rigorous Science and Political Philosophy," LS writes: "Let us see whether a place for political philosophy is left in Husserl's philosophy. What I am going to say is based on a re-reading, after many years of neglect, of Husserl's programmatic essay 'Philosophy as Rigorous Science.' The essay was first published in 1911, and Husserl's thought underwent many important changes afterward. Yet it is his most important utterance on the question with which we are concerned" (*SPPP* 34). In the same essay, LS also deals with Husserl's view of "Weltanschauung" (*SPPP* 36f.).

[2]The second part of this point was inserted in the margin.—Cf. G. W. F. Hegel, *Vorlesungen über die Geschichte der Philosophie II*, in *Werke*, edited by Eva Moldenhauer and Karl Markus Michel (Frankfurt am Main: Suhrkamp, 1986), vol. 19, 21f.: "Eine andere Schwierigkeit soll die sein: man unterscheidet exoterische und esoterische Philosophie. Tennemann sagt ([*Geschichte der Philosophie*,] Bd. II, S. 220): 'Platon bediente sich desselben Rechts, welches jedem Denker zusteht, von seinen Entdeckungen nur so viel, als er für gut fand, und nur denen mitzuteilen, welchen er Empfänglichkeit zutraute. Auch Aristoteles hatte eine esoterische und exoterische Philosophie, nur mit dem Unterschiede, daß bei diesem der Unterschied bloß *formal*, beim Plato hingegen auch zugleich *material* war.' Wie einfältig! Das sieht aus, als sei der Philosoph im Besitz seiner Gedanken wie der äußerlichen Dinge. Die Gedanken sind aber ganz etwas anderes. Die philosophische Idee besitzt umgekehrt den Menschen. Wenn Philosophen sich über philosophische Gegenstände explizieren, so müssen sie sich nach ihren Ideen richten; sie können sie nicht in der Tasche behalten. Spricht man auch mit einigen äußerlich, so ist die Idee immer darin enthalten, wenn die Sache nur Inhalt hat. Zur Mitteilung, Übergabe einer äußerlichen Sache gehört nicht viel, aber zur Mitteilung der Idee gehört Geschicklichkeit. Sie bleibt immer etwas Esoterisches; man hat also nicht bloß das Exoterische der Philosophen. Das sind oberflächliche Vorstellungen." ("Another difficulty is said to be the following: a distinction is made between exoteric and esoteric

6. Lessing—Leibniz—Spinoza (—RMbM)
7. Lessing'[s] intransigent classicism.

II[3]

7. Aristotle's "exoteric" writings.[4]
8. Cicero.
9. Xenoph. Cyneg.
10. Plato's Letters
11. Plato's dialogues. Phaedrus Rep Timaeus.
12. Plato on the poets
    and Hesiod on Muses.
13. Herakleitus
14. The big exceptions: Epicurus and Sophists. Cic. Rep. III

The questions: Why do they hide? and How can we decipher their truths will be discussed in[5] the continuation of this article. The historian cannot do more than to show that the ancient philosophers did hide their thoughts, that their works are—mixtures of truth and lies. The question of why they did it, must be answered by a philosopher.

---

philosophy. Tennemann ([*Geschichte der Philosophie*,] vol. II, 220) says: 'Plato exercised the same right that every thinker has to communicate only so much of his discoveries as he thought good, and only to those whom he credited with capacity to receive it. Aristotle, too, had an esoteric and an exoteric philosophy, but with the difference, that in his case the distinction was merely *formal*, while in the case of Plato it was at the same time *material*.' How simpleminded! This looks as if the philosopher is in possession of his thoughts in the same way as of external things. But the thoughts are something utterly different. Instead of the reverse, the philosophic idea is in possession of the human being. When philosophers elaborate on philosophic subjects, they have to follow [the course of] their ideas; they cannot keep them in their pocket. Even when speaking externally [*äußerlich*] to some people, the idea must be contained [in this speech], if the matter [*Sache*] has any content at all. It does not take much to hand over an external item, but the communication of ideas requires skill. The idea always remains something esoteric; hence, one does not merely have the exoteric [*das Exoterische*] of the philosophers. These notions are superficial.")

[3]The second part of this plan has been published previously by Heinrich Meier in the introduction to *Die Denkbewegung von Leo Strauss. Die Geschichte der Philosophie und die Intention des Philosophen* (Stuttgart/Weimar: J. B. Metzler, 1996), 15n4.

[4]Cf. *PAW* 28: "After the great theologian Schleiermacher asserted, with an unusually able argument, the view that there is only one Platonic teaching, the question of the esotericism of the ancient philosophers was narrowed down, for all practical purposes, to *the meaning of Aristotle's 'exoteric speeches'*; and in this regard one of the greatest humanists of the present day asserts that the attribution of a secret teaching to Aristotle is 'obviously a late invention originating in the spirit of Neo-Pythagoreanism.'" (My italics, H.K.) Aristotle refers at least eight times in his works to *exōterikoi logoi* (cf., for example, *Nicomachean Ethics*, 1102a26 and 1140a3, *Politics*, 1278b31 and 1323a22 as well as *Metaphysics*, 1076a28).

[5]LS first wrote "in a separate" but crossed it out.

APPENDIX G

LEO STRAUSS: LECTURE NOTES FOR "PERSECUTION AND THE ART OF WRITING" (1939)

Edited by Hannes Kerber

[1 recto] *Persecution and the Art of Writing.*

The purpose of this lecture[1] is to draw your attention to a certain approach to earlier literature—to an approach which, to my mind, has not been sufficiently considered. I do not say that the approach which I am going to suggest, is necessarily correct, but I believe that it is worth considering. As my starting-point, I shall choose certain phenomena which are accessible to everyone's observation, at least to-day, if not at all times.

Before I start, I want to point out one example of the questions which [2]originally[2] led me to consider the approach in question. You all know the *Don Quixote*[3]—you know the story and the characters—you remember how Cervantes interrupts his account of Don Quixote's fight with the Biscaianer[4] because, he says, he does not know the continuation—how Cervantes, as he recounts, was looking around everywhere for the continuation until he discovered by chance an Arabic MS. on the exchange in Toledo, how he got it translated into Castilian[5]—thus, the larger part of that immortal work claims to be translated from the Arabic, it claims to be written, not by Cervantes, but by Sid Hamed, a Muslim.[6]—Why does Cervantes

[1] Cf. p. 273n10..

[2] Inserted by LS in pencil between the lines or in the margin.

[3] According to German custom, LS prefaces the title of *Don Quixote* with the definite article, in order to distinguish for the listeners his mentioning the book from his mentioning the hero.

[4] That is, the Biscayan.

[5] Cf. Miguel de Cervantes, *Don Quixote*, chapter IX. Cf., for example, *NRH* 62; *CM* 158; *OPS* 169–70. See also "The Origins of Political Science and the Problem of Socrates," in *Interpretation* 23, no. 2 (1996): 152.

[6] Cf. LS to Jacob Klein, August 18, 1939, in *GS–3* 580f.: "Since we are talking about exotericism—epaggelomai [I announce] that I have understood *Don Quixote*. The key is this: the book is the work of two authors, of Cervantes and of Sid Hamed, *i.e.*, a Christian and a Muslim. Now take away the artificial

tell this obvious lie? Is this just a joke for joke's sake? Everyone admits that the *Don Quixote* is a *deep* book, Don Quixote is not just a fool, he *represents* something, certainly a folly, but a *great* folly, an *eternal* folly. What is then the reason that he makes such a strange joke concerning the authorship of the book, that he attributes the authorship to Sid Hamed? What is the *relation* of that strange joke to the eternal folly represented by Don Quixote?

Cervantes satirizes the books of chivalry. This is his professed intention. Accordingly the books of chivalry which drove Don Quixote mad, are burned by the priest and barber of Don Quixote's hometown, i.e. by the authority spiritual and temporal.[7] But, before they are burned, priest and barber discuss the merits and demerits of those books, and they find that they are *innocent*, and that quite a few of them are even good literature. Why does then Cervantes satirize the whole *genre*? Because of the idiotic imitations which abounded one or two generations before Cervantes wrote the *Don Quixote*? Are we to believe that a man of Cervantes' rank shall waste his time with satirizing an ephemeral fashion? No—for all good books are, and are *meant* to be, possessions for all times.[8]

We might be inclined to say: well, difficulties or inconsistencies of that kind occur in practically all great books—aliquando dormitat bonus Homerus[9]—May be. But may it not also be that we are somewhat *naive* as regards those books and their authors? That we underestimate the clarity of thought, the power of expression, the imagination, and, above all, the willingness and love for *work* (φιλοπονία)[10] of these men? If they were inconsistent and sometimes[11] insipid—may they not have *wished* to be inconsistent and insipid? may they not have *wished* to give us some riddles to solve? may it not be that the deficiencies of their works—all those

---

split of the one author, then you see that the author is Christian as well as Muslim, *i.e.*, neither of the two. The author is therefore a philosopher, and Don Quixote represents the founder of a religion and Sancho Panza the believer. In fact, Don Quixote is the synthesis of Christianity (sorrowful countenance) and Islam (holy war); he is superior to his predecessors in that he is furthermore educated and polite. Dulcinea is Mary. The allusions to the Reformation, for example, are abundant. Consider also the role of *books* in *Don Quixote*: Christianity and Islam are based on books. The deeds of Don Quixote are miracles. Read the book on occasion again, and you will see that this is the case."

[7] Cf. APT in *GS–2* 222: "Of Christian origin is, above all, Abravanel's general conception of the government of the Jewish nation. According to him, that government consists of two kinds of governments, of a government human and of a government spiritual or divine. This distinction is simply the Christian distinction between the authority spiritual and the authority temporal." Cf. *GS–2* 225. See also *NRH* 253–54.

[8] For the source of the expression, see Thucydides, *History of the Peloponnesian War*, 1.22.4 ("And, indeed, [the *History*] has been composed, not as a prize-essay to be heard for the moment, but as a possession for all time." Thucydides, *History of the Peloponnesian War*, translated by Charles Forster Smith (Cambridge, MA: Harvard University Press, 1962), vol. 1, 41. Cf., for example, *PAW* 160; *CM* 142–43, 157, 159, 228.

[9] "Sometimes [even] good Homer nods."—For the source of this proverbial expression, see Horace, *The Art of Poetry*, 358–60 ("...et idem / indignor quandoque bonus dormitat Homerus, / verum operi longo fas est obrepere somnum."). Cf. *PAW* 26.

[10] Cf., for example, Plato, *Republic*, 535d and *Alcibiades I*, 122c; Xenophon, *Oeconomicus*, 21.6. Cf. *XSD* 79 with 200.

[11] LS first wrote "somewhat" but later replaced it by "sometimes."

deficiencies exploited by 19th century higher criticism[12]—are *intentional* and *deliberate*? [2]At this point, we are helped somewhat by an experience we are unfortunate enough to make to-day.[2]

[1 verso]

<1. Persecution → writing between the lines.

2. Persecution in the past → writing between the lines in the past.

II 3. Of the danger of reading between the lines: what is the difference between legitimate reading between the lines and arbitrary guess work?[13]

Only if reading between the lines: more *exact* and more *exacting* than ordinary reading, can it claim any consideration.[14]

Reading between the lines as regards the books in question, is *necessarily* more exact than our ordinary reading: for a teaching transmitted between the lines, is addressed to *very careful* readers only.

Only the greatest care in reading can discover that teaching.[15]

But which are the cases in which we are entitled or rather compelled to read between the lines?

In all cases in which ordinary reading is not sufficient to lead to an adequate understanding. E.g. if we find insipid passages which a high school [boy] would be ashamed of having written, in books of first class writers.[16]

III 4. Two types of persecution-literature.[17]

Generalization of "persecution" › social ostracism.[18]

How far do earlier writers, *as a matter of principle*, conceal their most significant opinions?

Common to both types: conceal with regard to social conformity, which is either merely enforced (modern type) or even desired?>

[3 recto][19] <is opposed to the orthodox view in its entirety, although he pays lip-service to it on every page and in every sentence. If we read that author again, but more vigilantly, and less innocently, we can be certain that we find many more traces of his independence than the ones which struck us first.

[12] Cf. *PAW* 30–31.

[13] Cf. *PAW* 27, 30, 32; *WIPP* 224, 231; *OT* 27; ONI 351–52.

[14] Cf. *PAW* 30.

[15] Cf. *PAW* 144.

[16] Cf. *PAW* 30; *TM* 36; *WIPP* 223. The passage about the high-school boy may be an allusion to a statement made by G. W. F. Hegel in the introduction (§3) of the *Philosophy of Right*. (See *Grundlinien der Philosophie des Rechts*, in *Werke*, edited by Eva Moldenhauer and Karl Markus Michel (Frankfurt am Main: Suhrkamp, 1986), vol. 7, 39–40.

[17] Cf. *PAW* 33–34.

[18] Cf. *PAW* 32–33, *WIPP* 170.

[19] Unfortunately, the second page of the manuscript seems to have been lost.

In some cases, we are fortunate enough to possess *explicit* evidence[17] either by the authors or by intelligent philosophers[20] proving that the author hides his real views, and indicates them only between the lines.>[21]

Lessing to MM: "You are more fortunate than other honest people who can *destroy* the most loathsome structure of non-sense (sc. the orthodoxy in question) only by pretending that they want to give it a new foundation."[22]

Hobbes: points out at several occasions that he uttered certain "novel" views during the Commonwealth only, i.e. at a time when the Elizabethan laws against heresy were no longer valid.

and to Aubrey on Spinoza's *Tr. theol-pol.*: he had not *dared* to write so *boldly*.[23]

We have to base our interpretation of Hobbes preferably on the works published under the Commonwealth, and, in case we find two sets of statements, one nearer to orthodoxy and another, contradictory, more remote from orthodoxy—we have to consider the latter to be his true opinions.[24]

<"*Of Liberty and Necessity*" (London 1654, p. 35f.): "I must confess, if we consider the greatest part of Mankind, not as they should be, but as they are,...I must, I say, confess that the dispute of this question will rather hurt than help their piety; and therefore if his Lordship had not desired this answer, I should not have written it, nor do I write it but in hopes your Lordship and his, will keep it private.">[25]

4. Of the whole literature which teaches the truth concerning the crucial questions exclusively between the lines, there are two types.[26] The difference of these two types corresponds to the difference of attitudes men may have towards persecution.

a) The view most familiar to us, is that persecution is *accidental*, that it is an outcome of a bad construction of the body politic; according to that view, persecution *ought* to be replaced, and *can* be replaced, by freedom of speech; nay, persecution *will* be replaced by freedom of speech.

That view presupposes that the truth about the most important things can be made accessible to the general public, i.e. that popular science is possible (Hobbes: Paulatim eruditur vulgus).[27] Belief in *progress*. A man who holds this view of persecution, writes and publishes his books in order to *fight* persecution, in order to

[20] Inserted by LS between the lines. He first put "authors or by intelligent and benevolent contemporaries" but then crossed "and benevolent contemporaries" out and wrote "philosophers."

[21] Cf. *PAW* 32.

[22] Lessing to Moses Mendelssohn, January 9, 1771, in *Werke*, edited by Helmuth Kiesel with Georg Braungart, Klaus Fischer and Ute Wahl (Frankfurt am Main: Deutscher Klassiker Verlag, 1988), vol. 11.2, 146.

[23] See *Die Religionskritik des Hobbes* in *GS–3* 277n20, *HCR* 32n20, *WIPP* 274. Cf. *WIPP* 171 and *PAW* 183.

[24] Cf. *PAW* 185–86.

[25] See *The English Works of Thomas Hobbes*, edited by William Molesworth (London: John Bohn, 1840), vol. IV, 256–57. Cf. *PAW* 34n15.

[26] Cf. *PAW* 33–34.

[27] "Gradually the vulgar become educated." See Hobbes, *De Homine*, 14.13, in *Opera latina*, edited by William Molesworth (London: John Bohn, 1839), vol. II, 128. Cf. *PAW* 34n15; *NRH* 200; ONI 360; *Die Religionskritik des Hobbes*, in *GS–3* 348n243; *HCR* 94n243.

contribute to the establishment of freedom of speech. And he *hides* his view *merely* for fear of persecution, for fear of violent death or prison or exile.[28]

b) According to another view, persecution is *essential*, or necessary, and *will* not be superseded, and *ought* not to be superseded. What *we* call persecution, the adherent of that view would call: uniformity of thought as regards the fundamentals, among the citizens; such a uniformity, he holds, is a prerequisite of any [2]healthy[2] political life. And such a uniformity[29] ought not to be endangered by public utterance of divergent views, [3 verso] <however true>. <He holds that the requirements of political and social life are different from, and in a sense opposed to, the requirements of philosophy or science:

the principle of political or social life is: quieta non movere[30]

the principle of philosophy and science, of theoretical life is: quieta movere

Arts and sciences *ought* to progress—but laws and customs ought to remain as stable as possible.[31] This view combines then intellectual radicalism with political and social conservatism. An author of that kind hides his heterodox views not merely for fear, but as a matter of duty towards the Commonwealth. Therefore, his technique of hiding is much more elaborate than that of an author who is interested in political or social change. Therefore, his real views are much more difficult[32] to decipher, and, thus, his books are much more intriguing and interesting.[33]

[2]Generalization of our topic: *society and individual, thinking individual*—society and thought—How far do earlier authors, *as a matter of principle*, conceal their opinions? How far is earlier technique of writing *different* from present-day technique?[2]

Generally speaking, a) is modern, and b) is ancient and medieval. Yet, we find quite a few examples of the second type up to the 18th century.

I wish to speak mainly of the second type. For it is by far the more interesting and important. Not merely historically, but also for us: that type produced the very highest kind of literature in existence—a kind of literature which *has* provided men, and *will* provide men as long as they read at all, with the best and most solid kind of *education*.[34] By being silent to all but extremely careful and vigilant readers, they compel us to be as careful and as vigilant, as flexible and as resourceful as we possibly can. And thus, they educate us.>

If people hide their opinions, they will not *say* that they hide them, or at least they will not say it too loud—or else they would defeat their own purpose. Therefore, explicit evidence in support of the view that an author hides his opinions, is relatively rare. There is however a number of statements to this effect in existence.[35]

[28] Cf. SSTX 535: "It would, however, betray too low a view of the philosophic writers of the past if one assumed that they concealed their thoughts merely for fear of persecution or of violent death."

[29] LS first wrote "prerequisite" but later replaced it by "uniformity."

[30] Cf. above, p. 289n18.

[31] Cf., for example, *CM* 21–22.

[32] LS first wrote "hidden" but later replaced it by "difficult."

[33] Cf. *PAW* 34.

[34] Cf. *PAW* 37.

[35] Cf. *PAW* 32.

I have mentioned *Lessing* already. Lessing has written two treatises on the theology and philosophy of *Leibniz*,[36] which show that Leibniz had two kinds of teaching, a public and a private teaching. Lessing's interpretation of that procedure surpasses in depth everything I know of, written in the modern period. Another writing of Lessing's, *Dialogues on freemasonry*,[37] sets it beyond doubt that the method of Leibniz he analyzed in the 2 treaties mentioned, was used by himself as well: it was his settled principle not to state in his publications explicitly, what he really thought of the then crucial question. A few years after his death, a private conversation of his was published,[38] which gave people an idea, if a superficial one, that the ordinary reader of Lessing's writings, i.e. he who did not read between the lines, did not know Lessing's view concerning the most important questions at all.[39]

Montesquieu is another author of that kind. In a recent discussion of his *Spirit of [the] Laws*, complaint is made of the total lack of order of that work, and of the surprising amount of irrelevance to be met with in it.[40] An extremely intelligent contemporary of Montesquieu, d'Alembert, gives us some information about the apparent deficiencies of Montesquieu's work. "We say of the *obscurity* which one may permit oneself in a book of that kind, the same what we said of the *lack of order*. What would be obscure for ordinary readers, is not obscure for those whom that author had in mind. Besides, *voluntary* obscurity is not really obscurity. M. de Montesquieu had to present sometimes important truths, the absolute and direct statement of which might have offended without bringing any benefits; therefore he had the *prudence* to envelop them; and by this *innocent artifice*, he hid them from them [4 recto] to whom they would be harmful,[41] without making them inaccessible to the wise."[42] Another friend of M. speaks of the "wonderful, *if hidden* order" of the *Spirit of [the] Laws*.[43] That is to say: the first task of the interpreter has to be: to find out the reasons why M. discusses, say, this topic in this [2]strange[2] place.

[36] LS is alluding to "Leibniz von den ewigen Strafen" and "Des Andreas Wissowatius Einwürfe wider die Dreieinigkeit," in Lessing, *Werke*, vol. 7, 472–501 and 548–81. Cf. *PAW* 182.

[37] LS is referring to *Ernst und Falk*. Cf. Lessing, *Werke*, vol. 10, 11–66. An English translation by C. Maschler can be found in *Interpretation* 14, no. 1 (1986): 14–48.

[38] In 1785, Friedrich Heinrich Jacobi published *Über die Lehre des Spinoza in Briefen an den Herrn Moses Mendelssohn* (*On Spinoza's Teaching, in Letters to Mr. Moses Mendelssohn*). In this book, he reports a conversation with Lessing in July 1780. LS gives a detailed account of the controversy between Jacobi and Mendelssohn that followed the publication of the book (the "Spinozismusstreit") in his introduction to Mendelssohn's *Morgenstunden* and *An die Freunde Lessings*. The introduction, written in 1937, was first published in Moses Mendelssohn, *Gesammelte Schriften Jubiläumsausgabe*, vol. 3.2, edited by Leo Strauss (Stuttgart-Bad Cannstatt: Friedrich Frommann Verlag, 1974), xi–xcv; reprinted in *GS–2* 528–605; English translation in *LSMM* 59–145.

[39] In the margin, LS wrote "*Rousseau* p.m. 126, n. 2 and cf. *2nd Discours* p. 40–41 with *Contrat social* IV 8." The abbreviation "p.m." is short for "penes me" (in my possession).

[40] LS is probably referring to George H. Sabine's *A History of Political Theory*. Cf. *PAW* 28–29.

[41] LS first wrote "dangerous" but later replaced it with "harmful."

[42] This passage from Jean-Baptiste le Rond d'Alembert's *Éloge de Montesquieu* is quoted in *PAW* 29n11.

[43] Cf. *PAW* 29n11 with Stefano Bertolini, *Analyse raisonnée de l'Esprit des Lois*: "Voilà l'économie de cet ouvrage magnifique. A la peinture que je viens de tracer, quelque foible qu'elle soit, il est aisé de voir que dans ce livre de l'*Esprit des Lois* règnent la précision, la justesse, un ordre merveilleux; ordre peut-être caché aux yeux de ceux qui ne sauroient marcher que de conséquence en conséquence, toujours

Spinoza: one of the rules of life he set up for himself: ad captum vulgi loqui (to adapt his language to the language of the vulgar).[44] Tradition has it that the inscription of his signet is: "Caute."[45] It would be a mistake to think that Spinoza's *Ethics* is *not* written in the language of the vulgar. "Evasive".

Descartes makes this entry in his diary: "Up to now, I have been a spectator of this theatre of the world; but now being about to ascend the stage of that theatre, I put on a mask, just as the comedians do who do not wish that their feeling of shame would[46] become visible." ("Ut comoedi, moniti ne in fronte appareat pudor, personam induunt, sic ego, hoc mundi theatrum conscensurus, in quo hactenus spectator exstiti, larvatus prodeo." *Oeuvres* X 213).[47]

Accordingly, he demands that *some months* shall be devoted to the perusal of the 1st Meditation (VII 130).[48] *Writing* is an *action*, and as such subject to the political and ecclesiastical authorities; but *thought* recognizes no authority but *reason* (Discours VI in princ.).[49] The *real* views of Desc. are not to be found *in* his writings but *between the lines* of his writings.

---

guidés par des définitions, des divisions, des avant-propos, des distinctions, mais qui paroît dans tout son jour aux esprits attentifs, capables de suppléer d'eux-mêmes les conséquences qui naissent des principes, et assez habiles pour rapprocher et joindre dans la chaîne des vérités établies celles qui s'ensuivent, qui, aux yeux des connoisseurs, ne sont, pour ainsi dire, couvertes que d'un voile transparent." ("Here is the layout of this magnificent work. In the picture I have just sketched, however inadequate it may be, it is easy to see the precision, accuracy, and wonderful order that reign in this book, *The Spirit of Laws*. It is an order hidden perhaps from the eyes of those who can only proceed from consequence to consequence, always guided by definitions, divisions, forewords, and distinctions, but which appears fully illuminated to attentive minds, who are capable by themselves of supplying those consequences born of principles, and who are skillful enough to bring forth and connect to the chain of established truths those truths that follow therefrom, which in the eyes of experts, are, so to speak, covered only by a transparent veil.") The *Analyse* was reprinted in the *Œuvres complètes de Montesquieu*, edited by Édouard Laboulaye (Paris: Granier, 1876), vol. III, here 60.

[44] In his *Tractatus de intellectus emendatione* (sect. 17), Spinoza declares as one of his *regulae vivendi*: "Ad captum vulgi loqui, et illa omnia operari, quae nihil impedimenti adferunt, quominus nostrum scopum attingamus." (*Opera*, edited by Carl Gebhardt (Heidelberg: Carl Winters Universitätsbuchhandlung, 1925), vol. II, 9.) In the article "How to Study Spinoza's *Theologico-Political Treatise*," LS translates the sentence in the following way: "To speak with a view to the capacity of the vulgar and to practice all those things which cannot hinder us from reaching our goal (*sc.* the highest good)." (*PAW* 177, cf. 177–97.)

[45] Cf. *PAW* 180.

[46] LS first wrote "might" but later replaced it with "would."

[47] LS quotes the first few lines of the *Cogitiones privatae* in the edition by Charles Adam and Paul Tannery (Paris: Léopold Cerf, 1897–1913).

[48] LS is referring to the *Responsio ad secundas objectiones* in the same edition.

[49] Cf. Descartes, *Discours de la Méthode*, edited by Étienne Gilson. (Paris: Librairie Philosophique J. Vrin, 1939), 60 (beginning of part 6): "Or, il y a maintenant trois ans que j'étais parvenu à la fin du traité qui contient toutes ces choses, et que je commençais à le revoir, afin de le mettre entre les mains d'un imprimeur, lorsque j'appris que des personnes, à qui je défère et dont l'autorité ne peut guère moins sur mes actions que ma propre raison sur mes pensées, avaient désapprouvé une opinion de physique, publiée un peu auparavant par quelque autre, de laquelle je ne veux pas dire que je fusse, mais bien que je n'y avais rien remarqué, avant leur censure, que je pusse imaginer être préjudiciable ni à la religion ni à l'État, ni, par conséquent, qui m'eût empêché de l'écrire, si la raison me l'eût persuadée, et que cela me fit craindre qu'il ne s'en trouvât tout de même quelqu'une entre les miennes, en laquelle je me fusse mépris, nonobstant le grand soin que j'ai toujours eu de n'en point recevoir de nouvelles en ma créance, dont je n'eusse des démonstrations très certaines, et de n'en point écrire qui pussent tourner

Bacon. "I sometimes alter the uses and definitions (of the traditional terms), according to the *moderate* proceeding in civil government; where although there be some alteration, yet that holdeth which Tacitus wisely noteth, *Eadem magistratuum vocabula*." (Ann. I 3).[50] (Advanc. p. 92).[51]

Note his interest in *ciphers*.

The *arcana imperii* literature in the 16th century (Lipsius[52] etc.).

"Government...is a part of knowledge secret and retired, in both these respects in which things are deemed secret; for some things are secret because they are hard to know, and some because they are *not fit to utter*...even unto the general rules and discourses of policy and government is due a reverent and reserved handling." (205f.).[53] No wonder that he did not finish his utopia, *New Atlantis*, and that he omitted practically everything *political* from it.

The writers I have mentioned, are not the inventors of such techniques. They make use of a *tradition*, of the traditional distinction between *exoteric* teaching and *esoteric* teaching. An esoteric[54] teaching is *not*, as some present day scholars seem to think, a *mystical* teaching: it is the *scientific* teaching. Exoteric = popular. Esoteric = scientific and *therefore* secret.

---

au désavantage de personne." ("It is now three years since I completed the treatise that contains all these things, and began to review it before putting it in the hands of the printer, when I learned that certain persons to whom I defer, and whose authority over my actions can scarcely be less than that of my own reason over my thoughts, had disapproved of certain opinions in physics, published shortly before by someone else. I do not wish to say that I agreed with it, but since I had noticed nothing in it before their censure that I could imagine to be prejudicial either to religion or to the state, or consequently that would have prevented me from writing it if reason had so persuaded me, this made me fear that there might nevertheless be found among my thoughts some one that was mistaken, despite the great care I have always taken not to receive new ones among my beliefs of which I did not have very certain demonstrations, and to write nothing that could turn to the disadvantage of anyone." Descartes, *Discourse on Method*, trans. Richard Kennington (Newburyport, MA: Focus Philosophical Library, 2007), 48)—Cf. *PAW* 182–83.

[50] Cf. Tacitus, *The Annals*, 1.3: "Domi res tranquillae, *eadem magistratuum vocabula*; iuniores post Actiacam victoriam, etiam senes plerique inter bella civium nati: quotus quisque reliquus, qui rem publicam vidisset?" (My italics, H.K.) ("At home all was calm. The officials carried the old names; the younger men had been born after the victory of Actium; most even of the elder generation, during the civil wars; few indeed were left who had seen the Republic." Tacitus, *The Histories. The Annals*, translated by Clifford H. Moore/John Jackson (Cambridge, MA: Harvard University Press, 1962), vol. 2, 249.)

[51] Cf. Francis Bacon, *The Advancement of Learning*, edited by Michael Kiernan (Oxford: Clarendon Press, 2000), 81: "But to me on the other side that do desire as much as lyeth in my Penne, to ground a sociable entercourse between Antiquitie and Proficience, it seemeth best, to keepe way with Antiquitie *vsque ad aras*; And therefore to retaine the ancient tearmes, though I sometimes alter the vses and definitions, according to the Moderate proceeding in Ciuill gouernment; where although there bee some alteration, yet that holdeth which *Tacitus* wisely noteth, *Eadem Magistratuum vocabula*." Cf. *PAW* 183.

[52] For Justus Lipsius (1547–1606), cf. *CM* 144; *Hobbes' politische Wissenschaft*, in *GS–3* 100–4.

[53] Cf. Francis Bacon, *The Advancement of Learning*, 179: "Concerning gouernment, it is a part of knowledge, secret and retyred in both these respects, in which things are deemed secret: for some things are secret, because they are hard to know, and some because they are not fit to vtter: wee see all gouernments are obscure and inuisible. [...] Neuerthelesse euen vnto the generall rules and discourses of pollicie, and gouernment, there is due a reuerent and reserued handling." Cf. *PAW* 57n63.

[54] LS first wrote "exoteric" but later replaced it with "esoteric".

Tradition has it that *Aristotle* wrote two kinds of books: exoteric and esoteric books. But the content of the esoteric books was originally not destined for publication at all: they are still called *acroamatic*, oral.[55] Scientific teaching was oral teaching, because written teaching cannot remain secret. The truth cannot and ought not to be published—i.e. the truth about the highest things—what *can* be published, are things which *are* public in themselves, ἔνδοξα, moral and political things.

[4 verso]The story of the correspondence between Alexander the Great and Aristotle: Alexander complained to Aristotle that Ar. had published his oral teaching. Ar. answer: those *books are published and not published*; for they are intelligible only to those who have heard my lectures.[56]

This tradition may be spurious. But even spurious traditions are significant.

The attitude presupposed by that tradition, is certainly much older than the Christian period. We find it clearly expressed in the 2nd and 7th of the *Platonic* letters. I believe, they are genuine[57]—but even if not, the "forger" knew more of Plato than we know.

[55] Cf. Aulus Gellius, *The Attic Nights*, 20.5. Cf. above, p. 289n14.

[56] Cf. Aulus Gellius, *The Attic Nights*, 20.5: "Eos libros generis 'acroatici' cum in vulgus ab eo editos rex Alexander cognovisset atque ea tempestate armis exercitam omnem prope Asiam teneret regemque ipsum Darium proeliis et victoriis urgeret, in illis tamen tantis negotiis litteras ad Aristotelem misit, non eum recte fecisse, quod disciplinas acroaticas, quibus ab eo ipse eruditus foret, libris foras editis involgasset: 'Nam qua,' inquit, 'alia re praestare ceteris poterimus, si ea quae ex te accepimus omnium prosus fient communia? Quippe ego doctrina anteire malim quam copiis atque opulentiis.' Rescripsit ei Aristoteles ad hanc sententiam: 'Acroaticos libros, quos editos quereris et non proinde ut arcana absconditos, neque editos scito esse neque non editos, quoniam his solis cognobiles erunt, qui nos audiverunt.'" ("When King Alexander knew that he [sc. Aristotle] had published those books of the 'acroatic' set, although at that time the king was keeping almost all of Asia in state of panic by his deeds of arms, and was pressing King Darius himself hard by attacks and victories, yet in the midst of such urgent affairs he sent a letter to Aristotle, saying that the philosopher had not done right in publishing the books and so revealing to the public the acroatic training, in which he himself [sc. Alexander] had been instructed. 'For in what other way,' said he, 'can I excel the rest, if that instruction which I have received from you becomes the common property of all the world? For I would rather be first in learning than in wealth and power.' Aristotle replied to him to this purport: 'Know that the acroatic books, which you complain have been made public and not hidden as if they contained secrets, have neither been made public nor hidden, since they can be understood only by those who have heard my lectures.'" Aulus Gellius, *The Attic Nights*, translated by John C. Rolfe (Cambridge, MA: Harvard University Press, 1961), vol. 3, 433–35.) See also Plutarch, *Life of Alexander*, 7.

[57] Cf. LS to Jacob Klein, November 28, 1939, in *GS–3* 586: "By now, I am firmly convinced that *all* Platonic letters (even the first) are genuine: they are the Platonic counterpart [*Gegenstück*] to Xenophon's *Anabasis*: they are supposed to show that the author has not been corrupted by Socrates: while the author constantly veils himself in the dialogues, it is the purpose of the letters as well as of the *Anabasis* to show that the one who veils himself is absolutely harmless, absolutely *normal*. He unveils himself as normal by writing the first three and the last letter to a tyrant (Dionysius); moreover: the letters which are directed at philosophers deal *exclusively* with πολιτικά, philosophy is discussed only in letters to πολιτικοι, and in such a way that close reading fully destroys the fiction on which the whole matter is based: the seventh letter is precisely in the middle!"

[58] Cf. *OPS* 29.

Ep. II (314a–c).[58] Ep.VII (332d):[59]
a) the teaching cannot [be] "said" at all.
b) it can be "said" in writing or in speech, but well or badly.
c) saying it badly = stating it in *writing fully* to the *public*.

Plato's *dialogues*. The *Phaedrus* on the danger inherent in all writing. A writing does not know to whom it ought to *talk* and to whom it ought to be *silent* (276a6–7). This is so important *because* the truth is not fit for everybody. Inferiority of all writing to oral instruction. "It is hard to find the father of all things, but to *speak* of him unto *all men* is impossible." *Timaeus*.[60]

But Plato did write books about the most important topics: on nature, ideas, idea of the good, soul etc. How can we reconcile his refusal to write about such topics with his actual practice? Only by assuming that he did write and did *not* write about them at the same time. Just as Aristotle is said to have said of his esoteric works: they are published and they are *not* published. Books *do* speak and be [recte: are?] silent according to the capacities of the reader. Plato *did* write about the truth: but he did it *enigmatically*.

All Platonic writings are *dialogues*. Dialogues are a kind of *dramas* (dramas in prose and without women and nearer to comedy than to tragedy).[61] What is the characteristic feature of ²the² drama according to *Plato*? Drama is that kind of poetry in which the author *hides* himself.[62] By writing *dialogues*, Plato gives us to understand that he hides himself, i.e. his *thought*. *Plato* never said a word on his teaching—only his characters do. But his *main* character, Socrates, does *not*[63] speak when the highest topic, the κόσμος, or the being, is discussed: Timaeus or the Eleatic stranger.

Plato's *school*. The Academic philosophers, the successors of Plato, say: In order to discover the truth, one must dispute pro and con as regards everything. The adversary: "I should like to see *what* they have discovered." The Academic: "We are not used to show[ing] it." Adversary: "But what in the world are these *mysteries*? or why do you *conceal* your opinion, as if it were something disgraceful?" Academic: "That those who hear, will be swayed by reason, rather than authority." (*Lucullus* 60).[64]

[59] LS first wrote "314c–e" but later replaced it by "332d".—On the *Seventh Letter*, cf. ONI 348–51 with LS to Karl Löwith, August 15, 1946, in *GS–3* 663.

[60] Plato, *Timaeus*, 28c3–5. Cf. *PAW* 35n17 and FP 375n44.

[61] See *CM* 61: "Socrates left us no example of weeping, but, on the other side, he left us example of laughing. The relation of weeping and laughing is similar to that of tragedy and comedy. We may therefore say that the Socratic conversation and hence the Platonic dialogue is slightly more akin to comedy than to tragedy." Cf. *OPS* 279. Contrast LS to Alexandre Kojève, April 22, 1957, in *OT* 275: "All the Dialogues are tragicomedies. (The tragedian is awake while the comedian is sleeping at the end of the *Symp*.)"

[62] Plato, *Republic*, 393c. Cf. *OT* 32.

[63] LS first wrote "never speaks" but later replaced it by "does *not*."

[64] Cf. Cicero, *Academica*, 2.59f.: "Mihi porro non tam certum est esse aliquid quod comprendi possit (de quo iam nimium etiam diu disputo) quam sapientem nihil opinari, id est numquam adsentiri rei vel falsae vel incognitae. Restat illud quod dicunt veri inveniundi causa contra omnia dici oportere et pro omnibus. Volo igitur videre quid invenerint. 'Non solemus,' inquit, 'ostendere.' 'Quae sunt tandem ista mysteria, aut cur celatis quasi turpe aliquid sententiam vestram?' 'Ut qui audient,' inquit, 'ratione potius quam auctoritate ducantur.'" ("For my part, moreover, certain as I am that something exists that can be grasped (the point I have been arguing even too long already), I am still more certain that the wise man

It is *Cicero* who relates this little dialogue. Cicero himself was an academic. *Consequently*, he says of himself: "we have preferably followed that kind of philosophy (sc. dialogic philosophy) which, as we believed, Socrates has used, (and we did this) in *order to hide our own opinion*, to free others from error, and to investigate in each discussion what is *most likely to be true*." (Tusc. V 11).[65] There is a connection between *hiding* and arriving at a result which is only *likely* to be true, which is only a *likely tale*:[66] the *true* tale is hidden; it is revealed perhaps in a *dream* (*Somnium Scipionis*).[67]

[5 recto] Hiding one's thought is irreconcilable with a perfectly clear and lucid *plan*. A lucid plan does not leave room for hiding-places—as a consequence, an exoteric book will not have a very lucid plan.[68]

Cf. Lessing, Leibniz von den ewigen Strafen: "Ich will mich so kurz fassen wie nur möglich und meine Gedanken wenn nicht ordnen so doch zählen."[69]

Cf. the twofold discussion of poetry in Rep.[70]—
ib.: the interruption after the enumeration of the bad constitutions—

---

never holds an opinion, that is, never assents to a thing that is either false or unknown. There remains their statement that for the discovery of the truth it is necessary to argue against all things and for all things. Well then, I should like to see what they have discovered. 'Oh,' he says, 'it is not our practice to give an exposition.' 'What pray are these holy secrets of yours, or why does your school conceal its doctrine like something disgraceful?' 'In order,' says he, 'that our hearers may be guided by reason rather than by authority.'" Cicero, *De Natura Deorum. Academica*, translated by H. Rackham (Cambridge, MA: Harvard University Press, 1961), 543.)

[65] Cf. Cicero, *Tusculan Disputations*, 5.4.10–11: "Socrates autem primus philosophiam devocavit e caelo et in urbibus collocavit et in domus etiam introduxit et coëgit de vita et moribus rebusque bonis et malis quaerere: cuius multiplex ratio disputandi rerumque varietas et ingenii magnitudo, Platonis memoria et litteris consecrata, plura genera effecit dissentientium philosophorum, *e quibus nos id potissimum consecuti sumus, quo Socratem usum arbitrabamur, ut nostram ipsi sententiam tegeremus, errore alios levaremus et in omni disputatione quid esset simillimum veri quaereremus*." (My italics, H.K.) ("Socrates on the other hand was the first to call philosophy down from the heavens and set her in the cities of men and bring her also into their homes and compel her to ask questions about life and morality and things good and evil: and his many-sided method of discussion and the varied nature of its subjects and the greatness of his genius, which has been immortalized in Plato's literary masterpieces, have produced many warring philosophic sects of which I have chosen particularly to follow that one which I think agreeable to the practice of Socrates, in trying to conceal my own private opinion, to relieve others from deception and in every discussion to look for the most probable solution." Cicero, *Tusculan Disputations*, translated by J. E. King (Cambridge, MA: Harvard University Press, 1966), 435). Cf., for example, *NRH* 154–55.

[66] Cf. Plato, *Timaeus*, 29d. See, for example, *PAW*, 35 and *SPPP*, 166.

[67] Cf. Cicero, *De re publica*, 6.9ff.

[68] Cf. SSTX 523–24.

[69] Lessing, *Leibniz von den ewigen Strafen* (*Werke*, vol. 7, 481): "Ich will, was ich zu sagen habe, so kurz zu fassen suchen, als möglich; und meine Gedanken wo nicht ordnen, doch zählen." ("I want to try to express what I have to say as briefly as possible; and where I won't put my thoughts in order, I'll at least number them.") Cf. LS to Hans-Georg Gadamer, February 26, 1961, in: "Correspondence concerning *Wahrheit und Methode*," *The Independent Journal of Philosophy/Unabhängige Zeitschrift für Philosophie* 2 (1978): 6.

[70] *CM* 133: "Socrates suddenly returns to the subject of poetry, a subject which had already been discussed at great length when the education of the warriors was being considered. We must try to understand this apparently unmotivated return." Cf. *CM* 134–37.

the twofold discussion of education in *Laws*.[71] *Repetition*.[72]

the insertion of theology into penal law in the *Laws*[73] and into the discussion of noble lies in the Rep.[74]

the plan of Xen. *Memor*.[75]

Moreover, hiding one's thought is not reconcilable with absolutely lucid *expressions*: if everything is absolutely clearly expressed, there is no room for hiding places *within* the sentences.

A man who hides his thought will then accept the following maxim: "What is written beautifully and in order, is *not* written beautifully and in order." (Xen. Cyn[egeticus]. 13, 6).[76] This maxim occurs in a treatise on hunting with dogs, which is a rather good hiding place.

Hiding one's thoughts about the crucial things, when speaking or writing about those things, means making *misstatements* about those things—or: to *lie* about those things.

[71] Cf., for example, *AAPL* 23, 27 and 104–5.

[72] Cf. *OPS* 237: "General rule: there is never a repetition in Plato which is an identical repetition; there is always a change, though sometimes seemingly trivial." See *PAW* 16 and 62–64.

[73] According to LS's interpretation, books 9–12 of the *Laws* are "chiefly devoted to the penal law" (*AAPL* 64, cf. 126). With regard to the Athenian's natural religion in book 10, LS writes: "The Athenian is thus compelled or enabled to discuss what Adeimantos calls theology (*Republic* 379a5–6) within the context of the penal law, whereas Socrates discussed it within the context of pre-philosophic, nay, the most rudimentary education." (*AAPL* 140) Cf., for example, LS to Jacob Klein, February 16, 1939, in *GS–3* 567 as well as "Plato," in *History of Political Philosophy* (third edition), 85–86.

[74] Cf. *CM* 98, 102–03.

[75] LS's interpretation of the *Memorabilia* can be found in *XS* 1–126.

[76] Cf. *PAW* 29, SSTX 502, and LS to Jacob Klein, August 7, 1939, in *GS–3* 575–76.

CONTRIBUTORS

Gabriel Bartlett is Instructor in Philosophy at St. Xavier University, Chicago. He is cotranslator of Leo Strauss, *Hobbes's Critique of Religion and Related Writings*, and of Strauss, "The Place of the Doctrine of Providence According to Maimonides."

Nasser Behnegar is Associate Professor of Political Science at Boston College. He received his MA in economics and PhD from the Committee on Social Thought of the University of Chicago. He is the author of *Leo Strauss, Max Weber, and the Scientific Study of Politics* and is currently working on a book-length study of the liberalism of John Locke.

Jeffrey A. Bernstein is Associate Professor of Philosophy at the College of the Holy Cross. He works in the areas of Spinoza, German philosophy, and Jewish thought. He is currently at work on a book dealing with Leo Strauss at the borders of Judaism, philosophy, and history.

Timothy W. Burns is Professor of Political Science at Baylor University. He is author of *Shakespeare's Political Wisdom*; coauthor (with Thomas L. Pangle) of *Introduction To Political Philosophy*; editor of *After History? Francis Fukuyama and his Critics* and of *Recovering Reason: Essays in Honor of Thomas L. Pangle*; translator of Marcellinus's "Life of Thucydides"; and author of articles on Homer, Thucydides, Aristophanes, Strauss, Fukuyama, Putnam, Chesterton, and modern liberal republican theory.

Steven Frankel has taught at the American University of Paris, where he received the Board of Trustees Award for Distinguished Teaching in 2001, and now teaches at Xavier University in Cincinnati. His scholarly work focuses on the relationship between philosophy and religion; it has appeared in over a dozen journals, including *Archiv für Geschichte der Philosophie*, *International Philosophical Quarterly*, *Interpretation*, *Journal of Jewish Thought and Philosophy*, *Review of Metaphysics*, *Review of Politics*, and *Teaching Philosophy*. He is also the author of *French Culture and Politics: A Guide for Students*.

David Janssens is Assistant Professor of Philosophy at Tilburg University, The Netherlands. He is the author of *Between Athens and Jerusalem: Philosophy, Prophecy, and Politics in Leo Strauss's Early Thought* and of numerous articles on ancient law, philosophy and poetry, and the work of Leo Strauss. His current research focuses on the quarrel between philosophy and poetry.

Hannes Kerber is Research Assistant at the Carl Friedrich von Siemens Foundation in Munich. He is the author of a forthcoming study of Leo Strauss's hermeneutics and is currently preparing a dissertation at the University of Munich on Gotthold Ephraim Lessing's critique of the Bible.

Heinrich Meier is Director of the Carl Friedrich von Siemens Foundation in Munich, Professor of Philosophy at the University of Munich, and permanent Visiting Professor at the Committee on Social Thought, the University of Chicago. The author of eight books, including *Carl Schmitt and Leo Strauss: The Hidden Dialogue, The Lesson of Carl Schmitt: Four Chapters on the Distinction between Political Theology and Political Philosophy*, and *Leo Strauss and the Theologico-Political Problem*, he is also the editor of Leo Strauss's *Gesammelte Schriften*. In 2005 he was awarded the Leibniz Medal of the Berlin-Brandenburg Academy of Sciences. His studies on the theologico-political problem, on political theology, and in political philosophy have been translated into English, French, Italian, Japanese, Polish, and Spanish; furthermore, all of them are already or will soon be available in Chinese editions.

Thomas L. Pangle is the Joe R. Long Chair in Democratic Studies in the Department of Government at the University of Texas, Austin, where he directs the Jefferson Center for the Study of Core Texts and Ideas. He has published widely in the field of political philosophy, his 70 articles and book chapters and his numerous reviews addressing such topics as Socratic rationalism, the competing philosophic and scriptural understandings of wisdom and of moral and civic life; classical and modern republicanism; biblical politics; the Enlightenment as a theologico-political project; the Federalist-anti-Federalist debate, American constitutionalism, the moral basis of international relations; and postmodernity. He sits on advisory boards of centers and institutes for the study of constitutionalism, of public affairs, of democracy, of liberal education, and of Western civilization. He is the general editor of Cornell University Press's Agora editions, is on the editorial boards of three scholarly journals, including *Political Research Quarterly*. Pangle has published 15 books, the most recent of which is *Aristotle's Teaching in the* Politics. He is coauthor (with Timothy W. Burns) of the forthcoming *Political Philosophy: An Introduction*.

Joshua Parens is Professor of Philosophy and Dean of the Braniff Graduate School of Liberal Arts at the University of Dallas. He is the author of *Maimonides and Spinoza: Their Conflicting Views of Human Nature*, and of two books on Alfarabi—*Metaphysics as Rhetoric* and *An Islamic Philosophy of Virtuous Religions*. With Joseph Macfarland, he has coedited the second edition of *Medieval Political Philosophy: A Sourcebook*, whose first edition was edited by Ralph Lerner and Muhsin Mahdi. He has also published various articles on Alfarabi, Maimonides, and Spinoza.

Richard S. Ruderman is Associate Professor and Chair of the Political Science Department at University of North Texas. He has published essays on "Aristotle and the Recovery of Political Judgment," "Homer's *Odyssey* and the Possibility of Enlightenment," "Democracy and the Problem of Statesmanship," "Locke on the Parental Control of Education," "'Let Freedom Ring': The Abolitionism of William Lloyd Garrison and Frederick Douglass," and "A Slingshot Recoils: The Critique of Philosophy in Halevi's *Kuzari*."

Martin D. Yaffe is Professor of Philosophy and Religion Studies at University of North Texas. He is the author of *Leo Strauss on Moses Mendelssohn* and of *Shylock and the Jewish Question*; editor of *Judaism and Environmental Ethics: A Reader*; coeditor of *The Companionship of Books: Essays in Honor of Laurence Berns* and of *Emil L. Fackenheim: Philosopher, Theologian, Jew*; translator of Spinoza's *Theologico-Political Treatise*; and cotranslator of Thomas Aquinas's *Literal Exposition on the Book of Job*.

INDEX

CPSIA information can be obtained
at www.ICGtesting.com
Printed in the USA
FFOW05n1149050814